History of American Ceramics

Paul S. Donhauser
University of Wisconsin, Oshkosh

History of American Ceramics

The Studio Potter

KENDALL/HUNT PUBLISHING COMPANY
2460 Kerper Boulevard, Dubuque, Iowa 52001

Library of Congress Catalog Card Number: 78—52547

ISBN 0—8403—1864—2

Printed in the United States of America

401864 01

CONTENTS

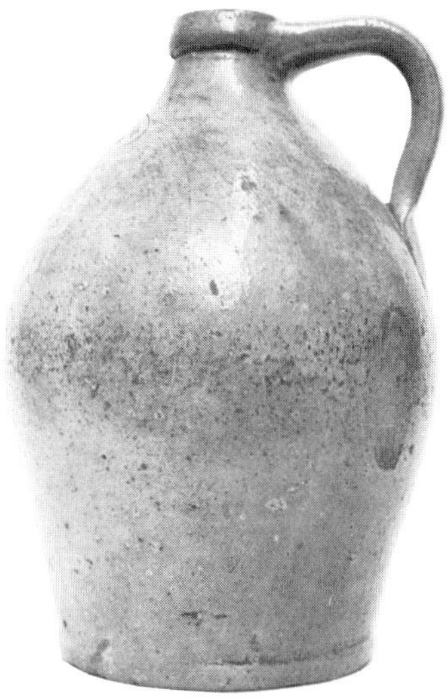

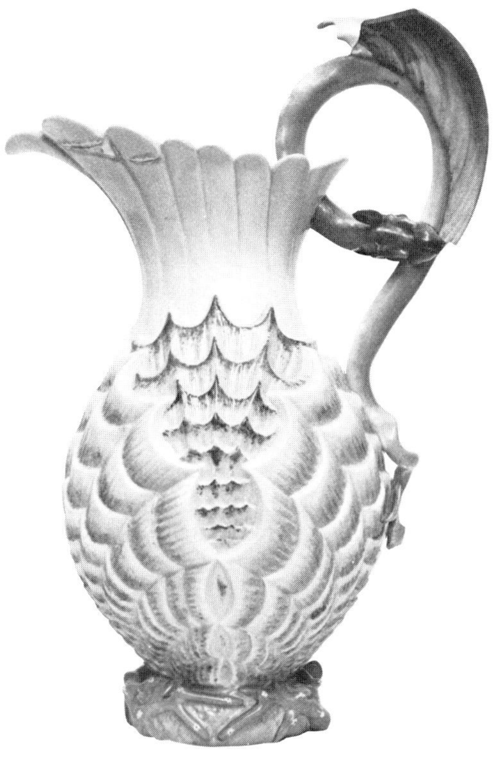

Contents

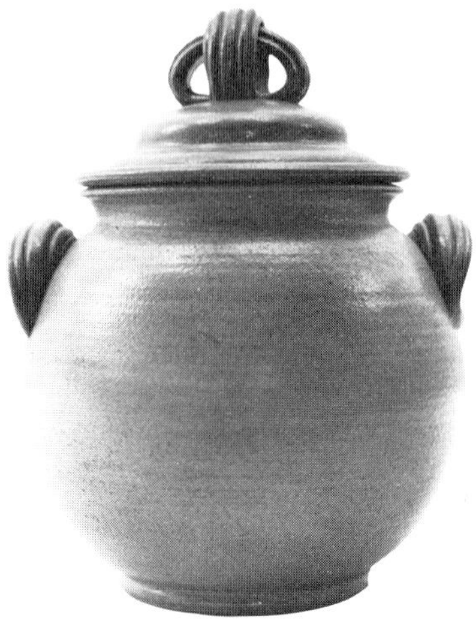

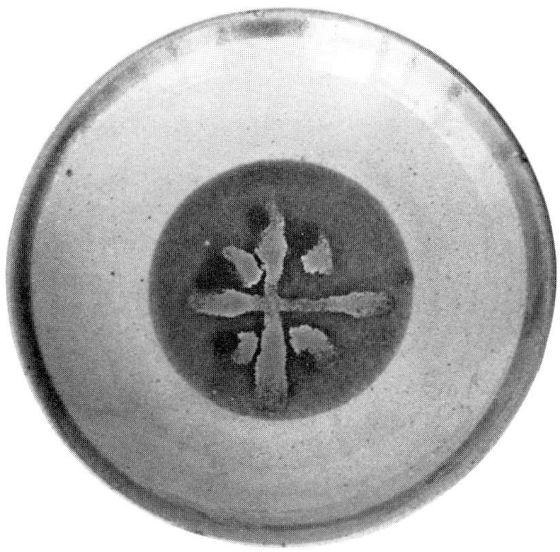

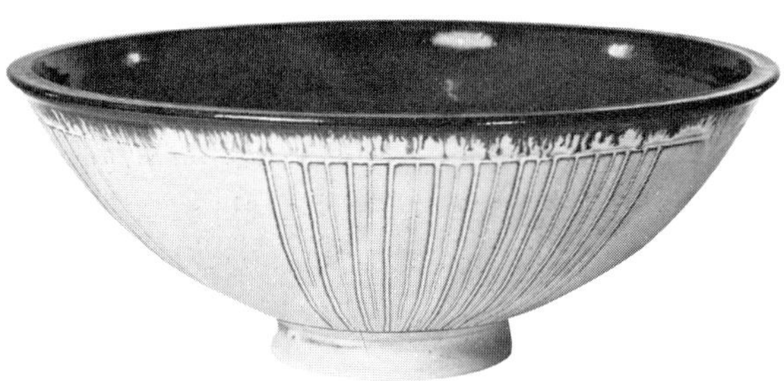

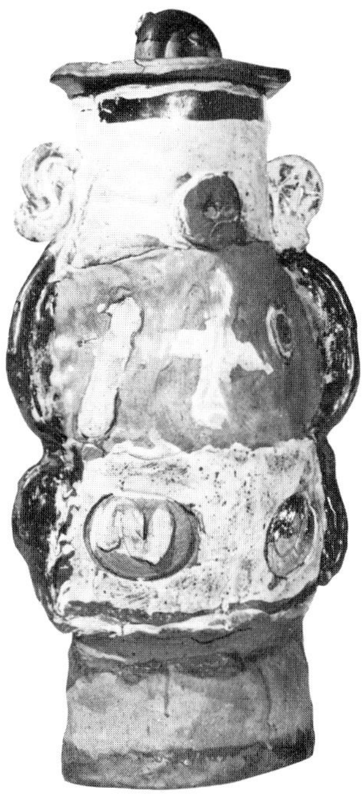

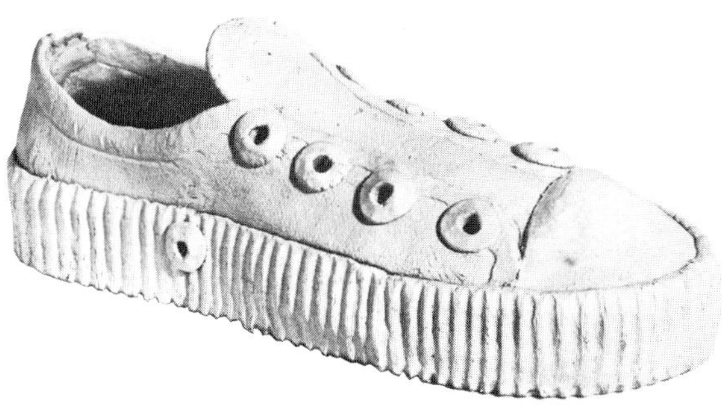

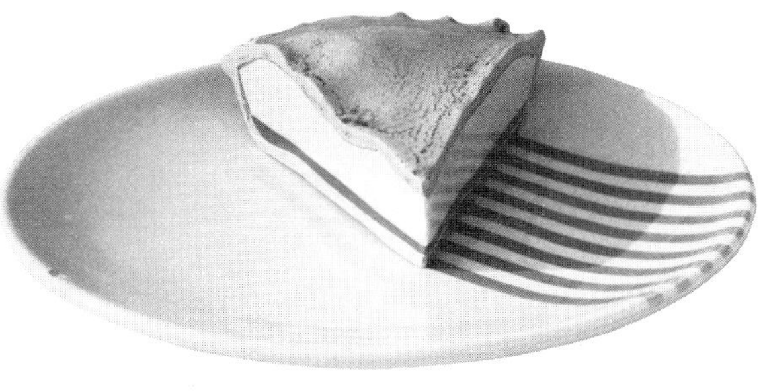

10. Expansion and Growth in Research, Publication and Schools 131

11. Changes in Form and Style After 1945 139

12. Developments During the 1960's 165

13. Individual Continuity in the 1970's 211

Contents

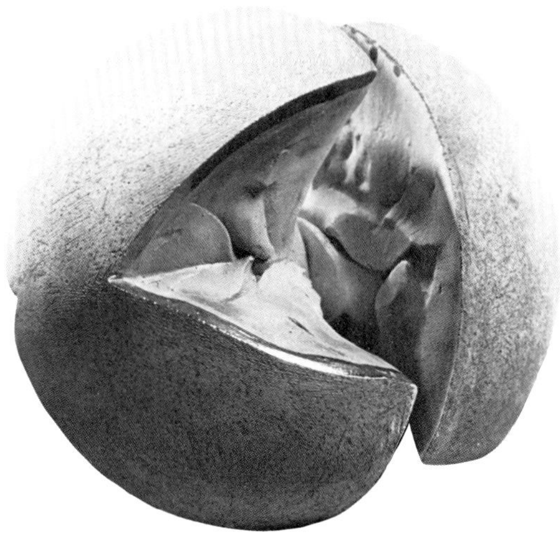

List of Figures and Colored Plates

Black And White Photos

Chapter 1

Chapter 2

Chapter 3

Chapter 4

Chapter 5

Chapter 6

Chapter 7

List of Figures and Colored Plates

Chapter 8

Chapter opening photo. Maija Grotell, vase, earthenware, wheel thrown, grey and white crackel glaze, 10 5/8″ × 8 1/8″, 1930. Collection, the Cranbrook Academy of Art Museum. (See page 92.)

Chapter 9

Chapter opening photo. Toshiko Takeazu, vase, stoneware, wheel thrown, brush decoration, 1958, 12 $3/4_0$ h × 9″ w. Courtesy, the Cleveland Museum of Art, Mary Spedding Milliken Memorial Collection, Gift of William M. Milliken. (See page 110.)

Chapter 10

Chapter opening photo. Susan Parks, "Instructional Mugs," 1975, cast earthenware, low fire glazes, overglaze enamels, decals, underglaze pencil, contact paper and wood; 12″ × 20″ × 4″. Courtesy of the artist. (See page 130.)

Chapter 11

Chapter opening photo. Peter Voulkos, untitled sculpture, stoneware, handbuilt, white and black slips, unglazed, approx. 6 ft. tall; 1958-59; Quay Gallery, San Francisco, California.

Voulkos' break with traditional pottery can be seen in massive sculpture that reflects an almost brutal explosion of handling clay and brush decorations. (See page 138.)

Chapter 12

Chapter opening photo. Robert Arneson, "Classical Exposure," Terra Cotta, handbuilt, 96″ × 36″ × 24″, 1972. Courtesy of the artist and Hansen Fuller Gallery, San Francisco.

Arneson, who has been regarded as one of the primary leaders of the California Funk art ceramics movement, often portrayed himself as an historical figure. (See page 164.)

Chapter 13

Description of Colored Plates
(Colored Plates Between pp. 126 and 127)

1. Pennsylvania Dutch Plate, wheel thrown, slip decorated, 18th century.
2. Rookwood Pottery, vase, underglaze decoration, transparent cover glaze, 1899.
3. Teco Pottery, vase, cast and handbuilt, green matt glaze, ca. 1910.
4. Karl Martz, bowl, earthenware, wheel thrown, slip decorated, 1937.
5. A.R. Deyer, plate, red strawberry glaze, wheel thrown earthenware; Leon Volkmar, vase, wheel thrown, copper green glaze, both 1948.
6. Gertrude and Otto Natzler, bowl, wheel thrown, stoneware, crater glaze.
7. Franz Wildenhain, plate, stoneware, wheel thrown, slip decorated, 1953.
8. David Gill, assorted pots, stoneware, cast and handbuilt, 1951.
9. J. Sheldon Carey, covered urn, incised decoration, stoneware, wheel thrown, 1958.
10. Peter Voulkos, Cross Pot, stoneware, handbuilt, low fire glazes, 1959.
11. Peter Voulkos, plate, stoneware, wheel thrown and altered, ca. 1957.
12. James Leedy, ceramic sculpture, handbuilt.
13. Timothy Mather, ceramic form, handbuilt, and wheel thrown, partially glazed, ca. 1963.
14. Robert Arneson, Landscape Cup, wheel thrown and handbuilt, low fire glazes, 1967.
15. Robert Arneson, Trophy, stoneware, handbuilt, low fire glazes, 1964.
16. Curtis Hoard, ceramic sculpture, stoneware, wheel thrown and handbuilt, low fire glazes and decals with lusters, ca. 1967.
17. Patti Warashina, Car Kiln, earthenware, handbuilt, slip decorated and lusters, ca. 1972.
18. Richard Shaw, ceramic sculpture, slip cast and assembled, decals, 1976.
19. Clayton Bailey, Kaolithic Fossil, stoneware, handbuilt, ca. 1973.
20. Roy Lichtenstein, ceramic sculpture, earthenware, slip cast and altered, low fire glazes.
21. Norris Dalton, Sandwich Plate, porcelain, handbuilt, 1973.
22. Victor Spinski, ceramic sculpture, earthenware, cast and handbuilt, multicolored low fire glazes.
23. Sandy Shannenhouse, Candy Box, earthenware, handbuilt, 1969.
24. Dick Hay, Woman's Club Sandwich, earthenware, wheel thrown and altered, low fire glazes and lusters, 1972.
25. Hui Ka Kwong, sculpture, earthenware, wheel thrown and altered, low fire glazes.
26. James Melchert, Mickey Mouse Plate, earthenware, wheel thrown and handbuilt, 1964.
27. Bill Farrell, sculpture, wheel thrown and altered, low fire glazes and lusters, 1970.
28. Robert Ransom, "B-Girls' " earthenware and mixed media, photo silkscreening, lowfire glazes and lusters, 1972.
29. Erik Gronborg, dish, stoneware, handbuilt, lowfire glazes, 1976.
30. Susan Stephenson, construction, handbuilt, low fire glazes, 1975.
31. Merilyn Levine, "Trents Jacket," stoneware, handbuilt, 1976.

Preface

Approximately two centuries ago American studio-pottery, as it is now known, was almost non-existent. Pottery making was essentially confined to utilitarian tasks or pursued as a leisure-time activity. Since that time, however, numerous and complex circumstances have influenced the evolution of pottery from a position of relatively minor importance as an art form to one of vital artistic self-expression.

The purpose of this book is to evaluate the events and people which were instrumental in the changing attitudes that have made ceramics an integral part of the American contemporary art scene. As such, it is not intended as a definitive study of every known potter, nor of every school, exhibition, publication or related events that have occurred over the past two hundred years.

Although the collector, connoisseur or scholar of ceramics may be interested in dealing with even more specific facts than are contained in this book, it may serve as a helpful guide for identifying prominent leaders and important movements both within and outside the field of ceramics that were instrumental in the growth and development of artistic ceramics. The student of ceramics and art history should find this study especially helpful, since there does not now exist a comprehensive overview of American studio-pottery. This study also supplements the large body of information that already exists in the areas of ceramic technology and design.

Photographs have been carefully selected in order to illustrate specific discussions in the text. Since the last two chapters deal more with a survey of the most recent trends, they contain more photographs than other chapters. At times, the photographs do not address themselves to a specific point in the discussion, but rather serve as a supplement to the general topic under consideration.

The Appendixes at the end of the book are designed as important additions to the various chapters where the information may have proven too cumbersome to be included in the text. They also serve as clues or items for further research for the interested student or scholar of American studio-pottery.

The reality of this book would not have been realized without the helpful guidance of Mr. James Wozniak, Professor of Art, the University of Massachusetts, Amherst, Mass., and the late Dr. Lillian

Dochterman of Illinois State University. Both provided highly professional evaluation and direction during the early stages of this difficult undertaking.

Acknowledgments of great gratitude also are extended to the numerous artists who have given permission to use photographs of their work which are cited in this book, and to those who consented to interviews and whose correspondence with the author form an invaluable part of this project. Special thanks are extended to the various galleries and museums who have provided important information and photographs—particularly to Dr. Peg Weiss and Magie Hughto of the Everson Museum of Art, Syracuse, New York, for their assistance in obtaining photographs from the Everson Museum collection.

A large debt of gratitude also goes to the Department of History of the Milwaukee Public Museum, especially to Mr. Leo Johnson of the Photography Department who gave generous assistance in securing photographs from the museum's permanent collection; Hazel Bray, Associate Curator of Art of the Oakland Museum, Oakland, California; the Fine Arts Museum of San Francisco and the Quay Ceramics Gallery of San Francisco whose help in procuring photographic examples of West Coast ceramics was of inestimable value.

Great appreciation is also extended to the staff of Kendall/Hunt Publishing Company for their skills in producing this book. Particular thanks go to Mr. James Martakes, the Associate Editor who coordinated production and to Dave Corona, Production Development and Design Manager, Wm. C. Brown Company Publishers, who was responsible for the book and jacket designs.

To my wife and children go special thanks for their patience during various phases of this project. My last and warmest expressions of gratitude go to my brother, Ted, without whose life-giving generosity of providing me with a kidney transplant, this book would not have been realized.

Paul S. Donhauser

History of American Ceramics

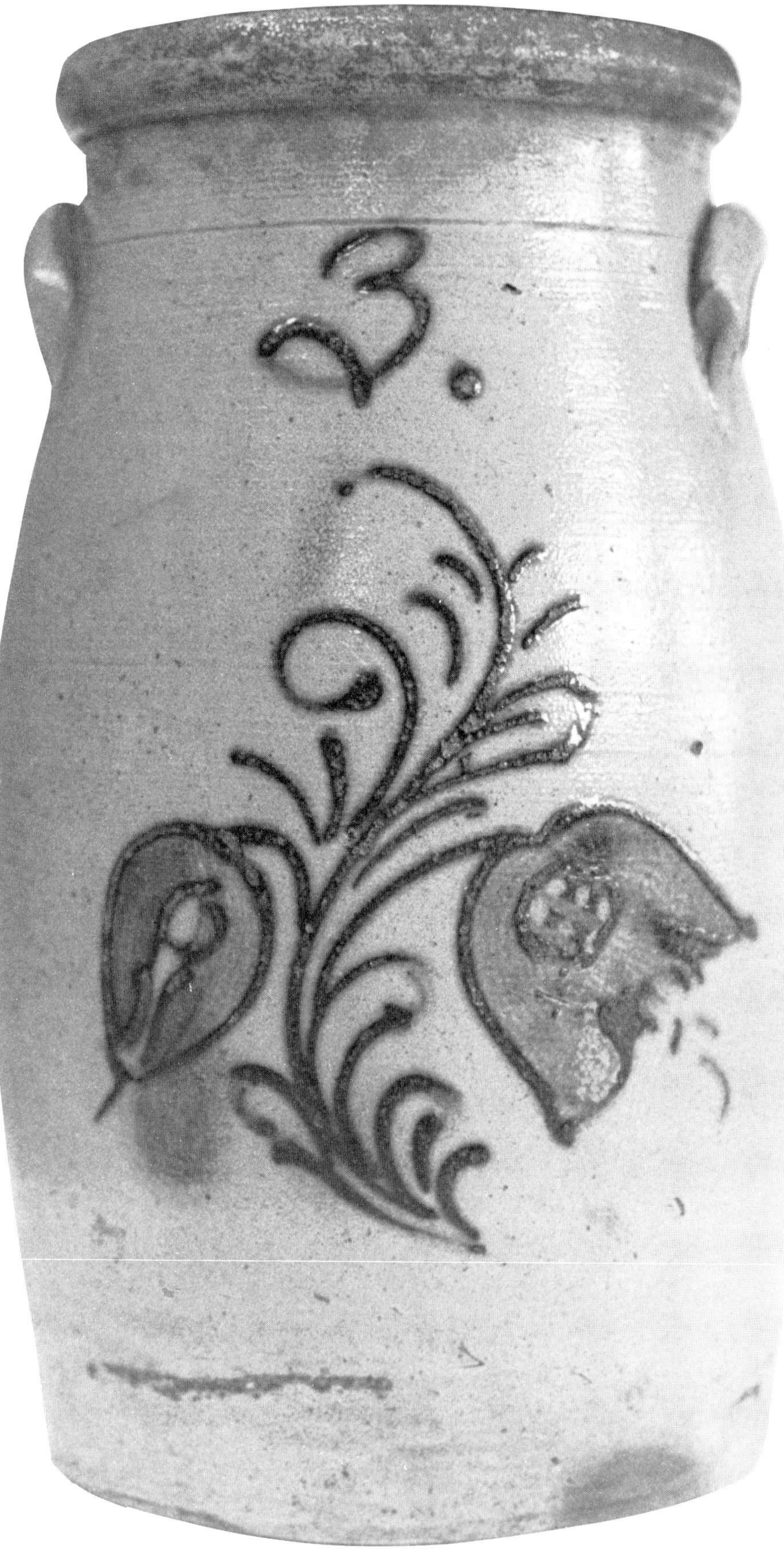

Anonymous

American Pottery of the 19th Century 1

Through a historical investigation of the development of American ceramics, beginning with colonial times and following through to the twentieth century, one is made aware of how the term "artist-potter" has changed. While this survey of the history of pottery will not be exhaustive, it will give prominent examples that were significant to the pottery movement. It will show how the term "studio-potter" or "artist-potter" has changed according to the potter's approach to designing forms, their intended function, their decoration—the potter's aesthetic.

Colonial Precursors

It has not been determined exactly when the first attempts at pottery were made in America by European colonists. The first pottery of any significance centered around John Remmey and William Crolius of New York in 1735. Three leading researchers in the field of ceramics, Edwin Barber,[1] John Spargo[2] and Warren Cox[3] differed in their opinions about the ownership and operation of the pottery which was complicated when Remmey and Crolius married two sisters. However, whether or not these two potters were in partnership is of no deep concern. The fact remains that theirs was the first pottery of significance produced in America.

The wares produced by Remmey and Crolius fell into the general category of utilitarian ceramics with stoneware jugs, storage jars, batter jugs, butter churns and teapots as the mainstay of their production. Most of their pottery was salt glazed and decorated with incised, stamped or cobalt brushed designs (Fig. 1-1).

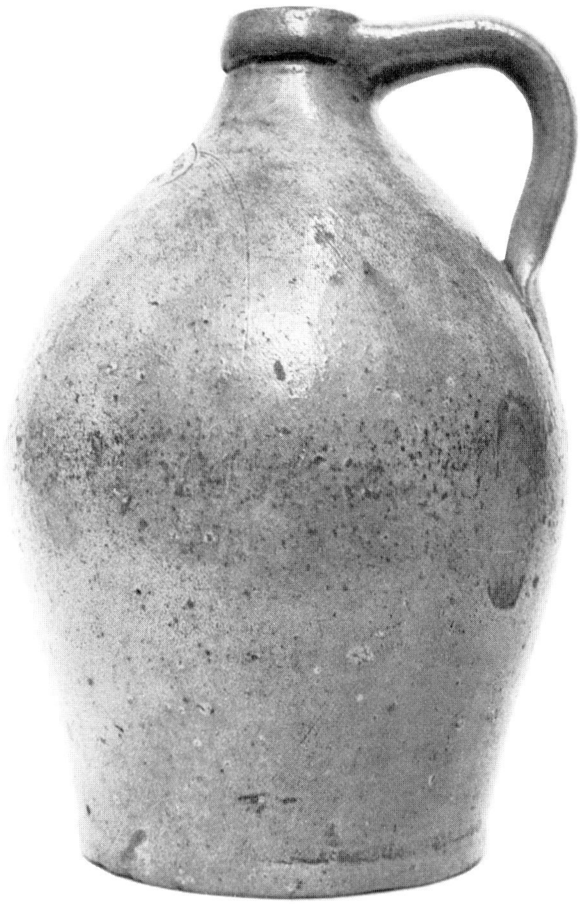

Figure 1-1. Anonymous, Jug, stoneware, wheel thrown, pulled handle, stamped "Milwaukee, 1835"; 11″ h × 7 1/2″ w. Courtesy, Oshkosh Public Museum Permanent Collection.

Most colonial pottery of this type was unsigned and undecorated. The potter often remained anonymous and made no claim to be recognized as an artist-potter.

This type of ware was common in early colonial potteries whose aim it was to fill immediate utilitarian needs. It was generally wheel-thrown. Pots were unsigned and often unmarked, except for occasional presentation pieces expressive of the skill and artistic bent of the potter. Sometimes the name of the donor, the date of presentation, and other data or appropriate sentiments were inscribed on the pieces especially made for gifts. But generally, the potter of the colonial period was anonymous and does not appear to have made overt claims to the status of an artist.

Pennsylvania Dutch ware represented an example of colonial pottery produced for decorative rather than utilitarian purposes. Pennsylvania was settled along the Delaware River first by Swedes, then by the English and Dutch. By 1655 the Dutch controlled these settlements and in 1664, the English. About this time the Mennonites arrived from Germany, the Lutherans and Reformed Church groups from Bavaria and Austria. The Swiss came in 1727 and the Scotch-Irish Presbyterians thereafter.[4]

The pottery produced by these people was, and is currently referred to as "Pennsylvania Dutch" slip ware or "Tulip" ware (Fig. 1-2). They are usually decorated with a variety of floral motifs including the tulip and the pomegranate. An additional distinguishing characteristic of this early American ware was the inscriptions on the plates and platters which were to be used primarily for decorative rather than utilitarian purposes. The sayings usually served as an interesting clue to ideas and customs of the various settlements.

These profusely decorated wares fell into two special categories, slip ware and sgraffito.

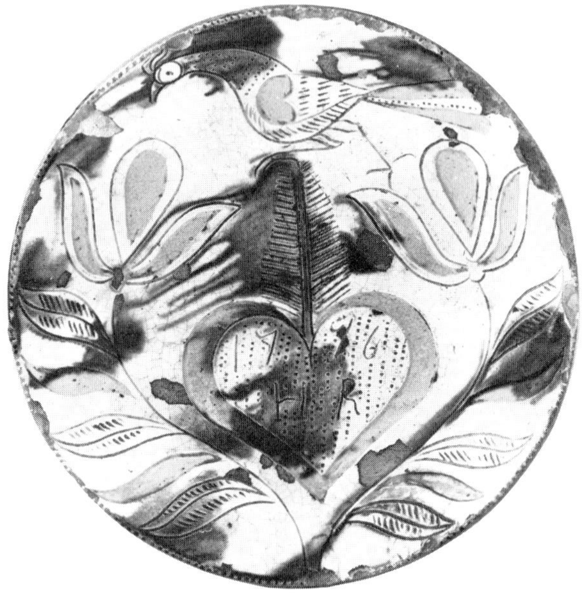

Figure 1-2. Pennsylvania Dutch Plate, earthenware, attributed to Henry Roudebuth, 1776, wheel thrown, slips and oxides, sgraffito decoration. Courtesy, The Henry Francis du Pont Winterthur Museum.

The former was usually accomplished by trailing a slip decoration of contrasting color on the red, earthenware body. The latter was first covered with a slip, usually white or yellow, and a design was then carved through it in order to reveal the dark, earthenware body beneath. Both types were then covered with a transparent lead glaze and fired at around 1,400 degrees Fahrenheit in an oxidation atmosphere (Plate 1).

In summary, the period spanning the time of the first colonial settlements to the end of the War of Independence in 1776 witnessed relatively little activity in the area of any large-scale pottery making. Small establishments were in existence, supplying the barest essentials. The records available do not indicate any more ambitious activity.

Pottery After the War of Independence

After American independence, a new direction in pottery emerged. Once the basic utilitarian needs were met, or at least the ability to produce these wares quite readily, more attention was directed to inventing pottery that reflected a higher standard of living and a change in taste. The new surge of nationalism which swept the country was reflected in pottery. This resulted in pottery that was highly decorated with patriotic slogans, portraits and various other embellishments such as stars, eagles and the American flag.

Having had no native pottery tradition, with the rare exception of Eastern Pennsylvania and some parts of Vermont, American manufacturers drew upon the European potteries for craftsmen with talent and skill. As a result, the smaller firms that were financially unable to recruit European talents for designing and decorating were eventually outdistanced by their more enterprising competitors. The larger, more financially stable companies were able to survive longer because of the ability to produce a ware of more diversified character, and at a more competitive price. Furthermore, they had obtained the best mold-makers, designers, decorators and chemists from France, Germany and England.

One important observation to be made of these pottery firms of the eighteenth and nineteenth centuries is that there was no individual who personally attended to the entire potting process. It is of further consequence that this division of labor kept the designer and decorator distinct from each other and from engaging in the numerous steps necessary to complete any one piece of ceramic ware. These people who were involved in designing and decorating for industry were loosely called "artist-potters."

The history of American ceramics of the eighteenth and nineteenth centuries is filled with innumerable examples of the rise and fall of pottery manufacturing plants. Ramsay, in his *American Potters and Pottery* included a list of over one hundred firms.[5] For this reason, the most obvious and largest concerns have been included in order to present a representative example of the eighteenth and middle nineteenth century setting. Smaller, less successful potteries existed but could not compete with the highly sophisticated and well organized European market. Generally, their inability to compete with the manufacturing skills of the larger companies resulted in financial failure.

At this time mass-production and its implications, i.e., quality control of materials and techniques, became the standard for excellence. In factory production the ceramic objects were designed by the sculptor of the molds in which they were made. Decorations applied to the pottery frequently became narrative in type, dealing with various historical events which were in stark contrast to the simplicity of colonial pottery. In giving less consideration to the nature of the materials, designers and decorators often sought to emulate the designs of other media such as silver, copper and pewter. The pottery, therefore, repeatedly assumed a peculiar similarity to the prototypes of the above mentioned materials. Typical copies in clay or porcelain were of silver and copper teapots, coffee pots, urns and pewter tankards. A similar approach was used with the more decorative forms.

After the Revolution, the first important American ceramic manufacturer was Captain John Norton. Various historians place the beginning of his pottery around 1793, in Bennington, Vermont. The business was handed down through at least two generations, and in 1845, Julius Norton, grandson of John, brought Christopher Webber Fenton into his business. The pottery firm has been variously known as Bennington Pottery, Norton and Fenton Company and the Edward Norton and Company.[6]

The company became famous for its Parian ware. This was the result of the discovery of a large bed of Kaolin near the location of the pottery.[7] The Parian ware of Norton and Fenton was similar to England's Jaspar ware produced by Wedgewood—no doubt because the firm employed the skills of John Harrison who had worked for Wedgewood as a modeller.

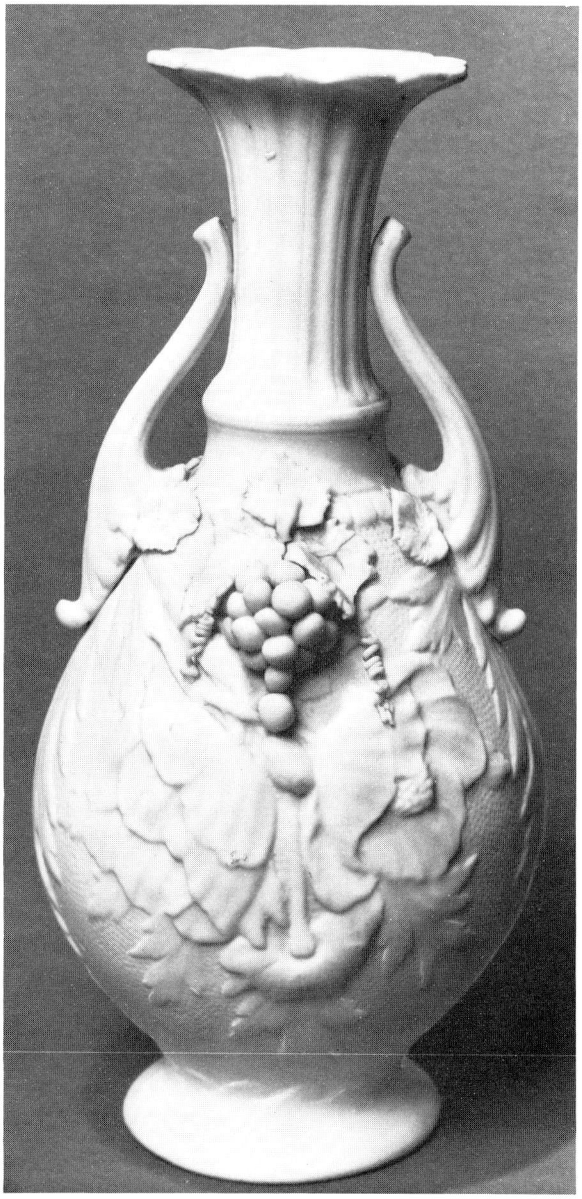

Figure 1-3. Parian Ware, Norton & Fenton, U.S. Pottery Co., 1850-58. Milwaukee Public Museum Collection. This piece illustrates how various skills of designers and modelers were required for the production of art pottery.

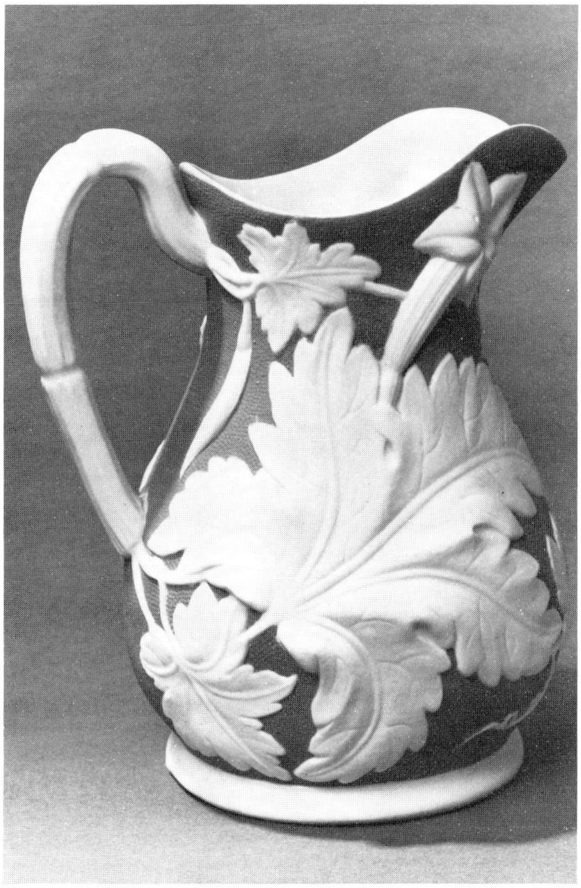

Figure 1-4. Parian Ware Pitcher, Bennington Pottery, ca. 1847, 10 1/2″ × 8 1/2″, white relief modeling on matt, blue background. Milwaukee Public Museum Collection. Most American ceramics produced by industry in the 19th century were imitative of the prototypes coming from Europe. This shows a clear influence of Wedgewood ceramics from England.

The Parian ware produced by Norton and Fenton was divided into two broad categories: utilitarian and decorative. The utilitarian wares were completely white and glazed (Fig. 1-3). The decorative pieces were executed in the traditional Jasper ware technique of blue and white and consisted of applied relief decorations on variations of Classic Revival vases, urns and pitchers (Fig. 1-4). These decorative treatments included sprigging and carving. Some parts of the pots remained unglazed, usually the colored background, which provided a strong contrast for the applied, three-dimensional relief decoration.

In 1849 Fenton left Norton and established his own pottery, naming it the United States Pottery. To it he brought the experience and knowledge of the Norton and Fenton Company, and improved the Parian ware to something more durable and colorful. Fenton relied heavily on European talent to improve the designs of his wares. Williamson pointed out:

> Modellers, designers, throwers, furnace men, all flocked to Fenton from all over the world. Outstanding among these was Daniel Greatbach who had modelled and designed for Wedgewood.[8]

The pottery produced by the United States Pottery was known as Flint Enamel or Rockingham ware. It consisted mainly of hound-handled pitchers which were Greatbach's designs, cow-shaped creamers, book flasks, candlestick holders and reclining animals. This first, large-scale American pottery was closed in 1858 for unknown reasons. The following year Fenton moved to Peoria, Illinois where he once more engaged in producing his famous white wares.

The importance of this firm lies in the fact that a high level of technological and artistic competence was achieved through the importation of European craftsmen. This is evident upon examining the ware it produced. The majority of its forms were not simply cast in one-piece molds. Instead, they often required two-piece molds; in addition, separate pieces had to be attached or added to the surface. The highly ornate surface treatments indicate that specialized talents were employed in the production of the initial molds.

Glaze calculation, which frequently concerned itself with reproducing colors and textures, also indicates a demand for a variety of skills. This is further evidence that a distinct division of labor was required to successfully operate and maintain a pottery during this period. Since there were no schools in America at this time which specialized in the area of ceramics, it follows that America's progress in pottery depended almost exclusively on imported talents.

Numerous potteries sprang up in the early and mid-nineteenth century but usually lasted for only a short period of time. Surviving the commercial competition both from the continent and from this country was the Jersey Porcelain and Earthenware Company. It, too, received the talents of Greatbach who continued to design the famous hound-handled pitchers. Many of its wares also depicted American slogans, portraits of national heroes and the famous American eagle-and-flag motif. This company was typical of the spirit of "scientific investigation" in the area of ceramics. It experimented with kaolin even before it organized into a large industrial concern, and in 1826 the Franklin Institute awarded it a silver medal for "the best china from American materials."[9]

In 1825, William Tucker and Thomas Hulme opened a pottery called the Philadelphia China Factory. The name of this firm was later changed to Tucker and Hemphill Works, and their products carried the firm's name. Their specialty was a hard-bone-china. Unable to recruit sufficient American talent, the company sent to France, England and Germany for potters, designers and painters. The skills of these craftsmen were reflected in the wares produced between 1830 and 1850 (Fig. 1-5).

> An imitation of some Sèvres wares was made with borders of roses and other flowers. Elaborate monograms, coats of arms, portraits of noted men, etc., were all made and later copies of well known works such as the Vaughan portrait of Washington by Gilbert Stuart and the Charles Wilson Peale one of Wayne ("Mad Anthony"). One ambitious piece shows Napolean watching the burning of Moscow.[10]

In addition to the Tucker and Hemphill Works, the only other significant porcelain manufacturing in the first half of the 19th century was carried on by William Boch and his brother, both immigrants from Germany. Their work was highly decorated, their subject matter being such events and motifs as the Boston Tea Party, Revolutionary soldiers and Indians. Sometimes it was difficult to distinguish their work from that of Tucker and Hemphill because of similarities in decorative motifs and their techniques of applying them. For their efforts the Boch brothers were invited to exhibit at the Crystal Palace Exhibition of New York in 1853.[11] Although no records have been located to indicate the number of other companies that also exhibited at this international event it can be assumed that the Boch brothers' work must have shown technical and aesthetic merit to have been included.

One of the earliest known ceramic factories producing specialty items such as buttons, door knobs, escutcheons, drawer pulls and umbrella handles was started by Charles

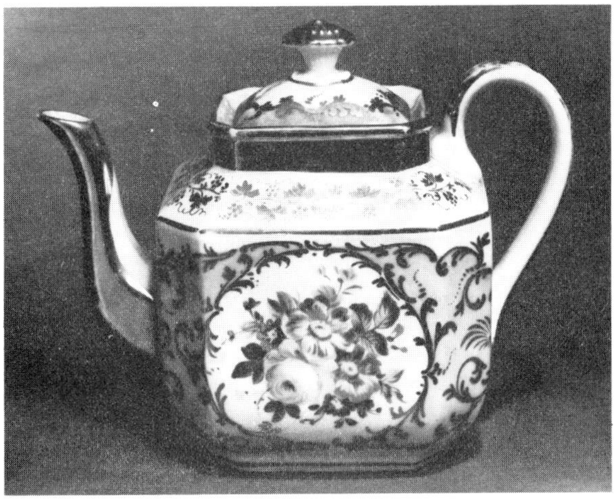

Figure 1-5. Tucker & Hemphill Porcelain Teapot, ca. 1826-30, 9″ × 7 1/2″. Many pottery manufacturers relied on the skills of talented decorators for embellishing their work with underglaze, overglaze, luster and decal decorations. Milwaukee Public Museum Collection.

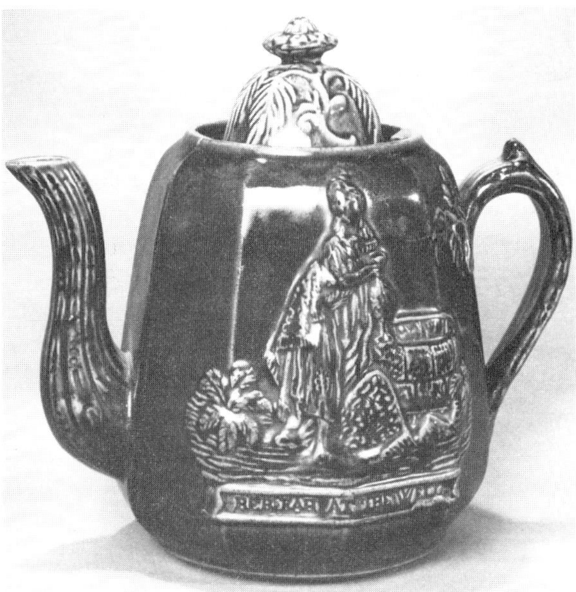

Figure 1-6. "Rebecca-at-the-Well" Tea Pot, 1860, E & W Bennett Co., Ohio, 9″ × 9″. Milwaukee Public Museum Collection. Decorators who made the original design in relief for commercial pottery were often referred to as "artist-potters" during the 19th century.

Cartlidge, who came from England in 1848. He sent for his brothers-in-law, both decorators at Staffordshire, and expanded his operation to include such items as portrait busts of Daniel Webster, Zachary Taylor and Chief Justice Marshall. Also included in this line were cameos, brooch medallions and miniature family portraits. But according to Barber—

> Work of this high order of merit was not in sufficient demand in the United States at that day to insure financial success and much money was lost in the enterprise.[12]

In 1839, an Englishman, James Bennet, found suitable clay near the banks of the Ohio River and sent for his two brothers to help establish a pottery which was known as the Bennington Pottery Company of East Liverpool, Ohio. Together they began the manufacturing of Yellow ware and Rockingham ware. Success came quickly, and the brothers looked for a location where better coal for their firing could be found, as well as a more economical means for transporting their goods. Accordingly, they moved to Birmingham, now a part of Pittsburgh, Pennsylvania, where they continued the manufacturing of, what was by then, the famous six-sided Rockingham pitchers.

A series of business maneuvers resulted in their moving to Baltimore, Maryland, where more elaborately decorated pitchers and teapots were made. One of their more popular items became the "Rebecca-at-the-Well" teapot. This complicated form and its relief decorations apparently required the abilities of highly skilled modellers and decorators (Fig. 1-6). Bennet's work received several honors at the Crystal Palace and Franklin Institute. An additional mark of distinction came to Bennet at the Chicago World's Fair of

1897. At that event several ceramic manufacturing companies displayed their work in one group exhibition, but the work of the Bennington Pottery Company was accorded the honor of having an individual exhibition.[13]

Another phase in America's move toward producing its own Art pottery was found in the Ott and Brewer Ceramics Company of Trenton, New Jersey. The company secured the services of a Mr. Broome from Liverpool, England. He was responsible for the introduction of vases adorned with figures that were modelled as free-standing sculpture and then fastened to various pots whose function is undiscernible to this writer. This company also obtained the skills of William Bromely and his relatives from Ireland. In 1882 the Bromely family came from the Belleek factory of Ireland and brought with them the trade secrets and decorating skills for this extremely fragile Belleek ware, originally invented by William H. Gross of Stoke-on-Trent of England.[14] The subsequent wares produced by the Ott and Brewer Company and the establishment in Belleek, Ireland are now more commonly known as eggshell china. It has become world famous for its extreme lightness and lustrous glazes.

In contrast to this delicate Belleek porcelain, there developed in America a more durable "hotel china." Its history goes back to 1854 and to the name of Knowles at East Liverpool, Ohio, which was reputed to be the largest center of potteries in the world.[15] According to Cox and Barber it was there that the famous stone china or granite ware was begun. This vitreous pottery lent itself to varying purposes, such as dinner ware and tea sets, as well as accessories for water closets. Most of these wares have opaque white glazes, applied over slight relief carvings.

Although none of the sources used by this writer referred to any of the wares produced at this time as "art pottery," it is possible that some form of the art-pottery movement found its beginning at the Knowles, Taylor and Knowles Company. It was there that the production of exhibition pieces came under serious consideration. Some pieces were sent to the Chicago World's Fair and Barber described them as follows:

> One of these is a nine-inch piece, made of the peculiarly translucent china body with soft, velvety glaze, which is designated by the manufacturer "Lotus" ware. The entire exterior surface is covered with an underglaze mazarine blue of a rich tone. While the subjects are not new (angels used as decorative subject matter) the treatment is original, the decoration is built up *over* the glaze instead of *under* it, as in the pate-sur-pate method. The neck of the vase is decorated in raised gold after the Renaissance style, while the handles are solidly gilded and chased.[16]

Regarding another, quite larger piece, Barber said:

> The ground color is a rich mazarine blue applied under the glaze. Flowers in relief coin-gold or various tints are applied to the surface, representing petunias, and on the side of the piece is an excellently painted pair of golden partridges. The neck of the vase and the pedestal are embellished with solid, raised gold borders in the Renaissance style.[17]

Thus, after the Revolution we find for the first time a genuine concern for the individual piece in terms of ornamenting it as a piece by and for itself. It could well be that the seed for the artist-potter was planted at this time. This may have come about through two considerations. First, the objects typical of Barber's description were manufactured for a rather select clientele and, secondly, they were also produced for purposes of exhibition at the annual expositions.

This artistic concern was exemplified more dramatically by the Chelsea Keramic Art Works of Chelsea, Mass. It was founded in 1890 and specialized in reproducing traditional European pottery, with particular attention given to ancient Greek forms. Of these the *amphora, lekythos, oenochoë, stamnos* and *krater* were favorite forms. This firm also strived to find the secrets of the much-sought-after Chinese *sang de boeuf* glaze. It succeeded in discovering the beauty of the unusual red color. Then, in order to make them available only to collectors who would pay a high price because of their rarity, the company produced only thirty pieces.[18]

In this survey of commercial ceramics, a changing role for the ceramic artist can be noted. Initially it was important for him to supply basic technical abilities. But as competition increased and public tastes became more varied, the ceramicist became more specialized in some artistic aspects of ceramic production. While he might re-create and even copy the styles and motifs of other countries, as well as other companies and past periods in history, it became increasingly important for him to develop an object of some uniqueness. This was accomplished most readily through hand-decorating in the form of painting, sprigging and carving. The individually adorned pottery, therefore, became a significant part of several companies' production.

The person referred to as an "artist-potter" of the nineteenth century consequently was one who specialized not only in a simple manual skill, but one who also helped to enhance a pot and add to it a characteristic of individuality, of preciousness. This quality was frequently found in people whose backgrounds went beyond the technical competence of ceramics, whose skills were also derived from a background in art training, especially painting and drawing. These attributes were found among the group of ceramic artists who have been referred to as china-painters or china decorators. It may be said that they were the earliest form of the studio-potter in America.

Notes

1. Edwin Barber, *The Pottery and Porcelain of the United States*, p. 28.
2. John Spargo, *Early American Pottery and China*, p. 84.
3. Warren Cox, *Pottery and Porcelain*, p. 51.
4. Helen Stiles, *Pottery in the United States*, p. 52.
5. John Ramsay, *American Potters and Pottery*, pp. 102-120.
6. Barber, p. 558.
7. The inclusion of Kaolin in Parian ware was necessary in order to obtain a pure white color which gave the pottery the appearance of porcelain.
8. Scott Williamson, *The American Craftsman*, p. 63.
9. Cox, p. 1002.
10. Ibid., p. 1003.
11. Ibid., p. 1005.
12. Barber, p. 162.
13. Ibid., p. 196.
14. Ibid., p. 215.
15. Stiles, p. 73.
16. Barber, p. 204.
17. Ibid., p. 205.
18. Ibid., pp. 267-405.

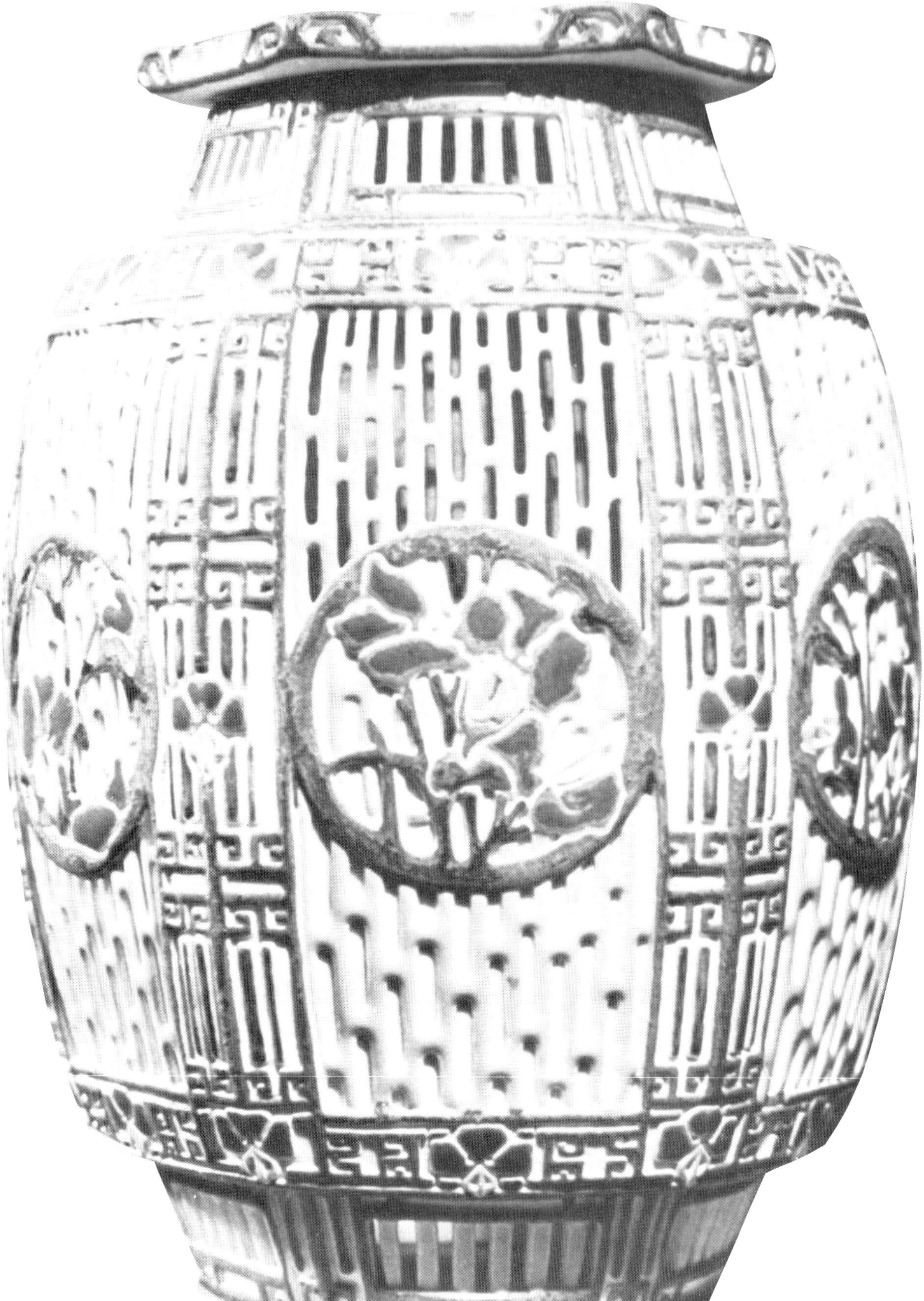

Adelaide Robineau

China Painting in America 2

China painting in America flourished contemporaneously with industry's imitations of European and Oriental styles during the period of approximately 1860 to 1920. It was from industry that the better skilled decorators came to serve as instructors to groups of ladies interested in china decorating as a leisure time activity.

A detailed history of the china painting movement is difficult to present due to the lack of dependable evidence, but an insight was provided by Edwin Barber.[1] He not only presented a sequence of how some prominent decorators arrived at their form language by copying the classic forms and decorations of Rome, Greece and China, but also how master craftsmen's talents were sought by ladies' clubs for the purpose of instruction. It was the latter whose influence Barber felt had an important role in helping to develop studio-pottery in the nineteenth and twentieth centuries.

Barber described at some length several commercial enterprises which dealt specifically with the various aspects of china decorating. These employed young men and women for the tasks of gold banding, gilding and other decorative processes. According to Barber, New York City was the center of most china decorating activity. With an increased demand for persons who were highly skilled in the decorating of ceramics, several large-scale manufacturers began to establish decorating departments. Since there were no professional schools in this country where one was able to acquire the necessary skills for decorating, it was up to several European craftsmen to establish informal classes in china decorating. Barber believed that Edward Lycett was among the first of these important persons.

Mr. Lycett was apprenticed to the ceramics firm of Copeland and Garrett of the old Spode Pottery at Stoke-on-Trent, England. It was there that he mastered the art of painting facsimiles of Greek vases. Some of the earlier examples of Mr. Lycett's decorating were exhibited at the first of the International Expositions at Hyde Park, London, in 1851. They were also reproduced in the illustrations of some of the art journals of that date.

Edwin Barber's evaluation of Lycett's influence on America's china painting movement is, in part, as follows:

> Mr. Lycett's artistic career in America may be said to represent the history of china painting in the United States. Not because he has been the only ceramic artist of ability that we have had, for there have been others, but because he has been continuously identified with the development and expansion of the art form from the beginning of the late Civil War to the present, covering a period of nearly three and a half decades. During all of this time he has kept fully abreast with the advance in public taste, and, indeed, has been largely instrumental in bringing about the recent remarkable revival of decorative art among the ladies from one end of the land to the other.[2]

Lycett's reputation as the pioneer of china painting rests not only on the fact that he brought with him from England an uncanny skill for reproducing the decorations of acknowledged masterpieces from Greece, Rome and the Orient, but also in his desire to teach the decorating methods to interested groups throughout the nation.

> The only place where painting of the finer kind was being done as a regular business was at Mr. Lycett's warerooms; and here many ladies resorted to study the methods employed and the materials required. This was the commencement of the first ceramic art movement in America, and in a short time many

> wealthy and prominent ladies were engaged in studying under Mr. Lycett's tuition. Some of these students afterwards became prominent as artists, and among Mr. Lycett's pupils have been daughters of many eminent public men . . . and a large number of women who later achieved distinction as leaders in ceramic associations in various parts of the country.[3]

The impact of Lycett in particular, and of other decorators like him coming from industry, had to be strong, if for no other reason than they were the primary source for technical as well as artistic information and guidance. This was appropriately illustrated when Barber continued:

> The founder of the celebrated Rockwood Pottery sent some of her earlier experiments to be fired at the Greene Street kilns, and Mr. George Nichols there watched the operation of firing, filling and drawing the kilns, and thus gathered much of the material for his book on "Pottery and How It Is Made."[4]

The importance of America's ceramic industry in providing the necessary guidance for the amateur china decorator was further illustrated when Barber stated that Mr. Lycett was invited to instruct a class in china painting at the School of Design, St. Louis, Missouri in 1877. He maintained this position for one year, after which time he accepted an invitation to teach decorating to a ladies' club in Cincinnati, Ohio.

Although insufficient evidence prevents an unequivocal conclusion regarding the significance of industry in relation to non-industrial china decorating, such as in ladies' clubs or classes at finishing schools, there are clear suggestions that china painting relied heavily on industry for technical and artistic guidance. The decorators depended on industry for bisque fired pottery to be decorated and for the pigments, glazes and kilns in which the ware was fired. Artistic guidelines were established by industry by furnishing the decorators with prototypes of accepted European and Oriental designs for imitation. The china painters' entire aesthetic, therefore, emulated the established patterns of the ceramic industry.

Despite these seemingly uncreative activities, it is important to note that through this close association with industry, efforts began to develop around 1880 which attempted to break with the dependence on, hence the stereotyped activities of, ceramic manufacturers. A reaction against industry was begun by several china painters, and attempts were made to establish an art-pottery movement which was based entirely on the abilities of individuals. Barber alluded to this possibility when he appraised the role of women decorators.

> It is true that china painting has heretofore been pursued largely as a pastime by the women of America, but Mr. Lycett sees in the near future vast possibilities for ceramic work, when women shall seriously engage in it. The great advantage they possess in their sex will enable them to work understandingly and in complete touch with consumers, thus adding a value to their work which the stereotyped decorations from the factory do not possess—where the principal interest seems to be to reproduce a prescribed and meaningless ornament of exact size and unvarying shades of color. The revival of original, appropriate and artistic work—the intelligent use of a sentiment, and idea, a quotation; the illustration of a historical event, seems to be reserved for the women of this country. The women decorators in all parts of the land are rapidly elevating the standards of this beautiful art, and much more may be expected of them in the near future.[5]

Although this prediction may appear to have been somewhat naive—since it did not come to pass—it nevertheless indicates a desire to strive for more individually created pottery. It is interesting to note, moreover, that the first well-organized and independent art-pottery movement did indeed begin with several women.

Activities in Cincinnati, Ohio

The pivotal point for the development of the American china decorating movement was in Cincinnati, Ohio. It was there that an early form of the artist-potter began to emerge from the china painters. Among the contributions that several of these new potters made was the solution of technical problems as they related to underglaze and overglaze decorations, glazes, clay bodies and the ability to reach high temperatures in firing. Of importance also was the fact that those who became identified as leaders within the china painting movement and who were involved in this type of research generally worked independently of the ceramic industry.

The first known occasion on which decorated wares of Cincinnati potters were shown in any quantity was in May, 1875 at the International Entertainment sponsored by the Women's Centennial Executive Committee of Cincinnati. The purpose of the showing was to raise funds to support the Cincinnati exhibition of china decorating at the Philadelphia Centennial Exposition.[6]

The group of ladies undertaking the task of decorating preformed pots at this time numbered only eight, but within a short period of time grew to almost sixty. Providing technical and artistic assistance was Mr. Benn Pitman of the Cincinnati School of Design. He commenced to teach various phases of decorating techniques in the summer of 1874. The first three to four years were spent in finding solutions to the problems of mixing pigments, application of decorations, glazing and the construction and firing of kilns. Kilns of commercial potteries were frequently used for firing the pottery decorated by these ladies.[7]

It was the Philadelphia Exposition of 1876 that served as a dramatic impetus to the American china decorating movement, for it was at that occasion that two of Cincinnati's china decorators became exposed to the ceramic art of Europe and the Orient. One was Mary Louise McLaughlin, the other Mrs. Maria Longworth Butler. Miss McLaughlin was impressed by the Limoges faience, which was shown for the first time in the United States, and Mrs. Butler by the Japanese ceramics. Both were familiar with over-glaze decoration which by this time had reached wide and popular acceptance not only in Cincinnati, but also in other metropolitan centers. Both ladies, however, were eager to venture beyond existing techniques.

Miss McLaughlin's interest in solving the various problems of decorating and glazing and their numerous ramifications marked her as an early leader in American ceramics. She knew that the Haviland's Limoges faience was decorated under the glaze rather than over it. But she also knew from her own experiences that when metallic oxides were applied on the bisque as colorants and then covered with a clear glaze, the fired colors usually ran with the glaze when it reached maturity. After several months of trial and error, she succeeded in solving the problem of underglaze decorations by investigating the decorative methods of commercial potters who used a colored slip on the green ware, thereby facilitating a more unified shrinkage of decoration and body. So successful was her "new" direction that several pieces were sent to the Paris Exposition in 1878[8] (Fig. 2-1).

The importance attached to Miss McLaughlin is two-fold. First, she was an example of the early phase of the American artist-potter. This can be seen in her struggle to solve aesthetic and technical problems while remaining essentially independent of industry. While commercial manufacturers were evidently satisfied in copying the forms and decorations of the past and of other countries and mass producing them, Miss McLaughlin sought to go beyond this. That she formulated her own clay bodies, decorating slips and glazes, threw her own pots, and in fact was instrumental in making independent decisions in the entire process, exemplifies her desire to be self-sufficient. McLaughlin's ceaseless inquiry also resulted in an avid interest in porcelain. Faced with the lack of published material concerning porcelain bodies or glazes, she once more proceeded to deal successfully with porcelain.

Most published material from 1880 to 1900 was concerned with soft-paste porcelain of Sèvres. Other porcelain bodies and glazes for higher temperatures were stated in empirical formulas instead of the batch recipe which would have given her the actual proportions of the raw chemical compounds making up the glaze or body. Thus, since she was not familiar with empirical formulas, she had to test clay bodies and glazes by trial and error.

In 1901, she solved the problems of a satisfactory porcelain body, glaze and a kiln that fired high enough for the maturing

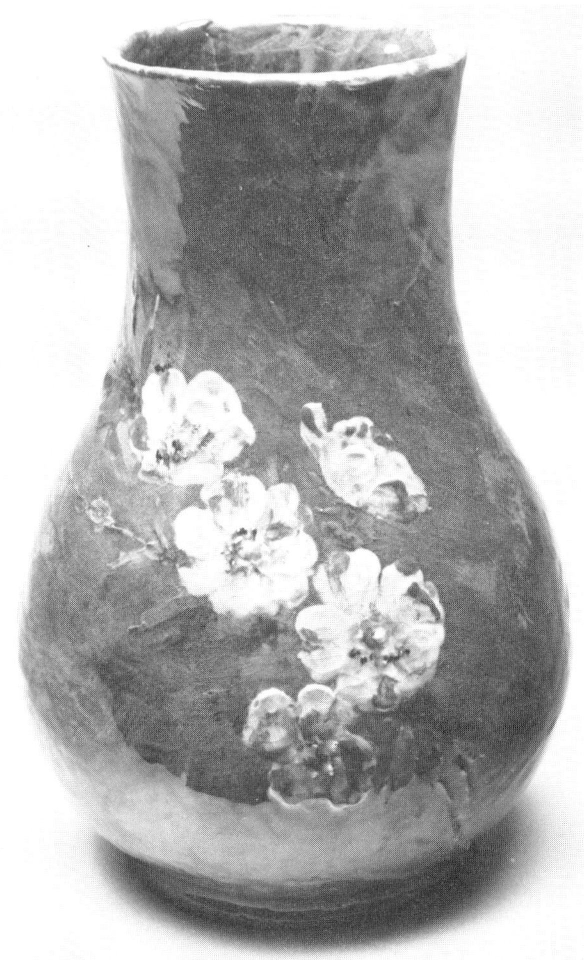

Figure 2-1. Mary Louise McLaughlin, "Cincinnati Limoges," vase, 8 1/2" × 5 3/4", 1879, Cincinnati Art Museum Collection. McLaughlin was one of the early leaders of the china decorating movement who struggled to find the various decorating and glazing secrets used by other countries, cultures and industry.

temperature of 2,400 degrees Fahrenheit. For this work in porcelain Miss McLaughlin was awarded a bronze medal for "American Porcelain" at the Buffalo Exposition of 1901.[9] Subsequent honors confirmed her status as one of America's earliest acknowledged studio-potters. In 1913 Dr. Charles Binns, then of Alfred University, praised her for her work in porcelain, stating: "You are so much to be commended for the manner in which you have overcome so many of the obstacles inherent to porcelain making."[10] In 1938 the American Ceramic Society awarded Miss McLaughlin an honorary membership for her accomplishments in the technology of underglaze, brush-painted faience and for her decorative, once-fired porcelain.[11]

Miss McLaughlin's second contribution to furthering the china decorating movement was her organization of the Cincinnati Pottery Club. It was founded by her in the spring of 1879 with twelve active and three honorary members. Each member had to be involved in some specialty within the ceramic process "or at least bringing to her work so marked an individuality as to characterize it with distinctive features."[12]

The organization sought to establish and maintain a high standard in its members' work. Each member had to have a specialty. In addition, all had to be capable of working with overglaze painting, incised designing, relief decorating, and underglaze painting. Although the pots were thrown by two men employed specifically for that task, the notion of versatility within a potter involved in the total ceramic process may have been unknowingly initiated at this time.

The club met three times a week to discuss its work, and in its continuing efforts to solve the vast array of technical problems, the organization soon became the largest, most active ceramic group in the country. The club occasionally held receptions to which visitors were invited. The first of a series of exhibitions was held in May, 1880, and not less than two hundred pieces were shown. A review of the show, in which several of the pieces were illustrated as well as evaluated, indicated that, by the use of various techniques, the reproducing of floral and animal motifs in as naturalistic a manner as possible was a main concern. Chinese, Japanese, Persian and Graeco-Roman derivatives were most popular.[13]

Seven years before The American Ceramic Society was founded, the organization headed by Miss McLaughlin sought, among other things, to—

> disseminate correct and practical information, so that many of the disappointments awaiting those who essay the work at a distance from competent instruction may be avoided.[14]

It has not been ascertained what specific influence this organization may have had on the china decorating movement or the American public in general. However, the group's efforts were notable for having promoted and advanced the art of the china painters, as well as for securing the best examples for the World's Fair. Moreover, through its membership of over ten thousand women who were reportedly active in pottery-decorating at that time, one has a good indication of the interest displayed in the field during the last decade of the nineteenth century.[15]

The second Cincinnatian who was influenced by the Philadelphia Centennial of 1876 was Maria Longworth Butler Storer. She had been a china decorator for some time, and was always somewhat partial to Japanese designs. Upon visiting the Japanese display at the Centennial, she became more enthusiastic about decorating pottery, and her father offered the use of a building for what he thought was a daughter's whim. It was in November, 1880 that the first kiln was fired with satisfactory results. The wares primarily consisted of underglaze decorations in blues and browns (Fig. 2-2).

Through Mrs. Storer's initial success the venture was operated on a more business-like basis and was called the Rookwood Pottery Company. Rookwood pottery was essentially concerned with imparting a feeling of individuality, a feeling that sought to oppose the impersonal character of other commercial manufacturies. It accomplished this through research in which native clays and chemicals were tested for use in the studio. As a result of this research, Rookwood became known for several unique glaze effects—the most notable having been called "Tiger's Eye" glaze. This glaze was developed by melting together several underglaze colors on the bisque ware. It was then covered with a transparent glaze and fired with a resultant opalescent quality.

In its attempt to produce individual, artistic pottery, Rookwood concerned itself with the uses of color in ceramics, such as oxides and stains in clay bodies, glazes and in under and over-glazes[16] (Plate 2).

An examination of a list of special glazes the Rookwood firm developed further points out its interest in creating a variety of unique glazes for its thrown shapes. These included the following:

> *Goldstone*, an effect resembling the glistening of golden particles in aventurine, but rather more limpid by reason of the glaze; *Aereial Blue*, a delicate

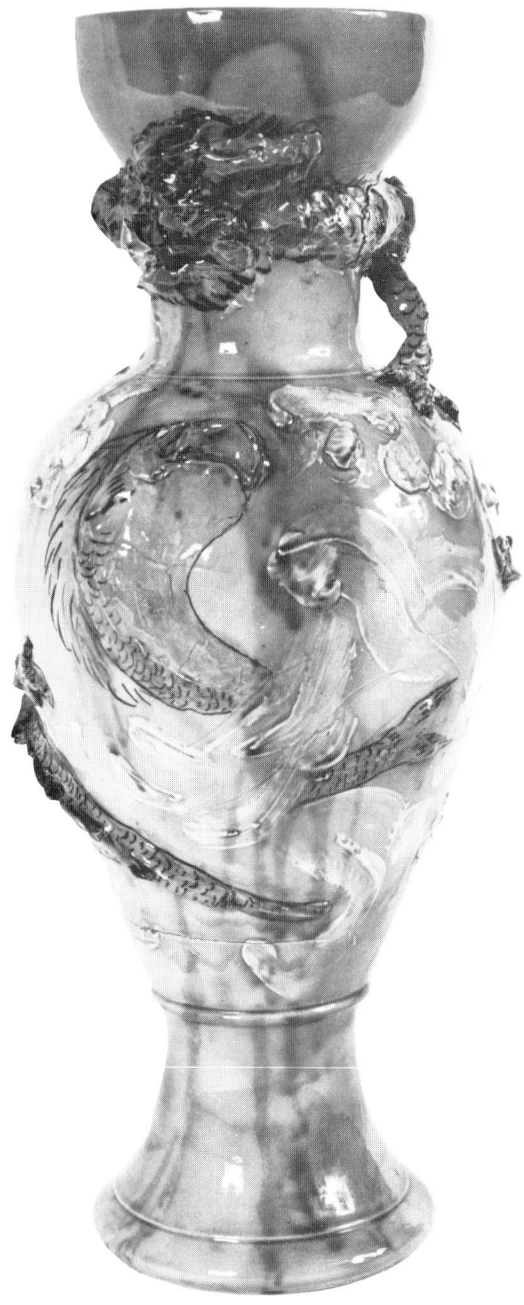

Figure 2-2. Maria Longworth Nichols, Vase, earthenware, 25" × 10 1/2", 1881, Cincinnati Art Museum Collection.

monochromatic ware with a quiet decoration in celestial blue on a cool grayish white ground; *Iris*, a class of effects with a considerable range of colors—pink, blues, greens, creamy whites, and yellow—based upon a warm gray tone; and *Sea Green*, a light-colored decoration varying from a mellow opalescent sea-green relieved by a few glowing warm touches, to a cooler green with bluish accents.[17]

For its work in pottery Rookwood was awarded a gold medal at the Paris Exposition in 1889, a "Highest Award" at the World's Columbian Exposition at Chicago in 1893, and a Grand Prix in Paris in 1900.[18] The list of awards is long and impressive and serves as one of the best indications that Rookwood was an exclusive collective body of craftsmen which represented America's art pottery in exhibitions in the United States and Europe.

Much of the success of Rookwood pottery has been attributed to the liberal attitude fostered among its decorators:

> being practically an enterprise for the production and sale of the work of forty or more individual decorators, who, in obedience to the rules of the pottery, constantly vary their shapes and never repeat their decorations.[19]

No efforts were spared to recruit the best decorators and throwers to further its aims. A goodly number of its designers came from the Cincinnati Art Academy. In its pursuit of the policy of liberality, the directors of Rookwood also sent to Japan for decorators such as Kitaro Shirayamadani. Although it is difficult to detect the exact pieces for which he may have been responsible, a more spontaneous, free-flowing brush quality is evident in examples of Rookwood pottery that was illustrated in an article in *Brush and Pencil*.[20] This is in strong contrast to the type of work with which Rookwood had been generally identified. The latter usually consisted of vases, bottles or jardiniers decorated with flowers or animals.

The concern for individuality in each piece produced at Rookwood is also seen in the stress on having the decorator's signature on every finished pot. In a booklet distributed by the company to its customers it emphasizes this point:

> A vase made at Rookwood under the conditions existing, is as much an object of art as a painted canvas or sculpture in bronze. And the artist's signature upon the vase is a genuine guarantee of originality. An object of art is immeasurably more precious when its owner knows there is no other just like it, that the particular artistic conception expressed there will never again be found quite the same. A Rookwood artist never does two vases alike, but carefully studies, composes and works out each piece for itself. It is that creative process which makes a piece of Rookwood an object of art.[21]

An examination of approximately 50 Rookwood pieces in the permanent collection of the Cincinnati Art Museum substantiates the claim made by the Rookwood firm regarding the signing of each piece. Although general repetition of shapes was found, a great variety of decorative motifs and techniques were evident. Each piece was signed by the decorator. The thrower, if not the same person as the decorator, stamped his personal monogram on the bottom of the pot, assuring the customer that the piece was entirely hand made.

The importance of Rookwood pottery was repeatedly recognized by writers in art journals when they evaluated arts and crafts exhibitions throughout the nation. The following comments represent a sampling of this viewpoint:

> Connoisseurs at home and abroad consider that in the Rookwood Pottery America has achieved its first and only distinctive artistic creation.[22]

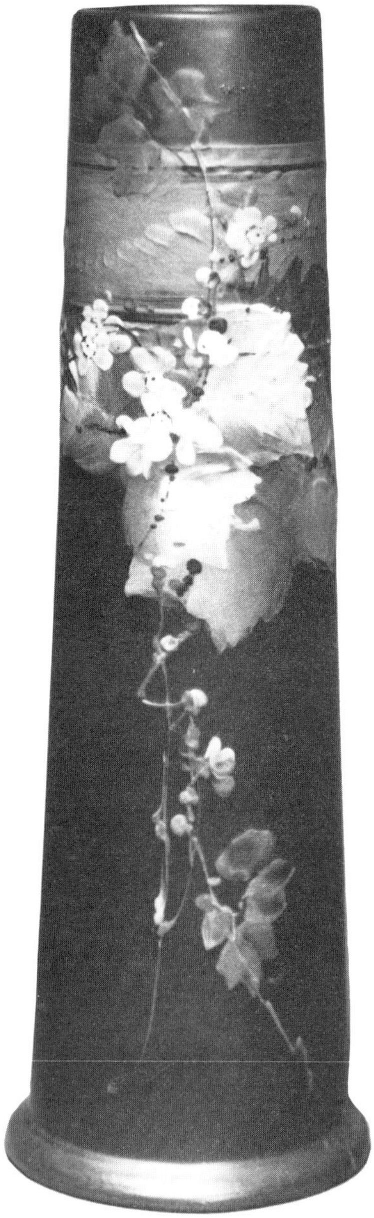

Figure 2-3. J.B. Owens, "Poppy" vase, 13" × 4", 1885, Zanesville, Ohio, Milwaukee Public Museum Collection. Once the problems of runny glazes was solved, decorators were able to deal more effectively with using underglazes for capturing the naturalistic appearances of a wide variety of subject matter.

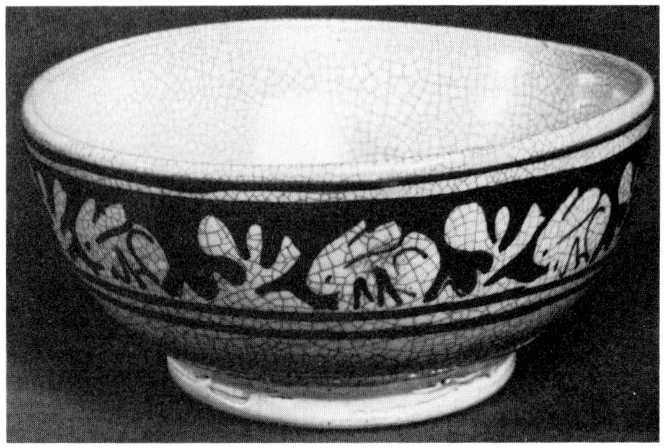

Figure 2-4. Dedham Pottery, bowl, wheel thrown earthenware, crackle glaze with cobalt wash decoration, 3" × 6".

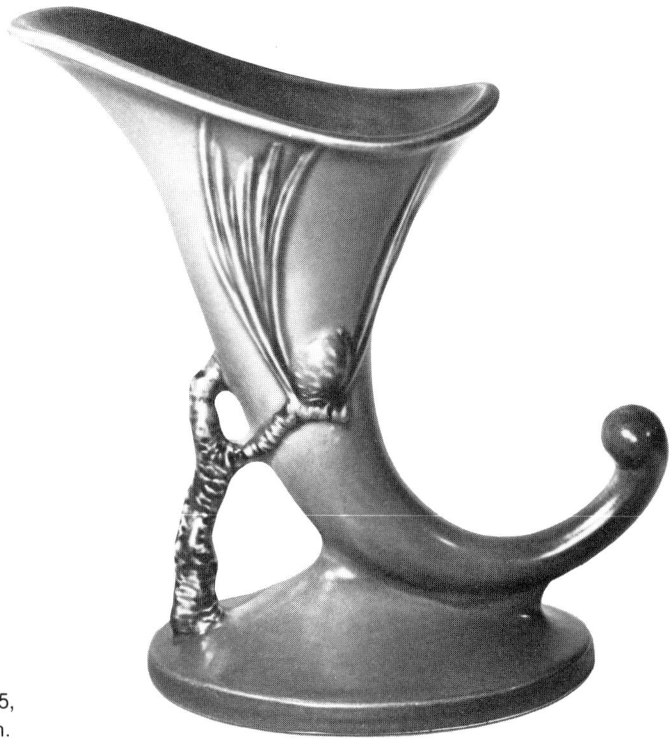

Figure 2-5. Roseville Pottery, Zanesville, Ohio, vase, cast and hand decorated, 1920. Milwaukee Public Museum Collection.

> There has been no real American ceramics with the exception of the Rookwood Pottery of Cincinnati, and its worth is too well known and its influence is too widely felt to be in any way confounded with the china-painter at large. Rookwood pottery and Favrile glass stand as landmarks in the advancement of American ceramics.[23]

It is difficult to estimate the effect that Rookwood ceramics had on contemporary tenets regarding the total form language of pottery. That it was hailed as America's first artistic pottery indicates that a conscious concern for individual distinctiveness had become an important criteria for excellence. This concern was demonstrated in the use of decoration which went beyond the mere reproduction of stencils or patterns supplied so abundantly to china decorators. The uniqueness attached to a hand-made pot was stressed by Rookwood. This quality was emphasized in the many favorable comments in various journals of the day and may have aided in creating more interest in purchasing that type of pottery.

However, the division of skills within the total pottery process was still evident. Several people in ceramics realized this situation and attempted to improve it by stressing the importance of being skilled in technical as well as artistic aspects of pottery-making.

Susan M. Frackleton

Susan Frackleton represents a typical example of the enthusiastic attitude toward china painting that existed from 1880 to 1920. Although the motivation for much china painting arose from a need to become involved in an acceptable hobby activity, it is important to note that in order to have been successful two requirements had to be met. First, one needed to possess the necessary talent with which to represent various naturalistic subject matter. Equally important, it required facilities for displaying the works, for publicity and for some type of a formal organization which served as the spokesman for these craftsmen. Susan M. Frackelton of Milwaukee, Wisconsin, attempted to fulfill both these needs.

Miss Frackelton was responsible for creating an organization which dealt exclusively with the activities of china decorators. In 1892 she became the first president of the National League of Mineral Painters, an organization whose primary aims were to—

> bring into closer relationship the overglaze painters in order to define lines of study and to aim in the development of a national school of ceramic art.[24]

Although the latter aims were not realized, the ambition to better "define lines of study" apparently met with some measure of success. In 1886 Susan Frackelton wrote her book, *Tried by Fire.*

A survey of books available at that time which were specifically written for the china decorator pointed out that Frackelton's book was the only one which dealt comprehensively with every aspect of china painting. She discussed in detail areas of design, tools for decorating, individual manufacturing of colors, and problems related to kilns and firing techniques. Although the book dealt with many facets of the decorating practice, her main emphasis was on inspiring the decorator to use original ideas for designs. In this regard she stated:

> Therefore I say, take that which seems most beautiful, and do with it according to your light. Your tastes and intuitions must be your safest guides, as the result to be obtained is a purely personal one.[25]

Frackelton's definition of originality apparently was equated with the ability to arrive at photographic reproductions of nature. This may have come about through her studies in painting under the Milwaukee painter, Heinrich Vianden, who came from Cologne, Germany in 1849. Three days a week she took lessons with Vianden. These dealt primarily with the rudiments of drawing, composition, color and rendering.[26]

Tried by Fire represents some viewpoints then held by studio-potters, especially those ideas that sought to equip the beginner with the requisites necessary to work independently. Miss Frackelton investigated the possibilities of a small, portable gas kiln that would be easier for the beginner to use. The new gas kiln was an outgrowth of a need to replace the cumbersome charcoal kiln that decorators used if there was no other means available for firing. The danger of manipulating the charcoal, the unpleasant odor of the kiln and the irregularity of heat distribution, according to Frackelton, made the old kilns a menace. Her newly designed gas kiln was more economical, safer and easier to operate. She said:

> When the kilns are lighted, it is not necessary to remain and watch them. When they are water-smoked, the gas may be turned on full; and when the proper number of feet [gas pressure] have been burned, turn the gas off.
>
> The smallest . . . kiln . . . can be set up in any room where a pressure of fifteen feet of gas per hour can be obtained. This amount of pressure is in the upper rooms of most houses. With gas at a dollar and a half per one thousand feet, the price per hour to fire it is not three cents. Which demonstrates that gas is not an expensive fuel, besides being perfectly cleanly [*sic*]. The kiln is attached to the gas-fixture by a little India-rubber hose, and no machinery, gas fitter's, or plumber's bill is necessary.
>
> I have owned and fired a large number, kind and variety of kilns, using both wood and charcoal as fuel, but find gas superior to them as the modern telegraph is to the old courier on horseback.
>
> All the terrors and mysteries of firing are smoothed away, and all the heavy, dirty, laborious work is no more. Under the present process, who ever can strike the match and turn the gas-tap has sufficient "force" to fire the china.[27]

An advertisement on the back pages of her book indicates that it was marketed. It was distributed nationally by the A. Satorius Company of New York.[28]

Susan Frackelton perpetuated the philosophy of china painters which held that it was considered an important accomplishment for fashionable young ladies to paint on china. But she went beyond the dependence upon industry for chemicals, colors, and kilns with which to work. She stressed that people should utilize their own resources for making pigments: especially the more expensive type such as gold and silver. Finally, she encouraged the china painters to seriously study drawing and painting in order that they would become more skilled in the techniques of decorating, as well as in the comprehension of what constituted good design (Fig. 2-6).

It was in the work of Susan Frackelton, therefore, that one could see implications for the development of a ceramic artist who insisted upon striking out in a different direction in order to express himself more independently in the medium of clay. Further developments in the complete process of pottery-making and interests in more personally conceived designs did not, however, come to fruition until after 1900.

Between 1899 and 1910 two events reflected a shift of emphasis in which attempts were

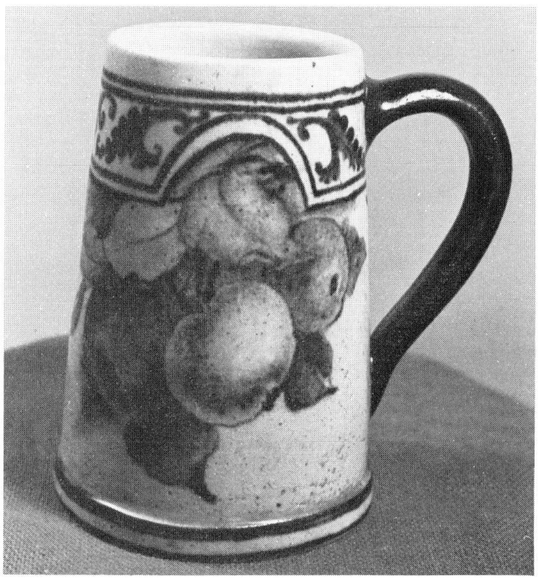

Figure 2-6. Susan Frackelton, mug, hand thrown, stoneware, underglaze and overglaze decoration. Milwaukee Historical Society Collection.

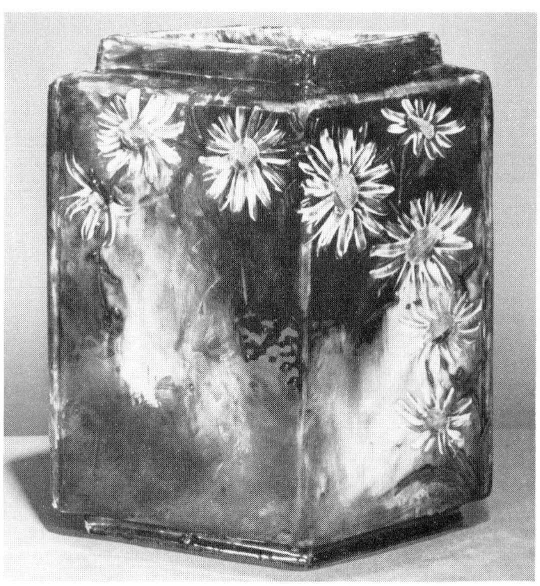

Figure 2-7. T.J. Wheatley & Co., Cincinnati, Ohio, hand-built vase, underglaze decoration with transparent glaze, ca. 1880. Milwaukee Public Museum Collection.

made to change china painting from a mere avocation to a serious form of artistic self-expression. First, several leaders established a school of ceramics which emphasized technical and artistic training for potters. Secondly, Adelaide Robineau, who was a popularly recognized china painter, started her magazine, *Keramic Studio*, in 1899.

Frederick Rhead and Developments at St. Louis

Relevant to industrial pottery and the china painting movement, there were people in the field of ceramics whose concern for elevating the artistic quality of American pottery resulted in several innovative attitudes and techniques for teaching ceramics. One person particularly noteworthy in this respect was Frederick Rhead. His importance lies in the fact that through his attempts to improve the quality of American pottery, several attitudes were brought more clearly into focus. One of these attitudes centered on equipping students with a more thorough knowledge of the entire ceramic process, in contrast to the china decorators or the industrial ceramist, both of whom usually specialized in only one or two aspects of pottery.

Rhead sought to implement his attitudes through his teaching, his magazine, *The Potter*, and his activities in the American Ceramic Society. His teaching was confined to People's University of St. Louis, Missouri. A detailed account of the development of this school and Rhead's part in it will point out his contribution and also provide additional insights into the disposition of studio-pottery during the first twenty years of this century.

Through the efforts of the Lewis Publishing Company of St. Louis and the American Women's League it was possible to create a school for the sole purpose of training students in the area of studio-pottery. In 1908 the forming of University City came under the joint sponsorship of the two organizations.[29] It was intended that the school was to be self-supporting within the city of St. Louis. Through the various chapters of the Women's League, as well as through donations from the publishing firm, funds were raised to construct a music library, a general library, a main building, an art school and an exchange. The Ceramic Art Institute, a division of the school, was directed by Taxile Doat. Doat was formerly chief designer and chemist of the Royal Sèvres Porcelain Manufactory of France.[30]

In order to attend classes or study at the university, one had to join the Woman's League. This merely required paying a yearly fee. Once the student was admitted to advanced training, he was considered an honor student. In art this meant that fifty percent of the profits realized from the sale of his work was contributed to the upkeep of the respective departments. Whatever work was not sold by the student was then sold through the League's exchange chapters which were located throughout the country, or was used for ornamenting the University or various chapter houses.

Taxile Doat was invited to the university in order to help plan and supervise the construction of the "most perfectly designed and equipped art pottery in the world."[31] He also supervised the creation of its curriculum which dealt with "ceramic arts, including every branch of glazing, decorating, *throwing* (?) and firing."[32] In order to assist Doat several other reputable potters were hired. These included Adelaide Robineau of the United States, Emile Diffloth from the La Louviere Pottery of Belgium, Eugene LaBarriere from France and Frederick Rhead from England.

Of these, the most interesting person in regard to the St. Louis plan was Frederick Rhead. It was through his efforts that the first correspondence course in studio-pottery was begun in the United States. The initial step in organizing this course was the creating of a text which the student used in the absence of instructors. The entire course was based on the premise that

> Pottery-making in this country, as practiced by the individual, is entirely a new art; and not only has there been no correspondence course embracing this subject but, as regards teaching the art in its entirety, there has been no systematic instruction whatever. Consequently, the lack of information and the difficulty in getting suitable instruction have given rise to false impressions regarding the difficulties of the work, and this has deterred many art students from attempting its practice.[33]

Upon registering for the course in pottery the student was asked to specify in which area he wanted to specialize. This ranged from decorating pieces cast from molds to learning to throw on the wheel. The student was, in fact, encouraged to learn all facets of the potting process. Most materials and tools were obtained from the Ceramic Art Institute of the university—including the kiln. One had to send in work sheets which indicated to the instructor the firing schedule, thereby enabling him to determine how the kiln was fired.

The correspondence text dealt essentially with the basic problems of clay preparation, throwing, coil building, slab construction, mold making, glaze preparation and application and firing techniques. Photographs were used for illustrating the processes.

No examples of work which have come directly from students at People's University are known to the author. But with the corps of instructors previously listed it is not difficult to imagine that the tastes and styles of nineteenth century European and traditional Oriental pottery were the standards for excellence. Nor is it known what effect this venture had in promoting a better awareness or understanding of studio-pottery in America. Frederick Rhead's prediction that

> it is safe to say that potters from everywhere will look with great expectations in the direction of University City, and there is every reason to think that they will not be disappointed

was not fulfilled.[34] In 1911 the creditors of University City began an investigation of its financial failures and after several litigations in court, the entire venture was closed, due to overextended credit and the fraudulent use of the mails by the founder, E.G. Lewis.[35]

However, it is significant that several leaders such as Rhead, Diffloth, Robineau and Doat devoted much of their time and energy attempting to organize the art of the studio-potter on an independent, professional basis. It is also important that, in their efforts to establish higher standards in ceramics, they placed special emphasis on training the student in the total ceramic process rather than merely encouraging him to become involved in isolated tasks such as mold-making, finishing, decorating or glazing. Thus, the entire St. Louis project served as an indication that several people tried very seriously to raise china painting from its position of a minor, almost non-creative craft to a position of importance as a meaningful form of self-expression.

Rhead's concern for improving American pottery was noticeable through two other means: first, through the magazine, *The Potter,* which he published independently and at his own cost, and secondly, through his severe indictments of the quality of American ceramic design through the *Bulletins* and *Journals of The American Ceramic Society. The Potter* was first published in December, 1916, but lasted only three years. The magazine was the first of its kind, despite *Keramic Studio,* because the former was intended exclusively for the studio-potter. As such, it dealt with every phase of pottery production. In each issue was an article which discussed specific aspects related to the technical and financial problems of operating an independent studio.[36] A series of articles also appeared under the heading of "Shape, Construction and Design," which analyzed the principles and elements of design in solving problems of creating "new" pottery forms.

Rhead felt that students should also acquire an understanding of the history of pottery. Articles that dealt with this covered everything from an analysis of the work of one of France's popular studio-potters, Bernard Palissy, to technical descriptions of Oriental pottery. Important supplements to this material were articles which informed the reader of ceramics exhibitions throughout the country, as well as reports about work done at schools in various parts of the United States that offered some form of ceramics.

Frederick Rhead, through his magazine, made an effort to place practical information related to ceramics at the disposal of potters. Through a more thorough acquaintance with every phase of ceramics and its numerous problems, it was hoped that a potter would be in a better position to work independently of the ceramic industry. Rhead nurtured this notion with enthusiasm. In order to provide potters the needed technical, artistic and historical material, he spared no efforts to obtain the best qualified teachers in several specialized areas to contribute material for his publication. For example, Dr. Edwin Atlee Barber, Director of the Pennsylvania Museum and School of Industrial Art, handled historical matters. Adelaide Robineau and Rhead concerned themselves with problems of design and taste, while William D. Gates of Teco Pottery dealt with technical aspects of clays, glazes and firing.

Despite the magazine's brief existence, it served to indicate the problems that plagued the potter in the first two decades of the twentieth century, and the efforts that were being made to alleviate them. This was a time when potters made attempts to strike out on their own, and in so doing, they depended for technical and artistic guidance upon the meager research performed by schools and people working independently of the ceramic industry.

Rhead's work with the American Ceramic Society further marked him as an early leader in the development of American studio-pottery. In 1920 the Art Division of the American Ceramic Society was instituted, and Rhead became its first secretary.

At its inception the Art Division served as a close adjunct to technical areas within the Society. Initially, the Art Division did not stress the developing of original designs because the accepted forms and decorations were still based on European and Oriental prototypes. The main concern of the Art Division was with providing adequate information and better training centers which could deal with a variety of techniques for the production and decorative processes already in existence. Toward this Rhead worked with devotion and enthusiasm.

Although his thorough knowledge of the entire ceramic process was reflected in a series of articles written for *Keramic Studio* from 1915 to 1920, as well as for his own publication, it was through his association with the American Ceramic Society that he was best able to make known his thoughts about the quality of American pottery. His initial concern was directed toward commercial pottery and the lack of facilities with which to train future ceramists. He expressed this concern in 1921 when he said:

> At the present time the factory is the only place where the student interested in ceramics can obtain a practical training in the various decorative processes used by the potter. I am not referring to the so-called crafts or student work taught in the schools and universities and entirely out of the range of commercial possibilities.[37]

However, Rhead also noted that there were a number of accomplished potters in America who were not directly associated with industry. Exactly one year later he praised the work of several American studio-potters whose work was displayed at an exhibition with the American Ceramic Society convention. The exhibition included, among others, the work of Charles Binns, Arthur Baggs and work from the Newcomb and Paul Revere Potteries. He pointed out:

> It is possible to name from a dozen to twenty schools and individual potters who can show the products of their kilns side by side with the work of European potters of high reputation without suffering in comparison.[38]

That he realized their importance and that he acknowledged it seemed important because in so doing he reversed his earlier opinion about American pottery and realized that there was meritorious work being done by some studio-potters. His appraisal of their work probably did not result in creating an enthusiasm in others to pursue the area of studio-pottery. But his role in having brought about an awareness of the high caliber of work done by these potters was surely a salutary contribution to the dedication of those who endeavored to work somewhat more independently of commercial pottery.

The importance of the St. Louis project and of Frederick Rhead in this study rests with the attempts made to alter the standards of American pottery. As has been pointed out, American manufacturers generally hired European ceramists, due, in part, to the lack of schools that could train qualified people for the ceramic industry. Most schools that taught pottery before and during the 1920's were so concerned with technical matters that artistic considerations became of secondary importance. Other schools considered only the problems of design, usually in the form of decorating, without providing a foundation in technology. Rhead and the people at St. Louis realized that it was imperative to combine these two elements in order to arrive at a solution to the problem of providing industry with sound designers. It was also noticed that most art-potters lacked a thorough knowledge of technical processes, and thereby may have limited themselves in their artistic efforts. In order to solve the dilemmas that faced both groups, attempts were made to train the potter thoroughly in technical, artistic and historic considerations. University City of St. Louis contributed by offering a diversified program in ceramics, while Rhead pursued his beliefs through his teaching, writing and activities in the American Ceramic Society.

There were others, to be sure, who were concerned with similar problems. The same subject matter was dealt with by several journals during the 1920's. The plea for training better artists who were also qualified to deal with industrial problems was heard from Paul E. Cox,[39] from Richard F. Bach of the Metropolitan Museum of Art,[40] and from L.V. Solon.[41] It is doubtful that their pleas for improvement in the technical and artistic quality of American ceramics were answered directly. For the most part art-pottery as it was known during the first two decades of the twentieth century was still being produced by the china painters. But it was from this group of artisans that some potters emerged who were aware of the limitations of china decorating. New considerations were encouraged regarding techniques and design. An individual approach to problem solving was fostered and the beginning of a new development in artistic pottery was established. One person who was closely associated with the china decorating movement and who began to implement new attitudes in studio-pottery was Adelaide Robineau. She has been regarded as one of America's first important studio-potters.

Adelaide Robineau

Mrs. Robineau had become dissatisfied with commercially made bisque ware which the china painters decorated. In response to her desire to learn more about stoneware and porcelain, her husband prevailed upon Taxile Doat to send her a series of lessons that dealt with the total ceramic process as practiced at Sèvres. The articles were translated from the French by her husband, and published in a series of articles in their magazine, *Keramic Studio*, from 1903 to 1904.[42]

Mrs. Robineau was primarily interested in forming by throwing. She alluded to this when she said:

> It goes without saying that to a connoisseur there is absolutely no comparison between the cast piece and hand work. Not only the cast piece had a different appearance easily detected by people having some knowledge of ceramics, but it is turned out in quantities.[43]

There can be little doubt that Mrs. Robineau represented an outstanding example of the philosophy of the early studio-potters of the twentieth century in the United States. Her desire to depart from the standard practices of the china decorators led her to investigate many aspects of producing pottery. She compounded her own clays and glazes; in fact she performed every step to completion, save that of firing, which was carried out by her husband.

Mrs. Robineau's interest in the individual pot as a statement of unique, total form was best exemplified by her untiring research into glaze chemistry and the meticulous decoration of a large portion of her work. She expressed her convictions about the individual approach to problem-solving in pottery when she said:

> The *art* of ceramics must be learned by personal experiment. . . . Unless materials were obtained from absolutely the same source and manipulated under exactly the same conditions, it is doubtful if two potters could obtain exactly the same results . . . the condition of the kiln which rapidly deteriorates under the high temperatures, the fact that two batches of materials are not always alike, and many other difficulties enter into the proposition.[44]

Her statements indicate that she was aware of the numerous variables which a potter needed to control in order to produce successful pottery—if he sought to work alone as a studio-potter.

Much of her work was influenced by Sèvres. This was understandable in view of her lessons received from Doat. Doat also published *Grand Feu Keramics* in 1910, a book which dealt with research in clay bodies and glazes conducted at the Royal Sèvres factory in France. But, according to Anna Olmstead, director of the Syracuse Museum of Art, who had a keen interest in Mrs. Robineau's pottery, she did not care for *pâté-sur-pâté* which was prevalent at Sevres. Mrs. Robineau herself stated that, although she was greatly indebted to the Sèvres formulas, she became more interested in considering other aspects of glazes, especially those of the problems of color at high temperatures.

> These [Sèvres formulas] I am still using, though I have developed several new and interesting types, and the beautiful color effects of my crystal glazes

have been commented upon favorably even in comparison with the best work of Sèvres and other European potteries. Some crystal effects, either of the needle type or the large flowery type, depend on a successful oxidizing firing and are very uncertain. . . . Of all oxides used in ceramics copper is probably the most fascinating because of the extraordinary variety of color effects it may give. Green in an ordinary oxidizing firing, under the influence of the flame and smoke of a reducing firing, will turn sometimes red, sometimes deep blue or turquoise. But most of all the color effects obtainable with copper, the most sought after and the most uncertain is the high fire oxblood.[45]

Robineau's lack of concern for the commercial market, in terms of not allowing it to dictate her personal standard, parallels notions held by a number of contemporary studio-potters. This can be seen in her severe self-criticism in accepting or rejecting certain pieces of work as they were taken from the kiln. In this regard she recalled:

I have tried firing after firing and combination after combination of copper glaze, but this does not mean at all that I have obtained a great number of good pieces. On the contrary, out of all these firings only a limited number of successful vases have come, but a few have been quite choice, among them a very small oxblood vase which compares favorably with the best Chinese blood, three or four others and somewhat larger examples of that rare blood color, several turquoise pieces of good quality, also vases with extremely interesting craquelé effect.[46]

Her untiring investigation of the endless possibilities of glazes resulted in the creation of some of the finest crystalline and luster glazes (Fig. 2-8). Excellent examples of these are housed in the permanent collections of the Syracuse Museum of Art, the Detroit Institute, the Boston Museum of Fine Art and several others.

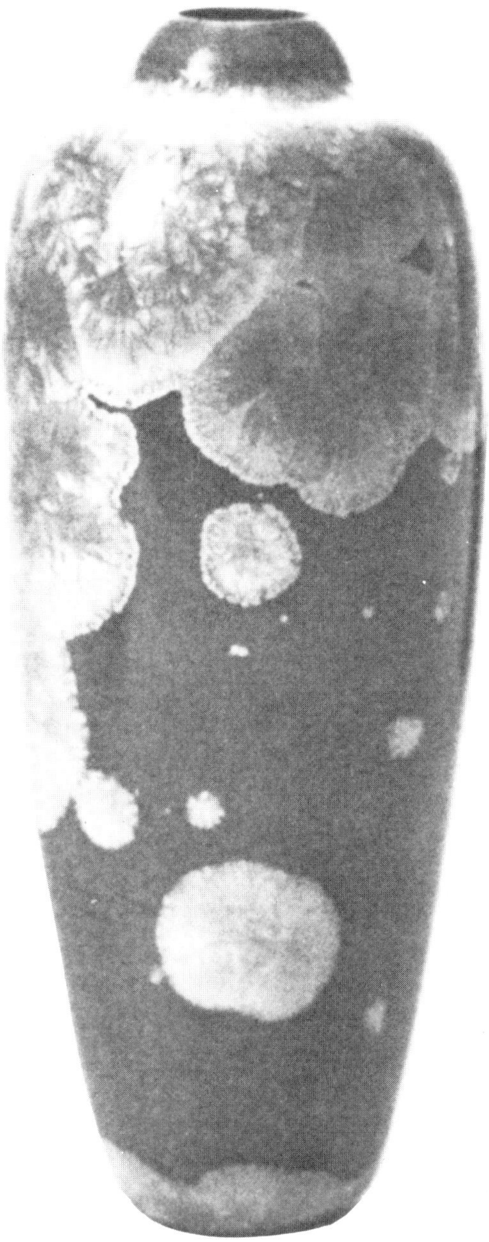

Figure 2-8. Adelaide Robineau, porcelain vase with crystalline glaze, wheel thrown, Everson Museum of Art Collection.

The crystalline and luster glazes were used on relatively simple forms, thereby achieving a concentration on the glaze which did not compete with a complex shape. This was in strong contrast to the overly-decorative forms so prevalent with the china decorators of that era.

Mrs. Robineau was also interested in Chinese ceramics, which led to additional possibilities of decorating the surface of her porcelain pottery through an incising process. Regarding this she pointed out:

> This slightly incised design, when covered with a transparent glaze, will show through with interesting decorative effects which are familiar to students of Chinese ceramics. In the use of sharp tools for the decoration of porcelain shapes I find my delight, but it is not exactly incising that I do. I much prefer to use the reverse process, technically called excising. Instead of the slightly cut design produced by incising the excising process consists in slowly cutting out the background so that at the end of the work the design will stand out in relief.[47]

The technique of incising and excising demanded care and patience, not only because of the amount of time that was required, but also because of the fragile nature of the green ware. The time-consuming element and careful control demanded of this technique was illustrated in Mrs. Robineau's "Scarab Vase," which took her one thousand hours to carve. After the first firing of this particular pot she discovered that it contained over two hundred cracks, all of which were tediously repaired and the pot refired before it was glazed (Fig. 2-9).[48]

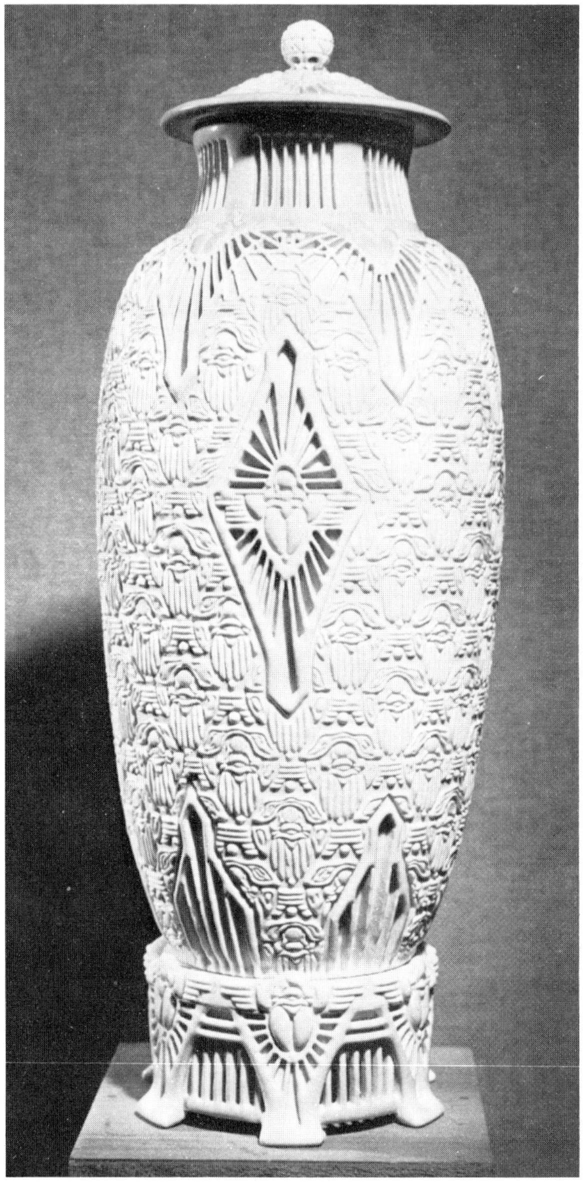

Figure 2-9. Adelaide Robineau, "Scarab Vase," porcelain, handbuilt, excised design with transparent glaze. This piece required over 1,000 hours to complete and was made for the St. Louis Exposition where it was awarded the highest prize for artistic ceramics.

It was through the spirit and work of Adelaide Robineau that the first outlines of studio-potters as they are known today began to be seen. Her departure from bisque-fired, pre-cast pots on which to decorate, her ceaseless search for improving glazes, bodies, decorative techniques and her critical appraisal of the work she produced all served to elevate the art of pottery-making above the contrived tasks of the china decorators. But her own productivity in pottery was only one phase of her contribution to the ceramic arts.

She was also involved in teaching, in publishing and in exhibiting her work in America and abroad. All of these activities helped in bringing recognition to ceramics as a "new" art form in twentieth century America.

Adelaide Robineau assumed added stature as America's first noted studio-potter because of the reputation she achieved through competitive exhibitions in America and Europe. A survey of available literature from 1890 to 1920 indicates that Mrs. Robineau was the sole representative of American studio-potters in European Exhibitions. Her principal purpose and desire to deal exclusively with each piece of pottery as a unique work of art brought her numerous rewards. The following list represents a sampling of prizes from exhibitions:

1. 1911, received Grand Prize at the Turin International Exposition.
2. 1912, exhibited at thè Paris Salon and the Musé de Arts Decoratifs, Paris.
3. 1913, received Grand Prize for the best craftswork in the Annual Exhibition of the Art Institute of Chicago.
4. 1915, received Grand Prize in ceramics at the Panama Exposition in San Francisco.

She was also awarded medals for her work by several Arts and Crafts Societies in America.[49] Mrs. Robineau collected an impressive list of one-man shows at leading museums throughout the country and in Europe, as well as having her work included in their permanent collections.

Keramic Studio, the periodical started by Mrs. Robineau in 1899, was also of importance. The early issues of the magazine devoted much space and material to the china decorators, aiding them with designs and painting techniques. However, after Mrs. Robineau's acquaintance with Taxile Doat, the magazine began to include information received from Sèvres which dealt with glaze compositions, forming techniques and firing procedures. Although the magazine reflected an enthusiasm for china decorating, it also encouraged those people who sought to work more on their own. For this reason Mrs. Robineau included numerous articles that dealt with clay preparation and other phases of pottery making. These articles were often accompanied with many photographs, illustrating whatever process was being discussed in the article. The advertising columns of the magazine were well supported by kiln manufacturers, ceramic chemical suppliers and manufacturers of tools for the china painters.

Throughout the issues a note of enthusiasm for the art of pottery decorating can be noted. This appeared in the form of encouragement to decorators to exhibit their works whenever possible at state fairs or when other opportunities presented themselves. Mrs. Robineau offered some of her own prized work as rewards for outstanding examples of student work. In the issues after 1910 particular attention was paid to the "learning of practically every possible process in studio pottery making."[50]

The importance of *Keramic Studio,* therefore, was not only in providing the novice with assistance, but also in its position as the largest, most enthusiastic spokesman for handmade ceramics. The magazine also included examples of ceramics from past periods and various countries, thereby exposing the reader to knowledge of the heritage of pottery.

The cumulative effects of china painting took several forms. It was the first broadly accepted art-pottery movement in this country. Although china painting depended on the ceramic industry for materials, tools and equipment, and also emulated its forms and decorations, this very association eventually brought about a shift in emphasis. This shift became particularly evident through the work of the movement's leaders such as Frackelton, Storer, McLaughlin, Rhead and Robineau. They realized that copying the accepted forms and designs of industry prevented the development of a meaningful form of expression. This motivated the notion of training a person in the total creative process in pottery. In so doing they provided the first break with the dominance of industry. Although a form of eclecticism still predominated, the idea of the individually handcrafted pot was nurtured.

That the best examples of china painting came from some of these leaders also suggested that it was necessary for a successful potter to have had training in other areas of the arts, particularly drawing. Thus, as the china decorating movement decreased in importance, efforts were made to encourage people to do more of their own designing and to learn to throw their own pots. The majority of china decorators probably did not succeed at this, but those who did represented a form of America's first studio-potters. Moreover, the leaders of china painting embraced some of the notions which have since become an integral part of potters' meaningful independence: a desire for freedom from the dictates of industry and a knowledge of all aspects of the craft. A spirit of independent investigation and testing was fostered, and to have had a sound foundation in drawing and design was also recognized as being important.

The successful participation by some members of the china painting movement in national and international ceramics exhibitions, furthermore, attested to their desire to be recognized as practitioners of a meaningful form of art. Those missionary efforts, in part, provided a basis for further developments in ceramics during the following decades.

Notes

1. Edwin A. Barber, "The Pioneer of China Painting in America," *New England Magazine*, 13:33-48 (September, 1895).
2. Ibid., pp. 36-37.
3. Ibid., p. 39.
4. Ibid., p. 42.
5. Ibid., p. 48.
6. Aaron Perry, "Decorative Pottery of Cincinnati," *Harper's Monthly*, 23:834-35 (May, 1881).
7. Ibid., p. 835.
8. M.L. McLaughlin, *Her Own Story*, Bulletin of the American Ceramic Society no. 17, pp. 218-19.
9. *Mary Louise McLaughlin*, Bulletin of the American Ceramic Society no. 17, p. 225.
10. Ibid., p. 225.
11. Ibid., p. 225.
12. Perry, p. 836.
13. Ibid., p. 837.
14. L.R. McCabe, *National Ceramic Association Founded in 1891*, Bulletin of The American Ceramic Society no. 82, p. 373.
15. Ibid., p. 373.

16. Lawrence Mendenhall, "Cincinnati's Contribution to American Ceramic Art," *Brush and Pencil,* 17:47-61 (February, 1906).
17. Walter E. Gray, "Latter Day Developments in American Pottery, III: Rookwood," *Brush and Pencil,* 9:359 (March, 1902).
18. *The Rookwood Book,* p. 6.
19. "The Rookwood Pottery," *Craftsman,* 3:248 (January, 1903).
20. Mendenhall, p. 55.
21. *Rookwood Book,* p. 2.
22. McCabe, p. 372.
23. T. McLennan, "The Art Industries of America-IV China Decorating," *Brush and Pencil,* 13:134 (June, 1905).
24. Myrtle French, "Pottery and Porcelain," *Encyclopaedia Britannica,* 14th edition, 1962, vol. 18, p. 373B.
25. Susan Frackelton, *Tried by Fire,* p. 14.
26. Mary Leader, "The Frackelton Story," *Exclusively Yours,* 13:6 (February, 1961).
27. Frackelton, pp. 72-73.
28. Ibid., p. 110.
29. It should be noted that this project has been referred to by other writers as the St. Louis Plan, People's University or University City. Within the University existed an Art Institute which housed the Ceramic Art Institute.
30. "The American Woman's League, Its Plan and Purpose," *Everybody's Magazine,* 4:1-5 (December-January, 1908-1909).
31. Ibid., p. 5.
32. Ibid., p. 5. (Italics and question mark by the author of the article. That the term throwing was italicized and a question mark placed next to it suggests that throwing was a relatively new aspect to be considered in pottery.)
33. Frederick Rhead, *Studio Pottery,* pp. 3-4.
34. Frederick Rhead, "America As A Ceramic Art Center," *Fine Arts Journal,* 22:193 April-May, 1910).
35. "University City," *The St. Louis Republican Newspaper.* (St. Louis, Missouri), col. 3, p. 15 (June 14, 1911).
36. "Planning and Operating a Studio Pottery," *The Potter,* 1:25-28 (December, 1916).
37. Frederick Rhead, *Research in Ceramic Decorative Processes,* Bulletin of the American Ceramic Society no. 5, pp. 330-31.
38. Frederick Rhead, *American Ceramic Society Exhibition,* Bulletin of the American Ceramic Society no. 1, pp. 15-16.
39. Paul Cox, *American Ceramics for Interior Decorating,* Bulletin of the American Ceramic Society no. 5, pp. 420-22.
40. R.F. Bach, *Art in Industry,* Bulletin of the American Ceramic Society no. 3, pp. 284-88.
41. L. V. Solon, "Sweden's Solution of the Art Industry Problem," *Architectural Record,* 65:375-76 (April, 1927).
42. Dorothy W. Perkins, "Education in Ceramic Art in the United States," Unpublished doctoral dissertation, The Ohio State University, 1956, pp. 178-79.
43. Adelaide Robineau, "American Pottery," *The Art World,* 3:155 (November, 1917).
44. Robineau, p. 153.
45. Ibid., pp. 153-54.
46. Ibid., p. 154.
47. Ibid., p. 154.
48. Ibid., p. 155.
49. Jonathan Rawson, Jr., "Teco and Robineau Pottery," *House Beautiful,* 33:151 (April, 1913).
50. Adelaide Robineau, "Hand Made Lunch Sets," *Keramic Studio,* 26:63 (July-August, 1922).

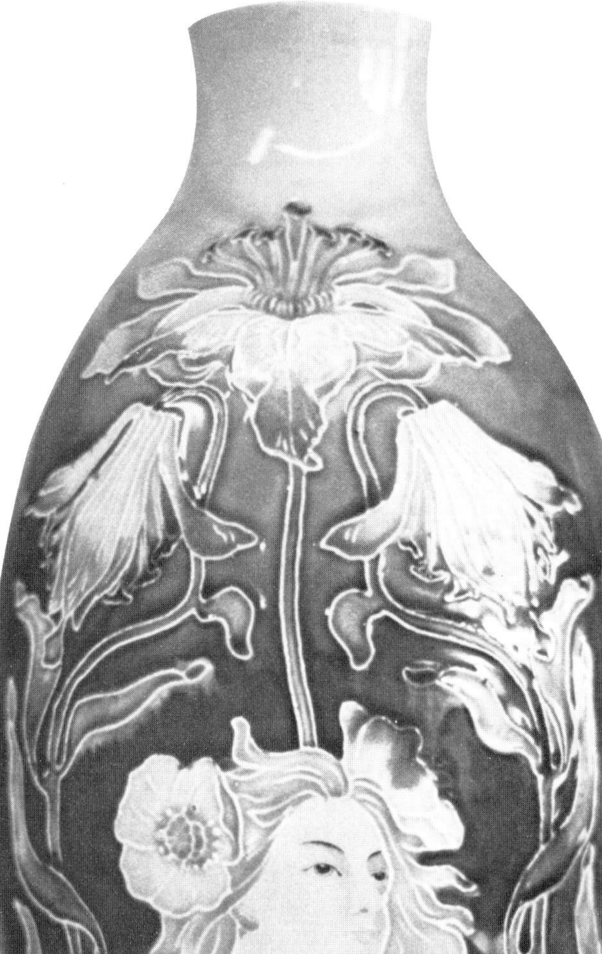

Anonymous

Art Nouveau in American Ceramics 3

During the years that china decorating flourished and as the notion of hand-made pottery was better established, a unique form-language emerged in several parts of the country. It was known as Art Nouveau and its influence in American pottery was most prominently felt from about 1889 to 1910. It affected the work of some potters who operated by themselves, as well as some commercial potteries. Schools were also influenced by this new style.

The pottery of Rookwood has been discussed in a previous chapter. The work of Newcomb College, Teco, Gruebey and Van Briggle is also noteworthy because it reflected the form-language of Art Nouveau as it came from Europe at the turn of the century. Although adverse feelings toward Art Nouveau were expressed by some elements that represented the Societies of the Arts and Crafts, there were, nevertheless, examples of Art Nouveau crafts published and discussed in magazines. The work seemed to have gained support primarily on the basis that it involved restoration of the dignity of hand labor.

Irene Sargent reflected typical responses to the insurgence of the Art Nouveau style in American crafts. She believed that art, when it was sincerely produced, always served as an index to aesthetic impulses of its time. In an attempt to dismiss the new, "revolutionary" Art Nouveau style as a decadent form of art she resorted to comparing it to the decorative motifs of the Egyptians and Assyrians. In their use of the lotus, the anthemion and other flowers she noted a close relationship, due to the dominance of natural elements as a basis for design and decoration. Art Nouveau artists, particularly those in pottery, in contrast, sought to stylize some plant, animal and human motifs in order that structure and decoration would result in a homogeneous whole. Sargent equated this with a lack of understanding nature, and she prophesied that this would cause the downfall of the "new movement" which was being acclaimed so enthusiastically in Europe. In this regard she said:

> For under the pretext of interpreting Nature by an advanced and subtle method, artists of great worth no longer observe the great mother of life. They attempt to subvert and destroy principles which are as permanent as the law of mathematics. They would have chaos in place of order. They are nihilists of aesthetics. They no longer observe Nature. They are blind to all save "the wavey line."[1]

Her criticism of Art Nouveau was typical of the opinions of one part of a divided attitude regarding the new form of expression. But equally strong voices were heard from writers that supported the new movement. Josephine Locke is a good example. She responded with a more enthusiastic and positive note than several of her contemporaries. She promised exciting things with the insurgence of this new style because it served as a distinct break with formerly-held "series of dry formulae." She felt that Art Nouveau consisted of a world of color and form-experiences which needed only the translation of those devoted and daring enough to surrender to the guidance of pure emotion. It seemed that Locke was speaking in regard to pottery when she said that intimacy with the medium resulted in significant art form, and that, because of this, Art Nouveau should be welcomed, not as frivolity, but as a step in a series of experimental movements toward a larger field for the play of human genius and the expression of personality.[2]

Newcomb Pottery

Newcomb pottery was a unique example in the development of American pottery for three reasons. First, it was an outgrowth of an economic and cultural dilemma of the South after the Civil War. In hopes of making New Orleans the cultural center of the South, Newcomb College, a part of Tulane University, instituted courses to train young ladies in the teaching of fine arts. But since there were not sufficient teaching positions in which to place its graduates, the school sought a more practical course of action. Some china decorating was done at the school, and it was felt that a course in pottery would fulfill the need for a more practical preparation of ladies who had to earn a living after leaving the school. Mary G. Scherer was hired in 1890 to conduct classes in the decoration and appreciation of pottery. Miss Scherer came from the Cincinnati Art Academy where she had obtained training in drawing and painting as well as in china decorating.[3]

A second reason for Newcomb's importance was its approach to teaching ceramics. Under Miss Scherer's supervision the students at Newcomb were urged to exercise the greatest amount of freedom in working out their own ideas for decorating pottery. This was in strong contrast to the usual approach to china decorating as practiced in other places at that time. A high standard of originality and craftsmanship was stressed. This was summarized by Professor Woodward, the first director of Newcomb's art school.

> Each worker in the craft is led to feel that the responsibility attaching to a signed design is the same as that which exists in the case of a signed picture, and that individual reputation may be gained by this as by other forms of art expression.
>
> It is not to be supposed that immature students are permitted to the privilege of working in the pottery. A pupil is required to take the full course of instruction, which usually extends about four years, and must be able to show by practical work that she is qualified to originate and execute independently. Having thus substantiated her claim to recognition by the directors of the pottery, she is admitted to the establishment without the payment of further tuition.[4]

The strong emphasis on originality and skill appears to have been influenced by the Arts and Crafts movement, begun in the nineteenth century by William Morris. Franklin Adams alluded to this when he said:

> In keeping with the principles inherent in this movement, against the Victorian Industrial Revolution and its lack of craftsmanship and design quality, Newcomb pottery, though to some degree "mass produced" was made entirely by hand and designs were never duplicated.[5]

In Newcomb pottery emphasis was placed upon choosing a design that most appropriately fit the form of the pot. For this approach to decorating, Newcomb ceramics became renowned. The reason for the pottery's distinctiveness was two-fold. First, the entire enterprise was directed toward developing indigenous qualities of the South. As such it relied on a clay body that was locally available, and the decorative motifs depended solely upon the flora of the immediate surroundings such as the cotton plant, the sugar cane and other floral forms of Louisiana. For the most part these elements were applied to the green or bisque pot with a simple white slip. These were then covered with an ordinary green or blue matt glaze. This combination of decoration and glaze became a popular trademark of Newcomb pottery.[6]

The work produced by decorators at Newcomb displays a complete departure from that of their contemporaries in other parts of the country. The designs, based entirely on plant motifs of the surrounding regions, were produced so that the plant is seen in its entirety, rather than as a small section or detail of a flower (Fig. 3-1). This encouraged a simplified rendering of the motif on an equally simple form which resulted in a rather robust, vigorous character. This is in strong contrast to the linear, somewhat frail decorations of most other decorators of that time, including those at Rookwood.

The third, and perhaps more important reason that Newcomb pottery assumed a unique position in American ceramics, was its adaptation, to some extent, of the principles of Art Nouveau design. Although Newcomb ceramics depended heavily upon the flora of the South for its decorative designs, it translated the southern botanical subject matter into highly formalized, clear, flat shapes outlined with the curvilinear treatment characteristic of Art Nouveau motifs (Fig. 3-2).

The ideals of art-pottery, as upheld by Newcomb College were reflected by the work illustrated in a catalog that dealt with an exhibition of Newcomb work from 1897 to 1917. Over one hundred works were listed as having been thrown by the same potter, but decorated by several different students. The work represented a stylistic departure from the methods and motifs of most other china decorators. In so doing, Newcomb managed to create some financial independence and an ability to create pottery which was able to compete with the best of the commercial ceramics of its day.

For their efforts to create distinctive, handmade pottery Newcomb potters were awarded

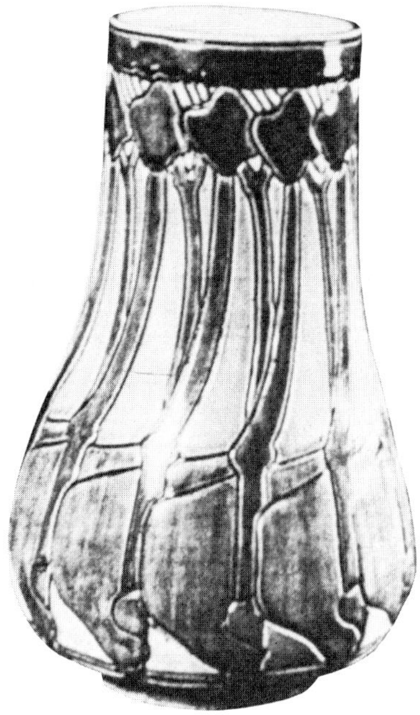

Figure 3-1. Newcomb Pottery, whiteware, wheel thrown with incised and raised decoration; ca. 1907. Courtesy, Newcomb College Permanent Collection.

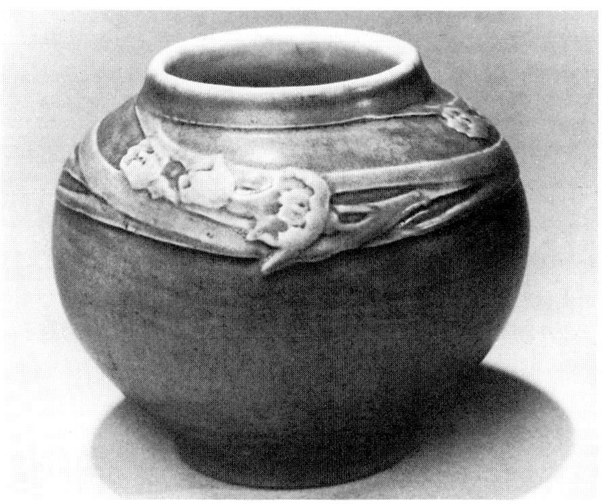

Figure 3-2. Newcomb Pottery, Newcomb College, New Orleans, La., 1896, wheel thrown, underglaze decoration, soft matt cover glaze, 4″ × 4 1/2″, A.E. Irvine, decorator and Joe Meyer, potter.

a bronze medal at the Paris International Exposition in 1900, and from then on for a decade, won a gold, silver or bronze medal in every international exposition and world's fair in which its work was entered.[7]

Because Newcomb insisted that its potters conceive and execute individual designs, the pottery represented the most indigenous product of ceramic art in America during the late nineteenth and early twentieth century. Other pottery had its individuality and special merit, but most were, in a sense, a reflection of the art of the Orient or of the Old World. In Newcomb pottery there was scarcely a suggestion of older, known wares. The pottery achieved renown through critical appraisals in several leading art magazines of its day. This recognition may have helped it to make its own contribution as well as fostering the idea of placing highest values on the hand-crafted pot.

William H. Gruebey

Writers of arts and crafts magazines in the first decade of the twentieth century regarded the work of William H. Gruebey as a high achievement in the potter's art. Although the author has been unable to determine the sources for Gruebey's designs, an examination of his work disclosed a close affinity to Art Nouveau form-concepts. This may have stemmed from the close association that Gruebey had with Louis C. Tiffany. The latter ordered bases for his lamps from Gruebey which he then covered with lamp shades of stained glass.[8] Gruebey's pottery was also sold at the Tiffany shops, and at times was even photographed alongside Tiffany's Favrile glass for advertisements and magazine articles.

Although Gruebey also produced a type of pottery that consisted of relatively simplified, classic forms, his most popular work seemed to have been influenced rather noticeably by Art Nouveau. Hence, a ware was created in which the three-dimensional, curvilinear surface decoration infused the basic shape and structure of the pot to a point where these two elements became totally synthesized (Fig. 3-3). Of interest was the hand-work required for decorative techniques which were important to the Gruebey enterprise. Walter Gray provided insights into the operation of the Gruebey business.

> This pottery is entirely hand-made, no molds whatever being used in the establishment. The designs being executed by Mr. Kendrick, the modeling for the most part is done by young women graduates from different art schools, particularly the Boston Art Museum and the Normal and Cowles Art Schools. After the separate pieces have been worked into perfect form, the enamels are laid upon the surface to the thickness of about one thirty-second of an inch, and the firing is then done. The whole operation is performed under the personal supervision of Mr. Gruebey.[9]

The Gruebey Faience Company was founded in 1897, and after three years became renowned as a producer of art-pottery. The credit for its success has been attributed to its founders, William H. Gruebey and George Kendrick. They were responsible for creating "the extraordinary beauty of its forms and the well-applied surface decoration in slight relief."[10] Gruebey supplied the glazes which were regarded as unique at that time because of their matt quality.

The surface of the ware is glossless, satiny, the soft dull surface being a wide range of greens, browns, yellows, and blues. In the manipulation of greens, however, the manufacturers have been most successful, and as a consequence greens predominate the output of the establishment.[11] (Fig. 3-4).

The development of matt glazes was especially important since they were rare in comparison to the glossy and semi-glossy glazes. When matt glazes were developed by potters who worked alone or by a commercial firm, the formulas were guarded with secrecy. This is understandable, since matt glazes did not become general knowledge until after Taxile Doat arrived in the United States in 1908. His book, *Grand Feu Keramics,* was not published until 1910, which means that Gruebey's development of matt glazes preceded the publication of Doat's book.

For their efforts to produce a ware that was distinctly different in comparison to the "mere decorated china . . . and clay vessels tricked out with designs borrowed from workers in other forms of art," Gruebey was awarded two gold medals at the Paris Exposition of 1900 and another gold medal at the International Exposition of Ceramics held in St. Petersburg, Russia, in 1901. Gruebey's research in glazes, which created a distinctive velvety appearance, furthermore gained him a personal gold medal from the French government at the Paris Exposition of 1914.[12]

The renown achieved by Gruebey through his new matt glazes and his unusual forms had its effect upon the production of American pottery during the early decades of the twentieth century. It was at that time that matt glazes came into vogue. These types of glazes, as well as the French-inspired Art Nouveau thus

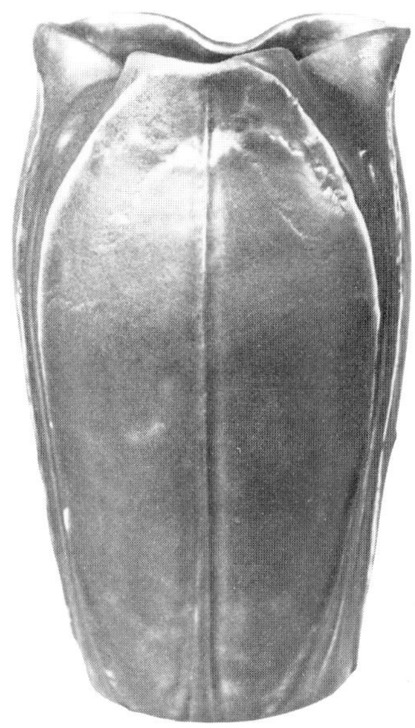

Figure 3-3. Wm. H. Gruebey, Gruebey Faience Co., 1897-1910, modeled by Annie V. Lingley, 8″ × 5″, Milwaukee Public Museum Collection.

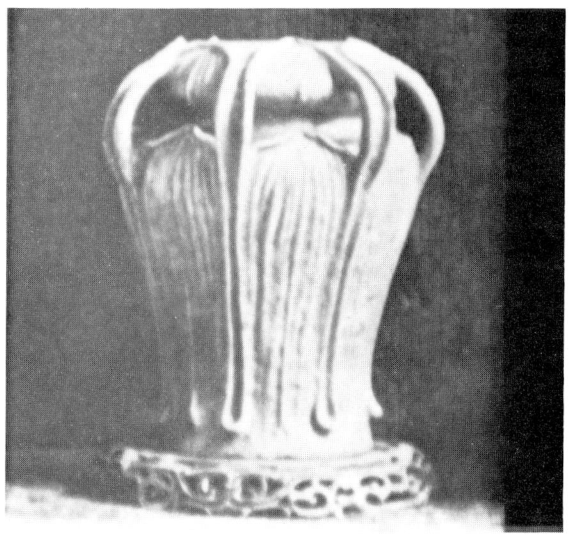

Figure 3-4. William H. Gruebey, Vase, stoneware, cast and handbuilt, matt green glaze; ca. 1902. Courtesy, the author.

became important in the works of other ceramists such as Van Briggle and in other potteries such as Rookwood and Teco.[13]

After Gruebey went out of business in 1907, Louis Tiffany carried on the tradition of the Gruebey forms in his own studios. Tiffany continued to use the unique and original designs and fitted them with shades of Favrile glass.[14]

In addition to the glazes he developed, Gruebey's pottery was also important because of his ability to arrive at unique designs in which the basic structure of pots became infused with the decoration, so that the two elements were often difficult to distinguish from each other. Indeed, the wedding of shape and decoration was at times accomplished to such a degree that it was possible to mistake a piece of pottery for a free-standing sculpture. The work of Artus Van Briggle also illustrated this design concept.

Artus Van Briggle

Artus Van Briggle was an example of a potter whose artistic success was an outgrowth of his enthusiastic acceptance of Art Nouveau principles. A trip to Paris in 1893 was the turning point of Van Briggle's career. Before this time he utilized his painterly skills at the Rookwood pottery firm in producing photographic-like reproductions of flowers, plants and animals on vases. These were painted in underglaze and overglaze decorations, as was so popular at Rookwood before the twentieth century.

However, while attending the Beaux Arts in Paris, he also discovered the beauties of Ming dynasty glazes. He saw these works in the permanent collection of the Louvre and was interested in reproducing them. In 1896 he returned to Rookwood and started to work with the Chinese glazes. After several years of ceaseless experimentation in a desire to find the secrets of these Oriental matt glazes, he finally produced something that resembled the finish of the Imperial Chinese treasures.[15]

The manner in which Van Briggle arrived at the matt glazes is not known, but pottery by Van Briggle has been examined at the Cincinnati Art Museum. The glazes viewed were of a matt, velvety nature. The colors were often muted so that a variegated effect of colors was created. Reproductions of his work also tend to substantiate this.

Van Briggle was famous for two very distinctive glazes that he developed at the turn of the century.

> Turquoise Ming-Luminous Blue. Not only is the word "Ming" to be associated with a celebrated Chinese Dynasty of the 14th Century, A.D., but in literal translation, it means "luminous."
>
> Persian Rose-Shadowy Rouge, a subtle double-tone. This is a color which may be said to pay homage to the Murrhine vases of Persia.[16]

In the summer of 1901 Van Briggle moved to Colorado Springs, Colorado. The skills of working independently in pottery, as he did in Colorado, was viewed as a rarity at this time. This was one reason for Van Briggle's reputation as a potter.

> Mr. Van Briggle can now devote himself entirely to the production of his wares. Although he employs an assistant, he is capable of doing any part of the processes from the first refining of the clay to the final glazing and firing of the vase.[17]

Despite the renown that Van Briggle gained through his discoveries of the matt glazes it was his total adaptation of Art Nouveau principles which made his pottery distinctive. Van Briggle was repeatedly singled out as one of the most modern and advanced potters of his time. This was in part due to the unusual subject matter selected for adorning his pottery. In a survey of written material, the following evaluation was typical:

> The vase is thirteen inches high and of the color of unbaked gingerbread—a disagreeable color to some persons—but its peculiarity is in the nude male figure which nearly encircles the lip. This figure is so posed that the profile of the face is seen relieved in light upon darkness of the interior; it is modelled with vigor and its pose is not without grace. As to the general scheme of an adornment found in the use of the human body, that and nothing else, combined with the piece, it is one with a vast amount of recent work in bronze, silver, block-tin and ceramic ware of different sorts, and forms part of a system of design which has spread all through Belgium, France and Germany.[18]

Thus Van Briggle became the innovator of a new style in American pottery when he utilized the human figure as a decorative motif in his highly unusual, distinctive technique (Fig. 3-5).

> The decoration of the Van Briggle pottery is something entirely new, and in one sense lends it a distinction which even the dead [matt] glaze cannot impart.[19]

Equally original was his method of executing relief decorations. In the past, the green clay was only carved when it was leather hard. But Van Briggle worked on his forms when they were plastic, thereby achieving the fluid, sensuous quality upon which the Art Nouveau style depended.[20] His mastery over this approach to pottery was readily acknowledged

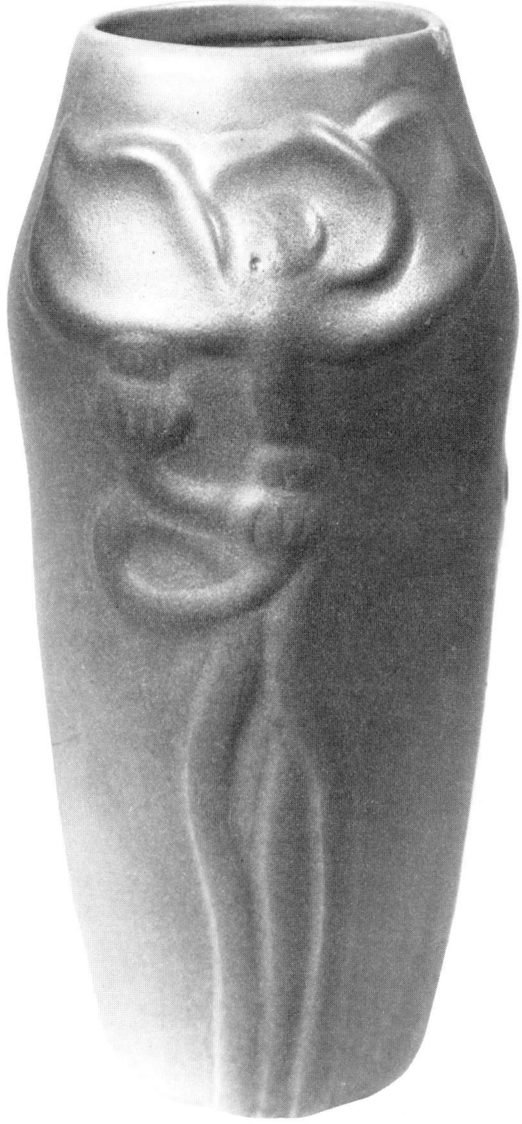

Figure 3-5. Artus Van Briggle, Colorado, vase, hand thrown and modelled, red matt glaze, 8 1/2″ × 3 1/2″, Milwaukee Public Museum Collection, ca. 1906. Van Briggle became nationally and internationally recognized as one of America's outstanding studio-potters for his distinctive Art Nouveau designs and use of soft, velvety glazes that were a closely guarded secret for several decades.

by writers who sensed in his work a quality that was indicative of tastes at the turn of the century. A description of Van Briggle's work follows:

> On a slender vase he will model the figure of a woman; her arms are clasped around its rim and she is gazing into the depths of it—a splendid conception, the working out of which none but a master would dare to undertake, for if unskillfully done the figure will be extraneous and so make the effort a failure. But Mr. Van Briggle makes the two one. Remove the figure of the woman, and there is no longer a vase, for her arms and head form the rim; her body, her hair, her drapery, make up the contour. With the most perfect feeling for form, he sees to it that the angles of her arms balance, that there is no salient point on one side of the vase without its complement on the other. The sweep of her hair balances the folds of her drapery; every line contributes to and preserves the harmony. Yet nowhere does this fine adjustment interfere one iota with the verisimilitude of the figure and pose, for then all would be lost.[21]

Van Briggle's form of personal expression in pottery met with recognition in America and in Europe. The exact number and types of awards received by him is not obtainable, but the following list is representative of the stature he achieved by the turn of the century: (1) the Saint Louis Exposition of 1904: one gold medal for his collective exhibit of pottery, one gold medal for Faience, one silver medal for pottery and clay bodies, and one bronze medal for decorated ware, (2) the American Pacific Exposition (Lewis and Clark Centennial) of 1905: one gold medal for finished pottery made from crude clay, (3) the Arts and Crafts Exhibition, Boston, 1906; "Highest Award" for pottery. The last two awards were given posthumously.[22]

A further example of the noticeable influence of Art Nouveau on American art-pottery and its subsequent ramification of dealing with each pot as a separate work of art was seen in Teco pottery of Terra Cotta, Illinois.

Teco Pottery

The work of Teco pottery is being considered in this study because it was the only pottery manufacturing company in the mid-west that dealt with the production of art-pottery during the 1910's in the style of Art Nouveau. Furthermore, it serves to illustrate how Art Nouveau helped in bringing about a type of artist-potter different from that of the previously described decorators.

The Teco company was originally formed in 1880 to produce architectual tiles and bricks. The growing demand for architectural terracotta increased the need for research and experimentation with colors and textures. Its owner, William D. Gates, also had an avocational interest in pottery, and upon the accidental discovery of luster and crystalline glazes, instituted a department which dealt exclusively with the production of art-pottery[23] (Fig. 3-6).

At first the company was satisfied with perfecting distinctive surface effects through glazes and textures on rather simplified forms.

> Whatever be the color adopted, the tones are so varied that with the different finishes produced an interesting collection of Teco pottery could be made in which one piece would scarcely suggest the same origin as the other. In this regard Teco ware is unique. Some of the most highly prized products of American pottery rely for their beauty on a given tone and a given finish, so that a collector having

> one piece as representative of the make would scarcely want another. No one piece of Teco pottery could be called representative of the company's output, a peculiarity that adds to the interest of the ware.[24]

In its spirit of experimentation the company also encouraged its employees to investigate possibilities of new designs for the shapes of vases. Operating under the assumption that beautiful surroundings helped to produce beautiful results, an effort was made to cultivate flowers, especially aquatic plants, on the premises of the factory. This was done with relative ease, since the pottery was located at the side of a small lake. Designers, decorators and modellers were urged to use motifs of the different plant forms and allow them to serve as inspirations for their work. As a result, Teco produced pottery of unusual design, not only in terms of shape but also in decoration[25] (Plate 3).

In February, 1902, examples of this new type of pottery were shown in an article which discussed the history of Teco pottery. The work shown illustrated a dramatic departure from designs produced by any other manufacturer or individual potter at that time. Whatever contacts the company or its designers and potters may have had with Art Nouveau sources is not known to the author. But a survey of the literature between 1890 and 1910 disclosed that Art Nouveau was a controversial and frequently discussed issue. The articles were frequently accompanied by illustrations of Art Nouveau designs. Attempts were being made to disseminate this new form language, to trace its origin and to evaluate it as a form of self-expression. A list of representative samplings of articles which articulated

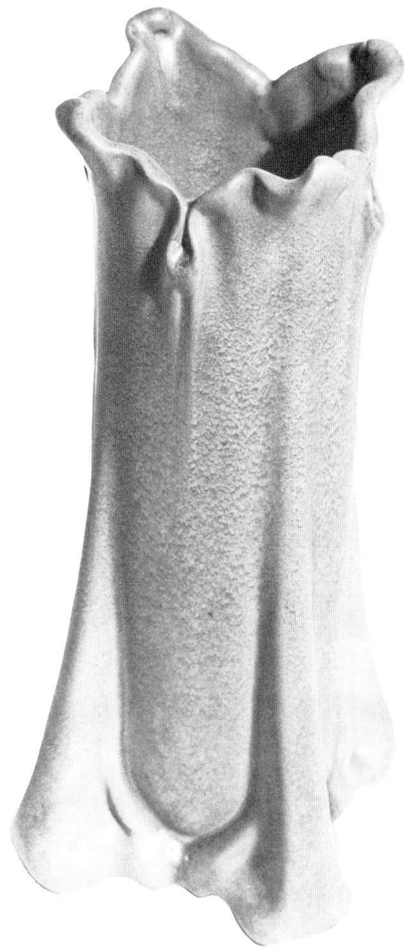

Figure 3-6. Teco Pottery, vase, stoneware with matt green glaze, ca. 1890. Chicago Historical Society Collection. A good example of the Art Nouveau influence which often resulted in an effective merging of form and decoration.

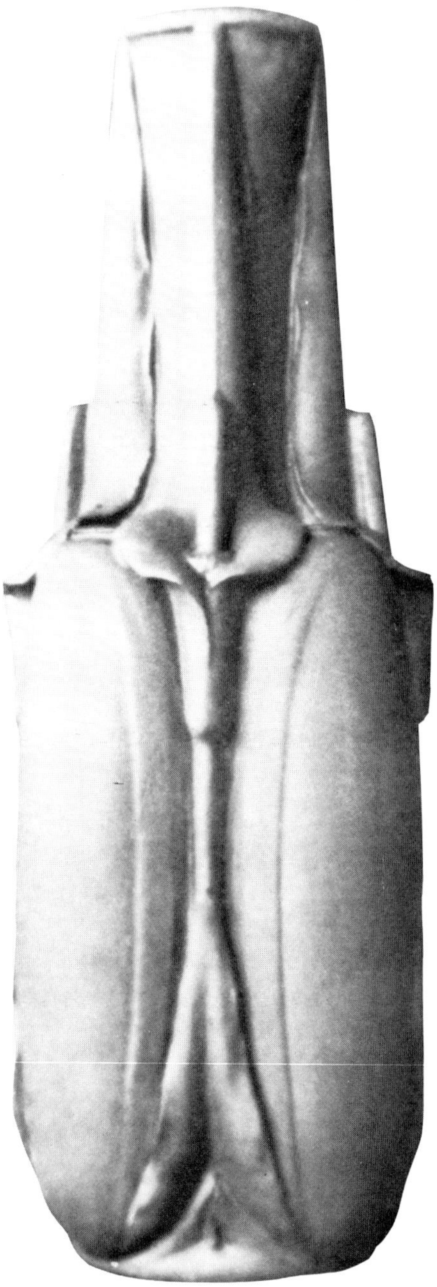

Figure 3-7. Teco Pottery; vase, stoneware, cast and handbuilt; green matt glaze; Fritz Albert, designer and decorator; ca. 1901. Collection of the author.

responses for and against the new form of artistic expression will be found in Appendix A.

It is surmised, therefore, that Art Nouveau designs produced by Teco came about both through the possible exposure to the large quantity of written material and through the inspirations and impetus provided by the president of Teco, William D. Gates. It is also of interest to note that Gates hired designers from Germany.[26]

In Teco work, particularly that of Fritz Albert (Fig. 3-7), Art Nouveau plant motifs were so dominant that the basic structure of pots became almost indistinguishable. The complete envelopment of some forms with aquatic plant motifs created a synthesis of structure and decoration. The forms designed and executed by Teco potters were all uniquely their own. Their work displays an extraordinary inventive and unconventional approach to pottery in which the exotic and the irregular prevailed. This was achieved through forming methods that demanded the skills of one person in the entire pottery process. Their pots were either thrown on the wheel or modelled by hand.

Although the venture of producing art-pottery was in no way anticipated as a commercial venture, William D. Gates did include Art Nouveau forms in his advertisements of regular pottery. In this regard he says:

> We are convinced that there is a large element of the public cultured of taste and in love with the beautiful who cannot afford to indulge in the luxury of high-priced articles of a decorative nature, and hence we feel that in putting Teco ware upon the market in artistic designs, and with finishes comparable with those of the more expensive ware, we will meet public want.[27]

Through the examples of Gruebey, Teco, Newcomb and Van Briggle one could see how, through the impetus of Art Nouveau, American potters involved themselves in bold and vigorous experimentation. This was particularly true in developing new design concepts, an attitude which became very important in the growth and development of studio-potters.

When Art Nouveau was one of the accepted idioms of artistic expression, from approximately 1900 to 1915, it lent itself to a certain amount of improvisation. Within the bounds of Art Nouveau styles occurred several variations. These were best distinguished in the pottery which has been discussed. All of them adapted some aspects of Art Nouveau principles, so that at times only decorative aspects such as under and overglaze painting or incising were considered. Others pursued the style further and were able to synthesize their work more completely with Art Nouveau designs. In those instances the shape and decoration were merged into one homogeneous unit. Hence the notion of expressing an idea subjectively by means of decorative pottery in the style of Art Nouveau created a unique form of American art-pottery.

Notes

1. Irene Sargent, "The Wavey Line," *The Craftsman*, 2:135 (April, 1902).
2. Josephine C. Locke, "Some Impressions of L'Art Nouveau," *The Craftsman*, 1:200-204 (August, 1902).
3. Perkins, p. 52.
4. Walter E. Gray, "Latter-Day Developments in American Pottery," *Brush and Pencil*, 10:36 (April, 1902).
5. Franklin Adams, "Two Decades of Newcomb Pottery; Pieces from 1897 to 1917," *Exhibition Catalog*, p. 3, February, 1963, Newcomb College, New Orleans.
6. Mary Scherer, "The Development of Decorative Processes at Newcomb," *Journal of the American Ceramic Society*, 7:645 (August, 1924).
7. Adams, p. 3.
8. Robert Koch, *Louis C. Tiffany, Rebel In Glass*, p. 140.
9. Walter E. Gray, "Latter-Day Developments in American Pottery," *Brush and Pencil*, 9:241 (January, 1902).
10. "American Pottery," *Scribner's Magazine*, 32:640 (November, 1902).
11. Gray, p. 421.
12. "The Potters of America: Examples of the Best Craftsmen's Work for Interior Decoration," *The Craftsman*, 27:302 (December, 1914).
13. "Forms From The Earth: 1,000 Years of Pottery In America," *Exhibition Catalog*, The Museum of Contemporary Crafts, New York, 1961.
14. Koch, p. 140.
15. The Van Briggle Art Pottery Company, Colorado Springs, Col., unpublished correspondence.
16. The Van Briggle Art Pottery Company, unpublished correspondence.
17. "The Van Briggle Pottery," *Brush and Pencil*, 9:2 (October, 1901).
18. "American Pottery," Scribner's Magazine, p. 640.
19. "The Van Briggle Pottery," *Brush and Pencil*, p. 4.
20. Ibid., p. 4.
21. Ibid., p. 5.
22. The Van Briggle Art Pottery Company, unpublished correspondence.
23. Walter Gray, "Latter-Day Developments In American Pottery—II," *Brush and Pencil*, 9:290-291 (February, 1902).
24. Ibid., pp. 293-294.
25. Interview with Arthur C. Jenner, General Superintendent, Teco Potteries, Terra Cotta, Ill.
26. Interview with Arthur C. Jenner.
27. Walter Gray, "Latter-Day Developments—II," p. 296.

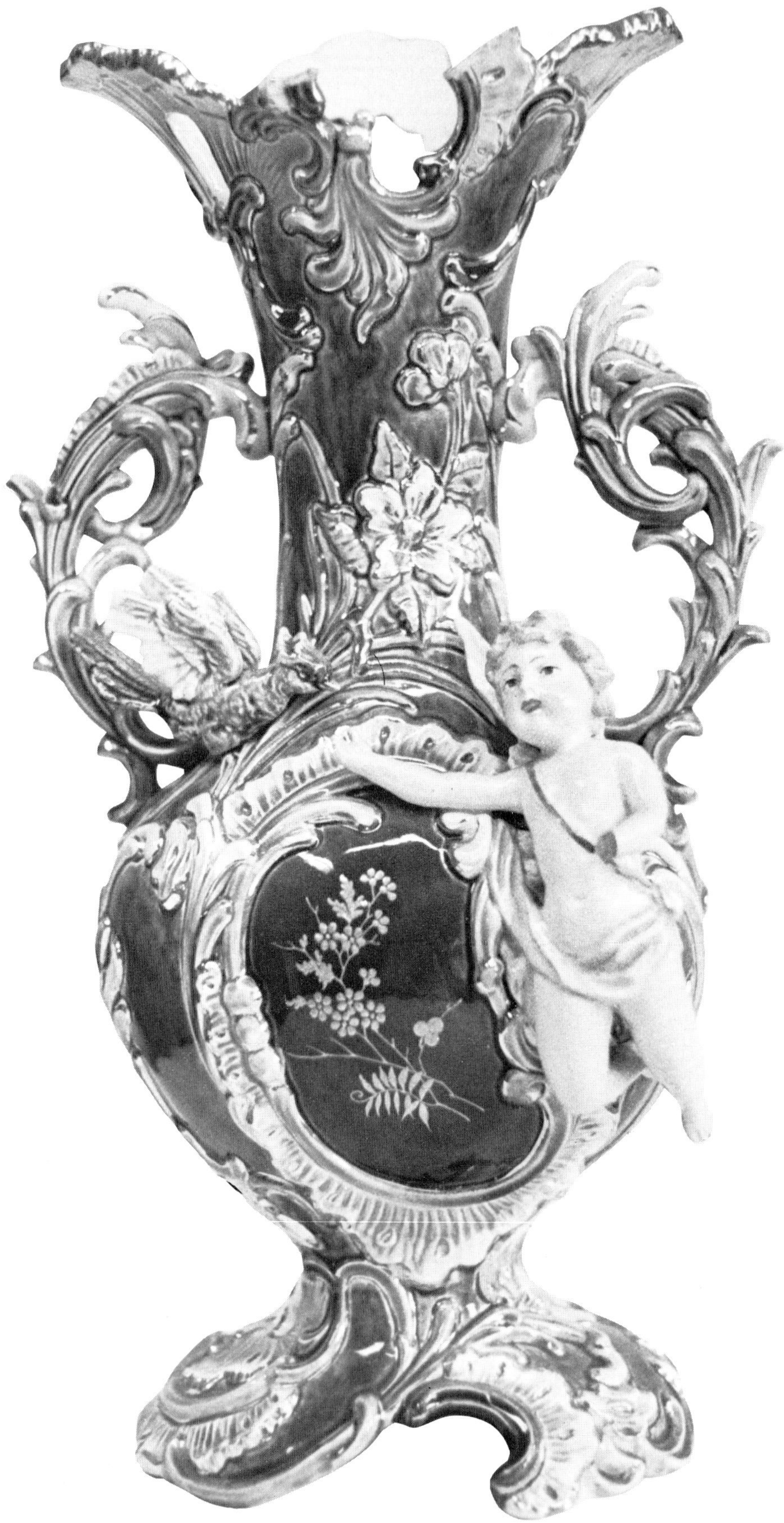

Anonymous

The Role of the Arts and Crafts Movement 4

The relationship of the Arts and Crafts movement to the development of American ceramics was significant. It provided several avenues for propagandizing the philosophy of the movement as it emanated from England in the late nineteenth century. This was accomplished primarily through the aid of three magazines, the *Craftsman, Brush and Pencil* and *Handicrafts.*

Important Literature of the Arts and Crafts Movement

The magazines mentioned were founded with the express purpose of supporting and perpetuating the doctrines of John Ruskin and William Morris, which stated a reaction against mechanical production. The *Craftsman* was rather general in its aims when it stated, "The *Craftsman* is an illustrated monthly magazine in the interest of better art, better work, and better and more reasonable way of living."[1] In so doing, the magazine strove to recreate something of the handicrafts of earlier days. The following statement included the guiding principles of the *Handicrafts* magazine and the Arts and Crafts movement in the United States.

> The motives of the true Craftsman are the love of good and beautiful work as applied to useful service, and the need of making an adequate livelihood. In no case can it be primarily the love of gain.
>
> The conditions of true Handicraft are natural aptitude, through technical training, and a just appreciation of standards. The unit of labor should be an intelligent man whose ability is used as a whole, and not subdivided for commercial purposes. He should exercise the faculty of design in connection with manual work, and manual work should be part of this training in design.
>
> When the designer and the workman are not united in the same person, they should work together, each teaching the other his own special knowledge, so that the faculties of the designer and the workman may tend to become united in each.
>
> Modern craftsmanship requires that the idea of patronage be superseded by that of reciprocal service and cooperation.
>
> The results aimed at are the training of true craftsmen, the developing of individual character in connection with artistic work, and the raising of beauty in objects of use.[2]

Broader views of Morris' aims, such as social justice, improvement of morals and cultivation of the powers of the mind have not been considered in assessing the development of American ceramics. Instead, the major contribution of the Arts and Crafts movement was its ability to generate an awareness of, and an interest in, the crafts in general.

Already mentioned were the important journals which the movement relied upon for spreading its ideology. In them were featured potters and their work, group exhibitions, articles that provided technical as well as artistic information and editorials which frequently criticized commercial ceramics.

But a note of contradiction has also been noted in examining the criticisms directed at American crafts by factions representing the Arts and Crafts movement. This was especially true in the area of pottery. On the one hand, it was felt that there was too great a reliance upon the designs and techniques of other countries and of past periods. The following excerpt was typical of this attitude.

> Good things are produced, very good things, but they are reproductions or copies of fine things done long ago. All we do is to adapt them to our purposes, to our needs, with very little, if any, alterations. The changes we make are rarely improve-

> ments, and our copies and reproductions are not so good as they ought to be. Our artists and craftsmen, the ablest of them have settled to a systematic imitation of historic examples, and the study of design is called the study of "historic ornament."
>
> The work which we do, when we follow our own impulses and disregard precedents, is often useful. It serves its purpose, but it generally fails in design or lacks technical perfection.[3]

On the other hand, the volumes of the afore-mentioned magazines were filled with examples that supported outright copying of designs and techniques. This was often regarded as a sufficient form of original or creative art. The following from an article which dealt with the recreating of a Turkish Coffee set is an example of this attitude.

> The decoration is the production of Mrs. Ruth Wilson Tice, a ceramic artist of Minneapolis, who is working along new and original lines. This decoration, which she calls enamel work, is individual with Mrs. Tice, quite her own invention, and has not yet been imitated. Indeed, it would be difficult to imitate.
>
> This set has had generous recognition wherever it has been exhibited, and took the gold medal at Atlanta. It was greatly admired in Cincinnati and was thought worthy of a permanent place in the Fine Art Museum of that city.[4]

On the basis of the quotation it is assumed that the Turkish Coffee set was copied from a picture or perhaps even from a commercially made prototype. The technique, too, was one that was known relatively well, although the use of enamels was not as widespread as was overglaze painting with oxides or engobes. Thus there remains little doubt that this was one of numerous cases of copy work. The practices of copying appears to have been supported in view of the hand-production involved. This seemed to be justified as an art activity, especially since the hand-crafted technique was in direct opposition to some mechanical practices in pottery (Fig. 4-1).

Other journals also gave enthusiastic support to the aims of the Arts and Crafts movement and helped to provide additional information that aided in the support of hand-craft operations throughout the country. In 1911, the *Magazine of Art* praised the efforts of the Pewabic Pottery of Detroit for promoting ideas that were similar to those at Rookwood, in which women produced individual pottery.[5] Similar support was given to the Paul Revere Pottery started in 1910 by Edith Brown. She sought to train young girls in the art of decorating pottery as a means for obtaining a livelihood.[6] *The Art World* magazine helped to promote the idea of hand-made pottery in its article that featured "The Saturday Evening Girls" as making a worthwhile contribution to American ceramics.[7]

In addition, other magazines which did not relate to the arts directly nor which were not formally associated with the Arts and Crafts movement, contributed to the increased interest in non-commercial pottery. They included *Scribner's Magazine, Munsey's Magazine, Good Housekeeping, International Studio, Living Age, American Review, Arts and Decoration, Survey,* and *Chautauquan.* Articles published in these dealt mainly with methods of building pots and decorative techniques. Over-generalizations and over-simplifications occurred frequently, especially when attempts were made to explain the complexities of throwing, glazing and firing. However, this did not necessarily emphasize the contribution they may have made in bringing about an awareness of artistic wares produced by some

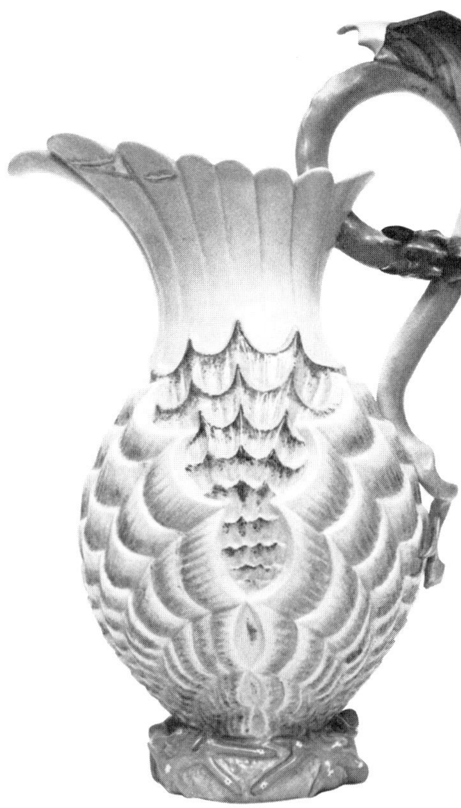

Figure 4-1. Anonymous, "Swan Pitcher," white earthenware, cast and handbuilt; hand decorated with multicolored underglazes and various overglazes; ca. 1918; 15″ h × 10″ w. Courtesy, the Oshkosh Public Museum Permanent Collection, Oshkosh, Wisconsin.

Copying the works of other countries, other periods and other cultures was an accepted practice by the Arts and Crafts movement, since it involved some form of hand-production.

potters. It remained for the various Societies of the Arts and Crafts to bring to the attention of the public examples of hand-made pottery. This was done through exhibitions, demonstrations and lectures.

Societies of the Arts and Crafts

The Societies of the Arts and Crafts developed in the late 1890's and early 1900's. A list of these organizations, found in Appendix B, is sufficient to indicate that an enthusiastic support for the Arts and Crafts movement occurred in the United States. The existence of these societies is viewed as having been important, since they offered a primary means by which artist-craftsmen were able to display and sell their work. Moreover, their membership was also indicative of the idea that crafts held an equally important position next to the fine arts. The following evaluation of the Society of the Arts and Crafts bears this out.

> The Society of Arts and Crafts, under whose auspices a number of local associations throughout the country have contributed to make this national exhibition of handicraft, was organized in 1897. It is not a mere local institution. In its membership of about 550 are included workers resident in nearly every American state. Its secretary, Frederick Allen Whiting, was director of the applied arts division at the St. Louis Exposition, at which for the first time the arts and crafts were given a place of co-equal importance with the arts of painting and sculpture.[8]

It is not known just which organization sponsored the exhibition. But it appears that the Society of the Arts and Crafts was among the earliest of the organizations that originated events in which the crafts were recognized to the same degree as were the other arts—and thereby may have begun to initiate more effectively the concept of the artist-potter.

The enthusiasm and support given to the crafts in general was furthermore reflected by the emergence of new organizations with aims similar to the Societies of the Arts and Crafts.

> So, as some things intended especially for permanent usefulness, to last a long time and not to be consumed immediately, are always best made by hand, the effort of the artist has been very generally expended upon reviving the hand industries. Hence, there has been in this country a recent growth of handicraft societies until now, according to a directory which has just been brought out by the National Society of Craftsmen, a newly organized society in New York, there are seventy organizations of this kind. The same compilation gives names and addresses of more than 1,100 workers, most of whom may no doubt be called artists in the arts and crafts.[9]

Charles F. Binns provided additional insights into the structure and operation of these organizations. He pointed out that in many cities the Society sought subscriptions from people who were interested in the crafts. With funds received through the membership, studios were rented and teachers hired. According to Binns, the active members of the club were men and women who had acquired the craft "notion," and who had at least one or more years of training in some sort of art school. They constituted the working force of the club(s) and, "they plunge[d] into the making of baskets, rugs, metal work and even pottery with an enviable enthusiasm."[10] Binns further points out that

> these societies have organized salesrooms which are intended to be self-supporting. That is, the commissions on sales are, for the most part, sufficient to pay rent and the cost of selling and packing. Each of these societies has a membership roll and members are entitled to a reduction in the commission paid for the sale of their work. A standard is set and supervision is exercised in order that the quality of the work may be maintained. The membership dues are used partly in the missionary efforts which every active organization must put forth.[11]

Among the important functions of the societies was, therefore, the providing of facilities for creating and displaying the work of active craftsmen. The necessity of furnishing studio space in which workers could gather is readily recognized. The desire to exhibit and sell the hand-crafted products is also of significance during these formative years of the development of the artist-potter. This became but another step in the direction of providing the potter with some measure of independence from industry.

The Arts and Crafts movement helped to supply a general philosophy without any specific methodology. Its emphasis upon the hand-crafted object was frequently confused with that of outright copying. No new form concepts were instituted. Nevertheless, it was an important event in the history of American crafts, because it served as the first, broadly-accepted source that deviated, at least temporarily, from the mass-produced pottery of industry.

In its desire to promote the handicrafts as a reaction against the "ugliness" of commercially produced wares it failed, however, to establish a standard of high quality. For this reason the exhibitions of the Societies of the Arts and Crafts frequently included a conglomeration of china painting, some thrown pottery, decorated ceramic tiles and ceramic sculpture. In addition, the lack of adequate teaching and the fact that most people associated with the Arts and Crafts movement were, in essence, hobbyists, prevented the emergence of any unique form language or the development of any concise, clearly defined philosophy.

But the missionary efforts of the Arts and Crafts societies did bring about an awareness and consciousness of the importance of crafts in general. This was accomplished through numerous exhibitions and organizations that held lectures and demonstrations throughout the country.

Preceding discussions, which included china decorating and Art Nouveau, have pointed out that several attitudes developed which were unique in the growth of American studio-potters. First, a resurgent interest in the crafts was noted. This came about through the Arts and Crafts movement which emanated from England and included some work by china decorators and some potters who emerged from that group as noteworthy potters. In America this movement resulted in the forming of several organizations and publications which were instrumental in promoting the work of several potters.

Second, the Arts and Crafts movement fostered the notion of hand crafted work. This found particular favor with a number of American potters who were seeking some form of independence from industrial standardization. One example was the work of potters who were sympathetic with the Art Nouveau aesthetic.

Third, it was important to note that those potters who were identified with the Arts and Crafts movement were the sole representatives of America's quest to create a distinctive form of art-pottery. Their work represented the United States in competitive exhibitions in Europe.

Finally, it became evident that the majority of potters were operating without any significant amount of information regarding the technical aspects of pottery. When new clay bodies or glazes were sought, for example, blind experimentation was generally the rule rather than the exception. In some instances, when research was carried on, the findings were usually kept secret and unavailable to others.

The lack of intensive research and the unavailability of existing facts required an organized effort to disseminate technical information as well as the defining of an aesthetic specifically for pottery. One way in which such information and ideas could be disseminated was through ceramics programs in colleges and universities. Alfred and Ohio State Universities were the first institutions to become involved in these tasks. Hence another type of studio-potter began to develop from 1920 to 1940.

Notes

1. *The Craftsman*, 20:1 (April, 1911).
2. "Principles of Handicrafts," *Handicrafts*, 2:2 (April, 1903).
3. Denman W. Ross, "The Arts and Crafts: A Diagnosis," *The Craftsman*, 7:335 (October, 1904).
4. Charlotte Whitcomb, "A Unique Turkish Coffee Set," *Brush and Pencil*, 8:135-136 (May, 1901).
5. H. Plumb, "The Pewabic Pottery," *Magazine of Art*, 2:64 (January, 1911).
6. "Story of the Paul Revere Pottery," *The Craftsman*, 25:205-207 (November, 1913), and Mary Northland, "Paul Revere Pottery," *House Beautiful*, 36:82-83 (August, 1914).
7. Livingston Wright, "Girls' Club Establishes Pottery and Ultimately Makes It a Financial Success," *The Art World*, 2:578-579 (September, 1917).
8. "Notable Arts and Crafts Exhibition." *Brush and Pencil*, 20:81 (February, 1907).
9. Ibid., p. 75.
10. Charles F. Binns, "The Arts and Crafts Movement in America," *The Craftsman*, 14:276 (June, 1908).
11. Ibid., pp. 276-277.

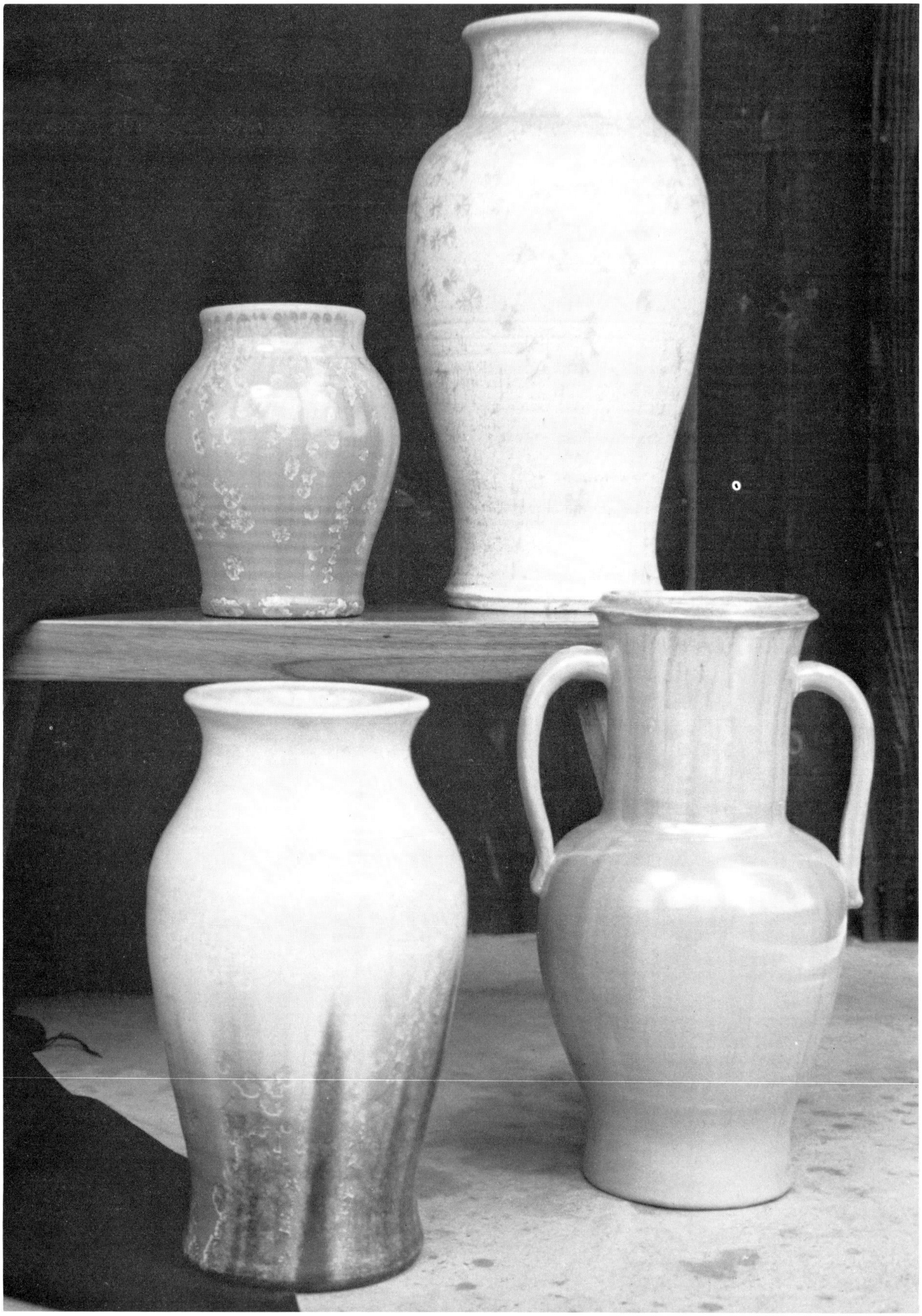

W.B. Stephens

Economic Effects on the Crafts 5

Parallel to and following the developments of China Painting, the Arts and Crafts Movement and Art Nouveau another force was developing which eventually became a significant catalyst in bringing recognition to the crafts. The movement emanated essentially from rural areas of the Eastern seaboard and several southern states. It was motivated primarily by socio-economic circumstances of the days before and during the depression. A more detailed discussion of its formation and growth will aid in obtaining a better insight into the expansion of the crafts in the United States and its relationship to the area of studio-pottery.

The League of New Hampshire Arts and Crafts

In 1907 the Society of the Arts and Crafts became so large that it expanded to include twenty states of the Union (see pp. 47 to 49). It was thereafter changed and known as the National League of Handicrafts Societies. In principle the purpose of the League was not unlike its predecessor in that it sought to become the main propagandizing force for the various crafts and its numerous practitioners. Among other things, the League sought to provide small traveling exhibitions which could serve as a set of standards; to provide to the various societies libraries of technical handbooks, and also help in co-ordinating lectures touching on a variety of topics related to the crafts for the numerous organizations.

One of the states which did not have membership in the National League of Handicrafts Societies was New Hampshire. Although it was not included in the League, it formed its own organization under the name of the League of New Hampshire Arts and Crafts. Its inclusion in this study stems mainly from its historical contribution in terms of the example that it set for other states in forming their own, particular organizational structures.

The village of Center Sandwich was actually the beginning for the New Hampshire League, since it was there that the various products of metal smiths, bookmakers, woodcarvers, glassblowers, potters and furniture makers were being exhibited and sold successfully. By the economic standards of 1928, the sale of five thousand dollar's worth of craft work by a group of largely amateurs, was viewed as admirable. The economic implications of this small venture prompted more investigation, so that by 1930 the League was beginning to obtain government support whose main interest it was to explore further the potential that the state's human resources had in it numerous craftsmen.

Experts in the field of the arts, crafts, government and business were recruited in order to help formulate fundamental matters of policy, markets, commissions to be charged, surveys of existing training schools and even to compile a bibliography of manual arts and handicrafts books to be made available to interested persons.[1] People from the Rhode Island School of Design, the University of New Hampshire and the Russell Sage Foundation all contributed to make this one of the enviable examples of how business, education and government could work co-operatively in making the crafts not only a viably functioning economic resource, but also serve as a means for retaining and upholding a dignified way of life for people who were steeped in economic and social depression.

By 1931 the New Hampshire League became

the first organization of its type to establish an arts and crafts service through the support and legal authority of its state government. More private support from people such as Mrs. Andrew Carnegie, as well as increased state aid helped in the growth of this group so that by 1932 it had over eight hundred members in twenty-one separate affiliations within the state.

So successful was the growth and expansion of the New Hampshire enterprise that other states sought assistance in forming similar groups. In 1937, therefore, the New Hampshire League called together representatives from the Southern Highlands and other areas of the Atlantic Seaboard to discuss mutual problems related to the status of the crafts. One of the results of this meeting was the formation of the first Rural Art Exhibition in the United States which was sponsored and supported by the Department of Arts and Social Work of the Russell Sage Foundation and the Department of Agriculture. At the same time, the 75th anniversary of the University of New Hampshire became a timely occasion for forming the New England Handicrafts Federation.[2]

The importance of the League of New Hampshire Arts and Crafts was two-fold: First, through the combined efforts of its monthly newsletter, its annual exhibitions, demonstrations, lectures and its permanent commercial outlets it was able to reach a large population both within and outside the state. The economic implications of these activities, especially for the practicing craftsmen, cannot be underestimated. Secondly, the League can be credited with having exerted considerable influence in aiding the formation of several other crafts organizations who sought to emulate the aims of the New Hampshire League. Numerous areas in New England designed their crafts organizations after the New Hampshire prototype. (See Appendix H for a more complete list of these organizations.)

The cumulative effect of the New Hampshire League's undertaking, as well as other organizations that followed its lead, is therefore viewed more in terms of the services, the financial and the moral support that it rendered to its numerous participants. It was not instrumental in any noteworthy artistic innovations. The most conspicuous contributions was the League's concern for bringing together men and women from every walk of life and to promote their efforts to produce individually made crafts.

Pottery in New England

A comprehensive survey of historical texts that deal with American ceramics will point out that before the Industrial Revolution over five hundred individual pottery studios existed in the New England area. An examination of their products substantiates the belief that, generally speaking, the styles coming from the majority of these studios were imitative of the forms and techniques brought to the American colonies from England and the European continent. This included the typical variety of low fired, lead glazed earthenware pitchers, jars, jugs, platters, plates, bowls, mugs and planters, as well as the stoneware, salt glazed crocks, bottles and cider jugs decorated with the familiar cobalt stains and slips. (See Chapter 1 for a more detailed discussion of this type of work.) Because of the demand for these types of pots, a high degree of uniformity was maintained regarding techniques of forming, decorating and glazing.

Not until after the 1930's was it noticeable that there were a handful of potters who began to concern themselves with creating unique and completely individual pottery. After 1935, pottery was being produced which was less provincial in character. This was especially conspicuous in the catalog of the 1943 Contemporary New England Handicrafts Exhibition, held at the Worcester Art Museum, Worcester, Massachusetts. Two distinctive types of pottery were selected to illustrate the efforts of New England potters. The first type dealt with almost exclusive utilitarian considerations which meant that the shapes of casseroles, tea pots, pitchers, cups and covered jars were generally uncomplicated and that there was also a notable absence of applied decorations to these forms. The work by Norman Arsenault, Lyn Phelan, Edwin and Mary Scheier and the potters from the Rowantree Kilns reflected a simple and direct approach to wheel thrown pottery.

The second type had a more pronounced emphasis on decorative considerations. The more interesting examples of this category came from the studios of Luman P. Kelsey, Lydia K. Winston and again Edwin and Mary Scheier. Their work was typical of the attitudes which existed throughout the United States during the 1930's and 1940's. Stylized motifs of animals, plants or human figures were very popular. The subject matter was often placed on simple shapes which allowed for the greatest variety of decorative techniques such as brush painting of slips, sgraffito, incising or low relief modelling.

In the latter category the work of Edwin and Mary Scheier of New Hampshire has been consistently distinctive for its individuality of form and decoration. They have been active in ceramics since 1939 and are one of the best examples of the studio-potter of the New England region. Although they have consistently produced utilitarian pottery, their more notable artistic contributions have dealt with more of one-of-a-kind decorative items in which surface decorations and glazes are featured in more important roles.

Large bowls, planters or compotes were the recurring shapes upon which the Scheiers have relied since 1940 for their highly individual surface treatments. Although stylized human figures were consistently used as the basis for the decorations of large, simple pots, they were always reduced to abstractions and repetitious patterns which helped to reinforce the simplicity and strength of the vessels' shapes (Fig. 5-1). A feeling of restraint permeates throughout their work. It becomes obvious that each piece was given careful consideration in its construction and decoration. Edwin Scheier alluded to this when he said:

> Pottery demands restraint. For a craft in which technique plays so vital a part, there is danger of virtuosity, bravura and precocity—the three greatest enemies of even the best potters.[3]

Although the Scheiers professed to be self-taught in pottery, their formal education did include involvements in drawing, painting, jewelry and puppet-making.[4] But their form language did not reflect the dogmas and activities of the middle 1950's, a time in which a more experimental approach toward asymmetrical shapes and highly textured surfaces started coming into prominence. Instead, their work espouses their love for masterful control of the wheel thrown pot which achieves a sense

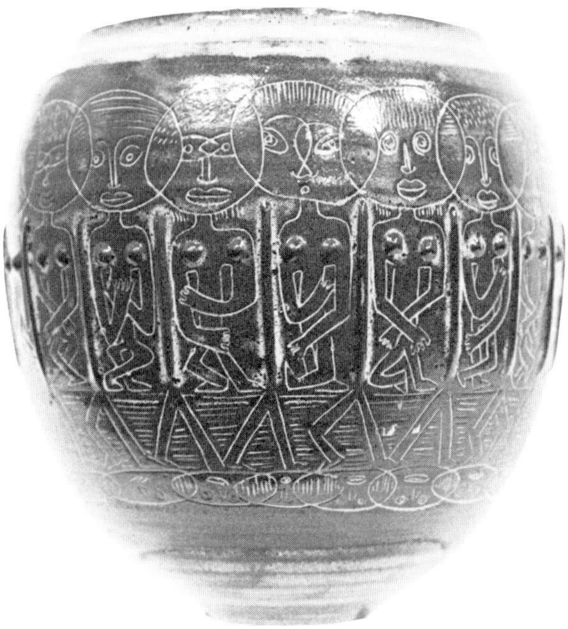

Figure 5-1. Edwin and Mary Scheier, Bowl, stoneware, wheel thrown, incised and raised decoration, 1949. Courtesy, the Everson Museum of Art Permanent Collection.

of timelessness through discriminating combinations of the pseudo pre-Columbian figurative imagery on uncomplicated pottery vessels.

Through their thirty years of teaching at the University of New Hampshire, and through recognition achieved by having exhibited in every major national ceramics exhibition in America and receiving awards in many of them, as well as having their works purchased by over thirty major museums throughout the world, the Scheiers became one of the earliest leaders of American studio-pottery within the New England area.

Revival in the Southern Highlands

Various researchers have placed the probable beginning of pottery in the Southern Highlands area anywhere from 1750 to 1800. The large array of material written on the subjects suggests that potters came from various parts of the United States and Europe to settle in the Southern Highland region in order to practice their crafts. Pottery making appears to have been a family affair which was handed down from father to son, generation after generation. It is therefore surmised that this type of training helped to perpetuate the established methods of working with the traditional shapes and quaint designs and decorations. Moreover, once the work of this isolated pocket of people was discovered, exploitation for the commercial market contributed to the continuance of this tradition.

> Possibilities were discovered for making saleable articles out of cornshucks, plentiful in every mountain household and already in use for everything

> from mattress stuffing to sausage casing, and when twisted tight, for chair seats and mule collars. The local chairmaker was pressed to make good settin' [sic] chair and gout rocker for sale to far-away shops. Whittlers whos pas [sic] and grandpas had made their own door latches with a pocket knife—good whittling seemed to run in families—were encouraged to carve the bears, squirrels, mules and pigs they knew so well, and the market responded. Potters' wheels whirred to fill orders and, as the smiths were drawn into the picture, wrought iron fireplace tools, toasting forks and candlesticks began to appear.[5]

It was not until well into the 1930's that a crafts, indeed, a way of life which originally existed to provide the basic and immediate necessities of life, became transformed into an activity of supplying a commercial market outside of its own region. This included keeping up with the demands of department stores, gift shops and tourist centers. Requirements for increased production soon became a problem. It was a time for organizational wheels to be set into motion if standards of craftsmanship and design were to be maintained. In 1930 the Southern Highland Handicrafts Guild was therefore formed with the proclaimed purpose to:

> . . . encourage creativeness in design and the use of materials, to preserve the traditional and indigenous craft thought, produced and sold in the area and to provide opportunity for the exhibition and sale of the crafts of its members.[6]

The mountain areas of Maryland, the Virginias, the Carolinas, Georgia, Kentucky, Tennessee and Alabama became the Guild's territory. The Guild has maintained selling centers in these regions even to this day, some of which are open throughout the year. The highlight of the Guild's efforts have been the Craftsman's Fair which has been held at various locations every year in the Southern Highlands. Little doubt remains that the aims of the Guild oriented themselves rather clearly around the idea of producing a saleable item which was to retain a distinct hand-made, indigenous character.

But the uniqueness that was once typical of the crafts originating from such a region, was gradually removed or lost by craftsmen who were not part of that long family or apprenticeship tradition. Some people who sought to fulfill their leisure time with some type of craft activity often came to their chosen crafts via some exposure of written materials, lectures, demonstrations or a class. A frivolous level of amateurism therefore often existed among the many other works which concerned themselves more with an unselfconscious effort to produce a simple, unpretentious craft item.

There exists the contention that the pottery which has come from the Southern Highland region has unique characteristics which distinguishes it from pottery produced in most other locales of the United States. One should realize, however, that the typical jug, butter churn, whiskey jug, pie plates and many other types of pottery made in the Southern Highland region were also made at that time, as well as now, by potters in various other parts of the country. Pottery referred to in the first chapter of this book, which were produced by the colonial potters in earthenware and stoneware were also created in the New England area. Although the East and South made these items in larger quantities than most other regions, a survey of almost any historical museum will readily point out that areas in the

Midwest (Ohio, Illinois, Wisconsin, Minnesota, Iowa and Indiana) also had a rather long tradition in producing similar types of pottery.

There is, in fact, little evidence which suggests that the crafts of the Southern Highlands exerted any appreciable influence in determining new styles or attitudes in the work of other potters that were working outside this region. The converse has been found to be true, in that "outside" pressures, related mainly to commercial markets, had a more direct influence in determining production methods and design in the work of Southern Highland potters. One of the notable ventures of attempting to regain and retain a local characteristic of Southern Highland pottery, but which failed, occurred with an enterprise known as Jugtown pottery.

Jugtown Pottery

One of the main industries of some Southern states, that of producing whiskey, gave an added impetus to the already existing pottery manufacturing which fulfilled the essential needs of one's household. As such, it provided a ready market for the famous "little brown jugs." It was during the last two decades of the nineteenth century that production of these jugs reached its highest point. North Carolina had between fifty and sixty individual pottery studios operating for that specific purpose. But the adoption of prohibition in 1908 curtailed this profitable craft which had been practiced over a long time.[7]

It was the curious mind of a Mr. Jacques Busbee to investigate the remnants of a once rich pottery tradition of the Carolinas. His inquiry eventually brought about an attempt to revive the art of the potter in that region. Busbee, who was a teacher of art, studied at the National Academy of Design, the Art Student's League and the Chase School, all of New York. He was, however, more interested in the promotion of the crafts rather than other areas of the arts such as painting or sculpture. Thus in 1919, as chairman of the Art Department of the Federation of Women's Clubs of North Carolina, he sought out the remaining potters in the hinterlands of that state as a first step in bringing about a revival in the art of pottery-making.[8]

In search for the older potters Busbee found that they had abandoned their craft which was heavily influenced by the laws of prohibition. A large number of potters who had at one time produced very actively had to toil on the farms and in the neighboring lumber mills. Consequently, there was a breakdown in the family tradition of training one generation after another in the skills of making pottery. Busbee realized that if steps were not taken to revitalize and resurrect this tradition it would become lost to the highly industrialized ceramic industry which was producing large arrays of unoriginally designed and garishly decorated ware.

Jacques Busbee therefore undertook the task of searching for old pottery which was once produced in the best local traditions. At the same time, he also sought to locate potters who would be willing to once more produce these fictile items in the hopes of stimulating a market for their sale. In order to create an interest in these pots and also find a profitable market, Busbee gathered his collection of pottery and established a store in Greenwich Village, New York, where he sold them.

In 1921 Busbee also purchased in Moore County, North Carolina, buildings for throwing, decorating, exhibiting and firing of pottery. The sight was named Jugtown. Local people were hired to perform the many tasks of running the pottery, and the Jugtown potters produced the traditional items in their customary designs. This included the usual platters, pitchers, pickle jars, crocks of various sorts, bean pots and butter jars. The absence of surface decoration and the use of yellow, orange and brown colors obtained through earthenware clays and glazes became the most distinguishing features of Jugtown pottery. Often the throwing process has remained as an indication of a rather direct, casual use of clay. The pulled handles were applied in an equally forthright manner (Fig. 5-2).

But the clientele of New York City to which Busbee sold these wares, was not content with merely utilitarian pottery. This prompted Busbee to become involved in researching the Oriental forms and glazes with which he was somewhat familiar and he taught some of the accomplished potters of Jugtown the use of his "new" ideas. During the 1920's Busbee took his master potter, Ben Owen, to various art schools and museums in order to study the designs and glazes of Chinese, Japanese, Korean and Persian pottery. With this new interest in decorative pottery, Busbee stressed form as the most important element with which the potter had to conern himself. He explained:

> North Carolina pottery is of no consequence in itself without beauty. Being made of North Carolina dirt adds nothing to its value unless it is embodied in the form of Art. For as a matter of fact the whole of art is form. We call it form in pottery and sculpture: proportion in architecture: good drawing in painting: feeling or soul in music: style in literature. Pottery without beauty of form cannot be made interesting by color, glaze or decoration.[9]

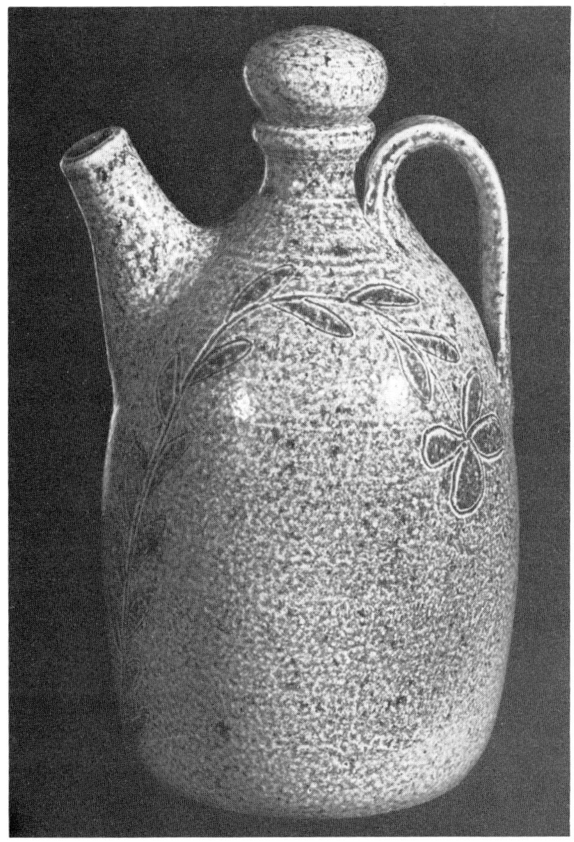

Figure 5-2 Jugtown pottery, covered pitcher, stoneware, wheel thrown, salt glazed. Courtesy, Sam Sweezy, Belmont, Mass.

Jugtown potters began to produce a variety of shapes which were copies of the Chinese Han, T'ang and Sung dynasties. The shapes that the Jugtown potters made reflect a high degree of throwing skill and a good ability to assimilate the total design concepts of Oriental pottery. Glazes used on these vessels were remarkable in their likeness to their prototypes (Fig. 5-3). Thus, the provincial character of the traditional Southern Highland pots which were Busbee's initial concern, were being rivaled in importance by the introduction of these distinctive Oriental forms and glazes.

Jugtown pottery, as well as other work from various areas of the Southern Highlands, was not without its national recognition. Examples of what was regarded as typically Southern Highland work was included in the permanent collections of major museums in the United States. More importantly, the work of Jugtown was frequently shown in exhibitions during 1925 and 1949. A small sampling of some major exhibitions attests to the nationwide recognition given the work of these potters. For example, the pottery was exhibited in May, 1925 at the Southern Exposition in the Grand Central Palace of New York. In March 1928, lectures, demonstrations and exhibitions were held at the Department of Ceramics Engineering, North Carolina State College. During November, 1937, their work was included in the National Exhibition of Rural Arts, sponsored by the Department of Agriculture, Washington, D.C., as well as in an exhibit at Howard University Gallery of Art, also of Washington, D.C. in March, 1940. During that same period examples of Jugtown pottery were part of an exhibition of "Contemporary American Crafts," at the Baltimore Museum of Art.[10]

The importance of the recognition received by the Jugtown potters lies mainly with the idea that it may have had a salutary effect upon the surrounding areas and its potters. But despite the widespread popularity of their work, much of which was also gained through publications such as the *Bulletins of the American Ceramic Society* as well as a number of other periodicals, it is doubtful that it helped in shaping the form concepts of other potters who were involved in ceramics in other parts of the United States. Certainly potters who were beginning to entertain the idea of "self expression" through their work did not turn to the eclecticism illustrated in most Southern Highland pottery. Although there has been a resurgent interest in recent years in dealing once again with a type of pottery which identifies with a "folk-art" notion, it has been generally inspired by the Orient, specifically that of the folk arts of Japan.

One of the few people from the Highlands area who has achieved renown as a studio-potter of distinctive work has been Charles Counts. Although trained in the art department of Berea College, the Southern Illinois University, the University of Southern California and the workshops of Pond Farm of Marguerite Wildenhain, Counts has retained a deep commitment to creating unpretentious, sound, functional pottery. But rather than continuing the practice of many other Southern Highland potters who are still working with the designs that have been handed down to them from previous generations, Counts has brought something of a personal vision and personality to his work. Mostly this manifests itself in a variety of decorative approaches on traditional forms. This gives his work a distinctively different quality from that of his numerous neighboring potters of the same region (Fig. 5-4).

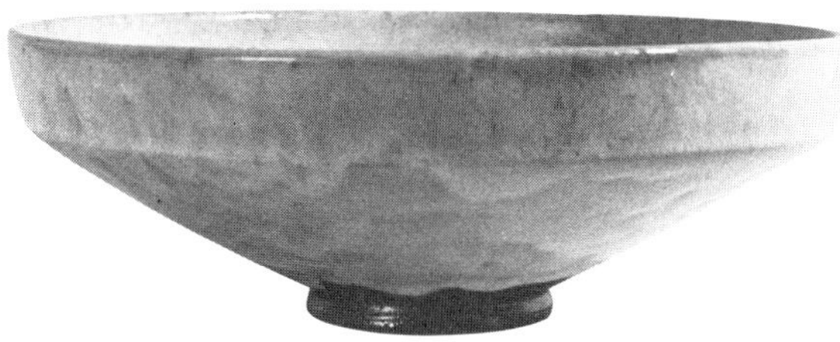

Figure 5-3 Jugtown Pottery, bowl, stoneware, wheel thrown. Courtesy, Sam Sweezy, Belmont, Mass.

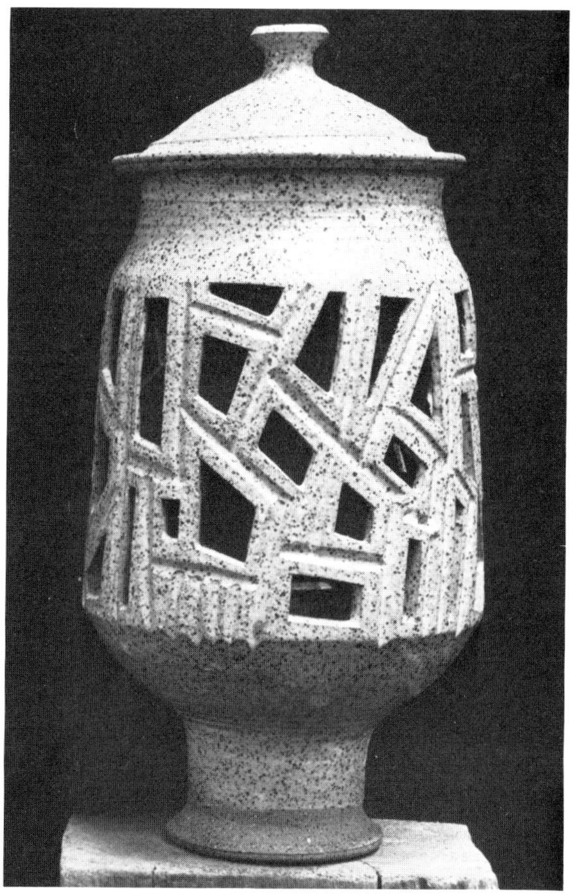

Figure 5-4. Charles Counts, covered lantern, stoneware, wheel thrown and cut design. The work of Counts is typical of how a small group of potters, working in the Southern Highlands region, have brought a contemporary sense of design to a tradition that is generally thought of as being typically folk-art pottery.

Equally important has been Counts' commitment to utilizing his time, energy and talents for helping others to wrest for themselves a respectable way of life. In 1965, for instance, he and his wife established an apprenticeship program with which to train young potters who might otherwise have to return to a life of poverty, ignorance and other degradations of the human spirit that accompany those conditions.[11]

The Depression and Its Relationship to Studio-Pottery

The crafts' movement of the New England area, as well as the developments in the Southern Highlands were undertakings essentially prompted by economic conditions before and during the depression. Among other outgrowths of this national dilemma were the creations of jobs and crafts programs for people who might otherwise have had to seek a less uncompromising manner of subsistence. The metropolitan areas of America were, perhaps, more visibly affected by the depression. Government assistance in helping to alleviate some of the hardships in these centers was therefore more evident.

Several ceramics programs came under the direction of the Works Progress Administration of the Roosevelt administration (see also pp. 88-89). It also created the National Youth Association in which ceramics played an active role. Both groups supported programs which trained men and women not only for industry, but also provided instruction in the crafts. In most instances the crafts served as a means to supplement one's income, except, of course, for the low-income groups in whose instances it was the sole means of support. It was therefore desirable for these people to accomplish as much of their craft work as was possible, at home.

Since ceramics required a great deal of expensive and space-consuming equipment, it is unlikely that the government sponsored crafts programs became involved to any large extent in the area of pottery. This observation is made despite the fact that several ceramics training programs were begun for the unemployed youth which ranged in ages 16 through 24. The pottery they produced was essentially used in federal establishments such as the National Youth Association resident centers, schools and other institutions. During the first years of the 1940's, dinnerware was also made by these groups for American military bases. But once the United States became fully committed to the war, this activity ceased.

However noble the efforts may have been of providing the destitute with facilities and personnel for acquiring some profitable and constructive skills, the emotional preconditioning of the times may have served as a strong undermining force. Moreover, the age factor was a serious deterrent to the successful implementation of the crafts programs. Most individuals in their late teens were not interested in becoming involved in the crafts. This is understandable in view of an economy which was having problems meeting the basic necessities for its population, leave alone the purchasing power for crafts items.

A typical account of the questionable success of government sponsored crafts training programs was given by Jack Smoot who reported his findings to the American Ceramics Society in 1942. The students involved were asked to give their reactions to the programs, and the following consensus was established.

> (1) Most of them could not draw; (2) they were not interested in learning to draw; (3) they felt that they were wasting their time; (4) they wanted to spend all their time in the ceramics department doing other work; and (5) they could see no practical application to what they were doing. It was evident that the actual construction of ceramic ware was being presented in an interesting manner but that the plan had definitely failed to interest the workers in artistic aspects of this work.[12]

Not all programs of this nature were failures, to be certain. The entire area of therapy, adult education and rehabilitation for veterans have all played a vital role in developing more fully the various crafts. The Rochester Athenaeum and Mechanics Institute was a typical example of how pottery was utilized as an effective means for exploring one's creative abilities in order to fill empty hours. It was at that institution where soldiers from World War I and unemployed people during the depression came to learn something about ceramics.[13]

In similar manner, the New York Museum of Modern Art established a War Veteran's Art Center in 1942 for the express purpose of aiding in the rehabilitation of soldiers returning from World War II. Victor D'Amico directed its educational program, and evaluated it as follows:

> . . . one thousand veterans have attended classes in painting, sculpture and ceramics, jewelry, woodworking, industrial arts, design, graphic arts, silk screen printing, illustrating, and orientation.
>
> . . . (the) faculty faced a student body from nearly every walk of life, all of whom had been through the unnatural experience of a war and many of whom had come out of this experience needing understanding and help. That these men and women found such understanding and help at the War Veterans' Art Center is demonstrated by their return week after week.[14]

D'Amico's book dealt with instructions for simple construction methods such as coil and pinch pots. No mention was made of problems related to designing or decorating. Good taste and guidelines for "correct" design were established by illustrating the work of Gertrude and Otto Natzler, George Fetzer, Laura Andreson as well as examples of Zuni Pueblo, Hispano-Moresque, Pennsylvania-Dutch, Peruvian and American Indian pottery from the Southwest.

It was through various government sponsored programs that the recreational, therapeutic and semi-professional aspects of working with clay may have generally succeeded. Whether there were any results that extended beyond these expectations is very doubtful. The general quality of work that has come out of those programs seems to cast serious doubts on the idea that anything of artistic consequence developed as a result of the numerous crafts programs. It is also very dubious whether or not the new directions of the 1950's were even remotely related to the activities of these programs.

But it is important that activities in the crafts did sustain themselves in some form during and after the years of the depression and the wars. At the very least it created new demands for qualified people to teach the various courses of the crafts. The effects of this requisite did not become clear until well after the close of World War II when noted increases occurred in enrollments, expansions of curriculums and enlargements of facilities at the college and university levels. This, in turn, created an exodus of artists and craftsmen to the teaching community at various levels. The relative freedom from financial burdens and the encouragement to become involved in a more experimental attitude, all of which are typical of academic situations, eventually became one of the more important contributing factors to the development of the studio-potter.

The significance of the Southern Highland potters, as well as that of the New England states, was not so much with their attempts to revive and sustain their indigenous form of art. The more important contributions to American studio-pottery was in its ability to bring about a keener awareness of the crafts in general and in the revelation that America did possess some type of ceramic heritage, however remote it may have seemed, excluding that of the American Indian.

The recognition of the crafts as a potential means with which to counter the financial burdens of the depression in rural areas was also important. The programs that arose from this economic dilemma had far reaching effects, especially in the areas of education, government support, recognition by major museums and the establishing of a number of organizations that strove to promote the work of craftsmen. These combined efforts aided in the American craftsman eventually wresting for himself a position of relative importance and dignity alongside other areas of the visual arts. A foundation was formed which enabled a number of craftsmen of succeeding generations to pursue careers in the crafts with challenge and enthusiasm.

Notes

1. Allen Eaton, *Handicrafts of New England*, Harper and Brothers Publishers, New York, 1949.
2. Ibid., p. 305.

3. Robert Scharff, "A Studio Session with Edwin and Mary Scheier," *Crafts Horizons,* XXI (May-June, 1952) p. 14.
4. Unpublished personal correspondence to the author from Mary Scheier.
5. *Crafts in the Southern Highlands,* Southern Highland Handicraft Guild, Asheville, North Carolina, 1958, p. 10.
6. Ibid., p. 11.
7. Juliana Busbee, "Jugtown Pottery: A New Way for Old Jugs," *The Bulletins of the American Ceramic Society,* XVI:10 (October, 1937) p. 415.
8. Jean Crawford, *Jugtown Pottery,* John F. Blar, Publisher, Winston-Salem, 1964, p. 10.
9. Ibid., p. 78.
10. Ibid., p. 58.
11. Jonathan Williams, "The Southern Appalachians," *Crafts Horizons,* XXVI:3, (June 1966) p. 58.
12. Jack Smoot, "Development of an Art Program at an NYA Resident Project," *Bulletin of the American Ceramic Society,* XXI (May, 1942) p. 77.
13. "Lulu S. Backus," *Bulletin of the American Ceramic Society,* XXI:4 (May, 1942) p. 61.
14. Julia Mamlin Duncan and Victor D'Amicao, *How to Make Pottery and Ceramic Sculpture,* The Museum of Modern Art, New York, Simon and Schuster, 1947, p. 5.

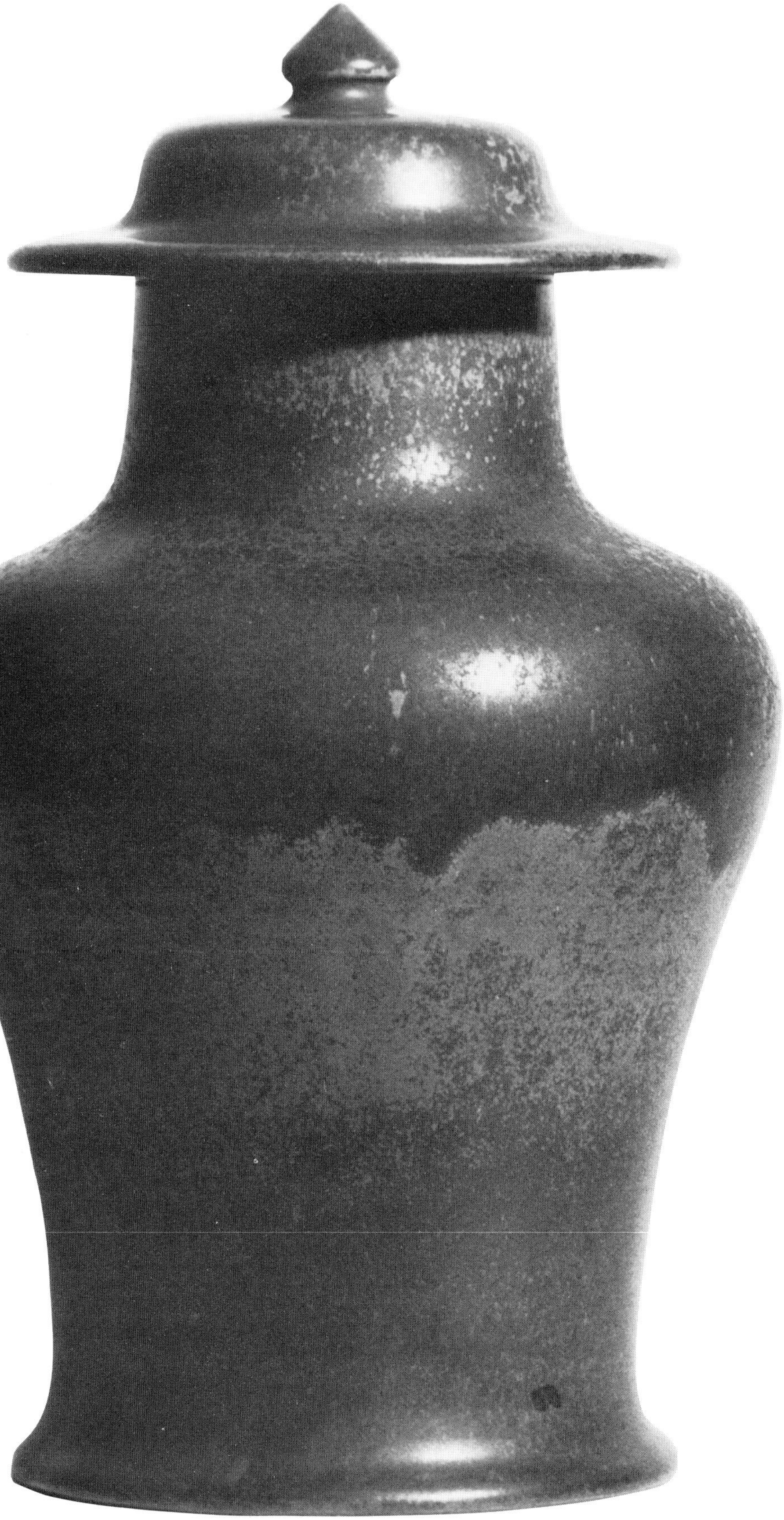

Charles F. Binns

Influences from Alfred University 6

Although Alfred University was not the first school that offered ceramics in America, it is discussed at this point of the study because it did institute America's initial Ceramic Art and Design course. A closer examination of its inception will provide an insight into the development of its programs and its relationship to the growth of studio-pottery from approximately 1910 to 1940.

Alfred University was founded as a small denominational school in 1836, in Alfred, New York. The inclusion of ceramics in its curriculum was decided upon because of financial necessity rather than through an overt claim to attempt to improve the standards of American pottery. Ceramics seemed a rather appropriate subject in the school's curriculum because two tile plants were in operation in Alfred, and because larger quantities of clay were available in the immediate vicinity. Theodore Roosevelt, then governor of New York, signed a bill bringing into existence the New York School of Clay Working at Alfred, New York, on April 12, 1900.[1]

The first classes in ceramics were offered in the spring and summer of 1901. The following summer a class was added which featured the use of clay in the teaching of art. The summer course was of some importance because it allowed students to pursue opportunities in pottery-making which would normally not have been available to them. These classes became so popular that in the fall of 1902 a student organization, "The Alfred Ceramic Society," was founded. The primary aim of this small club was to discuss artistic and technical problems related to ceramics.[2]

The New York State School for Clay Working gained momentum, and its enrollment increased rapidly. In a large measure this was due to the Leadership of Charles Fergus Binns, who has popularly been accepted as the "father of American studio-pottery." A detailed examination of his background and his contributions to American studio pottery will show that the title is clearly justified.

Charles Fergus Binns

The reasons for Binns' coming to the United States from England have not been established. It is known, however, that he did travel in America on a lecture tour, supposedly sponsored by an English Arts and Crafts organization, prior to his settling down in New Jersey in 1898.

Binns was apprenticed at the Royal Worcester Porcelain Works in England. There he learned every phase of pottery production, and after nine years was appointed the technical director of that company.[3] As such he was involved in technical research and in writing articles of a technical nature for England's top ceramic journals, the *Pottery Gazette* and *Ceramic Technology.* These articles dealt primarily with the problems of clay compositions, colors in glazes and kiln operation. It is in these articles that one senses an early interest in the dispersion of technical information. His interest in eradicating the secrecy which permeated the pottery industry was most important. Through his dissemination of the results of research, a large number of American potters were able to secure the "secrets" which were so necessary to the success of studio-pottery.[4] A representative list of his published material in the area of technical research is included in Appendix C to illustrate the wealth of information he made available.

The stress that Binns placed upon technical competence, especially in the area of glaze chemistry and clay bodies, was readily known. In this regard he said:

> The art of producing beautiful pottery is so closely interwoven with the ways of chemical combination that no one can hope to be a successful clayworker who has no knowledge of scientific procedure.[4]

Of equal importance, and of special significance in this study, was Binns' philosophy in regard to the artistic aspects of pottery. The technical considerations of pottery, however limited, were beginning to be taught at other schools. But Alfred University was the first to undertake the task of formally preparing a student in all phases of pottery-making, including design, in a program initiated under the direction of Charles Binns. His thoughts on the subject of preparing the potential potter with an artistic as well as a technical background were published in several journals. The following is a good example of his attitudes.

> It was necessary that some idea of form should be presented to them [the students]; many had scarcely seen a piece of decorative pottery, and certainly had no conception of making any such thing. A number of forms in plaster were therefore prepared and molds made. This had a double purpose. Molding, however objectionable artistically, is a fact and must be recognized, and by means of molding, primary students could learn to manipulate clay and study applied design before they had acquired the ability to create. This method of procedure had the effect of enlarging the horizon of students and setting before them the possibilities of their chosen art.
>
> Every student in art was set to study elementary and applied design with such simple drawing exercises as seemed necessary in each case. A course in simple chemistry was also deemed advisable, for intelligent design depends largely upon a knowledge of the material used. Then it was felt to be possible that some students be placed in a position where there would be no chemist to whom to turn for colors and glazes, so that for one to be able to make one's own combination was a distinct point of advantage.[5]

Herein lies the innovation of Charles Binns, and consequently of Alfred University. Although other schools had concerned themselves with producing artistic wares, the results were often arrived at through the efforts of at least two or more people. At Alfred this was not the case. All students, including women, were involved in all aspects of pottery, including the loading and firing of kilns.

The concern that Binns had for creating artistically sound pottery was of particular interest, despite his inclination toward technical considerations. He reflected the attitudes of the Arts and Crafts movement. The following excerpt offers further clues to his philosophy.

> Be it remembered that fine wares can not be made for money alone, that profit must not be thought of—at least in the beginning—if a world-wide reputation is to be made, it will be apparent why our manufacturers have not touched the question.[6]

Binns was aware that if studio-pottery was to be regarded as a fine art it demanded the same scrutiny and evaluation as practiced by painters and sculptors. A high standard of workmanship and design had to become an integral part of the potter's attitude. Binns emphasized this when he pointed out that—

> it is not enough to discern the good, the hand must follow the brain with diligent care. Furthermore, it is not enough to make things well, one must also make them good and know it. The artist-artisan

> must have courage to destroy that which is below standard, and self-denial to resist the temptation to sell an unworthy product.[7]

More specifically, he represented the idiom, "Truth to Material," when he urged that the nature of the material must be seriously considered. He was opposed to the idea of creating ceramics which did not reflect the intrinsic character of clay. To imitate objects of nature or the effects of other materials and media was, in effect, a denial of the nature of clay. Binns thought it equally superfluous to become involved in outlandish textures and colors.[8]

In keeping with his idea regarding fitness of material to form he also insisted that one needed to consciously concern himself with scale, design and weight of a pot. He felt these factors had to achieve an equilibrium which made the pottery appropriate for its intended use. For these reasons the appearance of the pot had to conform to the perceived estimate of what its weight would be.

With these attitudes in mind he set forth to teach the basic skills of pottery. Just how and what he taught is best seen in his book, *The Potter's Craft*. It is a reflection of his tastes and skills as an artist and teacher. Of particular interest is the section that deals with throwing techniques. A sequential pattern was followed in which each step of the throwing process had to be mastered before one became involved in the complexities of a completed form. The designs he prescribed were severe and their execution had to be achieved with accuracy. Emphasis was placed on walls of uniform thickness on which surface effects such as finger ridges, tooling marks or other signs of the forming process were not desired. Because of exceedingly careful throwing and precise trimming of the pot after it was leather hard, his work frequently assumed a character of having been cast rather than thrown.

Binns' way of working also suggested that large pots be thrown in several sections. These "large" pieces, according to Binns, apparently constituted anything over six inches in height. In regard to the throwing of large pieces he declared: "Work made in one piece is apt to be badly finished especially inside, and unduly heavy. Work made in sections can be thrown with thin walls and finished with proper care."[9] With meticulous care he would set out to make three or more pieces, carefully measured with a caliper and then assembled in their leather hard state. Photographs of Binns in *The Potter's Craft* illustrated this technique, and his strict adherence to it has been verified by Maija Grotell who worked with him after she arrived in the United States from Finland.[10]

Binns also recognized the value and possibilities of hand-building techniques. In an article for *The Craftsman* he wrote:

> The wheel was difficult, if not impossible, and molding was undesirable because of its lack of individuality. The study of Indian methods opened the way for clay building. In pottery which is fashioned by the hand method, there is a certain vibrant undulating of surface which at once removes it from comparison with tool work or machine finish. Not that the potter's wheel is to be classed as a machine; but in shaping a piece by the wheel there is an almost irresistible desire to turn and polish the clay until it assumes a mechanical quality.[11]

The article also illustrated numerous examples of hand-built ceramics which his students executed in the manner of Indian pottery.

Binns did not, however, dismiss the wheel as a valuable tool for creating pottery. He said:

> Clay in its responsive plasticity is so human, so living, that no one can wonder at the delights of the potter in caressing it upon the wheel. It is verily, not human but feminine. It has the coy resistance and the reluctant yielding of a blushing maiden.[12]

This romantic attitude was hardly detectable in Binns' own work. His attitudes concerning individual production were oriented around perfection in design, in execution and in surface decoration. The last was almost nonexistent in view of his predominant use of simple, single-colored glazes (Fig. 6-1). In his own work a distinct classical form is evident. The simplicity of his pottery was a radical change from the floral excessiveness that was so popular with the china decorators and potters who adopted Art Nouveau concepts as well as traditional European decorative motifs. Louise Avery evaluated his work as "restrained, subdued in tone, almost austere."[13]

Binns, therefore, created a relatively new concept regarding decorative possibilities of pottery. Instead of concealing the shape of a pot with decoration, he felt that the proper glaze on an appropriately shaped and fired body was a complete statement of art-pottery in itself. For this reason he became involved in considerable glaze research. Once he decided upon a desired glaze, he would set out to achieve the sought-after effects.[14] Particularly noteworthy were Binns' pots that emulated the simplicity of shape and glaze of Ching Dynasty pottery.

His encouragement of the hand-crafts in general, and pottery in particular, closely identified him with the Arts and Crafts movement. (See chapter 4) He frequently wrote articles for the *Craftsman,* which was one of the leading journals that supported the Arts and Crafts movement. The following statement is characteristic of Binns' views.

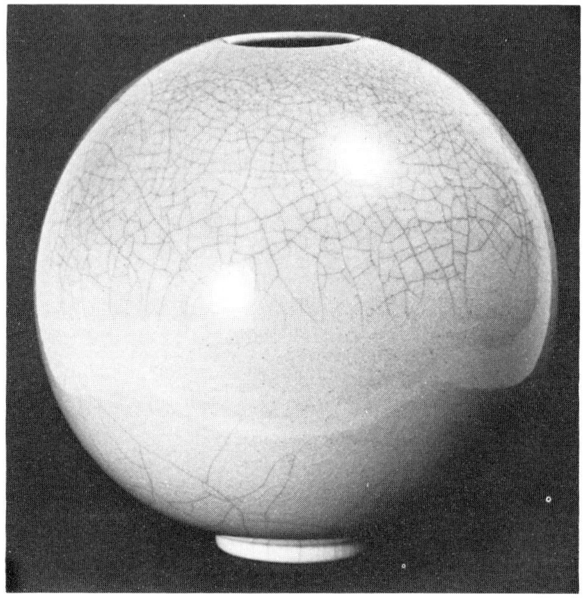

Figure 6-1. Charles F. Binns, vase, wheel thrown, porcelain. Courtesy, New York College of Ceramics at Alfred University, Alfred, N.Y.

> It is, however, in the studio and in producing objects of household service that clay is found at its best. This point has been reached through a long period of evolution. The struggle has been hard, but at length it seems that truth and simplicity are to prevail; that the artist is again to come into contact with his client and to impress his life upon many homes, without the intervention of machine and mold.[15]

The following quote has been extracted from an exhibition catalog which dealt with "Contemporary American Ceramics." In it he wrote of the dual purpose that ceramics must assume, which would be the utilitarian and decorative.

> Every craft should pursue the properties of the material. There are always facilities and limitations. A piece of pottery is essentially a vessel, and as such should lend itself to some useful service. On the other hand, such a piece should not need a bouquet or a spray of flowers to make it complete, but it should always be capable of such use. The same is true of a plate and indeed of every example of the potter's art. It need hardly be said that the basis of all craft work is design. A carefully considered form must be associated with some decorative feature or features, such as color, glaze quality, or line treatment, though in addition to these qualities, craftsmanship implies control over material and method.[16]

During Binns' stay at Alfred University, 104 students graduated in the area of Ceramic Art and Design.[17] Exactly what influences he exerted upon them is not known. It is surmised, however, that the graduates carried a sound technical knowledge with them. With them, too, may have gone the concept of the potter who was formally trained in aesthetic as well as technical aspects of ceramics. For fostering this concept Charles Binns and Alfred University deserve a prominent position in any history of the development of the American studio-potter.

Further, a sampling of contemporary American potters will indicate that Alfred University, because of its comprehensive training program, had graduated the largest number of well-known American studio-potters from approximately 1910 to 1940. (See Appendix D.)

Arthur E. Baggs

One of the earliest noteworthy graduates of Alfred University who became instrumental in furthering the cause of American studio-pottery was Arthur E. Baggs. Although he was associated for several years with commercial pottery, his importance in the area of American studio-pottery began when he was hired to take charge of the Department of Ceramic Art at The Ohio State University, Columbus, Ohio, in 1928.

Under Binns' guidance Baggs received the necessary skills and knowledge in pottery, enabling him not only to teach his craft, but also to establish a commercial pottery where he was in charge of all phases of production. With a recommendation from Binns, Baggs went to the Marblehead Pottery at Marblehead, Massachusetts. The pottery firm was started as a therapeutic aid for mentally-disturbed patients from a sanitarium operated by a Dr. Herbert J. Hall.[18] Baggs' duties with this pottery were usually required only during the summers. In the remaining months he attended the Art Student's League in New York, as well as Alfred University, to further his studies. This was supplemented with design courses at Harvard and some museum work at the Boston Museum of Fine Art and the Metropolitan Museum in New York.[19]

Pottery produced at Marblehead was commended by several writers for its beauty and simplicity. The previously cited article by Emerson included photographs of some work produced at Marblehead. If this was a representative sampling of the work produced, then it is appropriate to speculate that the influence of Charles Binns, and consequently of Baggs, had begun to be felt in the work of others. The examples shown illustrated form concepts that were being fostered at Alfred in its earlier years: that is, severely simple, almost completely undecorated, utilitarian wares. The impact of the work done at Marblehead must have been of some consequence, especially in view of the responses by several writers. The following evaluation was typical: "The Marblehead pottery stands for simplicity—all that is bizarre and freakish has been avoided."[20]

In 1925 Arthur Baggs left the Marblehead Pottery and joined the Cowan Pottery in Rocky River, Ohio. He was hired specifically to work in the area of research with glazes and clay bodies for commercial production. Among the other artists employed were Victor and Don Schreckengost, Russel Aitken, Thelma Frazier, Edward Winter, Wayland Gregory and Paul Bogotay.[21] From 1925 to 1928 Baggs also taught pottery at the Cleveland Art Institute, Cleveland, Ohio.

When Baggs became the director of the newly-formed Ceramic Art program at Ohio State University, his aspirations for the teaching of ceramics were best expressed in a letter he wrote when he was asked to submit some biographical data as the member of a jury.

> All my life I have been thoroughly interested in good, honest ceramic art, have some knowledge of its design and technology and a strong wish to help in the general improvement of American products.[22]

In his desire to improve American ceramic products, Baggs relied heavily upon principles similar to Binns', namely a thorough training in the technical aspects of pottery, as well as a knowledge of design. His success in these areas has been acknowledged by prominent students who have graduated from his department, and by the honors that Baggs has received for his work. His pottery is represented in the permanent collections of the Metropolitan Museum of Art, the Columbus Gallery of Fine Art and many others.

When asked about instruction received from Baggs, Herbert Sanders and Victor Schreckengost replied as follows:

> Emphasis was on sound craftsmanship, integration of form and decoration with careful consideration given to appropriate glaze treatment.
>
> Original conception of the pot as a completed unit with decoration and glaze as part of the original concept. Decoration and glaze should not be an after-thought. The whole should be a unified, creative expression of the individual.[23]
>
> A purist as regards glaze, form and decoration being each a part of one concept, the interdependence of each on the other for a complete whole; Craftsmanship; perfection so far as techniques were concerned.[24]

After evaluating Baggs' writings, almost all of which have been published in the *Bulletins of the American Ceramic Society*, it could be concluded that his first interest was in the area of technical research. But, though Baggs concerned himself with shortcomings in technical competence, he also was aware of the need to improve the design concepts of American potters. This concern was expressed shortly after he assumed the Chairmanship of the Ceramics Department at Ohio State.

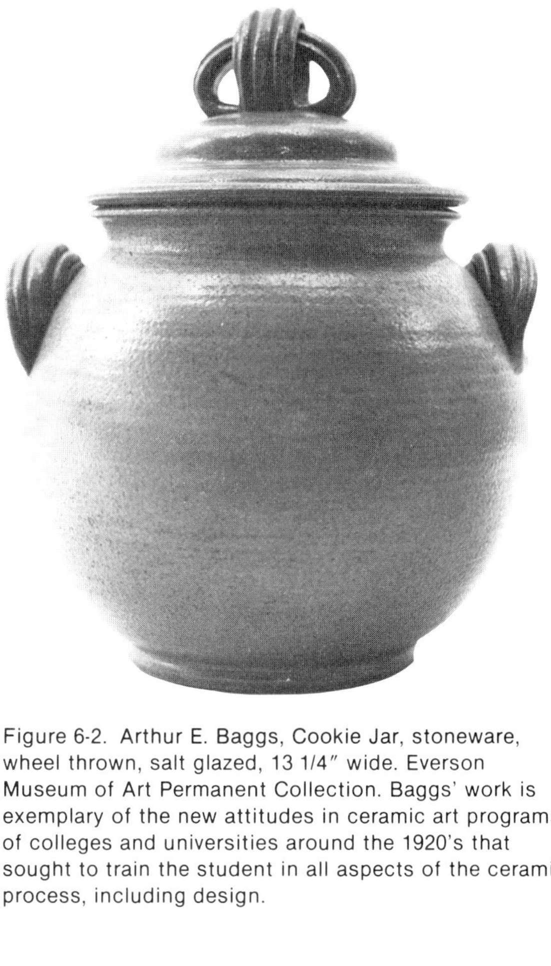

Figure 6-2. Arthur E. Baggs, Cookie Jar, stoneware, wheel thrown, salt glazed, 13 1/4" wide. Everson Museum of Art Permanent Collection. Baggs' work is exemplary of the new attitudes in ceramic art programs of colleges and universities around the 1920's that sought to train the student in all aspects of the ceramic process, including design.

> Artists can be developed in the shops to decorate very cleverly, but a ceramic artist who can conceive, produce, and decorate new wares has not heretofore been trained and only occasionally have our American works found a man who had the technical and artistic ability to create new wares, to appreciate and fill the technical and artistic requirements wanted by the trade.[25]

The above quotation is a clue to the philosophy that Baggs sought to implement in the ceramics program at Ohio State. It was indicative of a conscious concern for developing some balance between the potter's technical and artistic skills.

Arthur Baggs' own pottery reflected this philosophy. The author has examined a collection of his work at Ohio State University. The shapes were usually of a classic simplicity and the craftsmanship involved in throwing, trimming, decorating and glazing was precise and almost flawless (Fig. 6-2). Baggs' technical command of glaze chemistry is seen in the variety of glazes and decorative techniques used on vases and bowls. These included an array of colors and surface effects such as oxblood red, matt and semi-opaque turquoise, purple, lusters and salt glazes. Decorative approaches ranged from brush decorating, both under and over glaze, glaze inlays and sgraffito, to completely undecorated, single-glazed surfaces. Decorative motifs usually consisted of simple lines or circles or a combination of these, and were well integrated to complement the basic shape of the pot.

Carlton F. Atherton, a leading ceramic art historian, has described Baggs' work and given some clues to his virtuosity in the area of glazing. Among the glazes already mentioned, Atherton also described Baggs' mastery over effects such as lusters, crystallines, copper reds, apricot pinks and surfaces flecked with gold.[26] These accomplishments required a thorough understanding of firing and glazing techniques, important considerations not only in Baggs' own work, but in his teaching as well.

The high regard for craftsmanship, inherent in the scientific pursuit of ceramic technology, and reconsiderations of design problems were two reasons that Arthur Baggs and the ceramic art program at Ohio State gained recognition. Its graduates, as well as those from Alfred, perpetuated this philosophy and style in other schools throughout the country. These institutions were instrumental in establishing a new attitude toward pottery during the first forty years of the twentieth century.

Myrtle French

Another important early graduate from Alfred's Ceramic Art and Design program was Myrtle French. She has been acknowledged by other potters as a leader in the field during the 1930's and 1940's. Her Bachelor's degree was awarded in 1913, and she continued to work on her Master's at the same school. Her training at Alfred indicated a concern for all phases of ceramics, with an emphasis on technical knowledge, but also with attention to problems of design and the history of ceramics. Recalling her training at Alfred and the influence of Binns, she said:

> He [Binns] engaged in research himself; and he was an expert potter. His students were encouraged to follow his lead. Much that is everyday information now was not widely understood then (1900). At first, ceramic students followed instructions; a little later they studied museum pieces as a basis for laboratory work and art expression. They undertook to produce the colors, glaze types, decorative techniques, textures, etc., found there. This was not to use the knowledge of their own discretion. Students were disciplined to become intelligent, capable technicians and potters. They were trained to note relations of cause and effect.
>
> As the potters became more and more informed concerning pottery in museums, they began to be interested in raising the quality of industrial products. A secondary result of that effort was that the potter began to consider the functional quality of his own ware. This inaugurated the idea of making pottery for definite uses such as buffet suppers, vases to display flowers of a particular type, serving dishes, lamps, etc.
>
> Another influencing element was the explorations into the use of new raw materials—most of which were not chemically pure—such as Albany slip, Michigan slip, Barnard Earth, Volcanic Ash, Colemanite, impure colorants, crystallizing agents, etc. Along with this came a more thorough study of the effects of temperature changes. Many of these made the body or the glaze darker giving rich browns and grays. They prohibited whites and brilliant colors.[27]

A spirit of adventure, of scientific and historical investigation, as well as an awareness of attempting to develop a form language that did not depend on European precedents, began to become an important part of the growth of American pottery during the early 1900's. This was expressed by Miss French when she alluded to her early years in ceramics and recalled that the flurry of activity in ceramics "began to stimulate some artists in other areas to try their hand at ceramics."[28] Among them, she believes, were Henry Varnum Poor, George Biddle and Alexander Archipenko. The latter two were sculptors and Poor a painter before they were involved with pottery. In regard to their work she said: "Sometimes lacking knowledge of techniques, their ceramic wares were not professional, but their fearless approach encouraged the potters to become more venturesome"[29] (Fig. 6-3).

What effects these ceramic artists had on the attitudes and work of their peers is speculative, but a changing attitude did develop in regard to the purposes of teaching and studying pottery at the college and university level. One such attitude considered the possibilities of seriously studying other forms of art and their historical developments in the hopes of enriching and broadening the possibilities of the ceramic medium. Myrtle French represented this changing emphasis when she recalled that, while teaching at the Chicago Art Institute from 1930 to 1950, the study of art history had noticeable influences on the forms and surface treatments of student work. She further pointed out: "a class in pattern design and one in architectural modelling influenced their work. The students interested in abstract painting often carried their thinking into their ceramic work."[30]

French's attitudes scarcely reflected the teaching of Binns with whom she studied and with whom she taught for twelve years during summer sessions at Alfred University. Her encouraging the students to "think, experiment and direct themselves as far as they were able without missing unfamiliar new techniques and information which would be needed for future growth" was in strong contrast to Binns. The interest which must have prevailed in attempting to arrive at a synthesis of the technical and the artistic in pottery were further expressed when she explained that "a few students even hunted up local clays which they used for body, glaze or both."[31]

The stress on sound, basic skills with which to arrive at artistic form in pottery was,

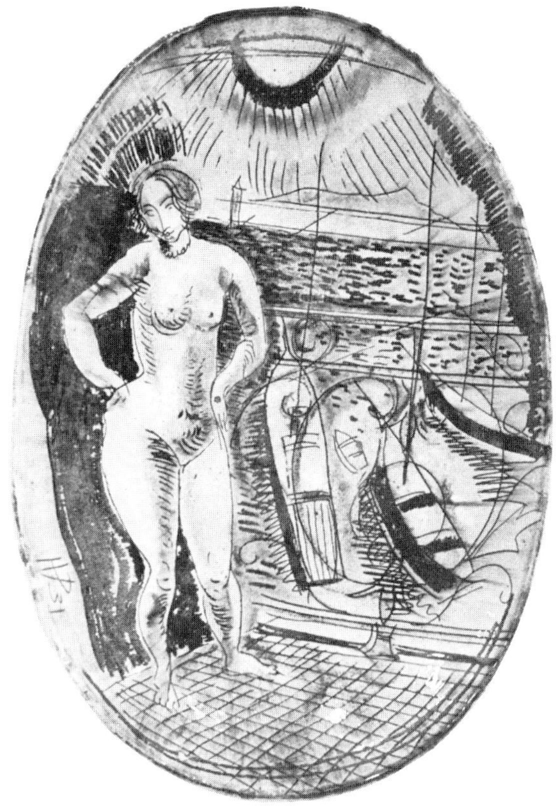

Figure 6-3. Henry Varnum Poor, dish, stoneware, underglazes and transparent cover glaze. Everson Museum of Art Permanent Collection, 1931. Poor was one of a handful of artists who were not trained as potters, but who brought a fresh approach to dealing with form and decoration which was in strong contrast to the more mechanical and precise approach practiced by most other potters at that time.

however, still the most important consideration. Experimentation currently upheld by many as a free search for a novel or different form-concept was always approached, in the first four decades of this century, with a sense of order and genuine purpose. This implied that the basic rudiments of throwing, glaze chemistry, glaze application and firing had to be well understood, if not mastered prior to becoming involved in experimentation.

William G. Whitford

William G. Whitford, also a student of Charles Binns and a graduate of Alfred's Ceramic Art Design Department, first taught pottery at the Midway Studios, the University of Chicago, in 1911. He upheld the typical Alfred philosophy of that time, which was somewhat in contrast to the more liberal position of Myrtle French. The conservative, restrained attitudes emanating at this time from Alfred were expressed by Whitford when he said that "the most important attention was given to the attainment of perfection in FORM. Secondary considerations were applied design, color harmony, perfection and variety in glazes and their application."[32]

Additional information offered by Mr. Whitford supports the belief that calculated control of the elements of design and a clear understanding of the nature of the material were regarded as prerequisites for arriving at sound pottery production. He emphasized this when he pointed out the following:

> The ideal pottery should, above all else, have the excellence of fine FORM. In addition perfection in glazes, both bright and dull or matt, harmony and variety in COLOR. Applied decoration that added interest to a ceramic piece, but all ornamentation should be secondary and not detract from the basic FORM.
>
> Such concepts were always stressed in class and lectures and aided me in establishing a rational philosophy regarding style and technique in ceramic art.[33]

The emphasis on a controlled, disciplined attitude regarding method and design in pottery may have been a result of earlier interests in commercial and industrial ceramics at Alfred. These principles were established by graduates who came from Alfred and assumed teaching positions in different parts of the country up to the 1940's. Although the majority of the graduates before that date remained in the East, some did move to the Midwest and West (Plate 4). For example, in 1920 Harold Nash went to the University of Cincinnati, Marion Heard started teaching pottery at the University of Tennessee in 1931, while Roger Corsaw became involved in ceramics at the University of Oklahoma in 1935 (Fig. 6-4). Hal Riegger graduated in 1938 and went on to teach pottery at the California School of Fine Arts, San Francisco, California. A number of potters attended Alfred's summer school to supplement their training in art. One such example was Winifred Phillips who taught ceramics at the Milwaukee State Teachers College, Milwaukee, Wisconsin. They were among the early leaders in pottery, and in part, were responsible for perpetuating the attitudes and ideas taught at Alfred.

More important, perhaps, was the image that these people created as potters, one quite different from their predecessors'. Although the improvement of commercial ceramics was

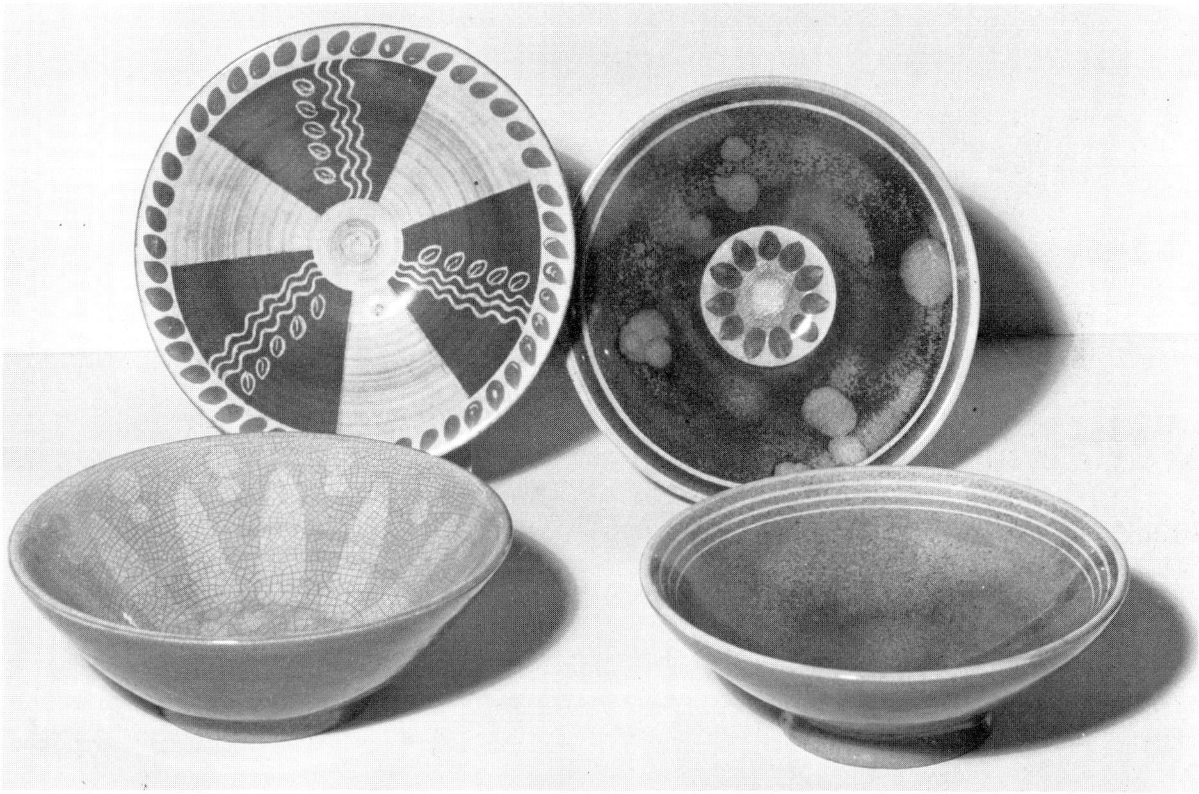

Figure 6-4. Roger Corsaw, Norman, Oklahoma, 4 bowl, earthenware with white engobe using brush and sgraffito decorations, 1937. Everson Museum of Art Permanent Collection. Prize winners in the 6th National Ceramics Exhibition, Everson Museum. This phase of Corsaw's work reflects the typical approaches toward precise throwing and decorating that was so popular during the 1930's and 40's.

of some interest at schools such as Alfred University, Ohio State, the Pennsylvania Museum School of Industrial Art, Pratt Institute and Syracuse, a changing emphasis was also beginning to appear in regard to the problems of studio-pottery (Plate 5).

Glen Lukens

Independent of the developments which gradually migrated from the East toward the Midwest and the West (via Alfred to Ohio State and the Chicago Art Institute, etc.) was the work of Glen Lukens who established himself as one of the earliest leaders of American studio-pottery on the West coast. Obtaining his training at the Oregon State Agricultural College in 1921, his most notable contributions in this country were made as a practicing potter and teacher at the University of Southern California.

While most other educational institutions before 1940 concerned themselves with problems of design and techniques growing out of industrial considerations, Lukens' primary interest centered around nurturing the creative needs and potentials of the individual. He was particularly interested for one to "follow his own tastes in creation, building modern shapes with emphasis on line, form and methods of surface enrichment."[34]

This relatively innovative approach to teaching is closely linked to his own enthusiastic development as an artist-potter. Of special inspiration was his first encounter with examples of ancient Egyptian Paste jewelry that he saw on a trip to Great Britain. Returning to California and realizing that the alkaline deposits of the arid Death Valley desert could be utilized in a similar way as did the Egyptians, Lukens set out to experiment and develop his own type of low-fire, Egyptian Paste ceramic jewelry.

His "discovery" was immediately recognized and acknowledged in exhibitions such as the Golden Gate International Exposition in San Francisco. Further research and experimentations led Lukens to develop for himself a highly varied and rich body of glazes which were especially distinctive for their exotic colors and surfaces. Gaining more insight into the problems of glaze chemistry and clay composition, Lukens continued to seek out the wide range of possibilities by utilizing native minerals found in various parts of the Southwest. Several glazes that he developed through independent research were aptly named to reflect his love for the natural, unpretentious and romantic interludes of the Arizona and New Mexico deserts. Among them were his now famous "Mojave Golden Amber." "Mesa Blue" and "Death Valley Yellow."

In the hands of a less sensitive or unskilled potter these glazes may not have been of any particular consequence. But Lukens combined these luminous, bright glazes with very simplified forms, sometimes glazing only the interior and allowing the exterior of the vessel's raw clay to serve as an effective contrast (Fig. 6-5).

By 1936 when most potters were still laboring under the eclecticism of European and Oriental influences, Lukens had developed a discernable style of his own. This was readily acknowledged when he was awarded the first prize at the prestigeous 1936 Ceramic National Exhibition held at the Everson Museum of Art in Syracuse, New York. This was followed by other honors, most notable of which was hav-

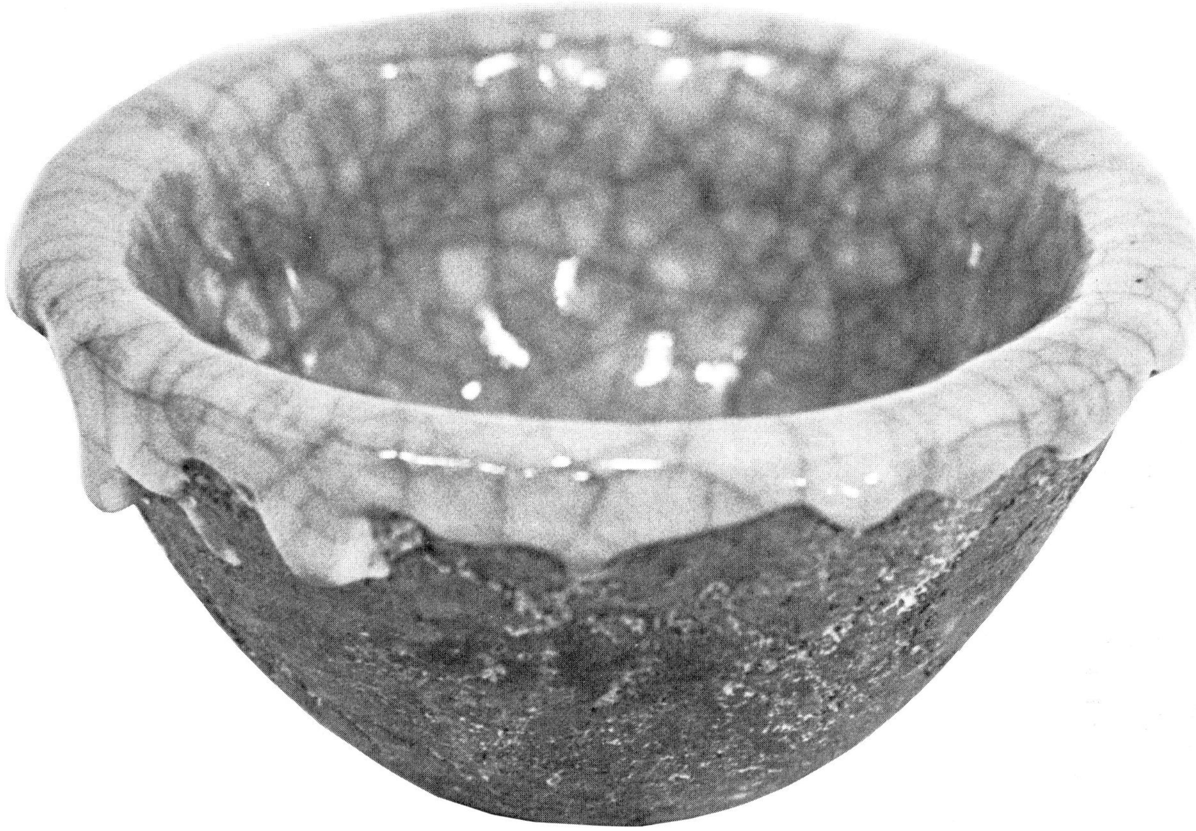

Figure 6-5. Glen Lukens, bowl, earthenware with light blue alkaline glaze. Lukens became one of the earliest, well established studio-potters on the West Coast through his highly individual use of glazes which were often compounded from minerals that he found in the New Mexico or Arizona deserts. Everson Museum of Art Permanent Collection.

ing his pieces represent the United States at the Paris International Exhibit of 1937 and at the all-California Ceramics Exhibition of 1938.

In addition to distinguishing himself as one of the early leaders of American studio-pottery, Lukens also achieved high respectability through his teaching and for sharing his ideas and information through various publications, particularly the *Annual Bulletins of the American Ceramic Society.* Imparting much of his researched information to his colleagues and his constant encouragement of his students, as well as continually pursuing high standards of artistic quality in his own work, gave stature to Lukens as a unique form of the studio-potter. His own work, his teaching, his dissemination of information, and his involvements in other humanitarian projects all served as an exemplary model for others who were contemplating the pursuit of pottery-making as a respectable, dignified human activity.

The apprentice system in pottery was practiced to some degree in America prior and up to the nineteenth century. But the industrial revolution soon eliminated the need for it. This meant that thereafter an aspiring potter had to receive his training in a college or university. Although an industrial orientation was adopted by most American schools that taught pottery, they had, at the same time, fine arts courses to which the students were exposed. It would assume too much to state that this alone may have been the determining factor which resulted in the students' venturing beyond industrial considerations. But it can be surmised, that the exposure to fine arts and the involvement in the problem solving of painting, design and sculpture, resulted in a design-concept that went beyond the limitations and requirements of dealing with the precision of creating work for mass production. Potters were still urged to exercise traditional judgments as regarded craftsmanship and design, but at the same time, an individual approach to pottery was established. This indicates that, as a result of a thorough understanding of all facets of the craft, one is better able to consider the problems of giving form to more personal ideas.

However, the abilities to accomplish this end were only one aspect of the studio-potter's development. Equally important were the means of obtaining recognition for his work. This meant exhibiting pottery in galleries and museums. That contemporary pottery would be shown in galleries and museums of fine art became significant in two ways: First, it brought the potter's work to the attention of the public on an international, national, regional and local level, and secondly, it aided in giving the potter added stature as an artist.

Notes

1. Nelson J. Norwood, *50 Years of Ceramic Education,* p. 5.
2. Dorothy W. Perkins, "Education in Ceramic Art in the United States," Unpublished doctoral dissertation, The Ohio State University, 1956, p. 87.
3. Norwood, p. 11.
4. Charles F. Binns, "Education in Clay," *The Craftsman,* 55:162 (June, 1903).
5. Ibid., p. 163.
6. Charles F. Binns, "The Progress of Ceramic Art," *Transactions of the American Ceramic Society,* 5:24 (1902).
7. Charles F. Binns, *The Potter's Craft,* p. 15.
8. Ibid., p. 4.
9. Ibid., p. 107.
10. Interview with Maija Grotell, Cranbrook Academy of Arts and Science, Bloomfield Hills, Mich., August 12, 1964.

11. Charles F. Binns, "Clay in the Potter's Hand," *The Craftsman,* 4:162-166 (May, 1904).
12. Charles F. Binns, "Craft of the Potter," *The Craftsman,* 9:856 (March, 1906).
13. C. Louise Avery, *A Memorial Exhibition of the Work of Charles F. Binns,* Bulletin of the Metropolitan Museum of Art no. 30, p. 108.
14. J. F. McMahon, *Charles F. Binns,* Bulletin of the American Ceramic Society no. 27, p. 176.
15. Charles F. Binns, "Clay in the Potter's Hand," *The Craftsman,* 6:164 (May, 1904).
16. "Exhibition of Contemporary Ceramics," Introduction by Charles F. Binns, *Exhibition Catalog,* W. & J. Sloane, New York (undated), although Maija Grotell, one of the exhibitors, date the show as having been in 1925.
17. Norwood, pp. 50-58.
18. Gertrude Emerson,"Marblehead Pottery," *The Craftsman,* 21:671-673 (March, 1916).
19. Carlton Atherton, "Arthur E. Baggs, Distinguished American Ceramist," *Design Magazine,* 19:10-11 (March, 1947).
20. Emerson, p. 672.
21. Interview with Paul Bogotay, Professor of Ceramic Art, The Ohio State University.
22. Atherton, p. 10.
23. Dr. Herbert Sanders, Professor of Art, San Jose State College, unpublished correspondence.
24. Victor Schreckengost, Cleveland, O., unpublished correspondence.
25. Arthur E. Baggs, *A Dream Come True,* Bulletin of the American Ceramic Society no. 6, pp. 286-287.
26. Atherton, p. 11.
27. Miss Myrtle French, Professor of Ceramic Art, Alfred University, unpublished correspondence.
28. French, correspondence to author.
29. French, correspondence to author.
30. French, correspondence to author.
31. French, correspondence to author.
32. Dr. William G. Whitford, Professor of Ceramic Art, retired, Midway Studios, the University of Chicago, unpublished correspondence to author.
33. Whitford, correspondence to author. (Capitalization by Whitford).
34. Susan Peterson, "Glen Lukens 1887-1967" *Crafts Horizons,* XXVIII:2 (March-April 1968), p. 23-25.

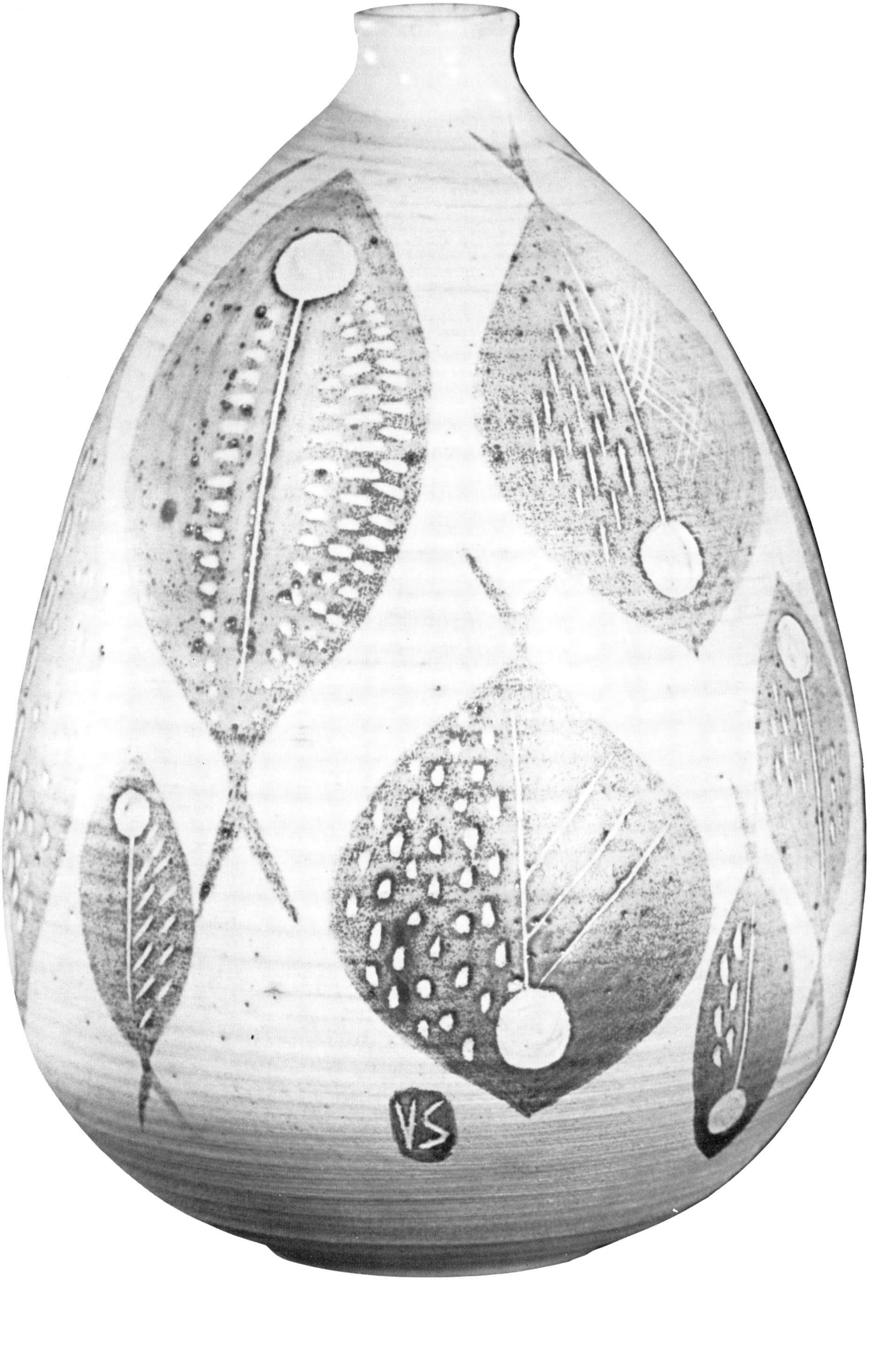

Victor Schreckengost

Exhibitions 7

The Robineau Memorial Ceramics Exhibitions

One of the forces that influenced the course of American studio-pottery was the wide exposure of ceramics through exhibitions. There had been a multitude of ceramics exhibitions dating back to the beginning of the organized china decorating movement. All of them probably provided some impetus to the studio-pottery movement. The effects of these exhibitions were three-fold. First, they brought about an awareness of the work done by craftsmen; secondly, they represented opportunities for the public to view original works by contemporary American potters; and lastly, the exhibits gave gallery status to the crafts of the time and by association placed them in contention with painting and sculpture. The latter may have played an important role in the lives of many potters. The recognition rendered by having had a piece of pottery shown in a museum of fine art must have seemed a notable achievement.

One of the earliest exhibitions that has been responsible for promoting the art of the potter in America was the Robineau Memorial Exhibition which was later re-named the Ceramic National Exhibition. Since its inception in 1932 these annual National Exhibitions have brought to the public throughout the United States the best efforts of the American studio-potter. A detailed history of its development will indicate the importance and the prestige of this, the largest, ceramic competition in the country.

Anna W. Olmsted, former director of the Syracuse Museum of Fine Art, initiated the first exhibition in honor of Adelaide Robineau in 1932. For this exhibition only potters from New York state were invited, but the response was so enthusiastic that it was decided to make the annual competition a national event. Therefore, in 1933 it was made an open show at which 199 pieces were exhibited by 73 artists.[1] The following years witnessed a dramatic increase in the number of potters whose work was exhibited at this event.[2] These shows became important to potters for several reasons.

A certain element of prestige may have been engendered by the fact that the initial exhibitions were sponsored under the auspices of the Syracuse Museum of Fine Art. That it was endorsed and promoted by the College Art Association probably added a touch of professionalism and importance, and since the jury was usually composed of renowned people connected with ceramic art, the exhibitions gained a competitive stature. In addition, the American Ceramic Society's recognition of these exhibitions as its official exhibition enhanced this event's importance. The American Ceramic Society outlined the following objectives for the National Ceramic Exhibitions. They are quoted in full.

> 1. To improve the ceramic art of America. Thru competitions we can stimulate our artists to do better work—with higher standards each year—and quality of work steadily improving (this had already proven to be the case in the history of our four exhibitions).
>
> 2. To educate the American public to take an intelligent interest in ceramic art and to realize that ceramics is a major art. It is a matter of history that Greek vases and Chinese porcelains ranked as major works of art, even as the Della Robbias and Joshia Wedgewoods were in the front rank as great artists in their times.

> 3. To make sales, secure commissions and positions for ceramic artists, and increase their income as well as their status as ceramic artists—all a part of educating the community to take an interest in the ceramic art of their contemporaries (as against "antiques") so that the good things produced will find a ready sale.[3]

Information received from several potters through interviews and questionnaires have indicated that, in some measure, the Ceramic Nationals have contributed to stimulating a more active interest in exhibiting the work of studio-potters. It has been pointed out that in an indirect manner the exhibitions have also helped to educate the American public in matters of studio-pottery. To be sure, sales have been made from the exhibitions. It is also reasonable to assume that a good record of having been included in this annual event may have been of some influence in procuring a teaching position at the college level.

The advancement by American studio-potters was dramatically acknowledged in 1937 when this country was requested to send the outstanding work of ceramic artists to Scandinavia. An exhibition was assembled by the Syracuse Museum of Fine Art. The work constituted a select group chosen from the previous Fifth National Ceramic Exhibition and included 183 pieces by 91 artists.

To have been invited by a foreign nation to exhibit the work of living American studio-potters was, of course, regarded as an honor. It served to bolster the prestige of American potters and the confidence of those who believed in their aspirations to develop a meaningful form of personal expression through pottery. Anna W. Olmsted reflected the pride that must have prevailed at the news of having been requested to send the best examples of American studio-pottery. In this regard she said:

> As Mr. Richard F. Bach has expressed it (regarding both to the Fifth National and to the special exhibition of American ceramics assembled by the Syracuse Museum upon official invitation from the Scandinavian countries): 'The Fifth National Ceramic Exhibition demonstrates consistent advance in artistic merit and ceramic skill and reveals a satisfying standard of quality as to form, color and understanding of material representative of American ability and comparable with modern work in Europe. That four cities abroad should invite an exhibition of work by American potters and that outstanding American Museums should gladly cooperate by lending exceptional pieces of modern American potters; and that several well-known museums in the east and in California should welcome an opportunity to display a collection of recent American pottery and sculpture—these are all endorsements that mature skill, patient training and thorough knowledge have brought to this important type of art in our country.'[4]

The high esteem with which this invitation was regarded was expressed in several magazines that carried the story of American studio-pottery to Europe. Ceramic sculpture was singled out, at times, as having been important in the exhibition, but this in no way detracted from the significance of the pottery. Excerpts from the following article are typical of the plaudits directed at American potters for their efforts to compete with the dominance of European pottery.[5]

> It was an invitational affair, with additional bids to show at the Kunstindustrie Museum of Copenhagen, the Roshska Museum at Gothenburg, the Swedish National Museum in Stockholm, and the Helsingfors Konsthall. Everywhere favorable comments indicated that European potteries, famous for centuries, tended to welcome to their ranks America's talented artisans in pottery and porcelain enamels.[6]

Anyone familiar with the field of pottery will easily recognize the names of the established artists that were included in this event.

They are names that have appeared with regularity in other ceramic competitions such as the "Fiber-Clay-Metal Show" at the St. Paul Gallery of Art, the "Young Americans" of the American Craftsmen Council, the "Miami National Ceramics Exhibition" of Coral Gables and many other shows which were of regional and local scope. A list of the names that comprised the representative body of prominent studio-potters as they appeared in various exhibitions is given in Appendix E. There were other ceramists, to be sure, but the above list represented consistent exhibitors and prize winners in the Ceramic National Shows until 1941. Some of these potters and their works have been discussed in previous chapters. Others will be dealt with in subsequent sections. It should then be possible to better see, through photographic examples included in the text, what the general attitudes were regarding style during the period from approximately 1930 to 1940.

It has been mentioned that one of the aims of the Ceramic Nationals was to attempt to educate the American public "to take an intelligent interest in ceramic art and to realize that ceramics is a major art."[7] One of the means for accomplishing this ambition was the national traveling exhibitions. These shows consisted of selected examples from each Ceramic National Exhibition.

The importance of the Ceramic National and its shows for the national circuits were readily acknowledged. William M. Milliken, director of the Cleveland Museum of Art appraised it in the following manner:

> The [Everson] Museum's sponsorship of ceramics as a Fine Art and its annual Ceramic Exhibition have given the American potter and ceramic sculptors an exhibition national in its scope. It has won for them in the exhibitions and in circulating exhibitions selected from these annual showings an ever increasing public.[8]

Over a period of six years many major museums and several universities throughout the United States displayed the best work of studio-potters through the traveling shows. A list of museums and galleries that exhibited these shows appears in Appendix F. It serves as an indication of the scope of the circuits. The list of museums and galleries which displayed the shows is evidence that a wider interest in ceramics as a fine art was developing. It is significant that a number of important museums, which in the past had gained their reputation mainly through collections of painting and sculpture, also accepted pottery as being worthy of receiving display space. This is especially interesting because prior to 1930 major exhibits of pottery in museums were usually works of past cultures and foreign countries, except for the posthumous exhibitions of such prominent potters as Robineau or Binns. The idea of exhibiting examples of the work of contemporary potters, therefore, became an important impetus in stimulating the studio-potter to arrive at unique designs.

A number of museums and galleries also started to accommodate pottery exhibitions of a type other than those which originated at the Syracuse Museum. Some of these shows were initiated by crafts organizations, ceramics departments of art schools or by one or two persons involved in pottery themselves. A representative sampling of such museums and the exhibitions they held is found in Appendix G. The list was compiled from the calendars of events published in various art journals between 1945 and 1955.

Equally important is the fact that, in addition to the museums already mentioned which accommodated ceramics exhibitions of various types, an increasing number of galleries and museums also started to originate other kinds of ceramics shows. Some exhibitions were invitational only, others were open to all professional potters as well as students; some were local, while others were designed to operate on a regional or national level.

Local and Regional Ceramics Exhibitions

One of the longest traditions in exhibiting crafts was established with the Toledo Area Artists Association. These artist-craftsmen exhibited their work annually at the Toledo Museum. Since the late 1940's and through the active work of Harvey Littleton who taught at the Toledo Museum School, this group's annual show has become an important event for potters in the vicinity of Toledo, Ohio. In similar manner, the Layton Art Gallery of Milwaukee, Wisconsin has accommodated a yearly competitive show of Wisconsin craftsmen dating back to 1920. In recent years the Wisconsin Designer Craftsmen Exhibition has become one of the largest state crafts shows in the midwest and has been shown at the Milwaukee Art Center. In 1933, the Albright Art Gallery of Buffalo, New York, started to show the yearly competition of "Western New York State Crafts Exhibitions."

After 1940, new exhibitions appeared in increasing numbers. In 1941, the Isaac Delgado Museum of Art, New Orleans, Louisiana, sponsored the first annual "Autumn Exhibition of Crafts." That same year the "Pacific Coast Ceramic Sculpture and Pottery Annual" was started at the Oregon Ceramics Gallery, Portland, Oregon, while in 1945 the distinguished Corcoran Gallery of Art, Washington, D.C., began its "1st Annual Area Exhibition" which included pottery. Ceramics also became an important part of the Butler Art Institute when it initiated the "First All-Ohio Ceramics Biennal" in 1945.

In 1947, the J.P. Speed Art Museum of Louisville, Kentucky inaugurated an annual "Art Center Association Show" that consisted mainly of pottery and other crafts. The M.H. deYoung Memorial Museum of San Francisco became one of the active centers for displaying crafts on the west coast when it held its first annual exhibition of pottery by Bay area artists in 1947, while the Silvermine Guild of Artists Gallery of Norwalk, Connecticut, in 1949, instituted a yearly competitive show of ceramics.

The Whitte Memorial Museum of San Antonio, Texas, was still another example. In 1951, it sponsored the "First Texas State Crafts Exhibition," and at the same time, the Baltimore Museum instituted its first annual "Maryland Crafts Exhibition." That same year the George Vincent Smith Art Center displayed its interest in the crafts when it held the first of several "Massachusetts Crafts of Today" exhibitions.

One year later the South Bend Art Association of South Bend, Indiana, commenced a regularly scheduled "Regional Ceramics Exhibition," and two years after that the University of Kansas started holding a yearly "Kansas Designer Craftsmen Show."

These examples do not include all of the new pottery exhibitions that were introduced from the late 30's to the early 50's. Certainly there were more shows, some of which were not held annually. But from the list one can ascertain the increased interest that was shown by galleries and museums of art in initiating crafts exhibitions. It remained for some of the national competitions to provide added stimulus, for in them one found keener competition because of a larger number of entries, and also because of increased sums of prize money offered. More prestige, due to the publicity rendered through national magazines, may also have been an attraction with the larger, national shows. The National Decorative Arts-Ceramics Exhibition of Wichita, Kansas that began in 1945 and the Miami National Ceramics Exhibition of Coral Gables, Florida, originating in 1952, were among the auspicious competitions in the nation.

The annual national events sponsored by the American Craftsmen's Council were important. In 1949 it held the first "Young Americans Exhibition" of crafts by American artists who were under thirty years of age. This exhibition was first held at America House in New York City and thereafter at the Museum of Contemporary Crafts. Four years later the Council instituted the "1st National Designer Craftsmen's Competition." These shows were supplemented by others such as those sponsored by the Smithsonian Institute, which held its "1st Annual International Exhibition of Ceramic Art" in 1953, and by the St. Paul Gallery of Art, St. Paul, Minnesota, whose annual "Fiber-Clay-Metal" exhibition has become an important event to potters since it started in 1951.

Some universities started holding national shows, although most of these were invitational. Several recent exhibitions such as the "American Craftsmen's Show" of 1955 at the University of Illinois, and the "American Artists in Silver, Jewelry and Clay" exhibition of that same year at the University of Iowa represent a proliferation of exhibits begun in the 1940's.[9] In recent years several other schools have instigated similar shows.

In addition to familiarizing the public with studio-pottery through exhibitions of the type sponsored by museums and galleries, there were other values gained. These shows were of particular importance to potters not only because of the prestige connected with them if one's work was accepted for exhibitions, but also because potters, teachers and students were actually able to see some changes of emphasis in design and techniques as they were taking place over the years. The exhibits were, in fact, one of the primary means with which people could determine just what was being done in pottery in various parts of the country.

Richard F. Bach, director of the Metropolitan Museum of Art, used the work of an international show, in which American pottery was also included, for determining the quality of design in contemporary ceramics. He praised the improvement of American pottery and credited the Syracuse Museum of Fine Art for its series of National Exhibitions of Ceramic Art, "for these have served, both as to place and procedure, to discover and discern design-quality and to aid it toward enhancement."[10] He further pointed out:

> At Syracuse and in these exhibitions ceramic artists and craftsmen have found not only a place for meeting, perhaps of contest, for their talents, but also a fair judgment, under favorable auspices, of concentration and a gauge of quality. Let us say this gauge is a barometer of design, and indicator of the character of today, but not only for today; rather a promise for tomorrow. For what is today's standard but a prediction?[11]

Henry Varnum Poor also used a national show as an index to the activities of American studio-potters. In regard to an exhibition held at the Corcoran Gallery of Art he pointed out:

> You must conclude that the medium [clay] really suits the temperament of American artists and craftsmen, for it is not just competence, you see here, but free, lively and genuinely personal expression thru the fluid art of shaping, glazing, decorating and firing of clay.[12]

Although several art periodicals aided in bringing about a better awareness of the studio-potter's activities and his products, it was in the exhibitions that one could see the results achieved by potters. This may have had educative benefits even to the potters themselves. For some of them an exhibition could have revealed a new technique, while to others the shows may have suggested new directions for developing their personal form-concepts.

The Role of Museum Schools

In connection with the museums' sponsorship and initiation of ceramics exhibitions, there was yet another consideration that aided significantly in the growth of studio-pottery. Some museums began to accommodate pottery in their regularly scheduled classes. This was unusual, because traditionally only drawing, painting and sculpture were regarded as essential subject matter in their curriculums. However, during the late 1940's and early 1950's more museums started to include ceramics classes as an integral part of their educational programs. Typical examples were the Toledo Museum School of Art where Harvey Littleton and Norman Schulman taught, the Brooklyn Museum Art School where Hui Ka Kwong was teaching after coming to the United States in 1948 and the Chouinard Art Institute of Los Angeles, California, which employed Vivika and Otto Heino during the mid-1950's.

Other noted museums that started an active pottery program were the Dayton Art Institute and the Fort Wayne Art Museum. Students could also study pottery at the St. Paul Gallery of Art, St. Paul, Minnesota. Alexius and Warren McKenzie started teaching there when the ceramics program was organized in 1948. Since then it has become a popular center for ceramics in that area of the country. The Los Angeles County Art Institute where Peter Voulkos taught for several years, starting in 1954, was still another example of the new interest shown by museums to include pottery in their art programs. The Chicago Art Institute, the Portland Museum School and the Cordova Museum of Lincoln, Massachusetts, are further examples.

A more exhaustive list is not needed to illustrate the important role that several major museums and art galleries played in holding various kinds of exhibitions, initiating competitive events and instituting classes in pottery. It is apparent that they provided significant opportunities for potters to obtain not only needed recognition, but also facilities for training. Thus, the museums and galleries were an important part in the development of American studio-potters. They were a source of inspiration for artists who worked to give form to a medium of self-expression which, for so long, had been relegated a position of relatively minor importance in the fine arts.

Perhaps one of the more notable museums that has carried on all of these activities for quite some time was the Cleveland Art Institute. A detailed treatment of its history will point out how the role of the museum changed in relation to the studio-potter and the effects it had on him.

The Cleveland Art Institute

The Cleveland Art Institute has been regarded as one of the major museums and art schools in America. It assumed a position of prominence in ceramics for providing a place where potters could be trained and as a center of stimulation and interest through the initiation of several important exhibitions.

In 1919, the First Annual Exhibition of work by Cleveland artists was held at the Cleveland Art Institute. At that time pottery was not included. At first this annual exhibition gained recognition essentially through the popularity and interest in painting and sculpture. However, with an increase of activities in ceramics in the vicinity of Cleveland, ceramic art became a part of the annual art exhibitions of the Cleveland Art Institute starting in 1925.

William M. Milliken, former Curator of Decorative Arts and Director of the Cleveland Art Institute, credited the close association of three organizations with the successful promotion of the art of the potter in the Cleveland area. These were the Cleveland Art Institute, the Cleveland School of Art, and the Cowan Pottery. The latter, although a commercial organization, was also concerned with the production of a non-commercial sideline in which the skills and talents of leading ceramists from the Cleveland area were utilized. For example, Paul Bogotay, Arthur Baggs and Harold Nash all worked for the Cowan Pottery before they assumed their positions on the art staff at The Ohio State University and the Cleveland Art Institute. Their work at the Cowan company usually involved either designing or making art-pottery.[13]

At first only ceramic sculpture was admitted for consideration in the annual Cleveland show. To illustrate how active the artists of this area were in ceramic sculpture, one need only count the entries in this classification which were included in the Ceramic National Exhibitions from 1934 to 1940. The largest number of entries in ceramic sculpture at these shows can repeatedly be traced to artists who were either residing in Cleveland at that time, or whose origin and training could be traced directly to Cleveland. Among these were Russell B. Aitken, Paul Bogotay, Stella Chester Jeske, Chester Nicodemos, Victor Schreckengost, Thelma Winter, Yetta Rosenberg, Harold W. Hunsicker, Edris Eckhardt, Virginia Crawford and Leah M. Lichtig. For example, nine artists from the Cleveland area were included in the Fifth National Ceramic Exhibition. They were also included in the show that toured the Scandinavian countries the following year. In the same show Alfred and The Ohio State University were represented by seven and five artists, respectively.[14] From this comparison it may be seen that Cleveland represented an active area in producing ceramic art during the 1930's.

Although several of the earlier artists represented in the Annual Cleveland Show were primarily ceramic sculptors, most of them have been more prominently identified in later years with studio-pottery. Most notable of these were Victor Schreckengost, Paul Bogotay, A.R. Dyer, R. Guy Cowan and Alice Ayars. Through their work Cleveland, Ohio became an active center for studio-pottery.

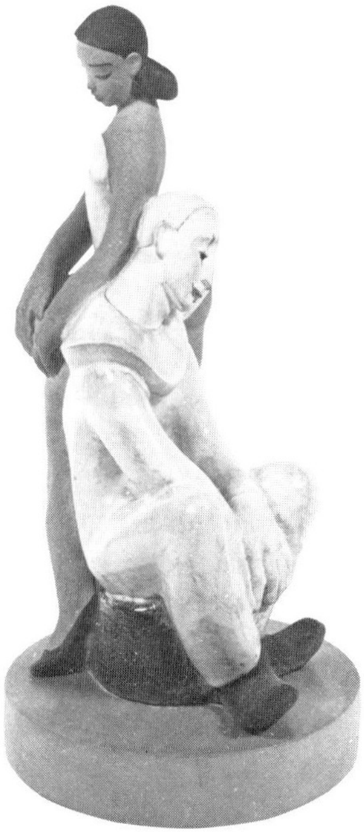

Figure 7-1. Edris Eckhardt, "Intermission," Terra Cotta, engobe and majolica glaze, ca. 1947. Everson Museum of Art Permanent Collection.

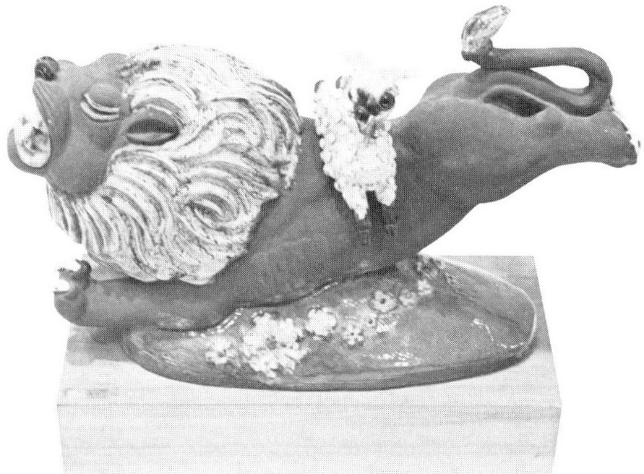

Figure 7-2. Victor Schreckengost, Sculpture, Terra Cotta clay, partially glazed, Everson Museum of Art Permanent Collection.

Additional interest in the development of studio-pottery in that area resulted from the work of Arthur E. Baggs before he assumed his position at The Ohio State University. For three years he worked as a potter in the vicinity of Cleveland. William Milliken appraised Baggs' importance in the following manner:

> Arthur E. Baggs is a past master in the use of glazes, and his experiments in that field and the work he did with R. Guy Cowan in the Cowan Pottery or with Mr. Cowan and Mrs. A.R. Dyer in the Cleveland School of Art laid a technical foundation of fundamental importance for Cleveland ceramics.[15]

The Cleveland area appears to have had an abundance of resources in the crafts. Supplementing the active interest in ceramics were craftsmen involved in enameling, such as Russel Barnett Aitken, Whitney Atchley, Kenneth F. Bates and H. Edward Winter. Each had a vital part in the growth of crafts in that area.

Cleveland was also the center of much activity in ceramics under the guidance of Edris Eckhardt who supervised the Cleveland branch of the WPA/FAP program.[16] Although no significant artistic innovations grew out of those efforts in the area of pottery, two noteworthy contributions did develop. Largely through her efforts from 1933 through 1940, more recognition was brought to the area of ceramic sculpture. Most work up to that time involved the creation of small-scale, figurative sculptures which was characterized by quaint and nostalgic overtones (Fig. 7-1). But once the potential of ceramic sculpture for its use on a larger, architectural scale was understood, a distinctive regionalist form began to emerge from the Cleveland area. Ceramic relief murals for various housing projects such as the Woodhill Homes and the Cleveland Public

Library featured stylized human figure and animal motifs, incorporated into narrative settings. Work by Louis Regalbuto, John Tenkas and Victor Schreckengost, among many, became recognized for their artistic efforts (Fig. 7-2).

In considering the talent concentrated in Cleveland it is important to realize that their success could not have come about without the conscientious institutions mentioned earlier and the roles they played in promoting the crafts, especially studio-pottery. The Cowan Pottery Company was particularly active in that regard. In addition to having hired local artists, the firm donated funds for awards at exhibitions. Alice A. Ayers, as Art Supervisor of the Cleveland Public Schools, may also have helped in bringing about an awareness of studio-pottery by stressing the importance of pottery in the classroom art activities. Moreover, the Cleveland Art Institute rendered substantial assistance when it undertook to sponsor annual ceramics exhibitions. It was this institution which has been especially distinguished in its efforts to support the work of Ohio's and especially of Cleveland's ceramic artists. Mr. Milliken supported this when he pointed out:

> All the prestige of the Cleveland Museum of Art was thrown behind the ceramic artist so as to encourage the creative; all the prestige of the Museum was impressed [sic] into service to encourage the patron.[17]

Through its enthusiastic support for ceramics the Cleveland Art Institute has established itself as one of the outstanding centers for the study and exhibition of pottery. As such, it has attracted some of the nation's leading ceramic artists who were, at times,

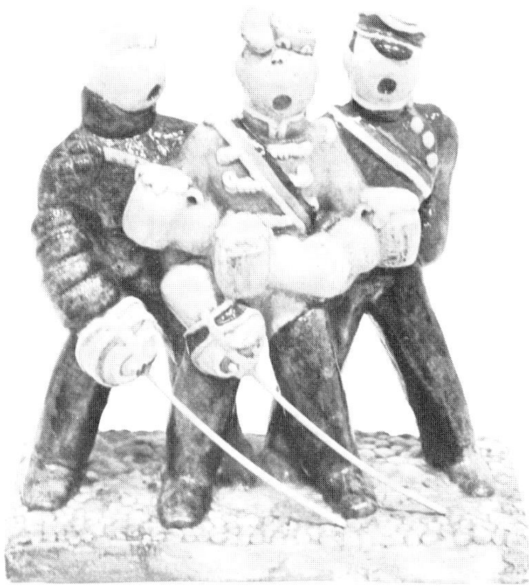

Figure 7-3. Russell Barnett Aitken, "Student Singers," earthenware, handbuilt, low fire glazes, from the "3rd National Exhibition of Ceramics, Everson Museum; Everson Museum of Art Permanent Collection.

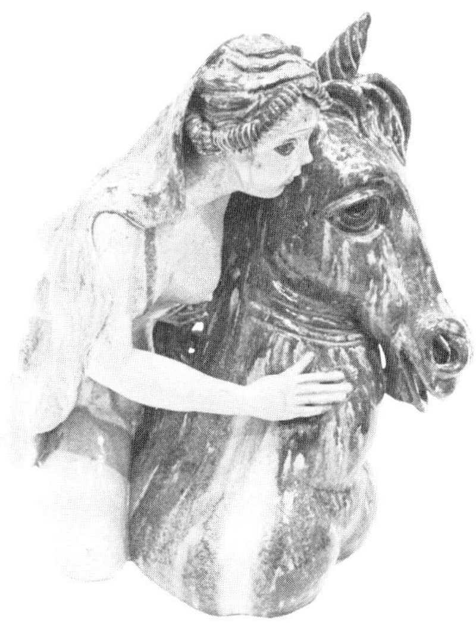

Figure 7-4. Vally Wiesenthaler, "Taming the Unicorn," stoneware, handbuilt, multicolored glazes, approx. 24″ × 28″; ca. 1941; from the "10th Ceramic National Exhibition," Everson Museum. Courtesy, the Everson Museum of Art Permanent Collection.

either students or teachers at that institution. Over a period of thirty years this has included, in addition to those already mentioned, such people as John Billmeyer, Charles Mosgo, Claude Conover, Mishka Petersham, Charles Lakofsky, Jane Parshall and Toshiko Takeazu. Some of them have been identified as leaders in studio-pottery while teaching at the Art Institute.

The Cleveland Art Institute is offered as a typical example of how a well-known museum has been instrumental in furthering the art of the American studio-potter. The director of the Cleveland Art Institute realized the museum's potential with insight when he observed that,

> All of those in America who are interested in preserving individualism and desire—and there is a greater individualism and desire for it than appears to the superficial observer—will be deeply concerned with the furtherance and development of similar efforts to gain national and international recognition for the creative efforts of the American ceramic worker.[18]

Beyond the financial awards and publicity afforded to the potter, there was another benefit which grew out of these ceramics exhibitions. Since many studio-potters have taught in a college or university art department it has been necessary for them to supply lists of exhibitions in which their work was accepted and awards received. Most potters would be interested in exhibiting their work merely as a matter of self-motivation and as part of their total involvement in ceramics. The fact cannot be dismissed lightly, however, that prestige gained from having been accepted in these competitive events may have prompted potters to participate more actively in exhibiting their work.

Little doubt remains that American museums started to participate more actively after 1940 in exposing the public to the latest efforts of potters. This was accomplished not only through the typical one-man or group shows, but especially through competitive exhibitions. Regardless of whether one accepts the system by which these shows were judged, they gave the studio-potter a certain amount of prestige and public acknowledgment, resulting from wide publicity given the exhibits through reviews in periodicals and other publications.

The leader in the area of pottery exhibitions was the annual Ceramic National at Syracuse at which large sums of money have been awarded to the most meritorious work of potters. Since 1945, interest in exhibitions has noticeably increased. Today numerous competitive and non-competitive exhibitions are sponsored at the state, regional and national levels.

Notes

1. Anna W. Olmsted, Foreword to the catalog of the *Second Annual Robineau Memorial Exhibition*, Syracuse Museum of Art, 1933, p. 1.
2. By 1937 the number had risen to 340. The exhibitions were discontinued during World War II and resumed in 1947. That year 247 entries were accepted for exhibition. Five hundred and nine were shown in 1949, 500 in 1951 and 428 in 1961. Figures were compiled from the catalogs of the respective exhibitions.
3. R. Guy Cowan, catalog of the *Fourth National Robineau Memorial Ceramic Exhibition*, Syracuse Museum of Fine Art, 1935, facing last page.
4. Anna W. Olmsted, exhibition catalog of the *Fifth National Ceramics Exhibition*, Syracuse Museum of Fine Art, 1936-37, p. 2.
5. Potters previous to 1936 had exhibited their work and also won awards. Particularly noteworthy were such people as Louise McLaughlin, Adelaide Robineau, Artus Van Briggle and others. Their work was frequently shown at

national and international expositions. But in comparison the late 1930's and 1940's, these events were relatively few. In comparison to the Europeans', America's representation in these events were usually small in number. Hence when a collective body of work was asked to be shown in Europe it was felt that American potters had established themselves as important artists.

6. John Lerch, "Yankee Pottery Goes Abroad," *Country Life*, 73:108-112 (December, 1937).
7. R. Guy Cowan, facing last page.
8. Exhibition catalog of the *Seventh National Ceramics Exhibition*, Syracuse Museum of Fine Art, 1938-1939, p. 2.
9. The list of exhibitions discussed have been compiled from *Art News, American Artist, Crafts Horizon, Design, Ceramics Monthly* and the *Art Index* from 1930 through 1960.
10. Richard F. Bach, "Foreword," catalog of the *Contemporary Ceramics of the Western Hemisphere Exhibition*, Corcoran Gallery of Art, March 4, 1942, p. 7.
11. Bach, p. 11.
12. Henry Varnum Poor, "Commentary," catalog of *Contemporary Ceramics of the Western Hemisphere Exhibition*, Corcoran Gallery of Art, 1942, p. 18.
13. The term "art-pottery" was frequently used to refer to pottery which was not mass-produced or which was made essentially for decorative purposes. This meant that commercial potteries such as the Cowan firm often developed a type of pottery that was entirely hand-made by one or two potters.
14. Exhibition catalog, *The Fifth National Ceramic Exhibition*, Everson Museum of Art, Syracuse, New York, 1936-1937.
15. William M. Milliken, "Ohio Ceramics," *Design*, 38:17-18 (November, 1936).
16. Karl Ann Marling, "New Deal Ceramics: The Cleveland Workshop," *Ceramics Monthly*, 25:6 (June, 1977) p. 25.
17. Milliken, p. 17.
18. Ibid., p. 41.

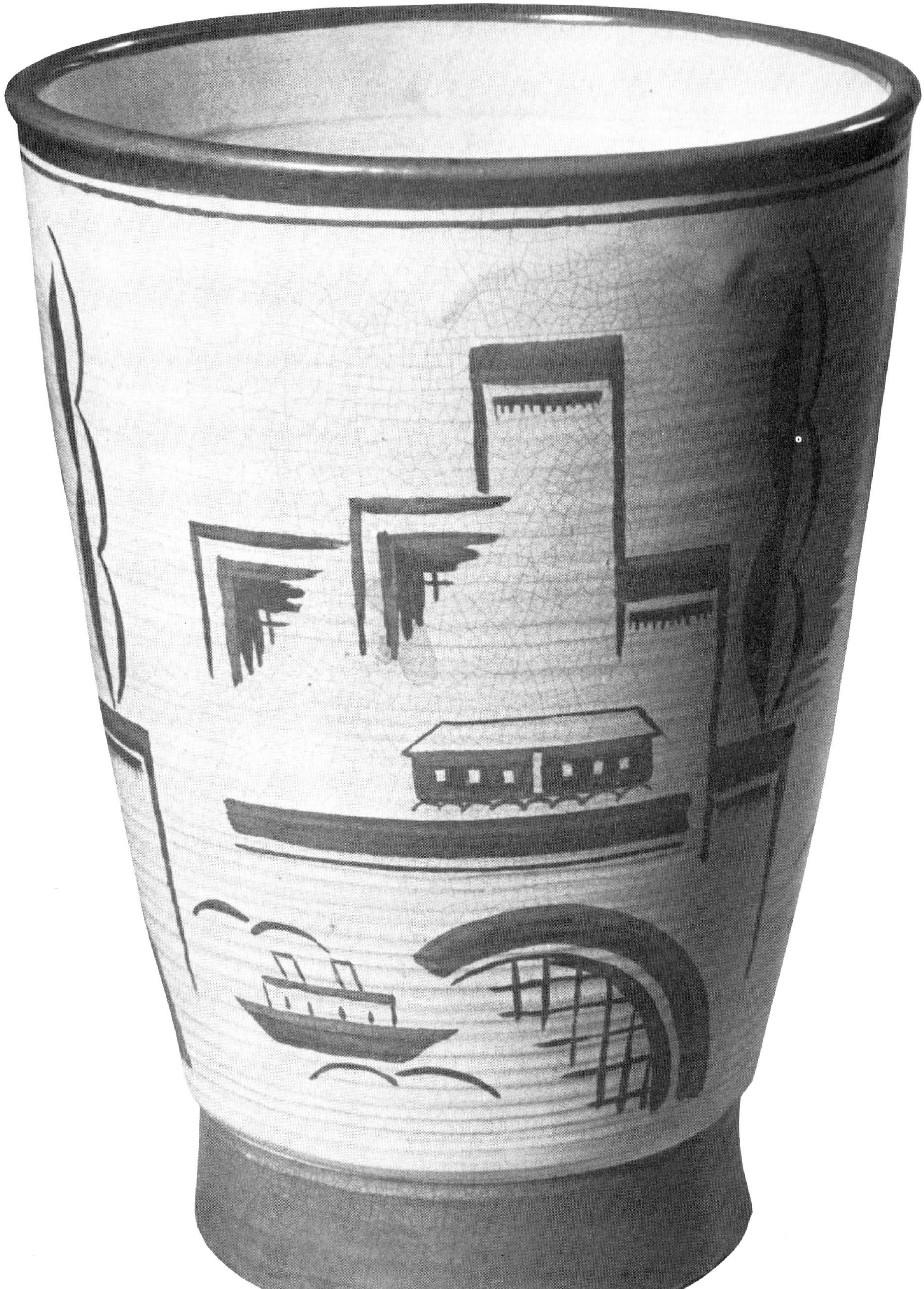

Maija Grotell

Foreign Influences on American Ceramics Prior to 1945 8

Several potters came to America from Europe. Many of them assumed teaching positions in art departments of colleges and universities. In their capacities as teachers some of these potters had noticeable influences on changing attitudes and philosophies regarding pottery. In some instances this occurred directly through students who studied with them and who, in turn, assumed teaching positions in other colleges and universities. Others had a less direct influence, but are included in this study because their presence in American ceramics has been felt through their work.

Maija Grotell

An important teacher who came from Europe to teach ceramics in the United States was Maija Grotell. She received her training under Professor Fitch, an Englishman, at the School of Industrial Arts, Finland. She arrived in New York in 1927 with no particular position in mind. After some searching, she acquired a position with the Inwood Ceramic Studio in New York City. Her work there was of a multiple nature, including making clay, firing kilns, teaching and producing.

In her desire to find out "how it [pottery-making] was done in America" she attended a summer-session at Alfred University under Charles F. Binns. She soon realized that in terms of attitudes toward pottery, the situation was quite similar to that in Finland.[1] Apparently she was referring to the methodical, precise and calculated manner in which the pottery process was approached. Although she respected Binns' philosophy, which she felt was still very much applicable, she also realized some limitations in his practices and teachings. Miss Grotell alluded to this when she described Binns' eight inch pot which was executed in three sections with calculated precision. She recalled that "he took great pride in making this pot which would take him over one week to complete."

Miss Grotell's desire to break away from the mechanical approach to creating pottery was demonstrated when, upon receiving some new wheels at Alfred, she undertook the throwing of several tall, cylindrical pots, only to be told by Binns that "in Europe one does not learn to make pots in that manner." Her desire to be more free was further pointed out when she related that inspirations for her work did not come from an attempt to perpetuate the established, accepted masterpieces of China, Europe or Greece. Instead, she relied upon sources outside the ceramic field to gain inspirations. Among them, she has stated, were the ballet and the theatre, as well as painting and sculpture where she sensed a quest for freedom to experiment. In addition, it was her teaching position at the Henry Street Settlement House in New York City which exposed her to another inspiration for her work. The people working there were mainly elderly ladies who had done a great deal of china decorating. Most of their work involved mold-making and imitations of other styles and designs. Miss Grotell felt that, because of this method, all the work was "so tight, so precise."

Nevertheless, in this group she found a person whose enthusiasm for a more spirited approach to working with clay was closely akin to her own desires. It was the ceramic sculptures of Vally Wieselthier that excited her because of the freedom displayed in her large, whimsical sculpture of people and animals.

Wieselthier came from the Wiener Werkstaedte in Vienna, and her vivid imagination and humor had gained her a favorable reputation in Europe after her work was seen at the Exposition des Art Decoratifs in Paris in 1925.[2] She maintained that ceramics, more than any other art, grew by experimentation, because it was rooted so deeply in man's simplest instincts.

Whatever influence Miss Wieselthier had on Grotell it was not reflected to any noticeable degree in the latter's own pottery. In an exhibition at the W. & J. Sloane Gallery in New York City Miss Grotell's work consisted of simply thrown platters decorated with highly stylized human-figure motifs which were placed in such a manner as to complement and reemphasize the completely circular form.

In 1938, Miss Grotell accepted a position at Cranbrook Academy of Art to take charge of the ceramics program. Although she exhibited continually in competitive shows before arriving in Cranbrook, it was there that she became best known as one of America's outstanding teachers of pottery and as a practicing artist. Her work was represented in almost every Ceramic National Exhibition including the "Ceramics of The Western Hemisphere" show and the "Contemporary Ceramics" exhibition at the Golden Gate International Exposition of 1939 (Fig. 8-1). In 1947, she was awarded one of the top awards for ceramics by the Encyclopaedia Brittanica Company, and was also given a "Special Commendation for Group of Pottery" in the "Eleventh Ceramic National Exhibition" held at the Syracuse Museum of Fine Art. Furthermore, her professional stature was recognized by invitations to serve as a juror for several Ceramic National Exhibitions.

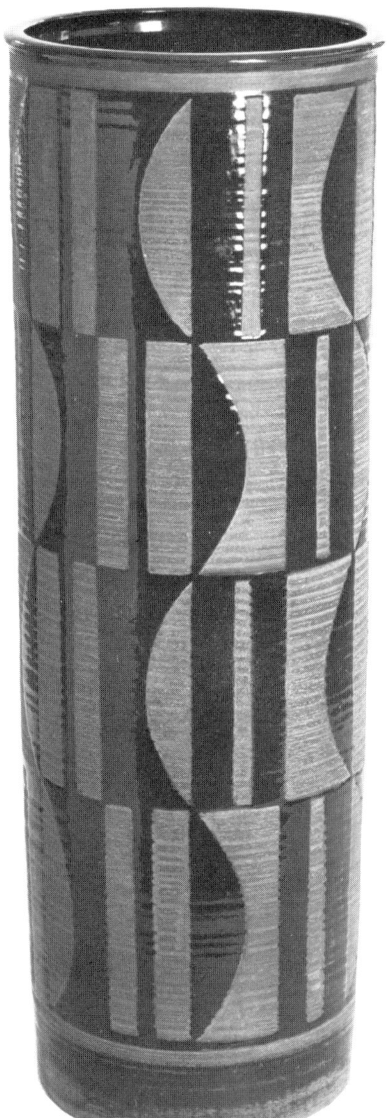

Figure 8-1. Maija Grotell, Stoneware Vase, 21 1/2" × 8", hand thrown, brown and black glazes, 1942. Cranbrook Academy of Art Museum Collection. Grotell was among a number of potters who were trained in Europe and who came to America during the 1930's. Their presence provided a wider diversity of attitudes toward form and philosophy for American studio-potters.

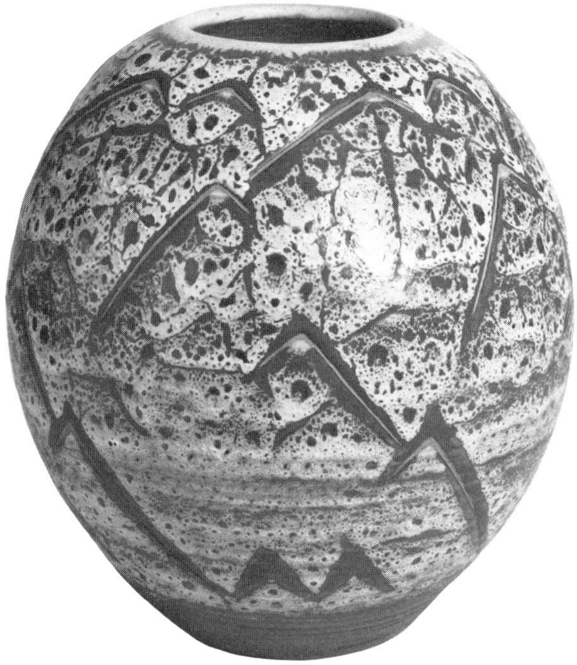

Figure 8-2. Maija Grotell, Vase, stoneware, hand thrown, orange and brown and white glazes, 12 3/4" × 12 3/4", 1944, Cranbrook Academy of Art Museum Collection. This vase shows how highly fusible slips or glazes break through a matt glaze to form an over-all, organic design. It was a technique that became popular with numerous potters during the 1950's.

Of special significance in this study, however, is Maija Grotell as the teacher of studio-pottery. Her reputation as a leading educator in the area of ceramics has been acknowledged by her former students, who have now assumed important positions in the field of ceramics as teachers and potters. Among them are Harvey K. Littleton of the University of Wisconsin, Toshiko Takeazu, formerly of the same institution and the Cleveland Art Institute, J.T. Abernathy of the Ann Arbor Potter's Guild, now operating his independent studio, Kurt Wild of the Wisconsin State University at River Falls, Wisconsin, Leza McVey of Cleveland, Ohio, also an independent artist and Edward Traynor of the Pasadena City College art department.

Upon arriving at Cranbrook, Miss Grotell did not orient her teaching to any particular point of view. She related that students at that time were not involved in any specific degree-granting program and were taking pottery mainly for leisure time activity. In recent years, she pointed out, her teaching has been directed more toward teacher-preparation for the college level. This meant a slight change of emphasis in her methods, so she insisted on certain basic competencies in throwing, glazing and firing. If these basic requirements were not met, she insisted that the student acquire them before he was allowed to go any further. In this regard she said: "I have to give them bitter pills now—things they have to do that they don't want to do." She was obviously referring to imposing on the student those skills which she deemed necessary in order for him to be able to exploit a more individual form of expression. This included a thorough knowledge of clay and glaze chemistry, firing and skillful execution of the various building techniques. In this regard Leza McVey related that Miss Grotell also stressed "an appreciation of craftsmanship and a sense of fitness of decoration to form."[3] When Miss Grotell was asked whether she felt that studio-pottery has been affected by a large number of potters coming from fine art and art education backgrounds she replied, "No. I don't think you can teach them to be artists. All we can teach them is techniques. Beyond that it is purely individual ability." Edward Traynor, of Pasadena City College, also pointed out that Miss Grotell placed a strong emphasis on good craftsmanship and design.[4]

When asked what influences the instructor had upon shaping his philosophy regarding style or technique, Kurt Wild, a former student of Miss Grotell, said:

> In an indirect way a great deal in that she encouraged and helped one in the development of his own views. I feel she had very little direct influence on style or techniques, but did encourage our development of our own style.[5]

In this respect Miss Grotell emphasized that she never consciously tried to influence a student, but instead, attempted to give form to an idea that the person might be trying to work out—even if it was contrary to her own philosophy. She tried not to explain an idea through her own work, but rather relied on the student's inventiveness to find out "what they are capable of doing."

These attitudes "stemmed from a great philosophy of life and views which one seems to experience rather than hear in terms of specific statements."[6] Mr. Wild added that Miss Grotell was very liberal in allowing nearly any type of work to be produced provided it was backed by some belief. The belief referred to apparently dealt with the student's conviction or total involvement with the ceramic medium as a worthwhile form of expression. Herein was the notable influence of Maija Grotell. Her philosophy, related as it is to sound skills in pottery with which the student and teacher could then begin to search for a more personal, specialized direction, has gained her a most respected position among American potters.

Marguerite Wildenhain

Another European-trained potter whose presence was felt in the development of American studio-pottery was Marguerite Wildenhain. She was born in France of German and English parents and was educated in France, England and Germany. Her early training was in sculpture at the School of Fine and Applied Arts of Berlin, Germany. In 1919, after some experience as a designer for the Porcelain Works of Thuringia, she went to the Bauhaus at Weimar and began her apprenticeship in pottery under Max Krehan and Gerhard Marcks. After seven years of training she accepted the job of chairman of the Ceramics Department at the Municipal School of Arts and Crafts in Halle, Saale, Germany.[7]

In 1933 she moved to Putten, Holland, where she and her husband operated their own workshop. At the same time, she produced production models for the Regout Porcelain Factory in Maasstricht, Holland. Upon her arrival in the United States in 1939 she taught at the College of Arts and Crafts in Oakland,

California. In 1942, she began her own workshop, Pond Farm, at Guerneville, California, where she produced her work and accepted selected students. In addition, she traveled extensively, giving lectures and demonstrations.[8]

Maguerite Wildenhain's influence can be described as of a philosophical nature, rather than stylistic. It is not intended to imply that her philosophizing about pottery was isolated from her work. Rather, her philosophy encompassed a way of making pottery, and indeed, a way of living. This was most clearly pointed out when she said:

> To learn a craft well is difficult enough, but the real difficulties start when you know your craft and want to express in your own way an idea that you visualize in your mind. First of all you have to make many pots—thousands—until your hands respond to the smallest, most subtle, most intricate or diversified feeling. Personal expression will come when you can really translate your innermost vision into the rough and so elusive material, clay.[9]

Through her background and training and her own involvement in creating pottery, Marguerite Wildenhain brought special vigor to American studio-potters. Daniel Rhodes appraised her early presence in the United States as follows:

> Her approach to the potter's wheel, a direct inheritance of the high standards of workmanship sustained by the German potters guilds, was a revelation to American potters, most of whom were clumsy and inept at throwing. Wildenhain's work was sharp, direct, well-made, and always had a natural beauty of surface, frequently resembling burnished rock.[10]

Whether American potters were clumsy in their throwing is, of course, disputable. But there is little doubt that Wildenhain's spirited approach to pottery provided an example of excellence and freedom not seen previous to her arrival in this country.

Marguerite Wildenhain's attitudes toward one's heritage in pottery was very unlike those who preceded her in America, especially when compared, for example, to Charles F. Binns who emulated the classic simplicity of China's Ch'ing dynasty pottery. She regarded a knowledge of the history of ceramics as an integral part of a craftsman's education and training, but not for reasons of enlarging one's repertoire from which to gain new ideas. Instead, she felt that "there is no need for Chinese glazes. It is much more important to be as basically honest as possible in one's search for artistic expression."[11] Her attitudes toward her work further indicated why her approach to potting was in distinct contrast to the calculated and restrained approach which was dominant previous to her coming to America. Explaining her more "unself-conscious" approach, she described her own work in the following manner:

> I have tried to find my own expression for the ideas I had without consciously forcing 'originality' and 'design.' Design starts for me when the clay is on the wheel and the pot grows; its volumes and lines change, clarify, and at the end balance, going out into space with bulges and hollows, light and shadow, with straight or curved lines, but never abstractly in formulae devised intellectually in advance.[12]

This in no way implied that an aspiring potter did not need to acquire the discipline of fully understanding every aspect of the pottery process, especially with regard to a keen insight into the nature of his material. In this respect she reflected the Bauhaus influence. Describing the limitless possibilities of clay, the various kinds of textures that could be achieved with it, even the different materials it can be made to imitate, she said:

> but in spite of all those near unlimited metamorphoses, there are only a certain number of forms and expressions that are truly characteristic of our material—clay.[13]

In regard to utility, she felt that there was no substitute for a clear understanding of the specific function that each form had, in instances such as tea pots, covered jars for cooking or storing, planters, bowls, compotes, cups or candleholders. To realize that certain functions demanded particular solutions was merely a matter of basic intelligence, she felt. But to order these separate considerations into a unified whole "is the ambition, the unending work and pleasure of a good potter."[14]

Examples of Marguerite Wildenhain's work reflect her European heritage. This is particularly noticeable in her large urns, some of which are decorated with the human figure somewhat in the manner of the Greek (Athenian, VI century B.C.) Lekythos. When there was an absence of this type of figurative work, motifs of leaves or plants were sometimes substituted. In a wine jug produced around 1950, she used such a decoration. The stylized plant design is well integrated into the pot and aids in reinforcing the curvature of the spout and handle. A white matt glaze, breaking over the incised design further helps in amplifying this approach to throwing and decorating pottery.

In the pottery produced after 1955, a severe reduction of the decorated and glazed surface could be noted. Textural effects were achieved through incising the clay with tools and through the inclusion of sand and/or grogs in the clay body. Whatever the theme of her decoration it was usually subdued and direct. The rich surfaces serve as an effective contrast to the direct and forceful contours of her pottery. The fusion of traditional form with her approach to decorating expressed Wildenhain's understanding of the nature of structure and design in pottery (Fig. 8-3).

Marguerite Wildenhain served as one of the most articulate spokesmen for the American studio-potter during the late 1940's and early 1950's. The enthusiasm with which she embraced her craft must have had some effect on the attitudes of her contemporaries. She beckoned the aspiring potter to consider his art form as a serious undertaking in self-expression. Realizing that there was certainly sufficient room for improvement in the area of commercial pottery design, she felt that

> it is increasingly important to again stress the value of the way of life of a craftsman and to try to educate young people to a basic understanding of the essence of life dedicated to an idea that is not based on success and money, but on human independence and dignity.[15]

In the course of this author's correspondence and in interviews with potters around the country, it was found that those who were trained after 1942 regarded Marguerite Wildenhain as an important teacher and studio-potter. It is also interesting to note that Marguerite Wildenhain was frequently identified with the Bauhaus. This may have been due to the fact that she was trained at the Bauhaus in Germany, and as a result, was an enthusiastic supporter of some of the Bauhaus' philosophy—such as the popular axiom that "form follows function."

Not all potters who came from Europe taught in schools. Some of them set up private studios where they worked. Their reputations as potters was gained mainly through competitive exhibitions or one-man shows. Most of them exhibited their work in galleries or shops throughout the country. Thus their influence may have been of a more indirect nature. One such example is the husband and wife team of Otto and Gertrude Natzler.

Gertrude and Otto Natzler

The Natzlers were born and trained in Vienna, Austria. Although they professed to be self-trained in pottery, their interest in the field came about through their exposure to the pottery workshop of Franz Iskra of Vienna.

Their influence in American ceramics began with their arrival in 1938. They have produced some of the most sophisticated glazes seen in the United States. Their traditional forms, supplemented with highly decorative glazes which included a variety of colors and textures, have brought them international recognition. The energies of this husband and wife team were divided, so that Mrs. Natzler concerned herself only with the throwing while Mr. Natzler performed all the glazing. In regard to their work they have said:

> A thorough knowledge of the potentialities of the medium, of its behavior under certain conditions and how to bring these conditions about, as well as complete mastery of every technical detail, is the basis from which we start.
>
> We are striving to combine this prerequisite with fantasy, inspiration and critical judgment, hoping it will result in the creation of a pot that will retain its timeless beauty as a work of art.[16]

It is doubtful that the Natzlers have had any significant influence in regard to ceramic forms. This is probably due to their concern for perpetuating a form concept that relies essentially on traditional designs. Instead, their most notable contribution is the invention of an extensive array of unusual surfaces and colors obtained through various types of slips and glazes. Years of experimenting and testing have produced glazes which range from inorganic, crater-like surfaces (Fig. 8-4) to numerous crystalline and luster finishes.

The intimate synthesis of form and surface brings them close to all types of analogies found in nature; exotic colors and engaging surfaces easily identify with precious rocks, minerals or surfaces that one might encounter on a celestial body. Without suggesting that the Natzlers looked to specific natural phenomenons for their ideas, Otto has pointed out, however, that identifying with nature in general has been of consistent inspiration. In this regard he has pointed out that

> I get my inspirations from walks in the high Sierra or in the desert or in the woods rather than from looking at books or pottery that has been made in the past.[17]

The Natzlers serve as a timely example of how an entirely new breed of potters in America viewed themselves and their work in relation to the *status quo.* Whether the work assumed a utilitarian, decorative or more "experimental" attitude, numerous potters like the Natzlers saw their commitment to creating unique pottery as

> . . . a rebellion against a civilization pervaded by mechanization, rebellion against it by confronting it

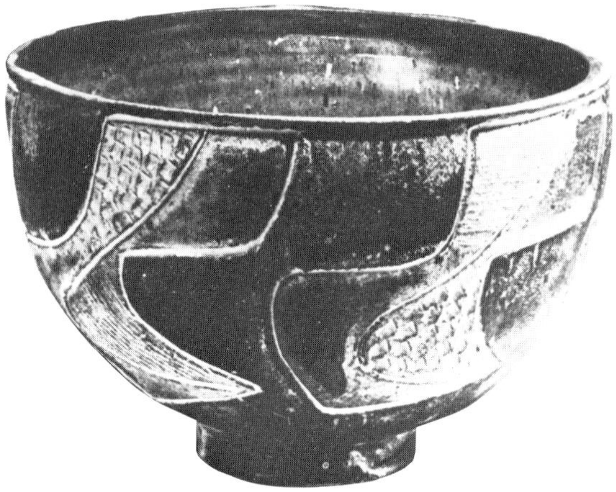

Figure 8-3. Marguerite Wildenhain, bowl, wheel thrown stoneware, 9 3/4″ diam., incised and sgraffito decoration, ca. 1968. Trained at the German Bauhaus, Wildenhain made American potters aware of new attitudes toward form, decoration and a way of life through her work and teaching after she arrived in the United States around 1939.

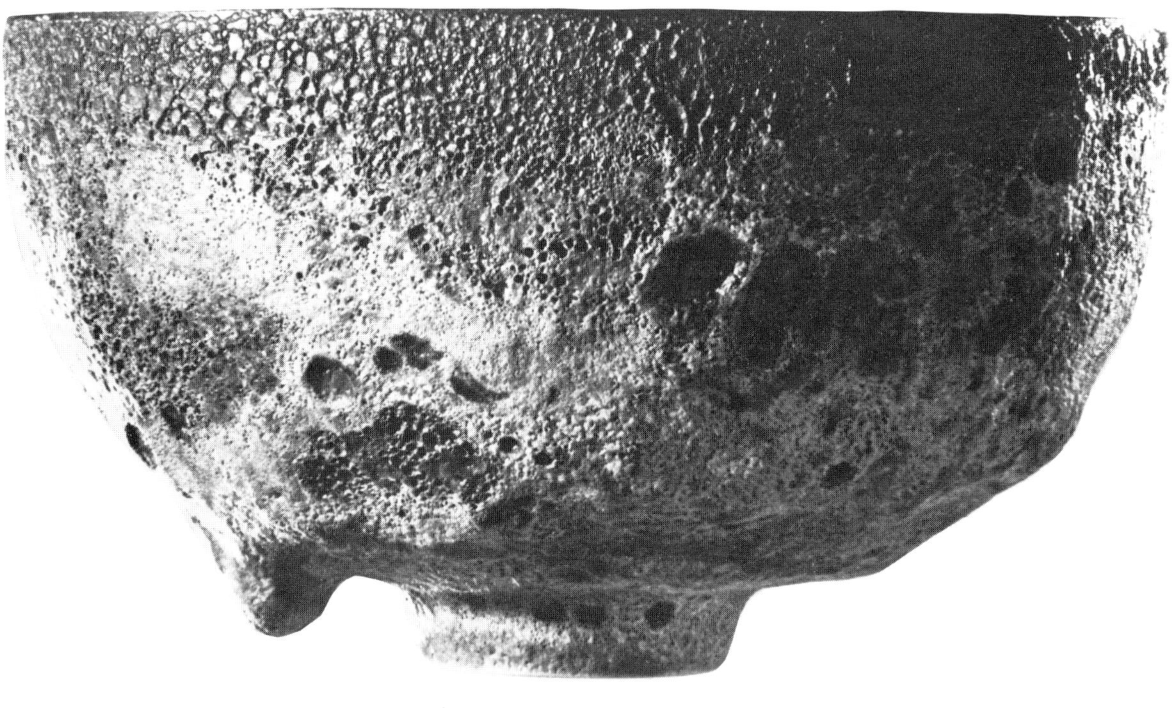

Figure 8-4. Gertrude and Otto Natzler, stoneware bowl, wheel thrown, Verdigris crater glaze with drop; 18 1/2 cm; 1961. The Museum of Modern Art, New York. Courtesy of the Artist.

> with our expression of an ancient art in which the imprint of the human hand is all important and preserved as part of the form.[18]

The Natzlers, like other potters who came to the United States from foreign countries, exemplify the diversification of styles and attitudes that existed in American ceramics before 1945 (Plate 6).

Franz Wildenhain

By the time he arrived at the Pond Farm Workshop at Guerneyville, California in 1947 and later at the School for American Craftsmen, Rochester Institute of Technology Franz Wildenhain had already established himself as a mature artist in Europe. Although trained at the Bauhaus in Weimar, Germany under Gropius, Klee, Albers, Kandinsky, Moholy-Nagy and Marcks, Wildenhain did not transmit in his teaching nor in his own work the over-used, and sometimes misinterpreted dictum of "form follows function." His own ceramics did not reflect a dehumanized, slick, machine-like quality that is sometimes erroneously associated with concepts of the Bauhaus design tradition.

Instead, his work is usually imbued with a strength and simplicity of form, with close attention given to appropriate decorations that reinforce the basic structure. These combinations exude a vitality that brings the work to a level of genuine art (Plate 7). They are not complicated by frivolity; they do not pretend to be any more than a simple testament to the ideal that, in the hands of a skilled craftsman and sensitive artist, a pot can become a vehicle of unique power and message. To this effect, Wildenhain has stated.

> A pot should be a pot, just a pot, and nothing more. . . . I use technical and professional skills, inventing my own technique—the one which I consider meaningful to me. What counts is vision. There are things which one may know fifty years, but it takes time to comprehend.[19]

Wildenhain's specific influences upon other potters may be difficult to ascertain. But the numerous exhibitions, both competitive and invitational, awards, fellowships and large, important architectural commissions, as well as having served on many juries for exhibitions, have all aided in giving prominence to him as an artist and teacher. His presence, like that of several other foreign potters, helped to give added stature to the development of American artistic ceramics.

Samuel Haile

Among the various foreign potters who made their presence felt both through their ceramics and their teaching was Samuel Haile from England. He and his wife arrived in America shortly after 1940 and Sam assumed teaching positions at Alfred University and the University of Michigan. Although they returned to England after the close of World War II, his short stay in America created a number of distinctive stoneware pots. Vigorously thrown on a relatively large scale and freely decorated with painted slips, this was not the type of work that American potters were used to seeing. Many of his pots were exhibited in various

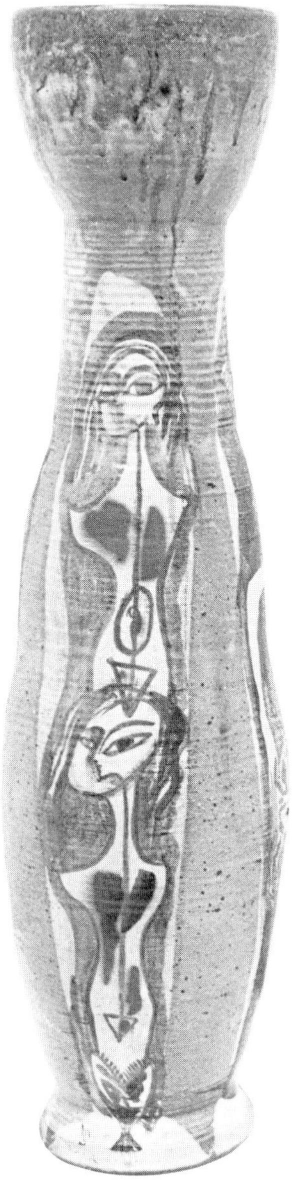

Figure 8-5. Samuel Haile, Vase, stoneware, wheel thrown and slip decorated. Everson Museum of Art Permanent Collection. Although Haile remained in America for only a short time, his vigorously thrown pots and freely painted decorations provided a fresh contrast for the more mechanical attitudes practiced by most American studio-potters during the late 1940's and early 50's.

shows and helped bring about a new awareness of the one-of-a-kind pot (Fig. 8-5). The importance of his ceramics rested more with the idea of uniqueness of personal expression than relying on the traditional dictum that a pot should grow out of purely utilitarian considerations.

Influences of Bauhaus Design on American Studio-Pottery

In addition to the previously discussed European influences which were directly attributable to specific persons that came to America before 1945, there were other sources of style and approaches to artistic problem solving. New design concepts and attitudes that developed around 1927 were generally referred to as the "international style." It found its greatest support with the Bauhaus of Weimar, Germany.[20]

Except for Marguerite and Franz Wildenhain no potters are known to have been trained as potters directly at the Bauhaus, either in Germany or in America. The Wildenhains' importance has already been discussed, and it was pointed out that their work did not exactly reflect the form language of the Bauhaus. Instead, they have been credited with contributing to American pottery a new philosophy and a new attitude which was directed toward re-examining the potters' relationship to his profession. Their identification with the Bauhaus has come mainly through virtue of having been trained at the school in Dessau, Germany, and because they have enthusiastically supported some aspects of the Bauhaus philosophy. Their support included the apprenticeship type of training, the serious consideration and intimate knowledge of the medium's character and careful examination of the proposed function of the form to be created so that it might serve as an important criterion for design and craftsmanship. The Bauhaus influence that is being considered at this point is that which dominated industrial design, starting approximately in 1927.

Design which emanated from the Bauhaus appeared in America several years before Moholy-Nagy opened the American Bauhaus (later School of Design) in Chicago in 1937. Several independent European and American designers operated design studios and provided industry with models which reflected the highly industrialized society of the twentieth century. For example, in 1927, Bel Geddes opened the first industrial design studio and shortly after that Walter D. Teague, George Sakier, Henry Dreyfus, Raymond Loewey, Harold Van Doren and others followed. Their designs for automobiles, locomotives, ships, airplanes, engines and machines, gas stoves, flat irons, pots and pans, knives and forks, cups and saucers, lamps, telephones and glassware were conspicuous for contours of simplified planes and fluid lines.

Almost every aspect of contemporary life seemed to have been affected by the new philosophy of construction and decoration. Three main areas of contemporary design, which have been identified with the Bauhaus, may have had some indirect influence in determining new approaches to ceramic art. First, the architecture of Gropius, Le Corbusier and Mies Van der Rohe exerted a strong influence with their developments of the light-weight constructions which featured plain facades, vertical accents of wall-dividers, panels, screens and light-weight furniture. The compressed design of building materials was an innovation that grew out of Bauhaus design concepts. Thus the development of less cumbersome and less centrally located lighting fixtures, less heavily decorated furniture and rugs and a more flexible use of open space began to appear. This resulted in an emphasis on the floating and lifting quality of much interior design, particularly in offices and stores, as well as homes and apartment houses.

Secondly, much of the contemporary affinity for the compressed, elongated forms that started to influence many aspects of design—including pottery—may have been related to aviation. A de-emphasis of earlier complex, linear forms appeared most aptly in the simplifications of aircraft bodies and the decrease of unnecessary weight and number of appendages. Similar considerations were noted in the work of some potters.

Lastly, the new, international style seemed to influence the design of the great number of advertisements found in various media of communication. For example, layout artists for advertising were reducing the amount of material placed within a specified area. Outdoor advertising also seemed to demand concise and simplified presentations. Hence the considerations implemented in these various areas may very well have influenced design concepts in other three-dimensional areas, including pottery. Lyle Perkins has advanced the theory that a great deal of design which has been associated with the Bauhaus has affected various aspects of contemporary life. Living space and accompanying furnishings have been deliberately compressed in structure and design in order to accommodate the scarcity of adequate room for living.[21]

The interest in this new style of designing interior and exterior forms for business, industry and the home became increasingly popular during the thirties. Major magazines in the country, including the homemaker's journals and magazines for school children, expounded on the merits of this newly emerging attitude toward design. Art journals discussed the Bauhaus aesthetic[22] while the home journals discussed innovative styles from the standpoint of the consumer.[23] New magazines analyzed the new design and its economic implications[24] and high school journals pointed out the progressive and challenging nature of a career in the area of design for those students who aspired to seek opportunities in that field of art.[25]

However, the effects of this trend in design was not generally felt by studio-potters until well into the middle and late 1940's. The ceramic industry was quickest to adopt the new design concepts. Leaders in the area of creating new forms for industry included Russell Wright who worked for the Steubenville Company and Eva Zeisel who designed for the Castelton China Company. Their work illustrated a complete re-thinking of problems related to tableware. Forms for utilitarian purposes became simple in contour, functional, undecorated and frequently used only one solid color without the usual floral motifs. Their work, as well as that by other manufacturers, was marked by a purity of form and simplicity of decoration and glaze. Hence potters were exposed to a type of work which was not based on external stylistic features but rather on intrinsic laws of material, technique and utility (Plate 8).

Several potters have pointed out that designs which have been associated with the Bauhaus did indeed influence the work of some American studio-potters. They did not indicate to what degree the new style may have affected their work, but it was important that potters were aware of this vigorous change in design.[26]

One of the earliest leaders in whose work the new style became manifest was Harold Nash. Several of his forms produced after 1936 reflect a concern for simple shapes and clean surfaces (Fig. 8-6). During subsequent years the work of several other potters displayed similar interests in form and decoration. The work of Glidden Parker was repeatedly chosen for awards in the Ceramic National Exhibitions. His compact and simply designed casseroles illustrate the successful solution of design problems set by the needs of easy handling, storing, building and shipping (Fig. 8-7). Bowls and trays made by Victor Schreckengost and William B. Ross also showed a concern for simplified, functional forms. Decorations applied to these shapes are usually linear and non-objective in character and are well integrated in the total design of the pot. Simplicity of design is furthermore reinforced by the use of uniform, semi-matt glazes.

Some potters may not have absorbed the influence of the Bauhaus until the early 1950's; in fact, some even may not have been consciously aware of the influences in their own work, even though their pottery did reflect the impact of Bauhaus design in the use of extremely simplified forms and the absence of superfluous decoration (Fig. 8-8). Influences that may have stemmed from considering Bauhaus developments could be seen in a prize-winning planter by Robert Turner made in 1949. It is another example of pottery which is notably simplified in contour and decoration. The absence of unnecessary surface treatment aids in strengthening the combined use

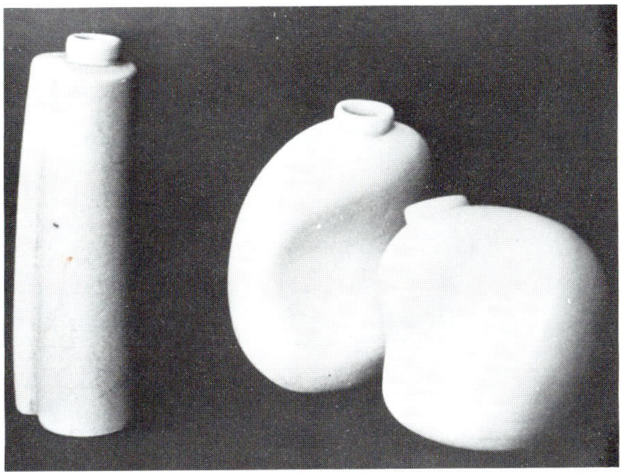

Figure 8-6. Harold Nash, Bottle forms, stoneware, handbuilt, majolica glaze, ca. 1939, collection of the artist. Nash's work shows clear influences of the "International Style" with its emphasis on simple lines and contours and the absence of any superfluous decoration. Because of its radical departure from accepted practices during the late 1930's and early 40's his work was often rejected from American competitive exhibitions of studio-pottery.

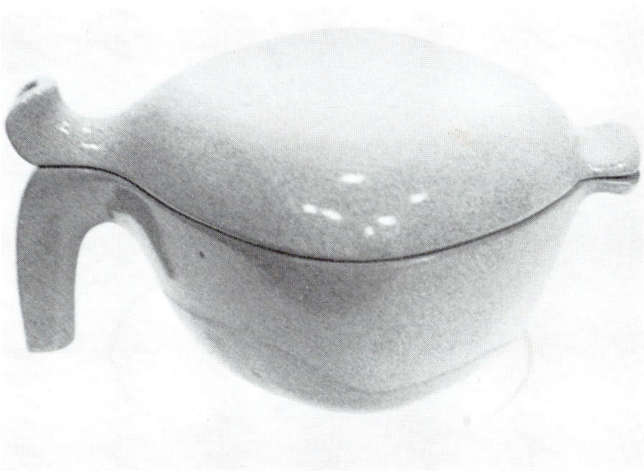

Figure 8-7. Glidden Parker, Casseroles, stoneware, handbuilt, Everson Museum of Art Permanent Collection. Parker's utilitarian ceramics illustrates the influence of Bauhaus design in its concern for integrating the final form with utilitarian function and good visual design.

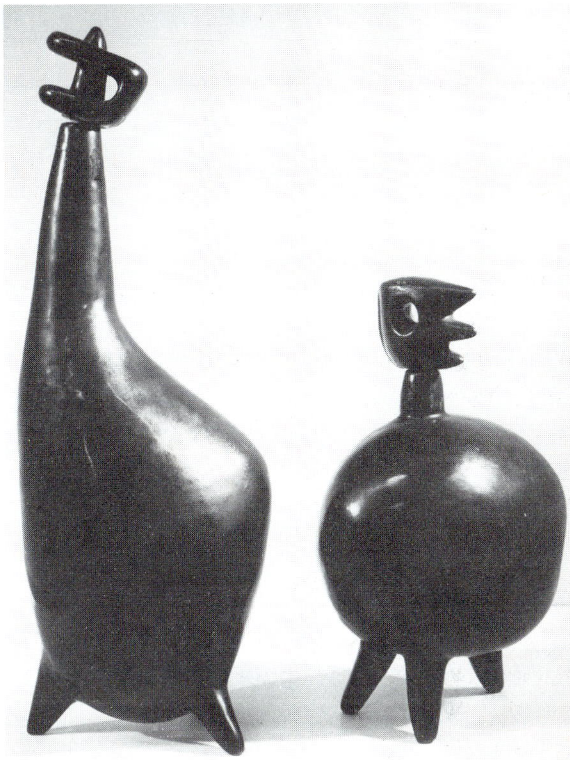

Figure 8-8. Leza McVey, "Ceramic Forms," stoneware, partially thrown and handbuilt. Everson Museum of Art Permanent Collection, 1951. McVey's work is a typical example of how numerous potters absorbed the influences of the "International Style" in fashioning for themselves forms that were simplified in contour and surface.

of severe lines and subtly balanced curves. It would be somewhat presumptuous to claim that Turner was directly affected by the insurgent interest in Bauhaus design. However, his work produced around 1949 and thereafter expresses most typically a form-language that identifies him closely with the Bauhaus. His simply designed vases, covered jars and bowls are primarily based on straight lines sparingly modified by subtle curves (Fig. 8-9). The predominant use of white and gray matt glazes further enhances the pots which were essentially created for use.

The utilitarian pottery of Gladys Crook reveals a similar orientation. Although her covered jars were produced in 1956, they are amplifications of a form concept reminiscent of machine art which was established during the 1930's and 1940's. Her pots, reduced to uncomplicated cylindrical forms, are conspicuous for their clean, untainted surface quality.

After 1949, an increased concern can be noted in the work of some other potters for creating pottery which relied specifically on the dynamics of the machine. Although pots were frequently thrown on the wheel, any clues as to this method of building were often obscured by painstaking efforts to finish the pot. This was particularly true in the porcelain work of Roland Lietzke whose decanter and cups could easily be mistaken for cast pieces. Some potters did, in fact, turn to casting. In some instances the forms were austere in shape, decoration and glaze. Sometimes students approached design problems of a particular type of pot by casting from molds. At the Rhode Island School of Design, students performed such experiments under the direction of Dorothy Perkins. The results are an unusual variety of pots based on simple vertical designs and adapted to several different kinds of functions. Some were altered to function as pitchers, vases, lamps, jars or candleholders. To deviate from the cast forms, some shapes were indented, cut or otherwise altered. Despite these changes a notable mechanistic character is still discernible.

The design work which has become identified with the Bauhaus style was another important foreign source for inspiration in American ceramics. Some potters assimilated the new trend quite readily, while others used it as a foundation for modifying certain aspects of their work (Fig. 8-10). In the latter instances, it may have meant that only a specific factor came under consideration, such as arriving at a better solution of utilitarian problems which were an outgrowth of the axiom "form follows function." For others the new approach to designing, building and decorating may have served as a liberation from the overindulgence in complex forms and frivolous decorations which had been so popular with some potters prior to 1940. As a result, the clean shapes and almost bare surfaces often created by machine art were a welcomed relief.

Ironically, this very innovation stimulated some opposition. Those who did not adopt the new style seemed to react against the mechanical, almost impersonal attitudes imbued in much of the work of the modern designers. Hence the influence of the Bauhaus did not make itself felt as a dominating force for any extended period of time in the work of studio-potters. Shortly after 1945, the romantic element reappeared as a contrast to the classic severity of the Bauhaus, machine art and industrial design inclination of the 1940's. More specifically, it meant that potters started to question the acceptability of the formal ap-

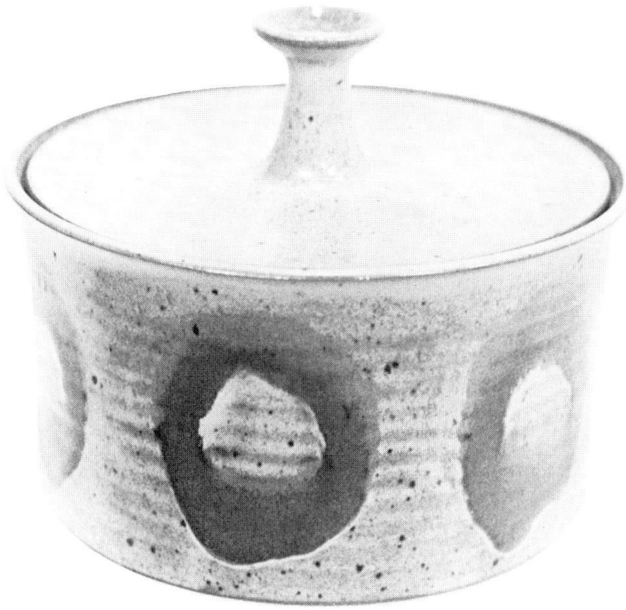

Figure 8-9. Robert Turner, Covered Jar, stoneware, wheel thrown, grey glaze with copper red decoration, ca. 1953. Everson Museum of Art Permanent Collection. The extremely simple shape is reflective of how some studio-potters during the 1950's responded to the International Style in dealing with more simplified forms and decorations.

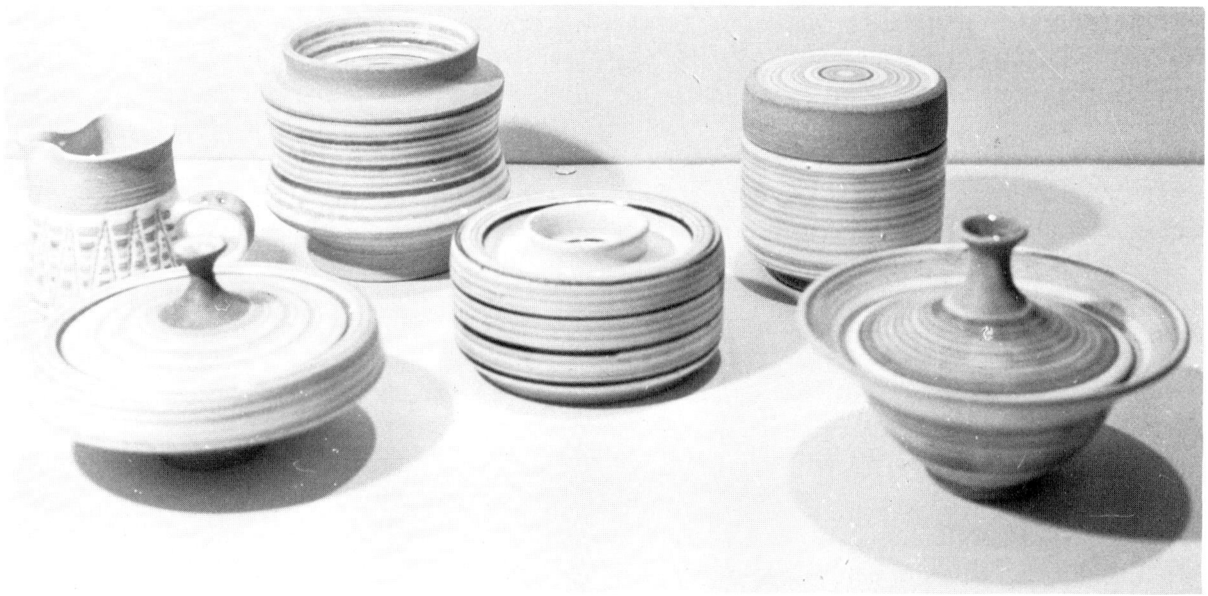

Figure 8-10. Dorothy Perkins, variety of wheel thrown forms, stoneware, average height 4″. Majolica banding on white, glossy glazes.

proaches to building, glazing, decorating and firing which had become an integral part of the aesthetic that was identified with Bauhaus design.

Notes

1. Interview with Maija Grotell, Cranbrook Academy of Arts and Science, Bloomfield Hills, Mich. (Unless other sources are cited, all information about Miss Grotell was obtained through an interview with the author.)
2. "Vally Wieselthier," *Design*, 39:46-47 (November, 1937).
3. Leza McVey, Cleveland, Ohio, unpublished correspondence.
4. Edward Traynor, Professor of Art, Pasadena City College, Pasadena, California, unpublished correspondence.
5. Kurt Wild, Assistant Professor of Art, Wisconsin State University, River Falls, Wis., unpublished correspondence.
6. Kurt Wild, unpublished correspondence.
7. "Marguerite Wildenhain," *Design Quarterly*, 42:63-64 (1958).
8. Ibid., p. 64.
9. Ibid., p. 64.
10. Daniel Rhodes, "The Twentieth Century," *Forms From The Earth: 1,000 Years of American Pottery in America*, Museum of Contemporary Crafts, New York, 1961, p. 10.
11. "Wildenhain," p. 64.
12. Ibid., p. 64.
13. "Marguerite Wildenhain," *Crafts Horizon*, 16:31 (November, 1956).
14. Marguerite Wildenhain, *Pottery: Form and Expression*, p. 68.
15. "Wildenhain," *Design Quarterly*, p. 64.
16. Gertrude and Otto Natzler, Biographical data from the catalog of *Clay Today*, Exhibition at the New Gallery, School of Fine Arts, State University of Iowa, December, 1963, p. 13.
17. "Natzler Retrospective Exhibition," *Ceramics Monthly*, 19:8 (October 1971) p. 14.
18. *Op. Cit.*, p. 14.
19. Franz Wildenhain, Foreword to the Catalog, "Franz Wildenhain Retrospective Exhibition," University Art Gallery, State University of New York at Binghamton, New York, December 1, 1974, p. 12.
20. The Bauhaus was moved from Weimar to Dessau on April 25, 1925.
21. Lyle E. Perkins, "An Investigation of Experimentalism as Applied to Creativity and Ceramic Media," Unpublished doctoral dissertation, The Ohio State University, 1956, pp. 42-47.
22. J. W. Higgins, "Design for Mass Production," *American Magazine of Art*, 26:40-41 (September, 1933).
23. L. Guild, "They Brought Style to the Machine," *House and Garden*, 65:54-5 (January, 1934).
24. "Gropius and His Bauhaus," *Newsweek Magazine*, 12:21 (December 12, 1938).
25. Harold Rugg, "The Creative Artist in Industrial America," *Scholastics*, 30:17-18 (April 24, 1937).
26. Those who acknowledged the presence of Bauhaus influence in studio-pottery included Ruth Randall, Herbert Sanders, Edward Traynor, Victor Schreckengost, Marion Fosdick, William Wyman, Val Cushing, James Wozniak, Myrtle French, Rudolf Stoffel and William Persick.

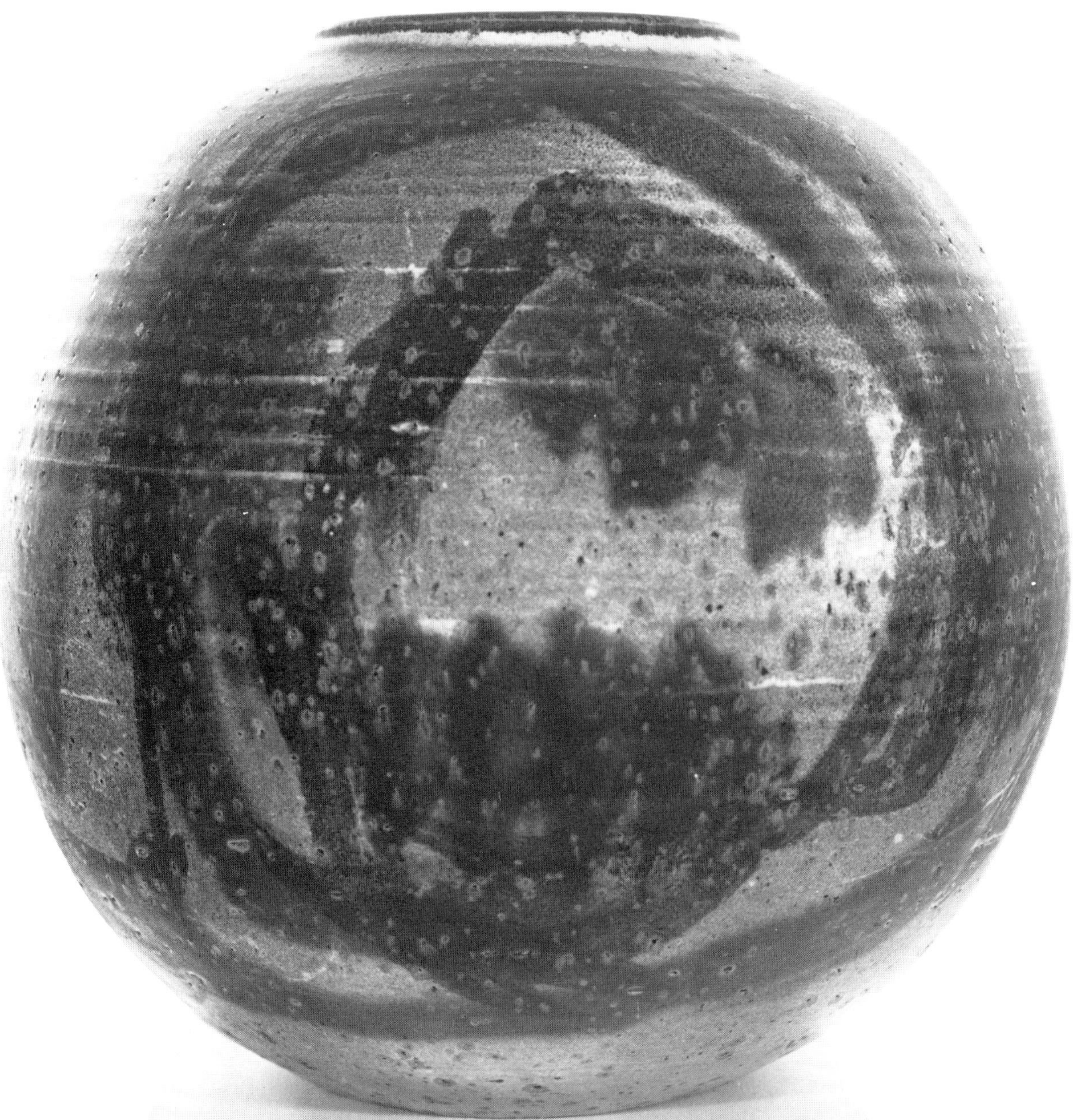

Toshiko Takeazu

Foreign Influences on American Ceramics After 1945 9

Oriental influences which became noticeable in the work of American potters after 1945 were of a different type from those which prevailed in much of the work produced from approximately 1880 to 1940. The pottery of china decorators, the Rookwood Pottery Company, Adelaide Robineau, Charles Binns and others, in some part, emulated traditional Oriental designs, as was manifest in the shapes of pots, their decorative motifs or glazes. After 1945 it was no longer important to imitate the strength and simplicity of Sung of Ch'ing dynasty forms, nor was there an urgency in spending endless hours in attempting to find the secrets of the famous oxblood, peachbloom or celadon glazes. Technical problems related to achieving these effects were mastered by the research of people such as Arthur E. Baggs and Edgar Littlefield, Charles Harder and Marion Fosdick. Their findings were published in two periodicals, *The Journal* and *The Bulletin of the American Ceramic Society* and were available to anyone who was interested in using them. Instead, it was Japanese folk-pottery which came to the attention of a large number of American studio-potters.

Bernard Leach

Bernard Leach was directly responsible for bringing the art of contemporary Japanese pottery to the attention of the potters of this country. This was achieved through his book, *A Potter's Book*, published in 1940. By 1960 it had gone through its eighth reprinting, which attests to its popular acceptance by American potters and students. It was the first comprehensive book which dealt almost exclusively with approaches to problems directly related to studio-pottery as Leach had learned them in the Orient and practiced them in England. Most previous books which dealt with Oriental pottery were generally approached from the standpoint of the connoisseur, and accomplished little toward giving an insight into the philosophy of building, decorating and firing stoneware pottery.

In his technical descriptions Leach shared with the reader all of the experience and information gained over his twelve years' stay in Japan. He provided recipes for clay bodies and glazes, techniques for firing and a multitude of other suggestions which included everything from pulling specific types of handles to the problems of how to market one's wares. Important technical information was included, such as a large body of facts about high-fire stoneware clays and glazes directly related to the introduction of a relatively new firing technique.[1]

Although stoneware had certainly been used before his book appeared, in most instances American potters were either still dealing with low or medium fired clays and glazes. This was in strong contrast to the type of work that Leach did himself and discussed in his text, since that work was fired at stoneware temperatures. This partially accounts for the appearance of different kinds of clay bodies, slips, glazes and surface effects in pottery after World War II.

When stoneware was worked in the past by American potters, it was protected from kiln gases by muffle boxes or saggars, thereby insuring a relatively well controlled oxidation atmosphere. This in turn enabled the potter to impose a certain amount of predictability and control over his work because the protective covering assured him that similar results could be repeated with relative ease. Open chambered firing which produced a reduction atmosphere, on the other hand, did not have the same "built-in" controls and assurances. Although potters could be reasonably sure of most of the desired effects, there were several variables which needed constant attention in order to insure specific results. For example, different types of fuel, the amount of oxygen intake, the ability of the flue to draw heat from the kiln, weather conditions and most important, the types of kilns used all influenced how the gases would travel through the unprotected pots and consequently the kinds of results one could achieve. The lack of control over these variables introduced an element of chance which became an integral part of the creative act in pottery.

In conjunction with the new type of firing, Leach also provided a number of glazes which had not been used previously to any great extent. Among them were iron saturated glazes which produced a variety of colors and textures, wood ash glazes which usually produced soft, variegated and matt surfaces, as well as a number of white and grey matts that created effects much like the qualities associated with various kinds of stones or rocks. Even the decorating slips which had been used earlier and often regarded as "dirty" or "impure" were again used with renewed interest and vigor. Albany and Barnard slip took on a more muted, stone-like effect when they were used in conjunction with the aforementioned glazes. Thus, since the introduction of Leach's text, stoneware pottery and its accompanying ramifications have become popularly accepted by a majority of studio-potters in America.

There was, however, a deeper meaning behind these physical phenomena. A certain amount of chance and a peculiar sense of drama associated with this new process found great sympathy with most potters. It seemed as if the newly emerging attitudes toward creating pottery served as a form of reaction against established principles of the past which upheld the industrial design concepts of the late 1920's and 1930's. The eager adaptation of new clays, glazes and firing techniques that embodied something of the unpredictable, in comparison to the reserved, clean and controlled glazes and techniques of previous years, thus became a romantic challenge for many studio-potters. This seemed especially meaningful after World War II, since, at that time and from then on, most potters were trained in fine arts departments where similar attitudes were being advanced in painting and sculpture.

Through a wide acceptance of the folk art tradition advanced by Leach a different type of pottery emerged in America. This assumed various forms, and because it has sustained itself as an integral style within contemporary pottery, it will be discussed in more detail.

During the early 1900's American potters had a tendency to decorate their wares in a formalized manner. In part this was due to the types of decorations and techniques employed, most of which consisted of incising, sgraffito, slip inlays, stencils, spraying, underglaze and overglaze decorations and banding. In those instances, precise care was taken in carrying out a preconceived decoration (Fig. 9-1). With

Figure 9-1. Various wheel thrown vessels illustrating a wide variety of decorative approaches such as slip trailing, brush decorating, sgraffito, wax resist and banding. These were among the popular decorating techniques enthusiastically explored by studio-potters during the 1950's. Courtesy, the American Art Clay Co., Indianapolis, Indiana.

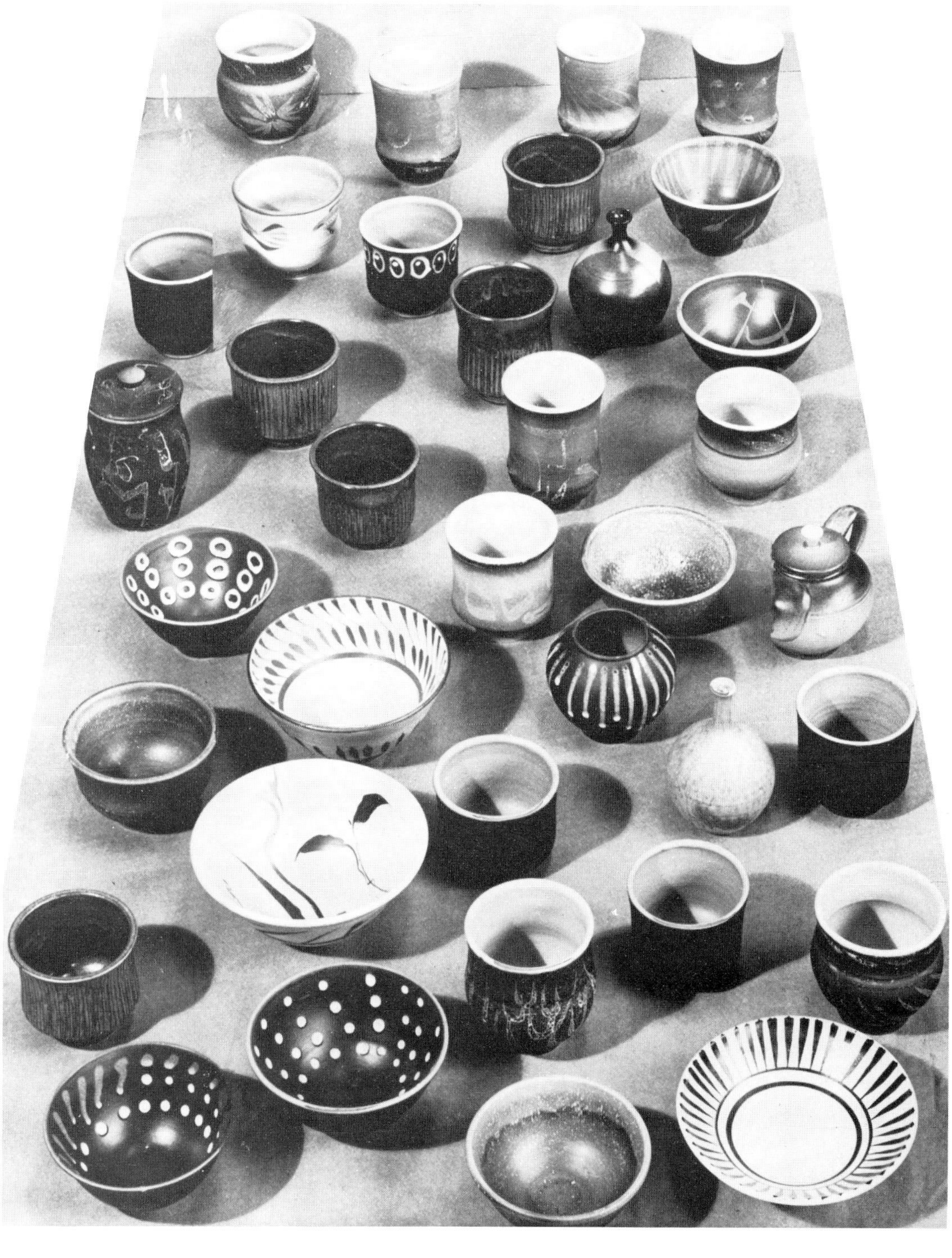

Leach's introduction of Japanese and Korean brush work, however, a new verve, a spontaneity and directness could be noted in the work of many American potters whose work in the past did not show this type of decorative approach. Leach illustrated several examples of Korea's Yi dynasty pottery as well as some specimens of Japan's folk-art pottery. In regard to the latter he pointed out, "The loose peasant pattern may be contrasted with the nervous energy and individuality of Tomimoto's brush work."[2]

Leach, himself a master of calligraphic decoration (Fig. 9-2), felt that the significance of any decorative motif was compromised by mechanical reproduction which suffered from the absence of any continuous, vital interpretation no matter how good the original design may have been. He pointed out, "That is why well painted pots may have a beauty of expression greater than pottery decorated with engraved transfers, stencils or rubber stamps."[3] Leach did not include examples of the masterful works of the Greeks, Hispano-Moresque, Delft, Cretan, Persian, Iranian or Pueblo polychrome pottery, all of which exemplifies a virtuosity and sensitivity of form and decoration different from that of the Orientals. It is unlikely that he failed to recognize their merit. Instead, he seemed to echo some aspects of William Morris' revolt against the Industrial Revolution which had manifested itself in pottery through mechanical, stultifying forms and decorations which were still very conspicuous during the late 19th and early 20th century in Europe and America.

Through Bernard Leach's introduction of the Japanese and Korean heritage came also a greater appreciation of the asymmetrical character of decorations. He stressed that

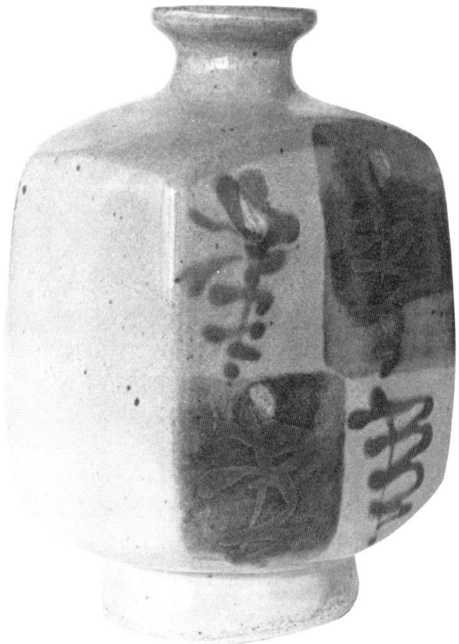

Figure 9-2. Bernard Leach, Bottle, stoneware, handbuilt and thrown, slip decorated, oatmeal glaze. Collection of the author.

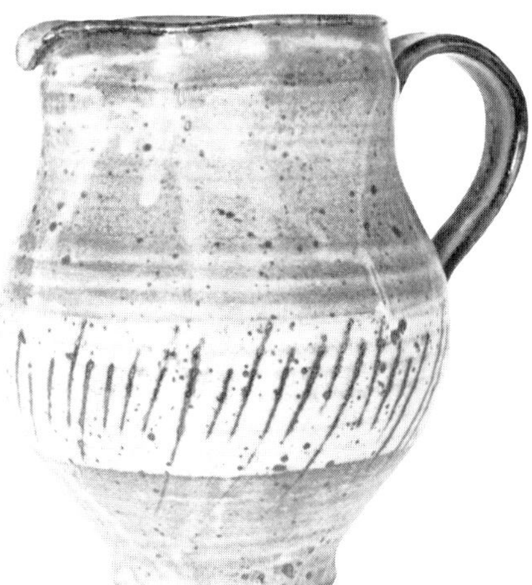

Figure 9-3. Harvey Littleton, Pitcher, stoneware, wheel thrown, wax resist and sgraffito decoration, ca. 1959. Collection of the author.

"regularity of form seems to call for an irregular element in decoration, and as an antithesis widens the range of expression."[4] This, coupled with a more vigorous approach to throwing, created pottery which was characterized by strength and simplicity. Typical of this new direction in making pots and in decorating their surfaces was Mini Negoro of Alfred University, whose three piece tea set executed in the typical Japanese style, complete with bamboo handles and swiftly executed brush work, won her one of the top awards in the 12th Ceramic National Exhibition.[5] Numerous potters were seemingly influenced in this new direction toward throwing and decorating and their work assumed an imposing, vital quality. Among them, for example, were Paul Volkening whose vases became fields for active calligraphic brush work. The simplicity of Harvey Littleton's pots were also reinforced by strong brush work and sgraffito (Fig. 9-3). Alix and Warren MacKenzie's work was supplemented by direct and spontaneous brush decorations (Fig. 9-4). Their work was conspicuous for its spirited thrown quality as well as for its brush work which was very much in the spirit of Oriental pottery, particularly that of the Japanese of which Leach had spoken so highly.

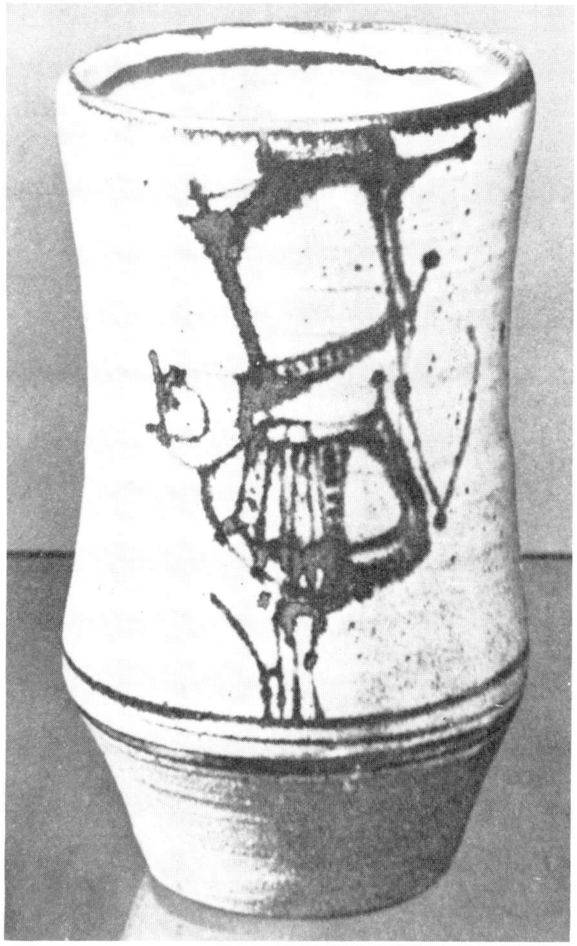

Figure 9-4. Alix and Warren MacKenzie, Vase, stoneware, wheel thrown, decorated with iron slip over white opaque glaze, 1951. Collection of the artist. MacKenzie's thrown pottery is often reflective of an unself-conscious attitude toward throwing and decorating which has been associated with the insurgent interest in contemporary Japanese folk-art pottery and through the exposure of Bernard Leach's ceramics.

Wax-resist painting was one of the popular decorative techniques which grew out of the mounting interest in brush work. Although it is difficult to determine when this technique began, Leach may well have been responsible for its introduction to American potters. In his textbook he discussed its uses and illustrated some exquisite examples by the Japanese master, Shoji Hamada. The use of wax resist as a decorative approach was adopted by numerous potters. A survey of several national exhibitions of the 1950's indicates that the examples of wax-resist in the work of Peter Voulkos, James McKinnel, Harvey Littleton and Carlton F. Ball were repeatedly represented. It was in fact, popularly adopted by many studio-potters and students who worked in the early 1950's (Figs. 9-5 and 9-6).

The significance of Bernard Leach and his influential book was not limited to providing the potter with a more extensive vocabulary to express himself. Of equal, if not more, importance, was an attitude toward pottery, indeed, toward a way of life for the craftsman which Leach brought to the attention of studio-potters. Daniel Rhodes observed that Leach's book was avidly read in this country not only because it offered some very constructive "how-to-do-it" suggestions, but also because he presented "a very strong personal philosophy about the making of pots and the honest use of materials."[6]

Leach felt that too much reliance on theoretical knowledge and not sufficient practical experience was one of the more serious dilemmas that faced the American student of pottery. In reading his text one became aware of his insistence that a sound understanding of this complex craft could only be achieved through a total and uncompromising commitment to the discipline. This was indicative of the apprentice system with which he was familiar, in which a student studied for several years under an acknowledged master and acquired the necessary skills in a sequential manner. Leach had served a rather severe indictment against the type of training in pottery which existed generally in Europe and America. He pointed out that, "In childhood a natural process of rehearsal and growth through experience is constant, but educa-

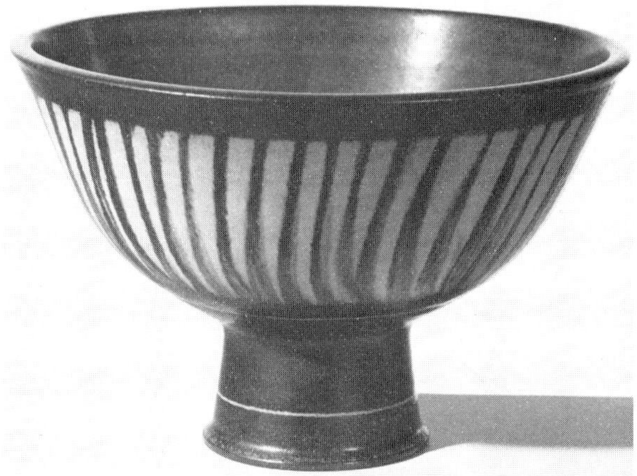

Figure 9-5. Harrison McIntosh, Footed Bowl, stoneware, wheel thrown, blue-green, black and gray glazes, wax resist decoration, 1959. Collection of the artist.

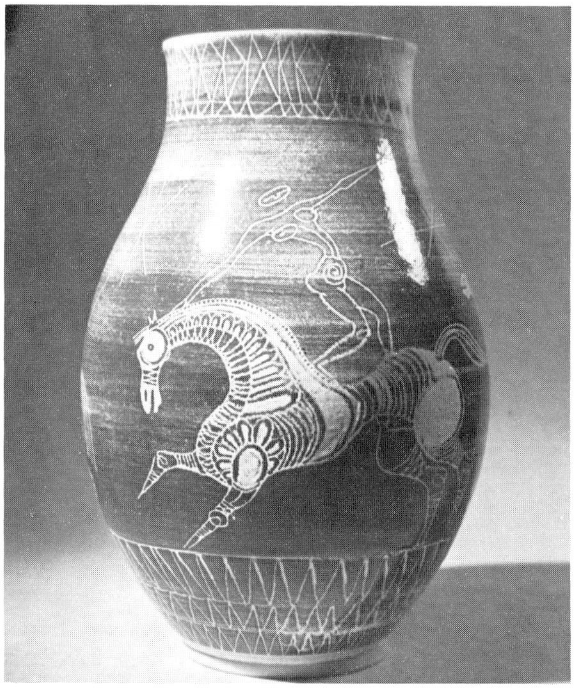

Figure 9-6. Carlton F. Ball, Vase, stoneware, wheel thrown, red slip, sgraffito design, transparent cover glaze, 1951. Collection of the artist. Thrown by Carlton Ball and decorated by Aaron Bohrod.

tionalists do not take this sufficiently into account in the teaching of pottery."[7] He was in favor of exposing the potential student of pottery to the fundamental methods of pottery, beginning with the digging of clays, of learning to throw similar forms in large quantities, of building his own kilns and preparing his own glazes. Above all, he felt it imperative that the student and the professional potter base their form concepts on the domestic needs of their surroundings, "for it is through local tradition that one gains a standard for form, pattern and color which embodies that deeper wisdom of beauty in articles of daily use which we have almost lost."[8]

Furthermore, Leach believed that formal schooling was a doubtful method of learning the potter's art. It was this very attitude which led him to be critical of American studio-potters and their work. In the Midwest Craftsmen's Seminar, held on November 17, 1952 at the St. Paul Gallery and School of Art, St. Paul, Minnesota, Leach expressed the opinion that American potters were unduly influenced by the work of China's Sung dynasty and by the work of the Pre-Columbian Indians. He also observed that Americans were, at the same time, too consciously concerned with the idea of producing "one-of-a-kind" pots. As a result of this concern for creating what is generally known as a "show pot," Leach felt that the majority of American studio-potters had fallen by the wayside.[9] It seemed evident to Leach that American potters lacked genuine cultural taproots, since our heritage stemmed from the fusion of perhaps thirty foreign countries. At the same time, however, he reminded his fellow potters that they did, indeed, possess a rich legacy in the work of their 19th century forefathers who had produced handsome wheel-thrown stoneware jugs and jars. The ceramic work referred to was one of the most obvious influences of Western Europe's medieval and folk-pottery heritage.

The second tradition which Leach pointed out as having genuine American taproots was that of the American Indian. It was from these two mainstreams of American pottery that he felt contemporary potters should have fashioned a more distinctive form language. In relation to this he explained that "the pot is the natural expression of the man or of the culture behind him."[10] Leach's criticism of America's failure to refine some past tradition as a way to create a truly distinctive form concept, aroused the ire of several potters around the country. Most outspoken of these was Marguerite Wildenhain. In reply to Leach's reproof she said:

> Roots are, of course, wonderful to have, but who has that one single 'taproot' you talked of? That single taproot no longer exists in our day. It is probable that it has never existed. No country, no single individual has only one root from which he draws strength.
>
> America has roots too, but there are many and come from all over the world, from all races. In this lies its uniqueness, its grandeur—this cementing together of a thousand parts. A country like America cannot have just one expression, one way of doing things. It must perforce have as many forms of expression as the sources of its life as a whole. That is America's beauty and greatness, and nobody would want to see just one single way of thinking grow on this continent. For our tradition is just the opposite: it stands for the free choice of each individual.
>
> It ought to be clear that American potters cannot possibly grow roots by implanting Sung pottery or by copying the way of life of the rural population of Japan. Conscious copying of the works of a culture

> unrelated to the mind and soul of our generation would only produce dubious makeshifts and turn our struggling potters into either diletantes or pure fakes. As creative craftsmen, we reject the tendency to force our generation into a mold that does not belong to it.[11]

In her reply to Leach, Marguerite Wildenhain seemed not only to provide an insight into the heterogeneous character of American pottery during the mid-twentieth century, but also appeared to forecast the temper and direction of pottery that was to follow during the late 1950's and early 1960's. In this regard Shoji Hamada, one of Japan's highly regarded potters who accompanied Leach to the seminars for throwing and decorating demonstrations, said, "The history of studio-pottery in America is yet quite green, but the unflagging endeavor of many honest artists certainly promises well for the future."[12]

Leach returned to the United States several times for lectures and demonstration tours, as did Shoji Hamada and Dr. Soetsu Yanagi, Head of the National Folk Museum in Tokyo. Of the three, Leach and Hamada appeared to have had a more direct and profound influence on the attitudes and habits of American studio-potters. In addition to publishing a wealth of factual and practical information Leach also suggested to American potters that the refinement of special and costly individual ceramics could be translated into simpler, functional pots, which, because of the repetitive process of throwing a large number of similar forms, could sell at prices within the reach of a far wider range of customers. Secondly, in view of the large number of pots which were being made from the standpoint of "one-of-a-kind," Leach stressed the idea that there was intrinsic merit in making pottery for a functional need, as had been natural and normal in the making of a great deal of outstanding pottery in the past.

Shoji Hamada

The influence of Hamada was equally forceful, especially through his lectures and demonstrations which continued until recently. His latest visit to America included a two-week workshop at San Jose State College during the summer of 1964. He also had numerous exhibitions of his work in the United States. At the workshops potters were exposed to the virtuosity of Hamada's throwing, his variety of decorating techniques and his reflections on individual potters' works. Through the exhibits and demonstrations, one became acquainted with his use of various approaches to decorating and glazing. Hamada dramatized in his work that which Leach had introduced through his text. He was, indeed, a living example of the book, for when one was exposed to Hamada and his work one was confronted with a completely new aesthetic derived from the pottery of Kenzan, Japan. This included an unselfconscious manner of throwing, a distinctive simplicity in the forms and a spirited approach to decorating and glazing (Fig. 9-7).

Hamada's decorations included slip trailing,[13] brush decorations with slips, raw metal oxides and wax-resist, patterns created by dipping the pot in glazes or by pouring glazes on parts of the pot, designs made with his fingers while the glaze was still wet, pressed, incised and combed patterns and an endless variety achieved through a combination of these tech-

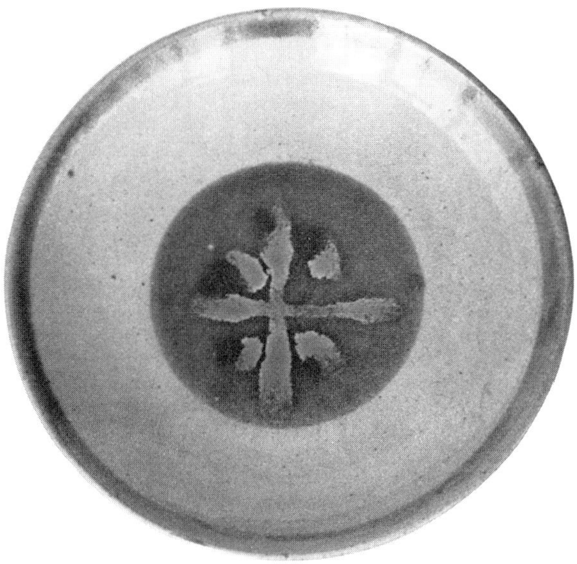

Figure 9-7. Shoji Hamada, Rice Dish, stoneware, slip decoration with opaque ash glaze. ca. 1962. Collection of the author. The casual attitude toward throwing and decorating as seen through much of contemporary Japanese pottery became an important influence in American studio-pottery during the 1950's.

niques. His glazes also included a number of distinctive types with which his work has become identified and which he has relied upon consistently over the years. They included the *Kaki*, an opaque, rust-brown glaze which turns black when used thin, *Tenmoko*, lustrous black iron glaze, *Hai-Kusuri*, an ash glaze, and *Tesha*, a variegated iron-brown glaze, as well as a number of other clear matt glazes. Most of these were used by a number of American potters after they were introduced in this country through Leach and Hamada, and they are to this day an important part of most potters' and students' repertoire.

Another manner in which the interests in Japan's folk-art tradition sustained itself in America was through the visits to Japan by several American potters. Their efforts to visit potters, village potteries and museums were prompted by a desire to gain first-hand knowledge of working methods, manner of living and ways of thinking in order to gain better insights into the long and colorful heritage of Japanese pottery. Among those who visited Japan during the 1950's were Paul Bogotay who went there in 1953, Herbert Sanders in 1956, Leon F. Moburg in 1957 and Marie Woo who was there in 1958 and several times thereafter. A number of other well established potters also visited Japan in the late 1950's and 1960's. These included Daniel Rhodes who went there in 1959, Karl Martz in 1963, Robert Sperry in 1965 and John Stephenson who returned in 1966.

Most of them wrote about their experiences in magazines such as *Craft Horizons* and *Ceramics Monthly*. Some of them also traveled to college and university art departments and presented slide lectures which dealt with their visits to Japan. Their topics usually included discussions of problems related to clay preparations, throwing, kiln construction, physical plants and other similar areas. They served as another means by which American potters gained further insights into the heritage and practices of Japanese pottery.

Toshiko Takeazu

In addition to Leach and Hamada and American potters who visited Japan there were others who came from the Orient to the United States who were influential in redirecting the philosophy of American pottery. Their work contained Oriental overtones, particularly in their approach to decoration. Among these were Hui Ka Kwong and Elizabeth Irwin who received their initial pottery training in China. Harue O. McVey, Henry Takemoto and Toshiko Takeazu came from Hawaii. Of these, perhaps none had a more direct and dramatic influence which affected attitudes and new styles than did Miss Takeazu.

In 1950, Toshiko Takeazu received her undergraduate degree at the University of Hawaii where she studied with Claude Horan. In 1951, she came to America and began graduate work with Maija Grotell at Cranbrook Academy of Art. At that time the influences of Miss Grotell were visible in Takeazu's work, especially in the geometric orientation of her surface decorations. Once Toshiko Takeazu left Cranbrook to assume teaching positions at the University of Wisconsin and the Cleveland Art Institute, a style of her own began to emerge. The work produced at Wisconsin and Cleveland consisted of forms which included simple ovoid vases, bottles and platters. These were enhanced with deftly brushed decorations of various kinds of slips, often of cobalt or copper used under or over matt glazes.

The pottery forms with which she has become identified were those which evolved over a five year period starting in 1951. This began with the idea of a tea pot which had similar designs for the spout and handle, varying only in their proportions. This design was further explored as a possibility for a wine bottle and finally resulted in a non-utilitarian, two-spouted bottle form. This in turn metamorphosed into a double vase which has been considered by some as Miss Takeazu's masterpiece. It was through the latter forms that she became well known as a potter. They were consistently accepted in competitive shows in this country and frequently singled out for awards (Fig. 9-8).

She continued to refine and simplify the form, so that at the end of the five year period she was again dealing with the previous forms, the single-spouted, closed pots. These were created by throwing a completely closed pot. When it was leather hard the pot was patted and altered so that the shape was subtly nonsymmetrical. The tops of some of these pots were accentuated with very small coils of clay. She contemplated the appropriate brush work and glazing which would enhance a particular form. The slip decorations on her pots illustrated an immediacy and confidence that can only be gained through careful consideration of the problem of where and how to apply a specific decoration. Once this had been decided, her execution of the design was swift. Conrad Brown observed her doing this and related the following:

> She does not plan the decoration of her pots until after the pots are made. To "free her hand" for the business of decorating she often goes through a ritual of uninhibited brush work on a tabletop, a kind of direct stimulation of her kinesthetic responses. The mental state she seeks may require 10 minutes of play with the brush, waiting until her hand is instantly transcribing the calligraphic ideas that go surging through her mind. She may even do very free pencil sketches right on the waiting pot—"but I never once followed the pencil lines with the brush."[14]

In a desire to find out more about her heritage and its relationship to her art, she traveled to Japan in order to study more intimately the meaning of Zen and "to meet some Japanese who had found serenity." She has said, "I always felt in anything that was good a sense of serenity no matter how alive the form or line might be."[15] During her stay in Japan she visited many of the country's leading potters. It was doubtful that her visit influenced her work stylistically to any great degree. She reflected on this when she said: "You don't hold onto this heritage because tradition can be deadening if you merely hold on to it—one has to go on once one has absorbed it."[16]

With this in mind she has continued to work at an increasing pace. She expanded her versatility in exploring the problems of colors at high temperatures, of searching for new forms and of resolving such problems as working with white glazes over thrown porcelain forms.

Miss Takeazu's place in the mainstream of American studio-pottery has been well established, and her influence has been deeply felt by students and other potters. Examples by Carlton F. Ball, Catherine Choy and Edward Cromey illustrate work in a similar vein by others.

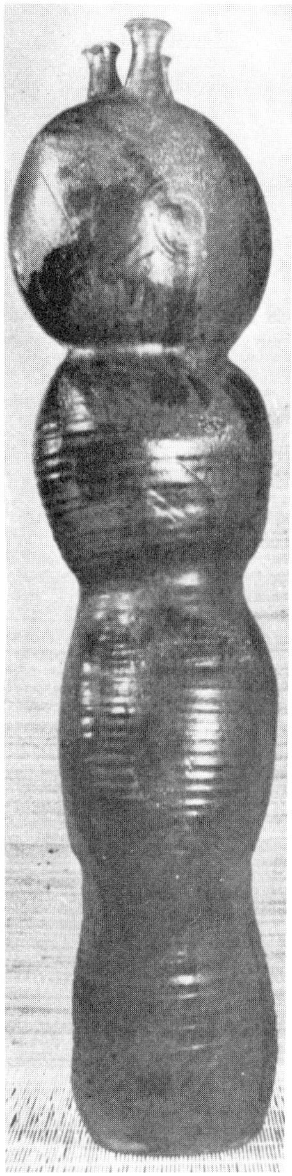

Figure 9-8. Toshiko Takeazu, Multiple Form, wheel thrown of several sections, slightly altered, bone ash glaze, ca. 1960. The use of several thrown forms which were stacked on top of each other and then topped with multiple spouts was popular with numerous potters during the 1950's.

More importantly, however, Takeazu aided in reinforcing the notion that

> a pot should be a flexibility in response to the developing piece which allows the creative impetus to shift from the dominance of the potter to the evolving shapes which the medium itself seems to desire.[17]

Indeed, the idea that the final result was dependent on the artist's intuition in regard to the proper balance of relationships seemed to be an integral part of her aesthetic. Her main contribution appears to have been the unpretentiousness and formal simplicity of her work.

Scandinavian Design

Contemporary Scandinavian design was another influence on some American potters. Finnish, Danish, Norwegian and Swedish crafts, particularly pottery, came to the attention of Americans in two ways: exhibitions sponsored by major museums and galleries and increased interest by retail merchants in handling Scandinavian products.

One of the exhibitions which exposed Americans to Scandinavian design in general and to pottery in particular was the "Good Design" show sponsored by the New York Museum of Modern Art in 1949. The major portion of this, the first of five annual shows, was devoted to Scandinavian crafts designed for daily use. Under the direction of Edgar Kaufmann the exhibit contained a listing of over 250 items which represented the best available examples of design and craftsmanship in modern home furnishings. This included wood, glass, silver, fabrics, porcelain, earthenware and stoneware. The exhibit traveled from New York to all major museums in America and terminated at the Merchandise Mart in Chicago, Illinois. Widespread exposure to the contents of this show was gained through wide and sympathetic press coverage.

Another comprehensive exhibition of Scandinavians' pottery and other crafts was sponsored by the American Federation of Arts in 1953. The show was titled "Design in Scandinavia" and traveled throughout the United States. Through events such as these Americans became more familiar with contemporary crafts being made in the Scandinavian countries. Potters began to recognize the names and work of ceramists such as Lindberg, Salmenhaara, Bengston, Hackman, Kage, Nylund, Stalhane and others. These artists, in part, represented the Scandinavian countries' most contemporary trends in ceramic design (Fig. 9-9). Of these, some highly popular work came from Sweden's Stig Lindberg and Finland's Kyllikki Salmenhaara.

Lindberg's utilitarian and decorative work in bone china, stoneware and earthenware appeared to be especially appropriate for newly designed homes and interior accessories which stressed the importance of function and structure as the basis of appearance. In his association with the Gustavsberg Porcelain Factory he created a seemingly unlimited quantity of highly original forms. Lindberg's significance to American potters was, however, related to the work he produced not for the factory but as individual pieces. It was in this capacity that he displayed his greatest versatility.[18]

Working on the wheel allowed Lindberg maximum freedom in experimenting with various forms. His work ranged from the whimsical to the primitive, and from informal-

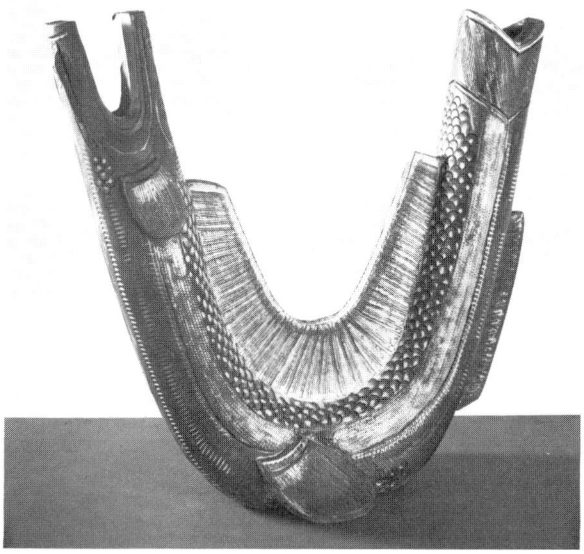

Figure 9-9. Wilhelm Kage, "Fish," stoneware sculptural vase, blue and brown slips, matt yellow glaze, 20″ × 21″, on view at the Metropolitan Museum of Art, New York, in the 1959 Ceramic International Exhibition. Everson Museum of Art Permanent Collection.

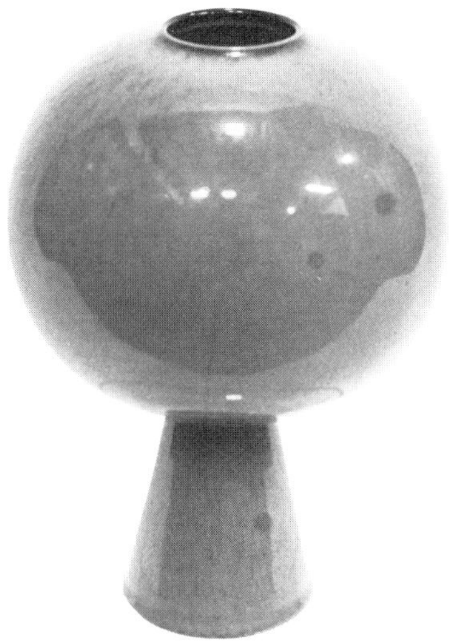

Figure 9-10. Stig Lindberg, Footed Vase, porcelain, wheel thrown, light blue porcelain glaze. Everson Museum Permanent Collection.

ly thrown pots to a machine-like quality achieved through precise tooling and finishing. The latter characteristics have identified his most popular pots. He created elegant forms and surfaces that were difficult to identify as thrown on the wheel or cast from a mold (Fig. 9-10). Especially conspicuous were the designs of pots which displayed an elongated, vertical thrust. The forceful direction of these shapes terminated with sudden changes at the top. Less dramatic changes were created by trimming the rims of symmetrical vases in a free-form manner, which provides a sharp contrast to the otherwise equally balanced proportions. An element of unity was achieved in all of his work through the use of uniform glazes and textures. Most variety in surface quality came about as a result of the glazes having collected at a particular part of the pot.

Lindberg's work received widespread publicity and exposure not only through exhibitions, but also through frequent articles in America's and Europe's popular interior design and crafts magazines. Among them were *Kontur, Form, Design, House Beautiful, Domus, Esquire* and *Crafts Horizons*. Another source of contact with Lindberg's, as well as other Scandinavians' work, was Bonniers of New York City. It has been and is today one of the distinctive retail outlets which sells the Scandinavian crafts.

Finland's foremost potter was Kyllikki Salmenhaara. Her work was notable for a vigorous quality which was not as dominant in the work of some of her contemporaries. Her pottery was thrown with a verve that contrasted starkly with the more refined work of Lindberg and other artists. Depressions from the fingers as the clay was pulled vertically on the wheel remained as an integral part of the pot's total design. Her approach to decorating and glazing was also unique. "Her own oxide glazes are reminiscent of birch bark, autumn leaves, reindeer lichens or the rugged surfaces of Finnish granite."[19] Simple matt glazes aided in revealing the impurities of the clay in reduction firing and further added to the straightforward, spontaneous handling of the medium.

Among other notable Scandinavian potters was Bernt Friberg. Like most of his colleagues, he preferred to work in stoneware. His pieces, most of which were decorative, depended mainly on glaze subtleties for special effects. Reminiscent of Persian influences, his bottles are characterized by sinuous, flowing, restful lines and smooth glazes. They vary in size from large floor pieces to tiny palm-sized bottles. Whatever scale his work assumes it does not detract from harmony of form, color and texture.

One of the oldest and best established potters whose work Americans began to know was Wilhelm Kage. His involvement in pottery dates back to 1917, but it was after 1930 that Kage became one of Sweden's important potters. By the late 1940's his reputation as a creator of unique and individual ceramics was well established. His experiments with glazes prepared by factory chemists are especially noteworthy. Seeking to go beyond the uniformity of these glazes, and having had no intimate knowledge of glaze chemistry, Kage started to "tinker them up" by various means. He was able to achieve unusual effects of color and texture.[20] His improvisations with glazes produced porcelain, stoneware and earthenware pottery of simple forms decorated with exotic glazes. These included variations of crystalline, irridescent, matt and opaque surfaces. His type of work seems to relate to pottery made by some Americans who were also dealing with utilizing exotic glazes of the past on relatively simple forms.

Several American potters have indicated that the work of the Scandinavians was of enough influence to become an integral part of the form language of a number of potters who were trained from approximately 1952 to 1956.[21] Irwin Whitacker recounted that "we were strongly impressed by Wilhelm Kage. In fact, Harrison MacIntosh still reflects the impact that Kage had on us all at that time."[22] The work of MacIntosh was a good example of one type of influence that was absorbed from the work of the Scandinavian potters. His pots were always designed for use in connection with the kitchen or dining room. At the same time, he allowed these forms to become the subject of various decorative techniques (Figs. 9-11 and 9-12). The contours of the pots were characterized by smooth flowing curves and the decorations, usually of a linear, completely abstract type, created a sharp contrast. The decorations were usually arrived at through variations of sgraffito, wax-resist or slip decorating. His work was also marked by a subtle use of rich, warm colors. This contrasted strongly with the exposed body of the white clay.

Referring to the Scandinavian work, Ernie Kim pointed out, "I was influenced at one time with the Scandinavian ware—slick and clean,"[23] while Glenn Nelson recalled that "my greatest influence has come from Scandinavia."[24] The emulation by some potters of Scandinavian designs became manifest in an insurgent interest in making clean, simple forms, particularly in the closed bottle shape with attenuated necks and small openings.

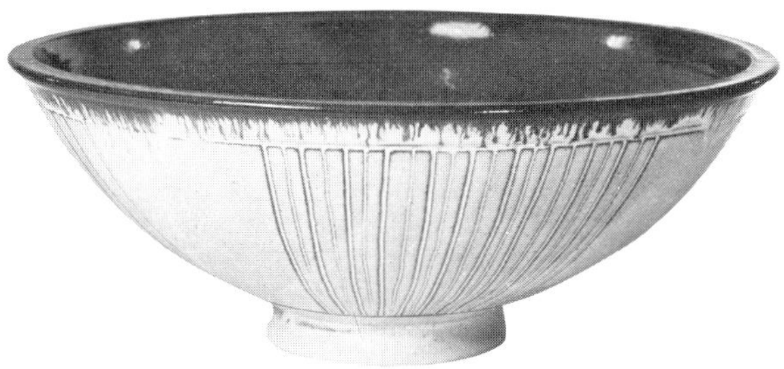

Figure 9-11. Harrison McIntosh, Bowl, stoneware, wheel thrown, beige mat glaze outside and dark brown glaze inside, 1954. Collection of the artist. Much of McIntosh's work reflects the influence of contemporary Scandanavian ceramic design with its emphasis on simple shapes and clear decorations.

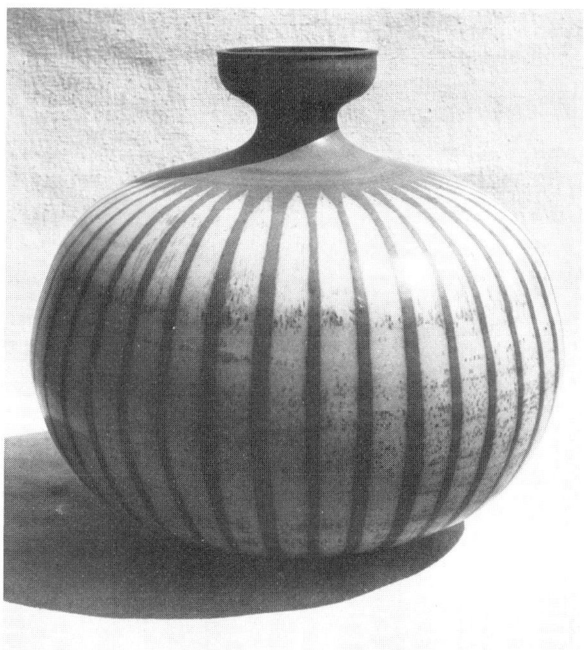

Figure 9-12. Harrison McIntosh, Vase, stoneware, wheel thrown, 13 1/2″ × 15 1/2″, ca. 1960. Everson Museum of Art Permanent Collection.

Additional European-trained Potters in America

The arrival of a number of European-trained potters in America, as exemplified by such people as Marguerite Wildenhain, Maija Grotell and Gertrude and Otto Natzler, continued into the 1950's. Dirk Hubers and Nicolas Vergette are two examples of potters who, through their distinctive form language, added to the diversity of style and attitudes which comprised the American studio-pottery scene during the 1950's.

Dirk Hubers

Dirk Hubers obtained his initial training in ceramics at the Amsterdam Arts-Crafts School where he came into contact with the traditional European method of working primarily with porcelain and plaster molds. The concern at that time, according to Mr. Hubers, was the ability to design specific forms and then to reproduce these through the use of molds. Equally important was the successful use of a vast array of "clever" glazes.[25] Upon his arrival in the United States he studied with Marguerite Wildenhain, whose idea of throwing numerous pots and keeping only one or two of the best examples was a completely new method of working. It was this specific influence which he felt "upgraded my personal standard of work to a much higher level."[26]

In addition to his contact with Marguerite Wildenhain his new interest in Pre-Columbian art served as a strong factor in re-evaluating his previous training in Europe, which he felt to be stagnant and stilted. Referring to his excitement about primitive art he said, "Clay functioned as a creative medium; these people used clay to express the phenomenal level of their culture."[27]

Mr. Hubers of the art staff at Newcomb College since 1955, represents another phase of the European-trained potter who reacted to industrial ceramics by creating individual forms in which a high degree of inventiveness and experimentation was sought. Hubers recalled the restrictions imposed by manufacturers and the schools that were preparing craftsmen for them. He pointed out that "despite their insistence on some fundamentals it all resulted in a reaction against it."[28] Mr. Hubers' pottery dramatizes this reaction quite vividly. His concern for creating large free-form pieces which are richly imbued with a variety of textures serve as vigorous statements against the sterile forms that are sometimes associated with mass-produced pottery.

Nicolas Vergette

Nicolas Vergette of Southern Illinois University represents another example of the European-trained artist, who, upon immigrating to the United States in 1957, added to the diversity of styles and attitudes already in existence.

Vergette received his training at the London University and Central School of Art, London. Most of his instructors were educated at Stoke-on-Trent, England, in the area of ceramics. They promulgated the notions of William Morris, and emphasis was placed upon producing "technically perfect work, incorporating traditional forms and modes of decoration."[29]

Although his early training in pottery resulted in "a great deal of technical knowledge and respect for the craft," it also served to create a reaction "against their point of view in regard to the nature, use of pottery and relation of the craftsman to society."[30] Vergette apparently refers to an overemphasis on technical matters and a de-emphasis on artistic problem solving. As such, his reactions were probably founded on the restrictions of this system. These limitations were noticeable in the denial of pottery as a medium for anything other than essentially utilitarian considerations. Although ceramic sculpture existed, the idea of creating a form that was derivative of a thrown pot, but made for purely decorative purposes in which any obvious utility was negated, must have seemed somewhat incongruous.

Even the work of Bernard Leach was not sufficient to provide a new direction for Vergette whose approach to pottery was very unlike that of his contemporaries in England. Well known studio-potters in England during the 1930's and 1940's were Michael Cardew, Staite Murray, Samuel Haile and Bernard Leach. Their primary concern was with perpetuating a tradition which represented a synthesis of English stoneware and some aspects of Oriental folk art.

After his arrival in the United States, Vergette was strongly influenced by Expressionist painters and sculptors. His pottery includes influences of both. Much of the pottery he created illustrates a rather conscious concern for highly textural qualities. Whether the forms he made were a departure from a classical bottle-shape or whether a completely non-utilitarian ovoid was created, the surfaces of these have an immediate impact (Fig. 9-13).

Plate 1. Pennsylvania Dutch Plate, 18th century.

Plate 2. Rookwood Pottery, 1899.

Plate 3. Teco Pottery, ca. 1910.

Plate 4. Karl Martz, bowl, 1937.

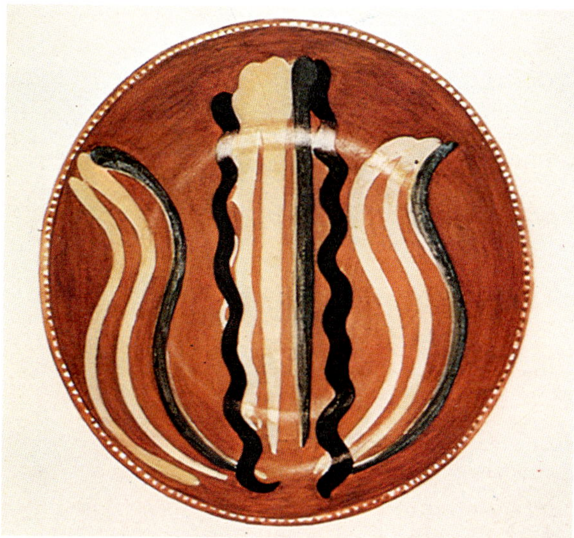

1

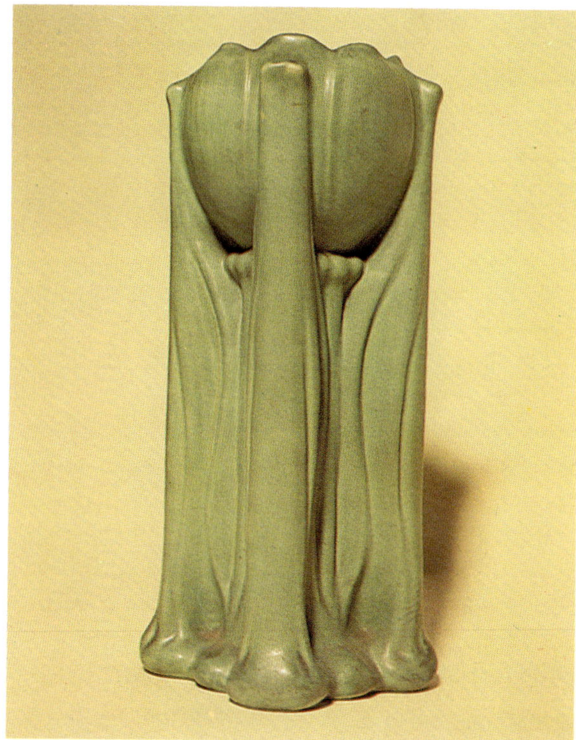

3

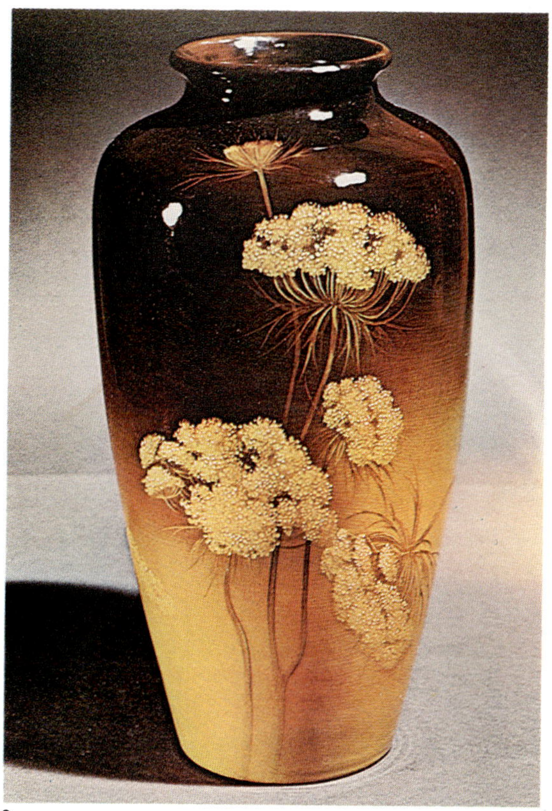

2

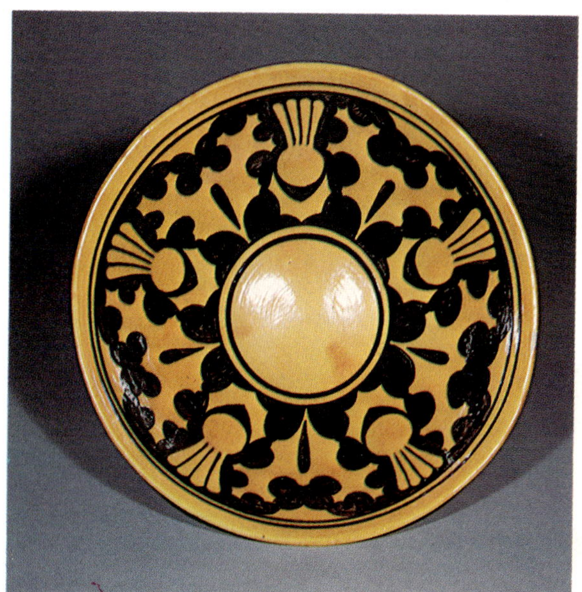

4

Plate 5. A.R. Deyer, plate; Leon Volkmar, vase, both 1948.

Plate 6. Gertrude and Otto Natzler, bowl.

Plate 7. Franz Wildenhain, plate, 1953.

Plate 8. David Gill, assorted pots, 1951.

Plate 9. J. Sheldon Carey, covered urn, 1958.

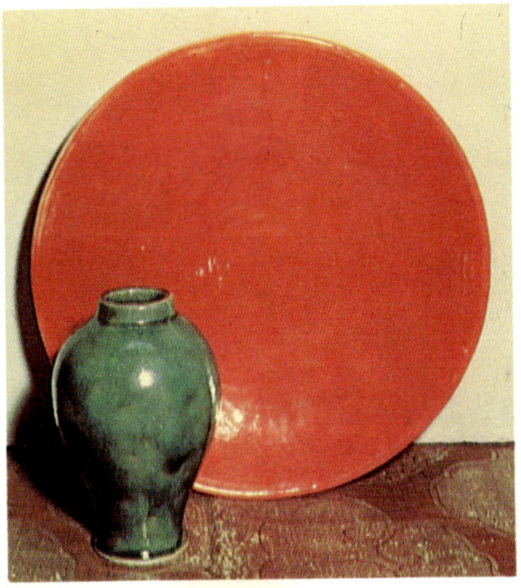

5

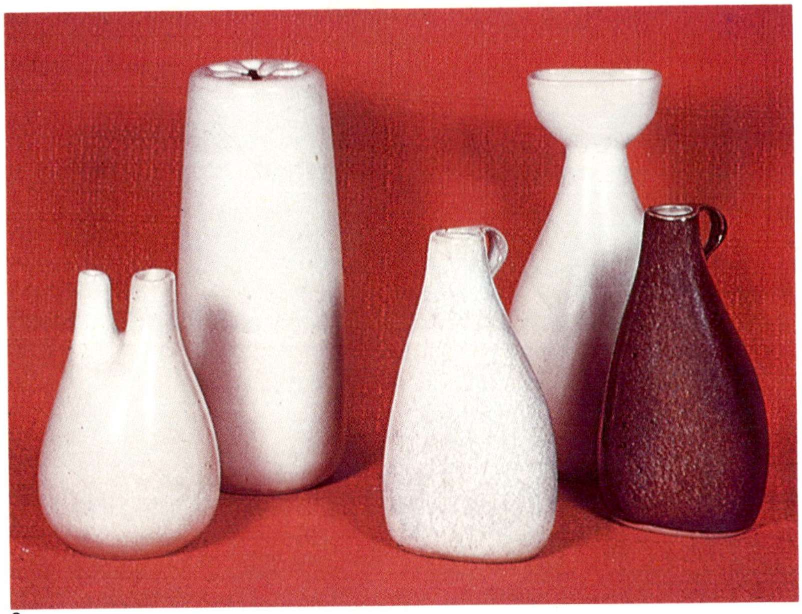

8

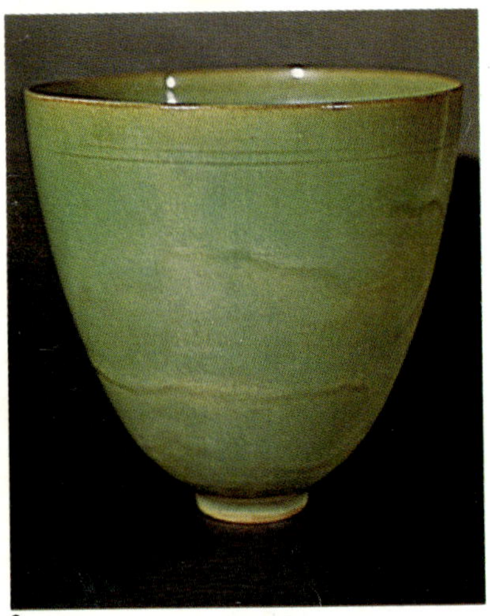

6

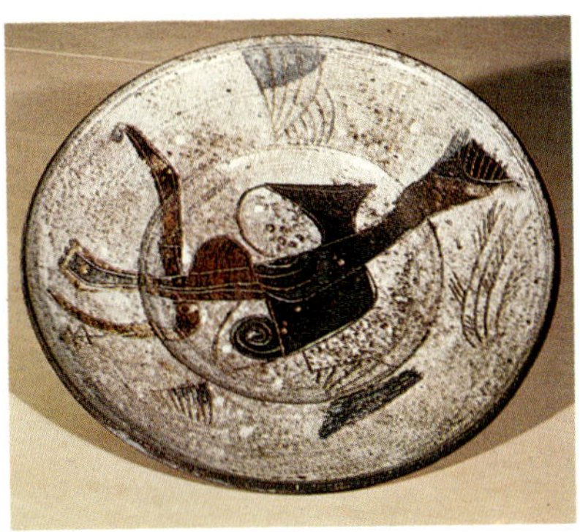

7

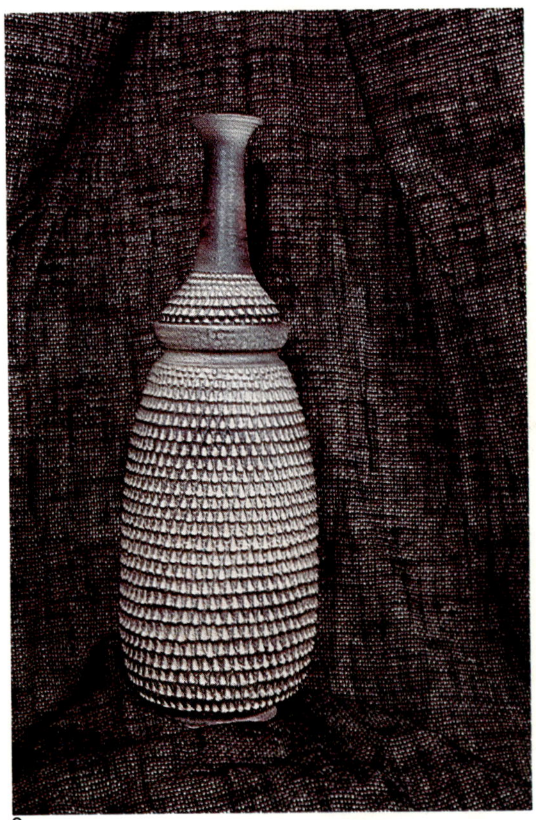

9

Plate 10. Peter Voulkos, Cross Pot, 1959.

Plate 11. Peter Voulkos, plate, ca. 1957.

Plate 12. James Leedy, ceramic sculpture.

Plate 13. Timothy Mather, ceramic form, ca. 1963.

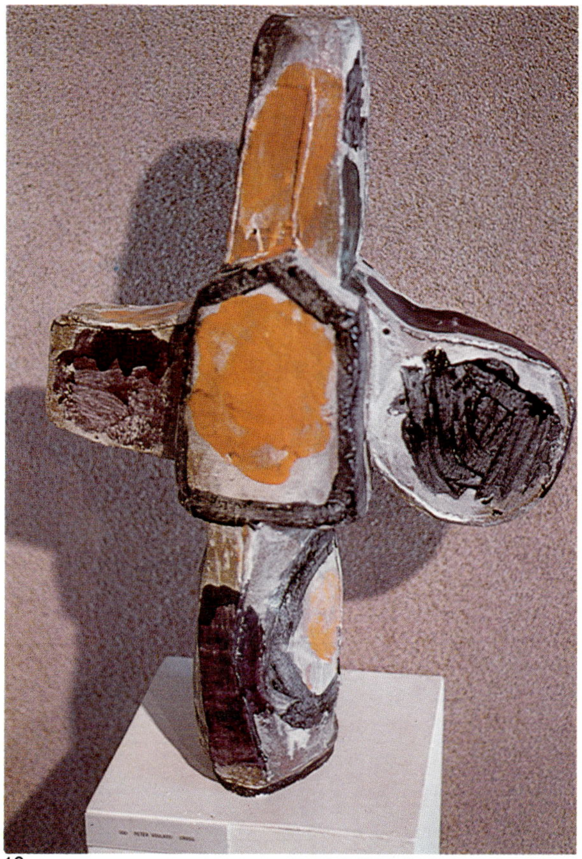

10

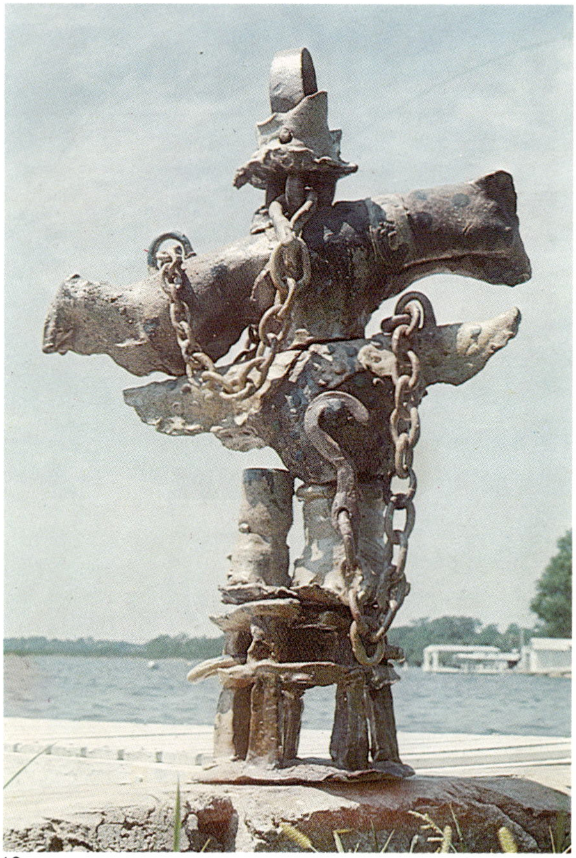

12

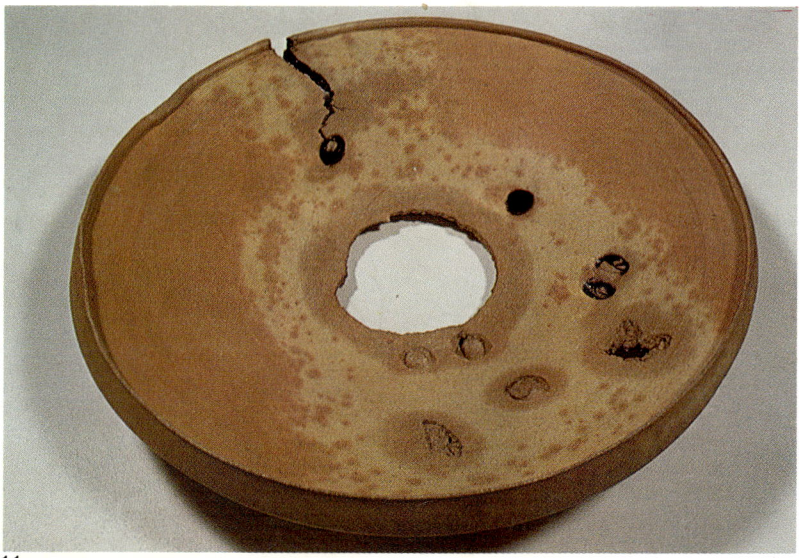

11

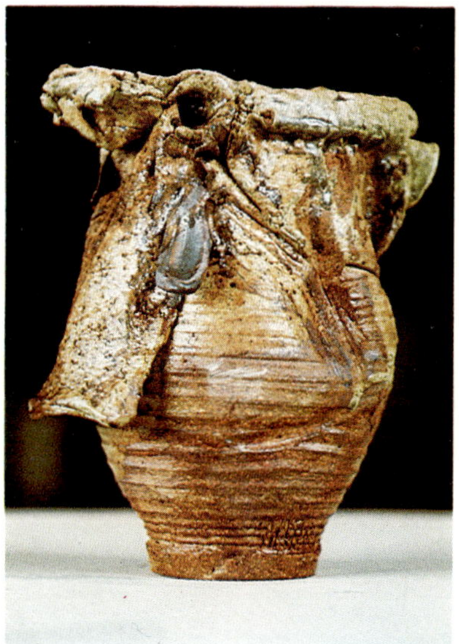

13

Plate 14. Robert Arneson, Landscape Cup, 1967.

Plate 15. Robert Arneson, Trophy, 1964.

Plate 16. Curtis Hoard, ceramic sculpture, ca. 1967.

Plate 17. Patti Warashina, Car Kiln, ca. 1972.

Plate 18. Richard Shaw, ceramic sculpture, 1976.

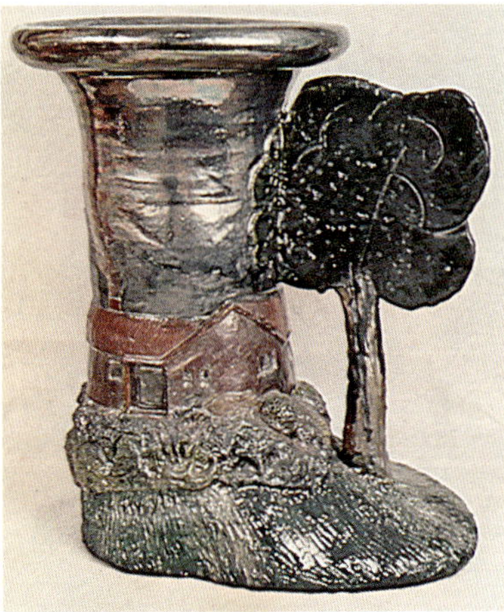

14

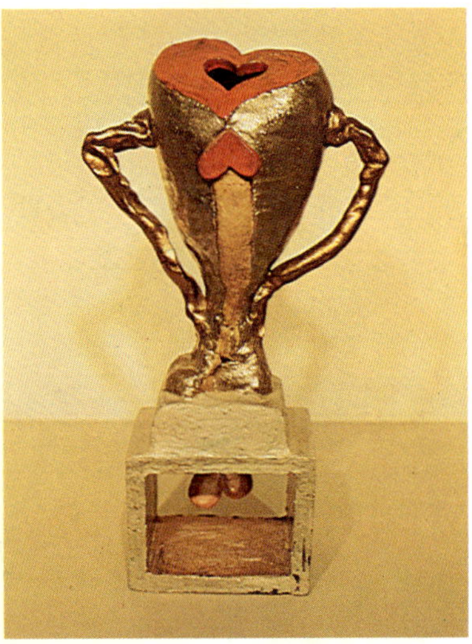

15

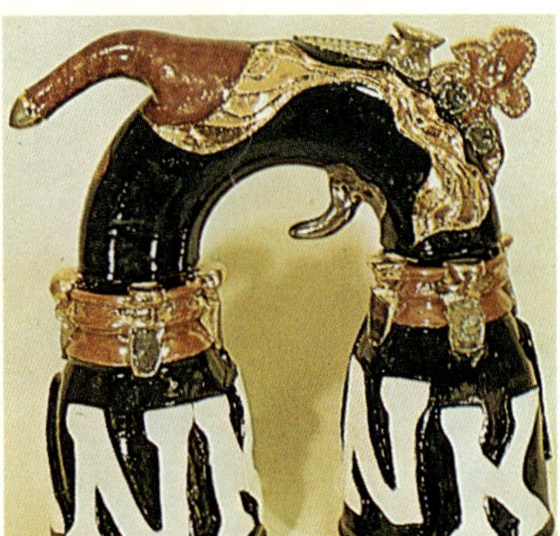

16

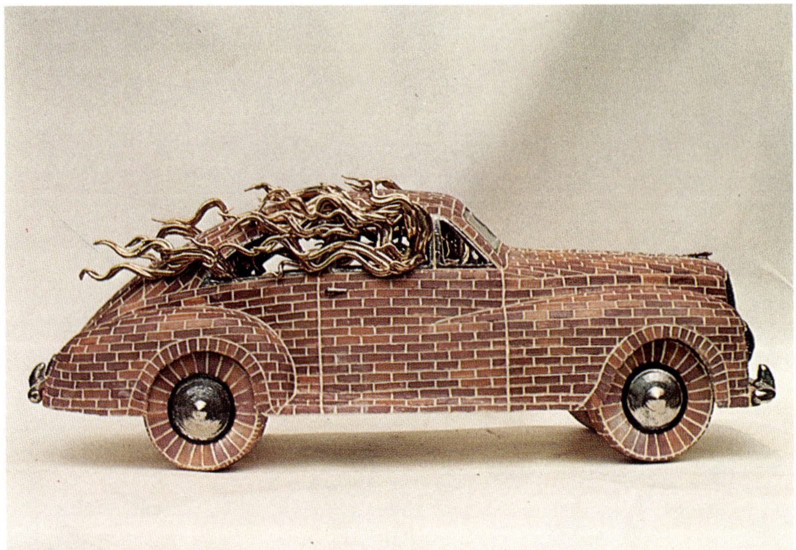

17

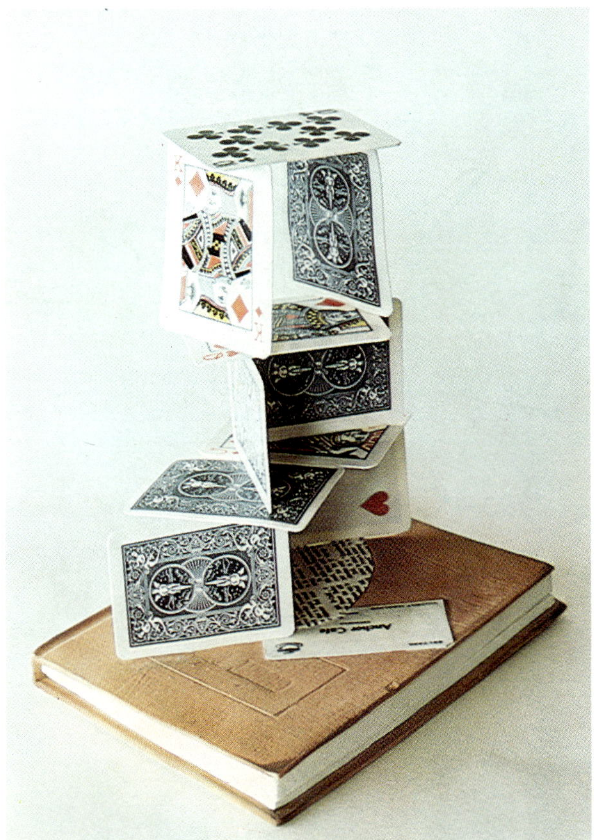

18

Plate 19. Clayton Bailey, Kaolithic Fossil, ca. 1973.

Plate 20. Roy Lichtenstein, ceramic sculpture.

Plate 21. Norris Dalton, Sandwich Plate, 1973.

Plate 22. Victor Spinski, ceramic sculpture.

Plate 23. Sandy Shannenhouse, Candy Box, 1969.

Plate 24. Dick Hay, Woman's Club Sandwich, 1972.

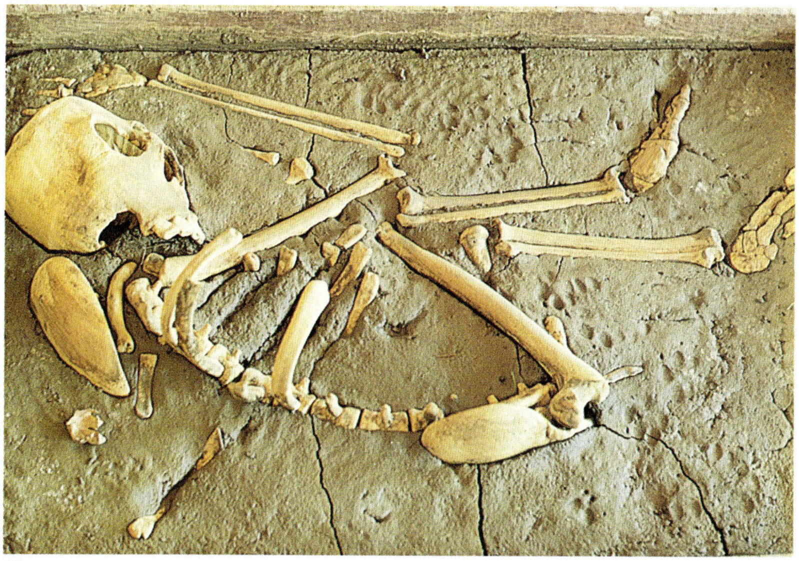

19

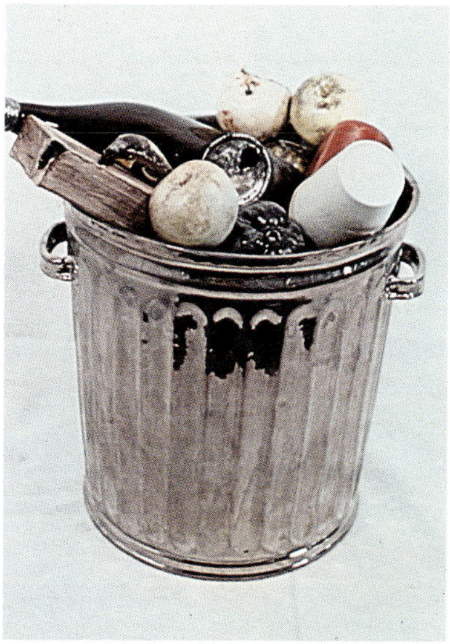

22

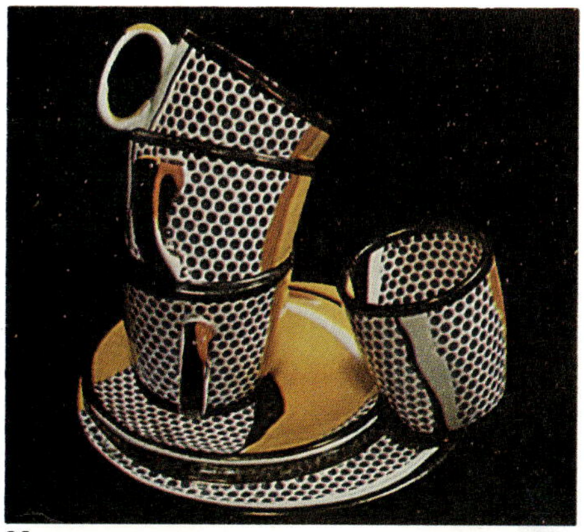

20

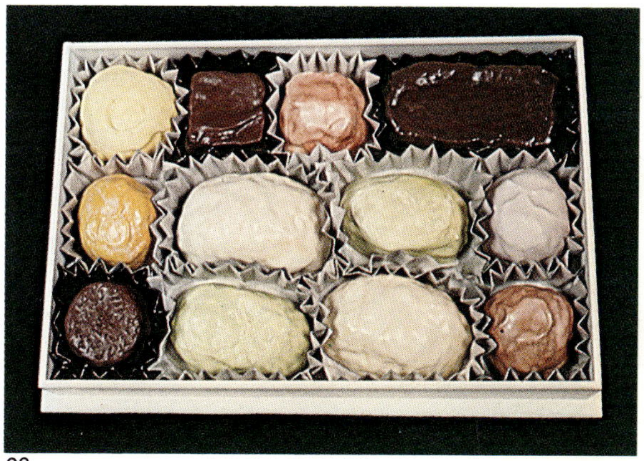

23

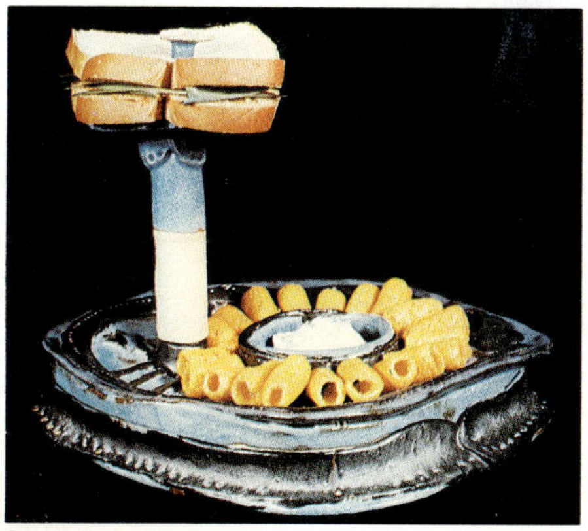

21

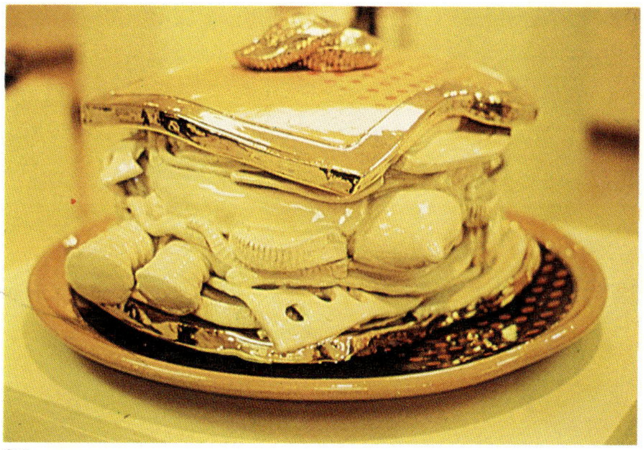

24

Plate 25. Hui Ka Kwong, sculpture.

Plate 26. James Melchert, Mickey Mouse Plate, 1964.

Plate 27. Bill Farrell, sculpture, 1970.

Plate 28. Robert Ransom, "B-Girls,' " 1972.

Plate 29. Erik Gronborg, dish, 1976.

Plate 30. Susan Stephenson, construction, 1975.

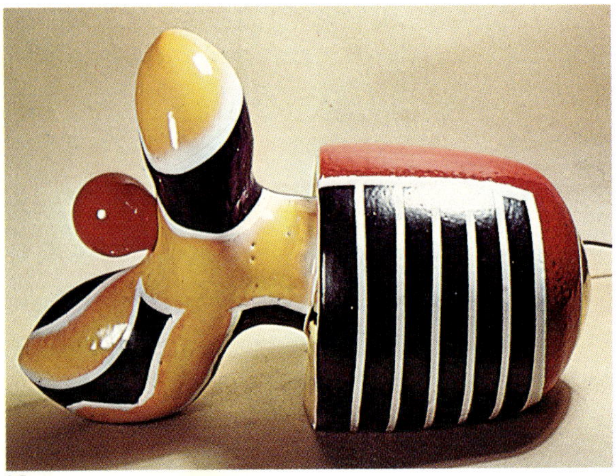
25

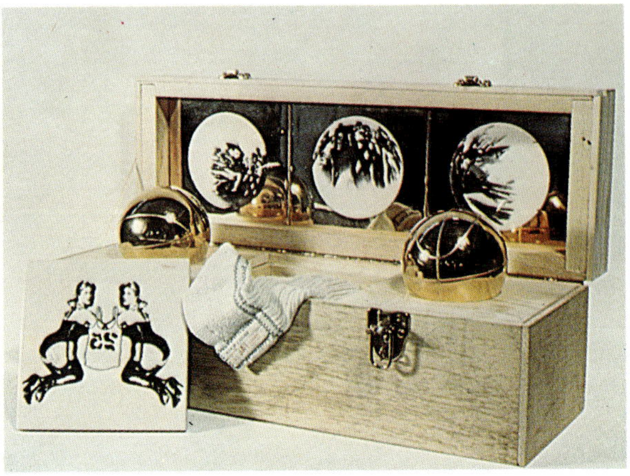
28

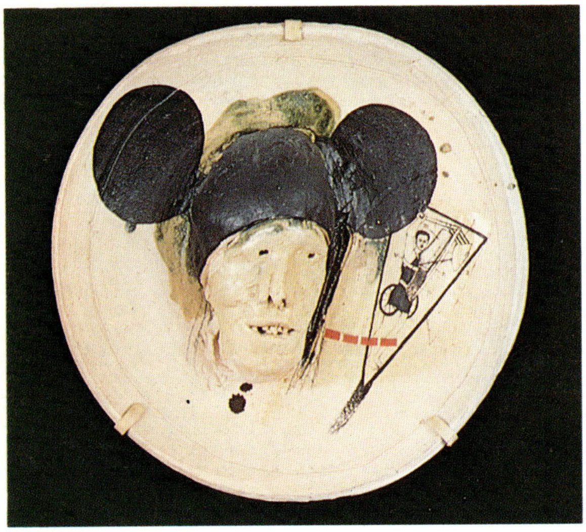
26

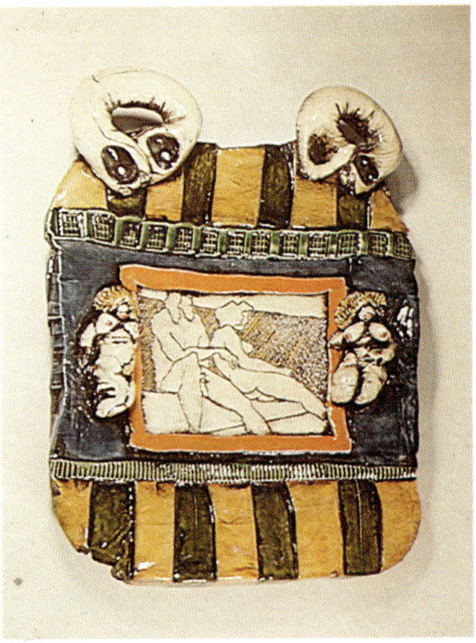
29

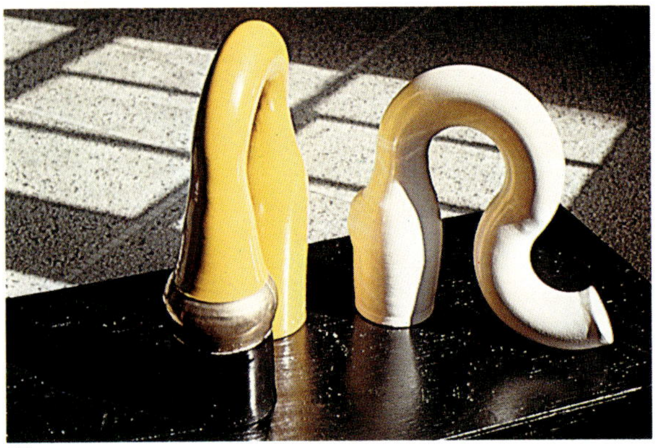
27

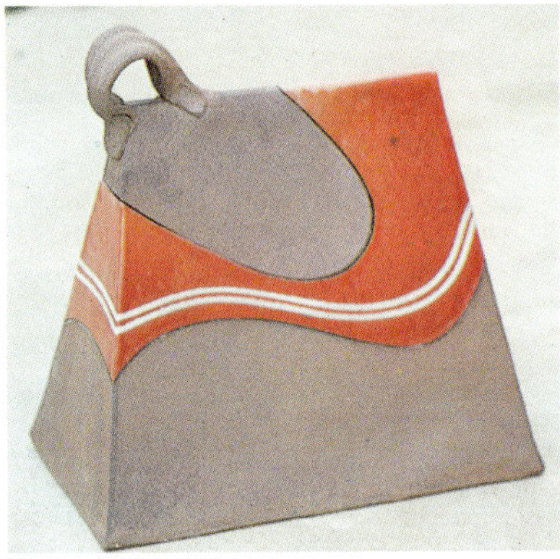
30

Plate 31. Merilyn Levine, "Trent's Jacket," 1976.

Plate 32. Ron Nagle, cup.

Plate 33. Ron Nagle, cup.

Plate 34. Gibson Strawn, covered jar, 1976.

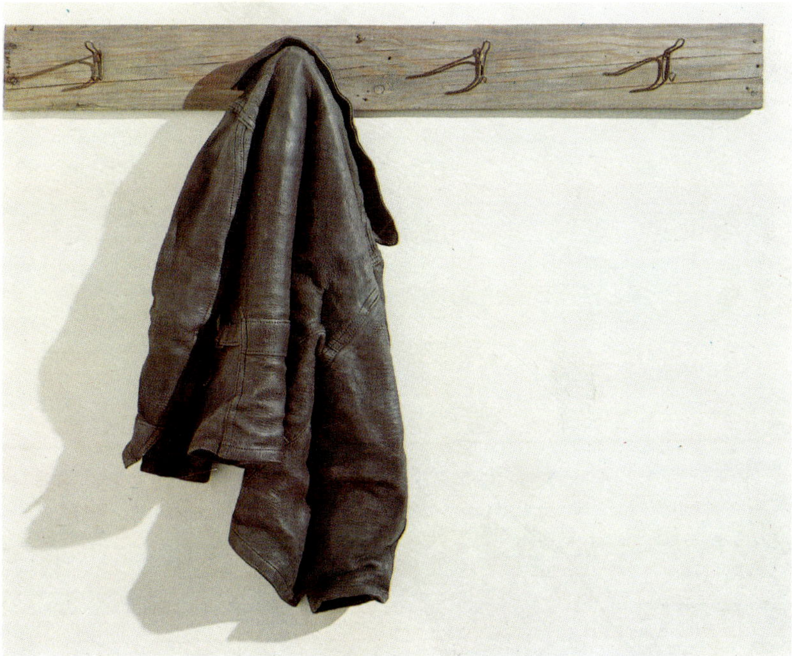

31

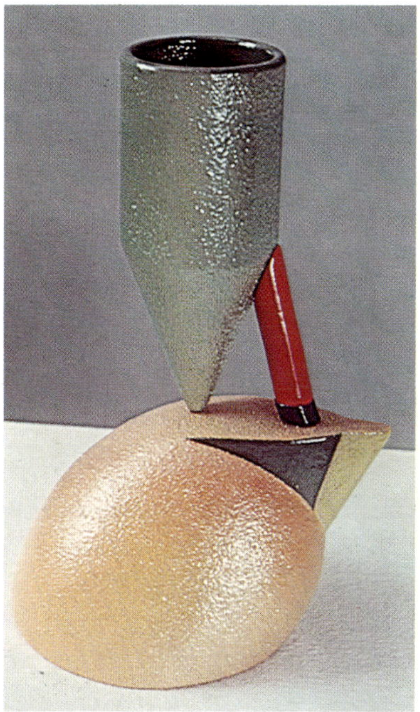

33

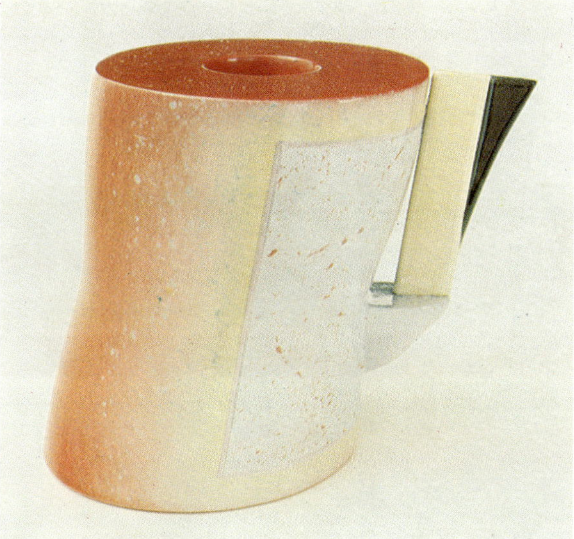

32

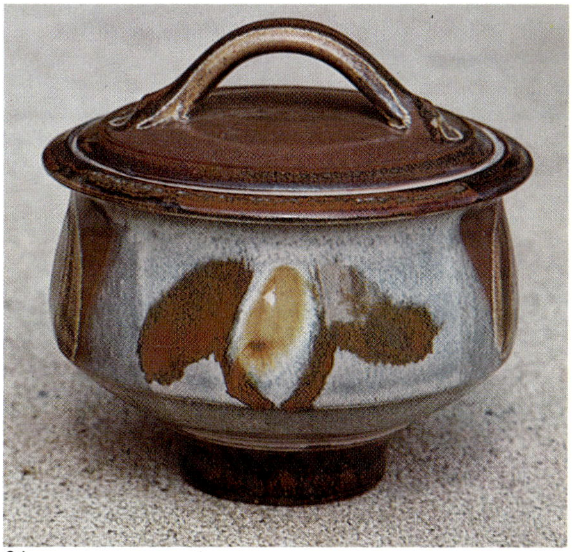

34

Plate 35. Donald Reitz, platter, 1974.

Plate 36. Margie Hughto, plaque, 1977.

Plate 37. Paul S. Donhauser, Sectioned Interior, 1977.

Plate 38. Paul S. Donhauser, spherical sculpture, 1977.

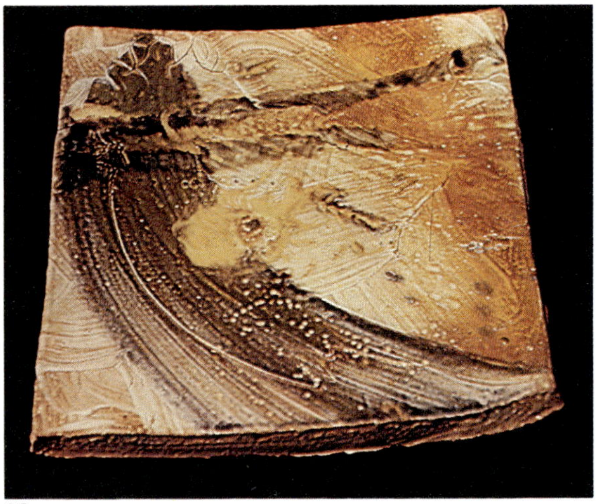

35

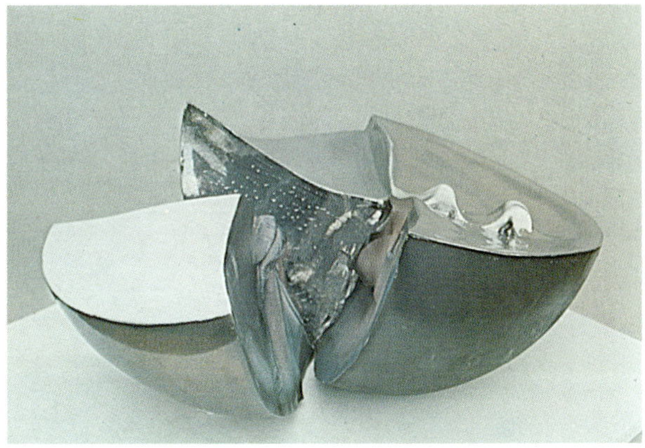

37

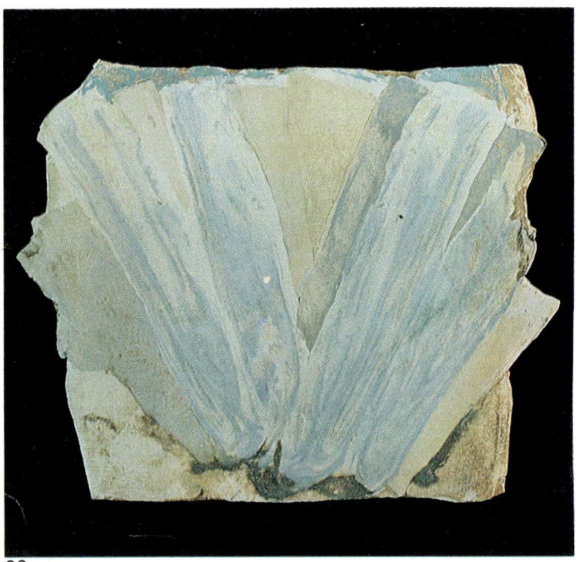

36

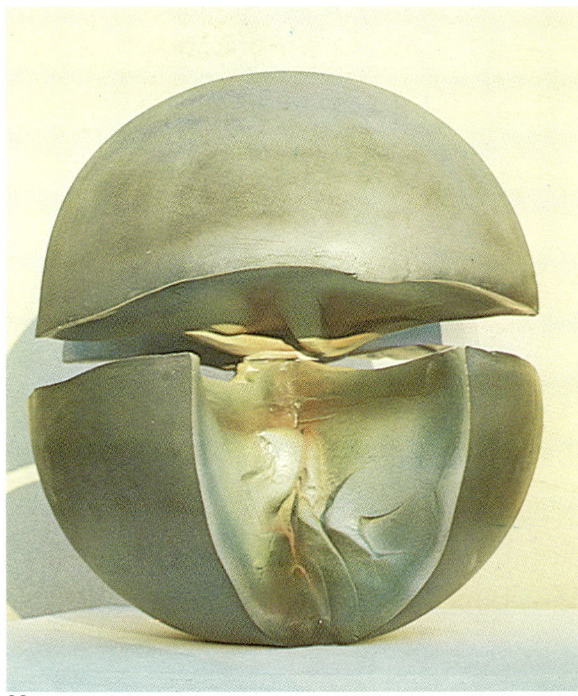

38

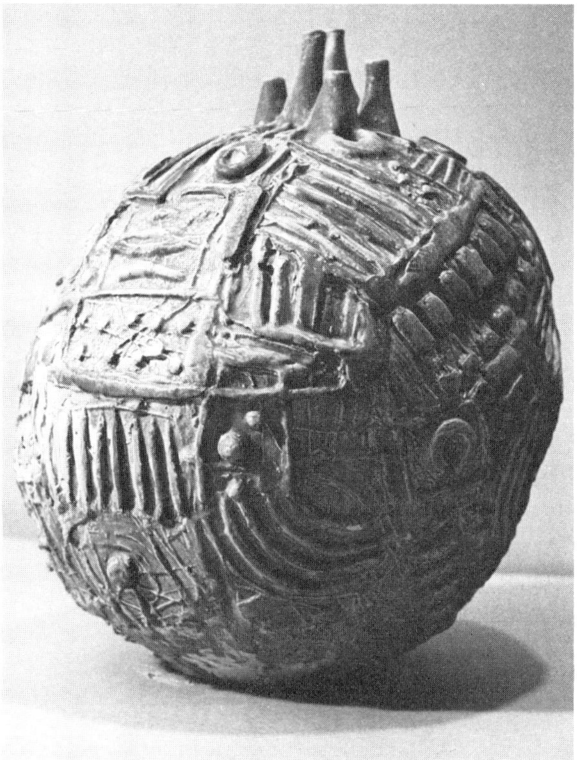

Figure 9-13. Nicholas Vergette, Ceramic Form, hand-built, stoneware, gray-blue glaze, 26″ × 23″. Courtesy of Mrs. Helen Vergette.

This was not arrived at merely through the manipulation of slips or glazes, nor through the introduction of various kinds of materials such as grog or sand. Instead, they are the result of molding, carving or incising to a degree which closely approaches a bas-relief. The relief was sometimes further accentuated through the use of slips and glazes.

Since 1950 Vergette's versatility and artistic competence in the area of ceramics has been acknowledged. He has served on numerous juries at the regional and national level, and has received several important architectural commissions. His work has been consistently accepted in major ceramics competitive exhibitions.

The Oriental and Scandinavian characteristics which have been discussed had several consequences on styles and attitudes of potters that worked after World War II.

The Oriental influence introduced through Bernard Leach, by potters who came to the United States with Oriental backgrounds or training and by Americans who visited Japan provided the studio-potter with a new aesthetic regarding clay bodies, slips, glazes and kilns. Techniques of throwing, decorating, glazing and firing which were quite different from those practiced by American potters in the past also aided in increasing the potter's vocabulary. With these new precepts American potters fashioned for themselves a distinctive form language in pottery. Oriental overtones were evident in many potters' work, but the new influences were quickly assimilated and redefined so that concepts and attitudes toward pottery were formed that were uniquely American. Although a number of potters created what had been referred to by some as pseudo-Oriental pottery, the important contribution of the Oriental influence, particularly that of Japanese folk-art pottery, was a new approach to pottery. This manifested itself in a more direct handling of material where one could note a more fearless approach to throwing, decorating and glazing. Perhaps more important was that these methods suggested new relationships in pottery which were contrary to traditional ideas of art-pottery. Asymmetry of design and decoration, splashed and poured glazes, accidents, pits, dark spots and "dirty" glazes, which were the result of impurities of the clay and glaze, were part of an enthusiastic reaction against previous influences of the industrial design syndrome. The influence of Oriental ceramics was one of the first important signs that American potters were moving in new directions.

It is important to note that pottery created by some Scandinavian potters provided an additional catalyst which served to revitalize American design in pottery. Despite the fact that this source of design was of relatively minor consequence—since the largest number of potters tended to lean toward the Oriental influences discussed earlier—the interest generated by Scandinavian pottery was a stimulus to some craftsmen in this country in reconsidering problems of design and technique. The Scandinavian example may also have aided them in reaffirming their own faith in the importance of their creations.

Notes

1. The new firing technique referred to involved the creating of a reduction atmosphere in the kiln. This meant controlling the intake of oxygen and gas (or whatever other combustible fuel was used) in order to produce an incomplete combustion, hence free carbon. When this was done at a specific time during the firing, slips, glazes and clay bodies would be affected. The reduction atmosphere usually caused the impurities of the clays and glazes to become prominent in the forms of dark spots and the clay, if it remained unglazed, yielded a warm, tan or brown color. These characteristics were often in keeping with the stone-like quality of natural rock which became much admired by potters.
2. Bernard Leach, *A Potter's Book*, p. 101.
3. Ibid., p. 101.
4. Ibid., p. 102.
5. Catalog of the *12th Ceramic National Exhibition*, Syracuse Museum of Art, 1948, p. 20.
6. Daniel Rhodes, "Contemporary Pottery and High Fire," *Ceramics Monthly*, 1:11 (January, 1953).
7. Leach, p. 27.
8. Ibid., p. 27.
9. James Brownson, "Midwest Craftsmen's Seminar," *Ceramics Monthly*, 1:10 and 28 (February, 1953).
10. Leach, p. 28.
11. "An Open Letter to Bernard Leach from Marguerite Wildenhain," *Crafts Horizons*, 13:43-44 (May-June, 1953).
12. Brownson, p. 28.
13. Slip trailing is a technique whereby a clay, usually made to a creamy consistency, is placed in a rubber bulb or syringe, and is then squeezed onto a leather hard or bisque pot. Glaze can be used in place of slip.
14. Conrad Brown, "Toshiko Takeazu," *Crafts Horizons*, 19:26 (March-April, 1959).
15. Ibid., p. 26.
16. Ibid., p. 26.
17. Ibid., p. 26.
18. Arthur Hald, "Stig Lindberg, Artist in Clay," *Crafts Horizons*, 14:11-15 (October, 1954).
19. H.O. Gummerus, "Wellsprings of Scandinavian Design," *Crafts Horizons*, 16:30 (July-August, 1956).
20. K. L. Boyton, "Trio at Gustavsberg," *Ceramics Monthly*, 2:14-16 (August, 1954).
21. Among those who expressed their awareness of Scandinavian pottery and who felt that it was of notable consequence, although not necessarily in their own work, were Rudy Autio, Ronald Du Bois, Olin Russum, Paul Soldner, George Fetzer, Stanley Zilinsky, Don Finegan, Angelo Garzio, Glenn Nelson, Erwin Whitacker and Ernie Kim. Correspondence to the author.
22. Irwin Whitacker, Associate Professor of Art, Michigan State University, East Lansing, Mich., unpublished correspondence.

23. Ernie Kim, chairman, Department of Ceramics, California School of Fine Art, San Francisco, Calif., unpublished correspondence.
24. Glenn Nelson, Professor of Art, University of Minnesota, Duluth Branch, Duluth, Minn., unpublished correspondence.
25. Dirk Hubers, Professor of Ceramic Art, Newcomb College, Tulane University, New Orleans, La., unpublished correspondence.
26. Dirk Hubers, correspondence to author.
27. Hubers, correspondence to author.
28. Hubers, correspondence to author.
29. Nicolas Vergette, Associate Professor of Art, Southern Illinois University, Carbondale, Ill., unpublished correspondence.
30. Vergette, correspondence to author.

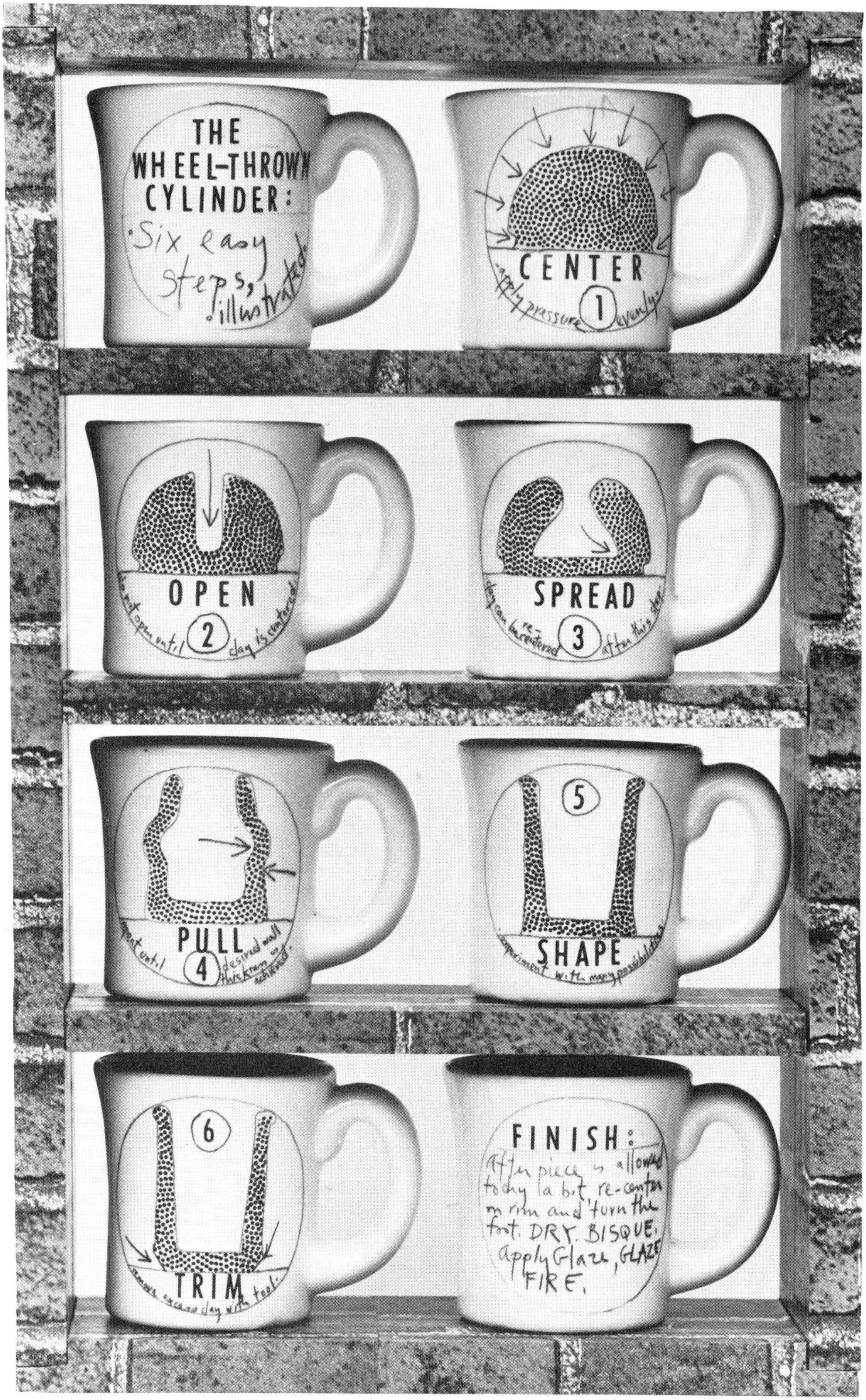
THE
WHEEL-THROWN
CYLINDER:
Six easy steps,
CENTER
1
apply pressure evenly
OPEN
2
do not open until clay is centered
SPREAD
3
clay can be re-centered after this step
PULL
4
repeat until desired wall thickness is achieved
5
SHAPE
experiment with many possibilities
6
TRIM
remove excess clay with tool
FINISH:
After piece is allowed to dry a bit, re-center on rim and turn the foot. DRY. BISQUE. apply Glaze, GLAZE FIRE.

Susan Parks

Expansion and Growth in Research, Publication and Schools 10

After 1945 studio-pottery expanded rapidly. This was due to several reasons. First, much of the research that had been carried on during the previous thirty years became the basis for several texts published between 1949 and 1959. Information contained in the texts was of significant assistance to students and potters. Secondly, the expansion of courses in ceramics at colleges and universities provided more opportunities for training. A more detailed account of these developments will help to provide insights into some of the causes that may have contributed to changing attitudes in American pottery from approximately 1948 to 1955.

Research and Publication

Limited research was carried on as early as 1910. Those involved in the investigations were usually connected with industry and therefore kept most of their findings secret. No significant texts dealing with pottery existed until Charles Binns published *The Potter's Craft* in 1910. The book contained much of his scientific research with clays and glazes, as well as some practical help for the beginner. It was the standard ceramic text for many years. Frederick Rhead's *Studio Pottery*, also published in 1910, offered helpful suggestions in all areas of pottery and was extensively illustrated. In 1922, Binns published his *Manual of Practical Potting* which was similar to his first book. George M. Forsyth wrote *Art and Craft of the Potter* in 1934. It was a highly condensed version of the information given in A.B. Searle's *An Encyclopedia of the Ceramic Industries*, published in 1930. Searle's book was a mine of information on clay bodies, glazes and kilns as they were used by industry. Between 1935 and 1949 relatively little publishing occurred in the form of texts which might have been useful to the potter or student. Leach's *A Potter's Book* of 1940 was a notable exception. However, beginning approximately around 1930 an increase in research began. This was carried on by industry in America and Europe, as well as by several people who taught ceramics in colleges and universities. Their findings were published in ceramic journals and other publications. These include *Ceramic Age*, *Ceramic Industry*, *Pottery Gazette*, *Keramische Zeitschrift*, and the *Bulletins* and *Journals of the American Ceramic Society*. Of these, the latter publication contained the largest amount of material related to problems of studio-pottery.[1]

For example, the availability and use of Feldspar for potters was discussed by Paul E. Knight.[2] Paul Cox reported on the matter of using a single clay rather than the combination of several types for composing a throwing body.[3] Glazes were also the subject of research by several people, many of whom were not potters. But their work supplied helpful suggestions to the reader of the *Bulletins of the American Ceramic Society*. The author compiled 83 references from the *Bulletins*, *Transactions* and *Journals* of this organization. These were published between 1920 and 1950, and each is a discussion of specific problems applicable to studio-pottery. The range of subject matter includes such items as crawling and crazing of glazes, Aventurine glazes, Bristol glazes, crystalline glazes, common defects in glazes, the use of engobes and slips, the use of fritted glazes, oxides in slips, matt glazes at various temperatures, ash glazes, wood ashes in low-fired matt glazes, porcelain bodies and glazes, turquoise alkaline glazes, the use of various chemicals such as talc, lithium carbonate and Rutile for special glaze effects, artificial reduction glazes, salt glazing, self-glazing slips, various types of stains for bodies, schedules for reduction firing, planning and operating an independent studio and many more topics.

Among those publishing research were potters who have become well established studio-potters, including Dorothy Perkins, Edgar Littlefield, Marion Fosdick, Arthur Baggs, Myrtle French, Karl Martz, Charles Harder, Theodore Randall, C.W. Parmelee, Paul Cox, Frederick Rhead, John Koenig, G.H. Norton, R.C. Purdy and others. The information in this accumulated research was the basis of several texts which started to appear with increasing frequency after 1949.

John B. Kenny's *Complete Book of Pottery Making,* published in 1949, was one of the standard texts for beginners. It contained a wealth of information about building processes, clays, glazes and firing, making it one of the best introductory sources. Ruth Home wrote *Ceramics for the Potter* in 1952. In it she discussed technical and artistic problems related to studio-pottery. F.H. Norton's *Ceramics for the Artist-Potter,* published in 1956 and Daniel Rhodes' *Clay and Glaze for the Potter* of 1959 presented a comprehensive range of data related to glaze chemistry, clay composition and firing processes as they applied to individual production. These texts were of a general nature and aided in supplying the potter with considerable technical information. It is difficult to imagine how potters would have operated without them. They were virtually the only means with which to translate the highly technical findings in glaze chemistry and clay compositions to a practical level where they could be used by studio-potters. For example, the conversion of equivalent weights to batch weights in glaze calculation has been of inestimable help to potters who may have had a limited working knowledge of glaze chemistry.

It has been difficult to ascertain how much and what type of influence this vast collection of material may have had on the attitudes and skills of potters during the 1950's. It is reasonable to assume, however, that the ready availability of information served to expedite the acquisition of a working knowledge of the various phases in pottery. Hence a potter was no longer forced to search for a particular clay body or a specific glaze. This was now common knowledge available in clear and well illustrated texts.

Equipment and raw materials were also more readily available. Texts written previous to 1950 did not contain significant sources for pottery supplies. Later, authors such as F.H. Norton and Glenn Nelson, who wrote *Ceramics for the Artist-Potter* and *Ceramics,* respectively, included in their books comprehensive lists of dealers and manufacturers from whom tools, equipment and materials could be purchased. The majority of these businesses dealt with large industrial concerns, but began to accommodate smaller orders. It was therefore possible to purchase relatively small quantities of glaze chemicals, clays, oxides, refractory materials and incidental tools and equipment without depending on local retail outlets.

Expansion of Ceramics at the College Level

After World War II an increase in American studio-pottery may be noted. In part this may have been due to increased enrollments in colleges and universities which were accommodating a sudden influx of veterans. A government survey of college and university enrollments indicated that "The total higher education enrollment for 1947-48 included more than a million veterans of World War II, whose education was partially paid for by the Federal Government."[4]

Ceramics courses at the college level also increased after the war. A survey by Dorothy W. Perkins indicated that between 1941 and 1951 an increase of ceramic offerings occurred at 92 colleges or universities. An additional 22 schools offered courses in pottery by 1955. This brought the total number of college art departments which taught some form of pottery to 187.[5] These findings substantiate the claim that ceramic education witnessed its most notable increase after World War II. This, in turn, may have accounted for more potters appearing on the contemporary scene.

Equally important were the aims of the ceramics programs. It is worth noting that the majority of these new courses were offered within fine arts curriculums, while previous to 1941 the preponderance of potters generally studied in industrial arts or other technical programs.

The significance of offering ceramics in a fine arts setting was that a changed emphasis began to develop in respect to methods, materials, tools, design-concepts and philosophy. Although the content within post-World War II ceramics programs was not altered significantly from those of previous years, the methods and emphasis did. For example, Perkins pointed out that of 365 ceramics departments queried in her study, 214 taught hand-building techniques, 197 throwing, 181 plaster mold making, 170 casting, 160 glaze preparation and 134 clay body composition and preparation.[6] It appears that more emphasis was placed on building techniques and less on the technical aspects of glaze chemistry, clay composition, kiln construction, and firing. Moreover, hand-building and throwing were stressed over other methods of construction. This was also substantiated by George Papas, who surveyed one hundred ceramics programs of colleges and universities in thirty-six states.[7]

Although most departments stressed at least a working knowledge of building processes, of raw materials, of glaze calculation and preparation, emphasis was given to their creative use. This meant that once the rudiments of pottery were accomplished, encouragement was given to explore further the possibilities of new forms which did not rely on precedent. It is not implied that heritage was dismissed as part of the guidelines for the development of taste and design, but now the stress was placed on investigating the intrinsic characteristics of the medium in order to deal more individually with form, color and decoration. This attitude may have found more popular acceptance because a majority of potters were trained and worked in other areas of the arts, such as sculpture, painting, drawing, design and graphics.

It was of no small consequence that more frequently people brought to the field of pottery the visual perceptions, the questions, challenges, imagination and conceptual abilities inherent in the basic training as an artist. This enabled and encouraged many potters to consider problems in pottery within the framework of its relationship to contemporary art. That the majority of pottery courses were being taught in university art departments may have aided in changing the emphasis from one of essentially utilitarian tasks to one of investigating clay as a potential medium of more expressive possibilities.

Role of the American Crafts Council

Perhaps no other "institution" in America has been more influential in advancing the cause of contemporary crafts in general, and ceramics in particular, than has the American Crafts Council and its official publication, *Craft Horizons Magazine.*

Founded as the American Craftsmen's Cooperative Council in 1943, and headed for many years by Aileen O. Webb, this organization and its magazine have been largely responsible for providing American potters with a form of professional identity, a means of national and international communication and a true spirit of communion among fellow artists. The latter is viewed as being of inestimable value to potters, not because the ACC has sponsored numerous conferences throughout America where potters may have encountered new information related to their specific problems—these could have been dealt with in other ways, most likely in their studios or in the private discussions with other potters—but more importantly, because these occasions have served as periodic reminders that artist-potters were not alone in their search for an identity amidst the anonimity of the post-industrial culture. Although new information was always made available for the latest products, techniques and equipment, the real significance of these gatherings is attached to the idea that there was always a genuine expression and concern for the life of the craftsman—that he was not alone, not isolated, not forgotten. The overriding sentiment was, in fact, that as a practicing craftsman he was respected, acknowledged and very much needed.

If any one organization and journal was willing and able to focus on the idea that a new era in the crafts had emerged and become an integral part of contemporary American culture, it was the American Crafts Council and *Craft Horizons.* Through its first National Conference at Asilomar on the Monterey Peninsula of California in 1957, to its most recent meeting (the 7th National Conference) at Winston-Salem, North Carolina, the ACC has served as a kind of clearing house for ideas, attitudes and concepts concerning the production potter as well as the maker of "artware." Through these many gatherings of the ACC these two seemingly divergent groups in the field of pottery often met in a spirit of genuine interest, coming away with a better understanding of each others' problems, ideas and philosophies—hence, a better awareness that both parties are part of the same system which they have helped to nourish and is nourishing them.

Craft Horizons was started in 1941 in the form of a small mimeographed newsletter for artists who were selling their work in New York City's America House. It has served as one of the more important means for disseminating and distributing vast amounts and kinds of information for artists of various crafts, designers, architects, gallery directors, shop owners, teachers, students and researchers.

By 1947 it moved from infancy to maturity with a professional cover, a name and a staff of dedicated writers and researchers. In addition to bringing to its readers information about exhibitions of the most current artists in America and from abroad, the magazine also assumed the responsibility of serving as a forum for open discussions related to the role of the craftsman, quality of design and purposes and methodology of educational programs.

Above all, the importance often attached to having one's work reproduced or reviewed in *Craft Horizons* (or other magazines such as *Ceramics Monthly*) cannot be overlooked. With over 30,000 subscribers in 1966, growing to a readership of over 400,000 by 1977, it is easy to see the influence of the magazine in promoting the growth and development of the artist-potter. Helping to communicate new ideas, new forms, new techniques and introducing new personalities in the field, as well as rediscover forgotten leaders, *Craft Horizons* has played a vital role in dealing more directly with the realities and the dreams of aspiring American ceramic artists. To have one's work reproduced, a technique illustrated, an idea discussed or a workshop or conference publicized was of immeasurable importance to the evolvement of the art-pottery movement, especially since this was being communicated to regions where much of this information and many of these activities were not otherwise available.

The ready accessibility of information and materials freed the potter of technical involvements, such as having to develop a clay body or glaze. These problems had been well mastered so that the potter was able to become intimately involved with clay, with the tools and materials. Other developments such as the expansion of college art departments, the inclusion of pottery courses in fine arts programs and students coming to pottery with diverse backgrounds in art further aided in the growth of the American studio-potter after World War II.

These activities were instrumental in creating the notion of training the student as an artist. Hence the contemporary potter was variously referred to as an artist-potter, artist-craftsman, craftsman-designer, designer-artist, or, as in this study, studio-potter. This designation is not indicative of a more specialized person. Instead, it points to a more diversified individual—one who was not only trained in the complete process of making pottery—but one who, due to his exposure to other studio problems, approached pottery from a more creative standpoint, particularly as related to design. It is, therefore, theorized that the diversification seen in total form concepts, beginning during post-war years, related directly to the training of potters within the structure of fine arts programs. This seemed to offer new sources for creative stimuli.

The potter began to reflect his total personality, his environment and his aesthetic choices. Starting around 1948, these new developments were making themselves felt in the work of potters. This work was characterized by a new exuberance, by a spirit of experimentation and a challenging and questioning of established concepts regarding design and craftsmanship.

Notes

1. A survey of its publications has served as an index to the research activities of American potters. In this regard several noteworthy people have already been discussed, such as Charles Binns, Charles Harder, Arthur Baggs, Edgar Littlefield and Myrtle French. Although their inquiries varied, a majority of their published reports dealt with technical aspects of glazes and clays. Several others,

not directly related with studio-pottery also provided additionally helpful information over a period from 1930 to 1950.

2. Paul F. Knight, *Commercial Feldspars in the United States,* Bulletin of the American Ceramic Society, no. 13, pp. 532-33.
3. Paul E. Cox, "Why Use More Than One Clay in a Body Mixture," *Journal of the American Ceramic Society,* 29:48 (March, 1946).
4. Federal Security Agency, *Statistics of Higher Education; Biennial Survey of Education in the United States, 1947-48,* Chpt. 4, p. 5.
5. Dorothy W. Perkins, "Education in Ceramic Art in the United States," Unpublished doctoral dissertation, The Ohio State University, 1956, pp. 265-77.
6. Ibid., p. 275.
7. George Pappas, "Ceramics Teaching in American Colleges," *College Art Journal,* 16:332-35 (1957).

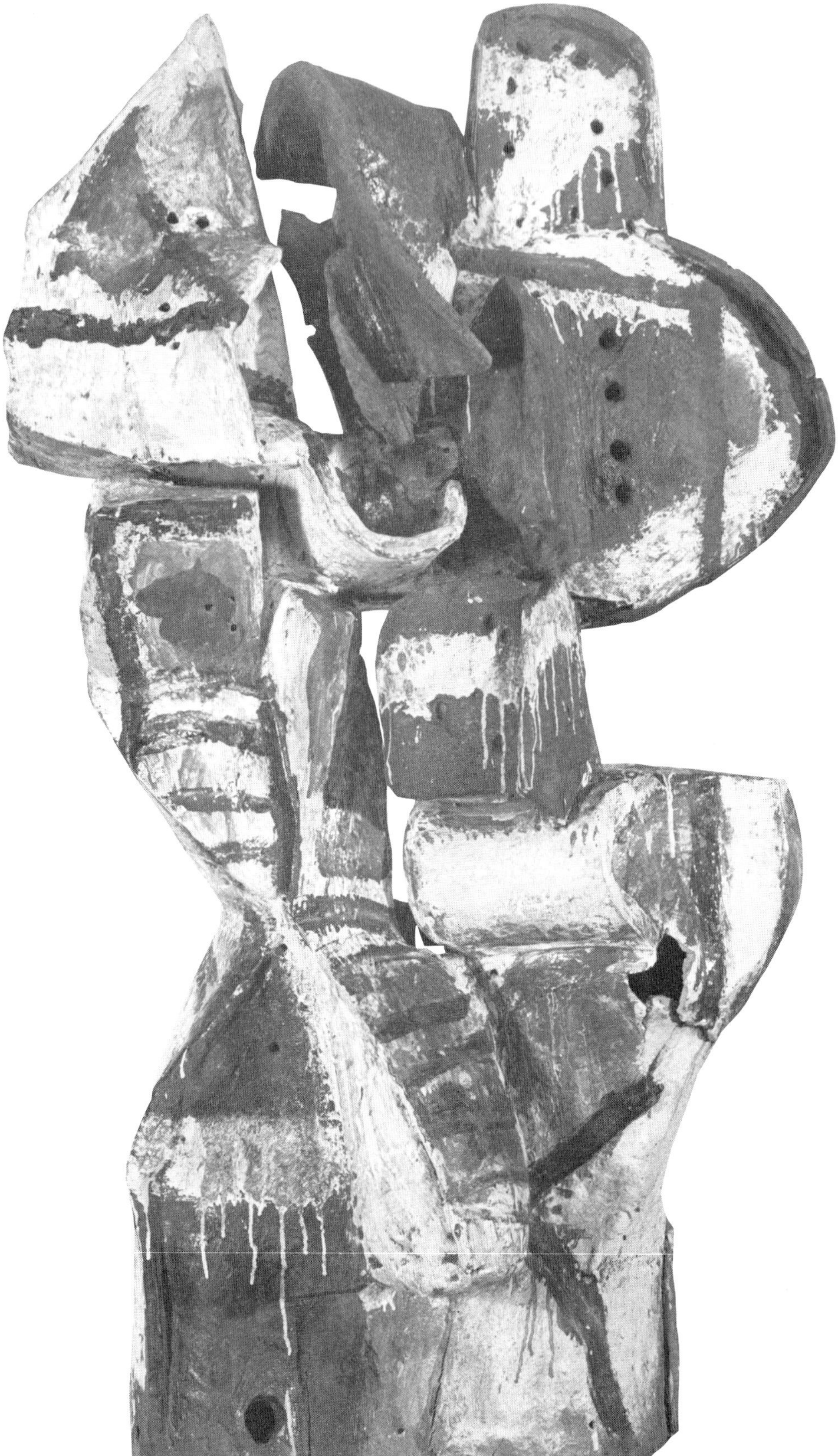

Peter Voulkos

Changes in Form and Style After 1945 11

During the early 1950's one began to see manifestations of ideas which were developed over the past eight to ten years. Among the first signs which disclosed that new attitudes were being actively nurtured in studio-pottery was the implementation of innovative approaches to decorating pottery.

Exploration in Decoration

An interest in brush decorating was typical of new attitudes in decorating pottery. It reflected the immediacy of a sketch in which conceived designs were executed with swiftness and forcefulness not witnessed in previous work. Indeed, the freedom experienced in brush decorations appears to have been a synthesis of post-World War II activities in art. In this instance contemporary painting seems to have supplied an expanded vocabulary of abstract decoration and fresh meaning to the accidental effects of dipped, splashed, poured and freely brushed slips and glazes.[1]

Some potters began to improvise with various types of materials in order to achieve special surface effects. Sometimes a distinctiveness in color or tecture was created through the use of local materials. Several potters exploited this idea more than before. Ted Bielefeld typifies the interest in using local materials. He points out:

> Until this year I have been using coarse grained fire clays and foundry clay, heavily grogged with chunks and fines from about 4 mesh earthenware body. This year I have switched to a local, low firing earthenware body, about cone 6 tops, and have been using beach washings of tiny pebbles and quartz chips for grog.[2]

In this same regard Dennis Chaseck says:

> Black Michigan sand which gives a mottled texture increasing in darkness with reduction fire is characteristic of all our work. When we glaze we use mostly maple leaf ash glazes (40% ash) which are soft matt and pick up the black sand from the clay when reduced.[3]

Potters were interested in further exploring the inherent qualities of their materials. The textures, impurities, colors of clay, its earthiness and touch, became important. It seems as if the refinement and perfection of surfaces as seen in Sung Dynasty pottery, and perpetuated in much American wares prior to World War II, were being rejected. During the late 1940's and through the mid-1950's the interest of potters turned toward somewhat less refined surfaces, such as salt glazed pottery and the work of contemporary Japanese potters. In some instances, if the clay was relatively free from impurities and consequently inactive during the firing, attempts were made to supplement it with various types of grogs, oxides, shales or other ingredients. Angelo Garzio of Kansas typifies this attitude. He recalls:

> Because of the similarity to the generic source of clay, I enjoy loading the clay with a superabundance of both grog and large feldspar granules. These, when fired in reduction high temperatures in the cone ranges of 10-13, melt and fuse in a quasihomogeneous mass, producing a skin structure closely akin to stone.[4]

The result of introducing foreign material into the clay has been that visual and tactile qualities of pots became more pronounced. At times this was combined with a more free-form approach to embellishing the surface with thick slips, as seen in a large bottle by George Roby (Fig. 11-1). The mottled surface created an effective unity of form and decoration.

In the work produced by William Wyman from 1956 to 1958, one is introduced to another approach to surface treatments. He popularized a method of applying sand and grog to the outside of the pot while it was still moist (Fig. 11-2). This is a technique which has since been used extensively.

Equally interesting are the surfaces of pots whose textural possibilities were exploited through the use of poured slips and glazes. Paul Soldner of California, Marie Woo of Michigan and Dean Strawn and Peter Voulkos, also from California, all used variations of heavily applied slips and glazes in order to create interesting graphic results. The endless variety of textures and decorations possible through the manipulation of slips and glazes was also of pronounced importance in the work of Maija Grotell, produced between 1956 and 1958. The surface of one of her large vases shows the fluidity of the slip as it matured under the cover-glaze (Fig. 11-3).

Lastly, Gertrude and Otto Natzler established the use of glazes and slips as a means of developing textures. Their application of "crater glazes" on simple bowl forms created surfaces that closely approximate the erupted contours and surfaces of quickly cooled molten ores (see Fig. 8-4, page 100).

These examples, produced during the 1950's, illustrate the knowledge, skill and imagination which potters utilized to achieve a variety of surfaces. In addition, other methods, related to structure as well as to surface, became important in the potter's decorative treatment of his work. Surface interests were also achieved by allowing the building processes to dictate the

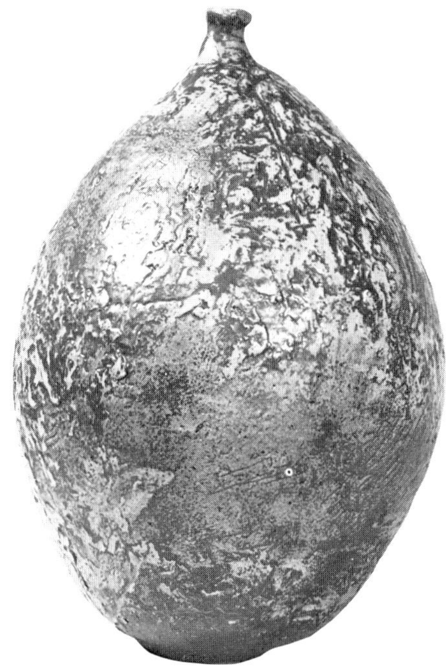

Figure 11-1. George Roby, Stoneware Bottle, handbuilt, decorated with thick slips and glazes which were wiped away in some areas to reveal the clay body. Everson Museum of Art Permanent Collection.

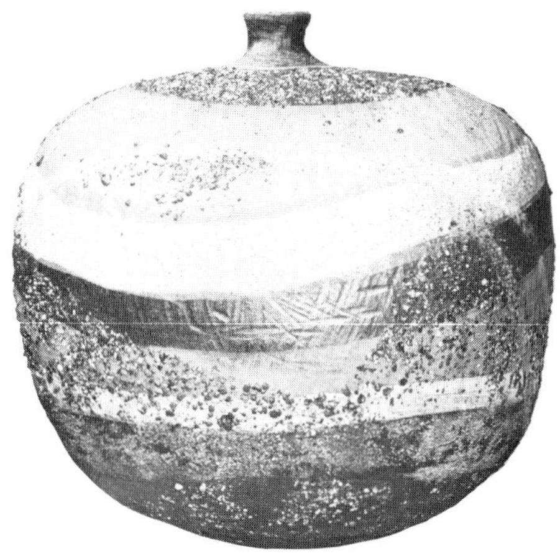

Figure 11-2. William Wyman, Stoneware Terrace Bottle, handbuilt and thrown, 20" × 20", Prize winner in the 21st Ceramic National Exhibition. Everson Museum of Art Permanent Collection.

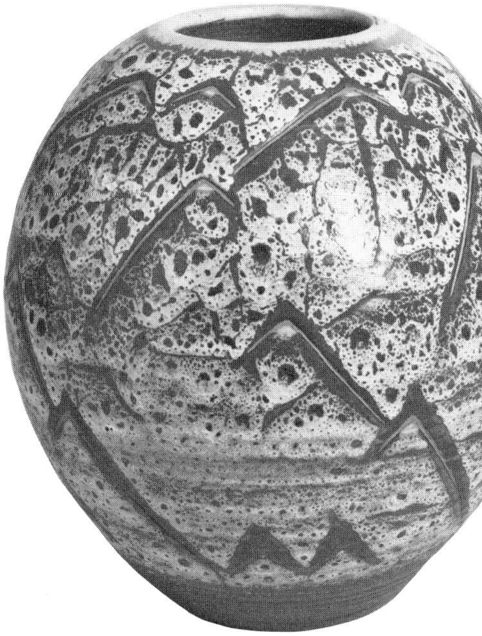

Figure 11-3. Maija Grotell, Vase, stoneware, hand thrown, orange and brown and white glazes, 12 3/4″ × 12 3/4″, 1944, Cranbrook Academy of Art Museum Collection.

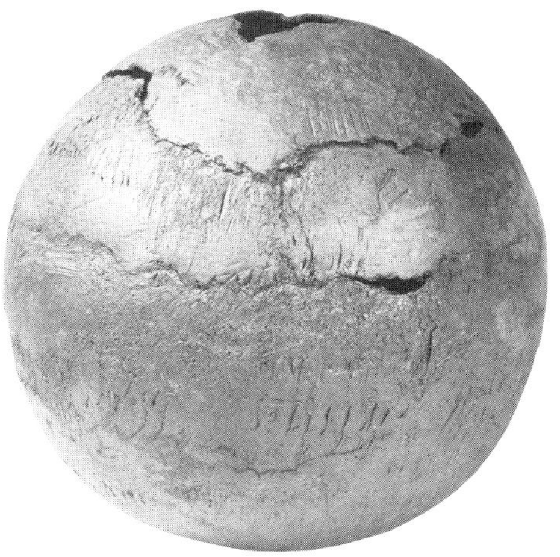

Figure 11-4. Thomas Shafer, Globe, stoneware, handbuilt with slabs and coils, iron and cobalt oxide stain, 1960, Everson Museum of Art Permanent Collection.

decoration. Imprints which were the result of methods of construction, such as joining, attaching or cutting, were frequently allowed to remain. Although this had been in evidence in the work of previous cultures, such as the Pre-Columbian and some American Indian pottery, it did not appear to any great extent in the work of American potters until the late 1950's. Previous to this, efforts were made to eliminate most signs that indicated the building method, but now the tooling or finger marks were considered as possibilities for surface embellishment. The idea that the evidence of tools and processes used in making pottery should remain was a keynote in pottery during the early 1950's. This is aptly reflected in a statement by Hal Rieger.

> I like to hammer clay with a piece of wood. I like to cut it into strips and I like to pound it with my fist too. Then make it into different shapes, into an object that might be all clay or might combine with wood, metal and rope. Obviously my methods show that I'm trying to work with freshness and spontaneity and if I want to make a cut into clay, for instance, I want to do it with deftness and not touch it again. If the clay is cut with a sharp knife I want it to look as though it had been cut that way. If I used a bamboo edge to cut it I want it to look slightly softer. I don't see a need to hide things about the craftsmanship of clay working. If the craftsmanship is craftsmanship it should speak clearly and beautifully of itself.[5]

To many potters, the plastic character of clay was of prime importance. Its pliable nature invited direct manipulation by hand or tool. This inherent aspect of clay generated a search for new possibilities of treating the surface of pottery as seen in a large stoneware vessel by Thomas Shafer from Iowa (Fig. 11-4). Traditional techniques were explored and expanded within the idiom of the contemporary aesthetic, thereby increasing the potters' decorative vocabulary.

The slip-decorated pottery of Charles Lakofsky from Ohio is illustrative of a new handling of traditional techniques. In some instances slip was applied immediately after throwing and worked into with a tool, while at other times slip was slashed freely onto the pot with a brush to retain a fresh sense of spontaneity (Fig. 11-6). The combination of his freely thrown and decorated, yet well controlled, pots convey freshness and directness.

Not all decorative processes were approached with the spontaneity and vigor previously described. Some potters explored more calculated surface treatments after the clay was leather hard. Particularly noteworthy was the work of J. Sheldon Carey from Kansas. His urns and vases demonstrate a meticulous, carefully executed treatment of the surface. This resulted in a relief texture of depressed areas contrasted to a raised clay edge (Plate 9).

A number of potters achieved a sense of boldness through patterns created by carving and sgraffito (Fig. 11-7). The renewed interest in sgraffito reflected the potter's growing awareness of decorative possibilities conceived from clay and executed prior to glazing. Although this was not a new technique, several potters began to use it with renewed vigor and inventiveness.

The production of Clyde Burt was dominated by variations of sgraffito, incising, latex resist or inlays of slips. In a large, covered urn he painstakingly painted abstract patterns onto the bisque pot, glazed it, removed the latex design and then filled it in with a contrasting slip and glaze.

A different manner of working the surface of pottery appears in a piece by Irwin Whitaker.

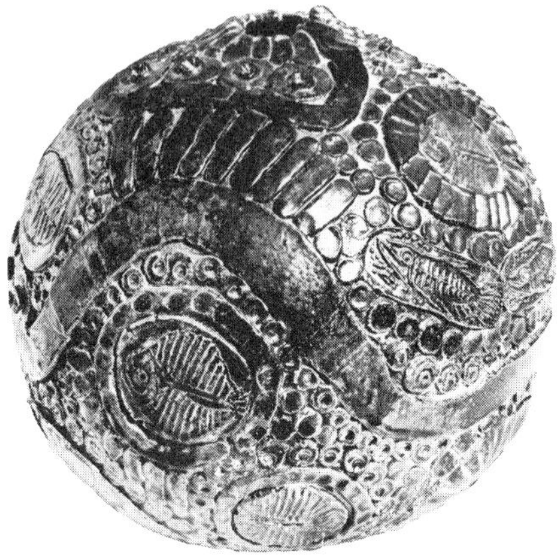

Figure 11-5. Richard Peeler, Pot, stoneware, handbuilt with applied and stamped decoration. A simple vessel shape became an active field for graphic surface treatment with the use of coils, stamps and balls of clay which were enhanced by the free wood ash floating through the kiln and depositing itself on the pot. It is a technique still very popular with today's studio-potters. Collection of the artist.

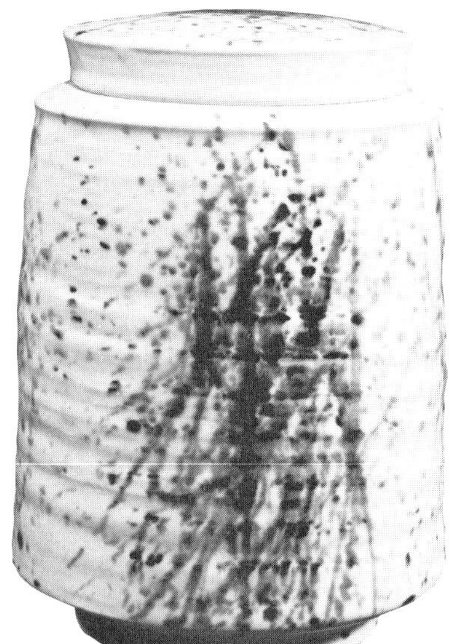

Figure 11-6. Charles Lakofsy, Covered Jar, porcelain, wheel thrown, slip decoration under transparent glaze. Mary Spedding Milliken Memorial Collection, Gift of William M. Milliken, the Cleveland Museum of Art.

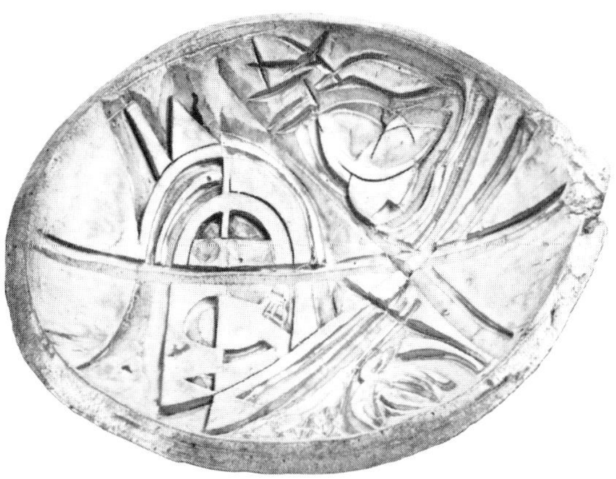

Figure 11-7. Henry K. Gernhardt, Baptismal Font, stoneware, handbuilt, incised decoration with applied clay, white opaque glaze.

The leather hard clay often allowed the potter to vigorously cut designs into the form or to add to it slabs of clay for decorative purposes.

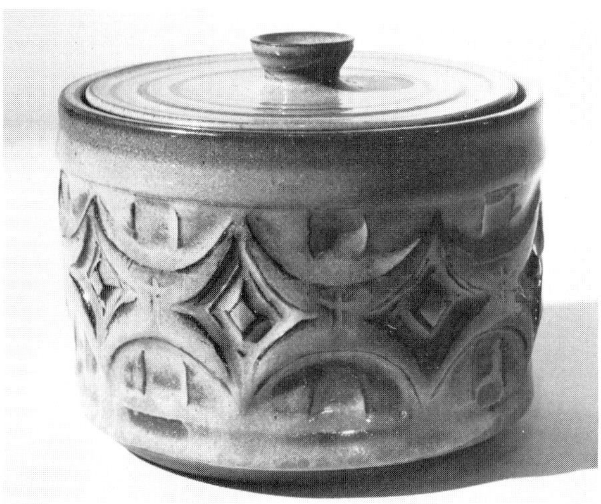

Figure 11-8. Irwin Whitaker, Covered Jar, stoneware, wheel thrown, 4 1/2″ high, 1950. Collection of the artist.

Many studio-potters during the 1950's and 60's explored the possibilities of carving deep relief decorations into rather traditional forms.

His simple cylindrical covered jar was deeply carved and resembles a contemporary bas-relief. The profusion of decorative activity is set off against quiet bands at the top and bottom, and the over-all glazing of the pot helps to emphasize the relief and strengthen its decorative impact (Fig. 11-8). It serves as a further example of the variety of decorative techniques explored during the period.

Another investigation of surface treatments was indicated by a new use of color. Previously, color was used in glazes applied over the entire pot. Around 1955, some potters began to abandon the traditional use of colored glazes, engobes, slips and enamels. In some instances, commercially produced enamels and colored glazes were used in a more inventive, spontaneous and almost blatant manner. Majolica glazes were given new meaning through exploitation of their possibilities as a painting medium. In 1957 and 1958, Henry Takemoto created a series of large platters which he decorated with a variety of raw reds and greens over the cover glaze. Joan Pearson explored traditional media such as this with a more contemporary approach. She explains:

> In my experiments with color at temperatures of 2,300 Fahrenheit I have been able to get Majolica color as brilliant as the low temperature ceramic color in Italy. Glaze colors now used predominantly are pale blue glossy glaze on black clay—depending for its effect on the color in the clay—and a black crystalline glaze on a white mat glaze with multicolor Majolica application on the red clay.[6]

The use of low-fired glazes was revived. Several potters began to work at lower temperatures where a larger variety of brighter color was possible. Although the dark, earthy tones of reduction fired stoneware were still dominant, a concern for other potentials of color was evident. This was observed, for example, in an exhibition of work by leading American potters at the opening of the Museum of Contemporary Crafts in New York.

> Colors were brighter, especially in pottery which saw a number of top U.S. ceramists relaxing the rule that the *sine qua non* of pottery is ultra-high-fired stoneware. Turning out work in the cone three range, which permits brighter colors, the work of two Chinese-Americans formed a case in point: Katherine Choy's blue and white vases, Fong Chow's greens.[7]

A more direct use of color is noted when low-fired, brightly colored glazes and enamels were applied to isolated areas on otherwise unglazed surfaces. These serve as a strong contrast to the earthy, unrefined color and texture of the raw clay as seen, for example, on pots by Peter Voulkos made around 1958. The use of raw metal oxides diluted in water and applied directly over the cover glaze is a further indication of how some traditional techniques were reconsidered for decorating. In the past, this method was used with some restraint and careful planning. By 1960 this decorative technique was used in a more straightforward and spirited approach, much in the same manner as seen in some painting of that time (Plate 10).

Influence of Painting and Sculpture

The activities of twentieth century painters and sculptors were important to potters. Particularly noteworthy was the spirit of experimentalism which prevailed in painting and sculpture, characterized by critical appraisals of traditional values as regarded form, texture, color and craftsmanship. Of particular interest were the involvements in ceramics of European painters such as Miro, Leger and Picasso. Their exploits into clay, though usually rather temporary, were pursued with great interest by not only the leading crafts journals of the time such as *Craft Horizons* and *Ceramics Monthly*, but also by other leading magazines of the arts such as *Arts*, *Art International* and *Art News*. The publicity attached to these international artists' involvement in ceramics led to some serious reconsiderations regarding purposes and methods of expression in American ceramics. Perhaps most notable among these is Picasso. The work he did, starting after the second World War, was one of the forces leading to the significant explorations of form during the subsequent decade.

Pablo Picasso

In 1946, Picasso rented a studio in Golfe Juan on the French Riviera. A local painter invited him to visit the Poterie Madoura in the village of Vallauris. During this visit Picasso became fascinated with clay and began his prolific production of plates, plaques, jugs, vases and human and animal shapes. Most of them were fashioned from thrown forms.[8] His work fell into three main categories: (1) those modelled by himself or (2) fashioned into shapes by someone else under his supervision, and (3) limited editions of forms from molds that Picasso had carved himself and stamped "Edition Picasso," which were copies or interpretations of designs he had originated at other times. Within these three categories, the most imposing work was that which he created directly himself. This included animal and human figures produced from thrown pots. Bottle forms were sometimes set on their side and reworked to resemble animal forms. Some forms went through several alterations. Thus, any reference to a pot made on the wheel was destroyed.

Other forms had gone through a less radical change in structure and therefore retained the basic characteristics of bottles, vases, bowls and platters. These shapes became vehicles for two-dimensional decorations, often linear configurations of human or animal heads. Through these decorations, done with the use of interplaying light and dark slips and carved lines, the basic concept of the pot was altered. Particularly noteworthy were some vases and plates which display his verve in creating satirical images on rather static forms (Fig. 11-9).

At other times the shapes themselves suggested a particular theme which he further explored by supplementing the pot with direct, spontaneous brush work. One such form was apparently derived from the ancient Peruvian Mochica stirrup pot. This was adopted as the basic shape for a bird form which Picasso embellished with profuse light and dark slip (Fig. 11-10).

Within this large body of work, a variety of other approaches have been seen, all of which signaled a radical departure from the work of past European potters. In viewing Picasso's prolific production, one becomes aware that his ability went beyond merely decorating the surfaces of pots. The shapes appear to have been carefully chosen, and through his manipulation, were transformed into totally new pottery forms. In a wry manner, Picasso was able to impart a sort of joke that potters have delighted themselves with in the past as,

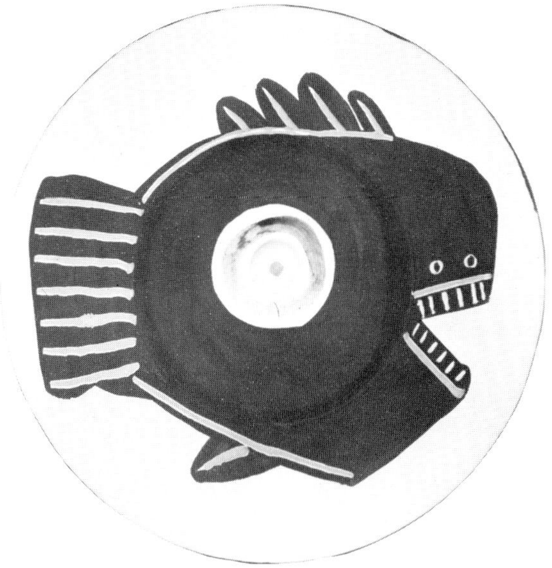

Figure 11-9. Pablo Picasso, dish, "Le Gros Poisson Noir," earthenware with slip decoration, Vallauris, France, 1958. Courtesy of the Cooper-Hewitt Museum of Decorative Arts and Design, Smithsonian Institution.

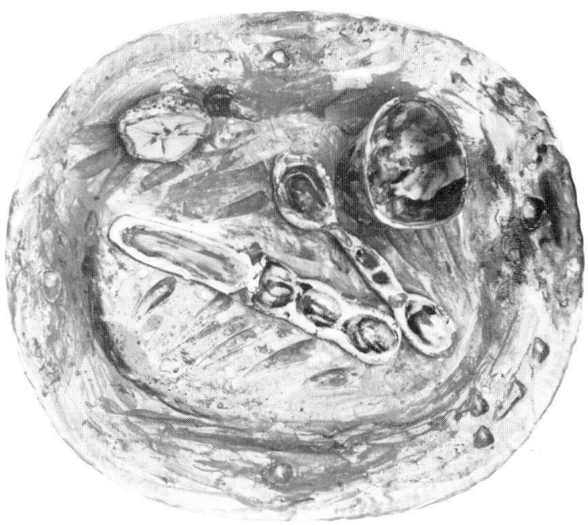

Figure 11-10. Pablo Picasso, Plate with Still Life, Modelled polychrome glazed ceramic in relief, unique, 2 7/8″ × 14 3/4″ × 12 1/2″, 1954. Collection, The Museum of Modern Art, New York.

for example, in instances such as the English Tobey mugs, the German Bellamine salt-glazed pots, or some of the plates of the Dutch. The traditional function of a vase or plate was negated for a more personal, unique expression. Picasso developed statements of delight and good humor in this versatile medium. Indeed, it was his playfulness, his experimentation in the broadest sense of the word, which provided a stimulus to sonie American potters.

By 1956 Picasso's ceramics gained unprecedented popularity. During that year, and in 1957, the New York Museum of Modern Art, the Smithsonian Institute, the Cooper Union Museum and the Brooklyn Museum sponsored exhibitions of his work. Moreover, in 1958, David Duncan's *Private World of Picasso* provided additional circulation of Picasso's ceramics produced during the preceding 12 years.

Several potters have expressed the viewpoint that Picasso's influence added impetus to the revitalized direction of pottery during the 1950's. Among them were William Wyman, Paul Soldner, Charles McKee and Stanley Rosen. The latter expressed a typical attitude about Picasso's influence on American pottery when he pointed out that, "Picasso . . . suggested a wider range for ceramics."[9] The wider range suggested is interpreted as meaning that new possibilities were now being recognized, that the potter's course was directed into exploring the limits of his material—that the potter was to manipulate the clays, slips, glazes, and other materials, and his tools, in order to create more personally expressive forms—that, in order to create new relationships of form, color, line and texture, the potter had to break with the past or make attempts to reform it.

Picasso's involvement in pottery suggested new possibilities. The stimulation provided by the Spanish master for the development of Peter Voulkos as an artist in ceramics provides a relevant example. At the same time, the activities of painters, both in Europe and America, who were working in the modern spirit of Abstract Expressionism added to the complex influences that affected the course of American studio-pottery.

Influences of Abstract Expressionism and Action Painting

Complementing the improvisations of Picasso was the increased popularity of Abstract Expressionist painting. Potters' exposure to, and interest in, this school of painting enabled them to expand their scope of self-expression. Already discussed were precepts of asymmetry and imperfections of contemporary Japanese pottery, the informality and spontaneity of Oriental pottery in general, the innovative attitudes of people such as Picasso, and the more venturesome attitudes borne out of increased knowledge and skill with materials. It is surmised, therefore, that the impact of Abstract Impressionism was more of an aesthetic nature than a physical one.

It seems that Abstract Impressionism provided new attitudes, feelings of greater intensity, and a heightened awareness of rhythms, tensions and forces of contemporary life. Of equal importance was the new meaning given to accidental effects of line, color, texture, in fact the total form, by relying on the free invention and dynamic automatism as displayed in the work of Pollock, de Kooning, and Kline. Some painters began to abandon the smooth, untextured two-dimensional surfaces and take into account the feasibility of building and modelling their surfaces. This included some work coming from Pierre Soulages, Alberto Burri, Marco-Relli and Bernard Dubuffet. The individualism and sense of freedom expressed in their art began to make itself felt in the work of a number of American potters.

Numerous potters have indicated that Abstract Expressionism was an important catalyst in freeing the potter from tradition, convention and limitations of materials and techniques. Following are some insight provided by potters who felt that Abstract Expressionism had noticeable effects on their own work or on the field of pottery in general:

> Abstract Expressionism shook loose from the pottery tradition a strong group of artists who were hungry for a way to speak through their work in more abstract and poetic term than functional considerations would allow.[10]

Val Cushing pointed out that "Abstract Expressionism led to pottery's becoming an 'art form' in which function was removed from the pot."[11] Roger Corsaw was somewhat more specific when he said, "It seems that the Abstract Expressionist painter with his action of paint application has had considerable effect both on form and surface."[12] Robert Sperry also agreed that Abstract Expressionism exerted a strong influence on pottery, while Glenn Nelson cited, in addition to this movement in painting, other areas of contemporary art expression that were of consequence to the potter. He stated:

> The cult of individual self-expression developed by painters has brought about the *no pot* idea. Junk sculpture and raku idea of pseudo-primitive are important influences.[13]

Wesley Mills explained that "the experimental pot whose only value is that of shock has a place today because of the nature of our lives."[14] Rudy Autio pointed out that "Abstract Expressionism initiated a new freedom from the sometimes rigid disciplines of the potter's wheel,"[15] while Ward Yowry felt that it "has provided the environment in which parallel directions in pottery are also found."[16] Some potters declared that it affected their work very directly. Among them were William Wyman and Louis B. Raynor. Wyman felt that it had a "very big influence on my work and an opening of what I would call the expressionist school of ceramics."[17] Wyman's large, slab-constructed bottles typify an abstract expressionist approach toward surface decorating (Fig. 11-11). Raynor explained, "Experimentalism by painters and their freedom has helped me to free myself from some of the traditions, etc. which have become pretty firmly ingrained."[18]

Studio-Pottery of the 1950's

An important indication that the limitations of the symmetry of the potter's wheel would be re-evaluated occurred after World War II. Several potters used the wheel as a means for creating forms, which were altered when they were leather hard. For most potters it was enough to change the form only slightly, perhaps by gently pushing in two or more sides of a pot, or by twisting a certain section into subtle contortions.

An example of how a number of potters combined new attitudes toward altered forms and free, extemporaneous approaches to decorating is seen in the work of Charles

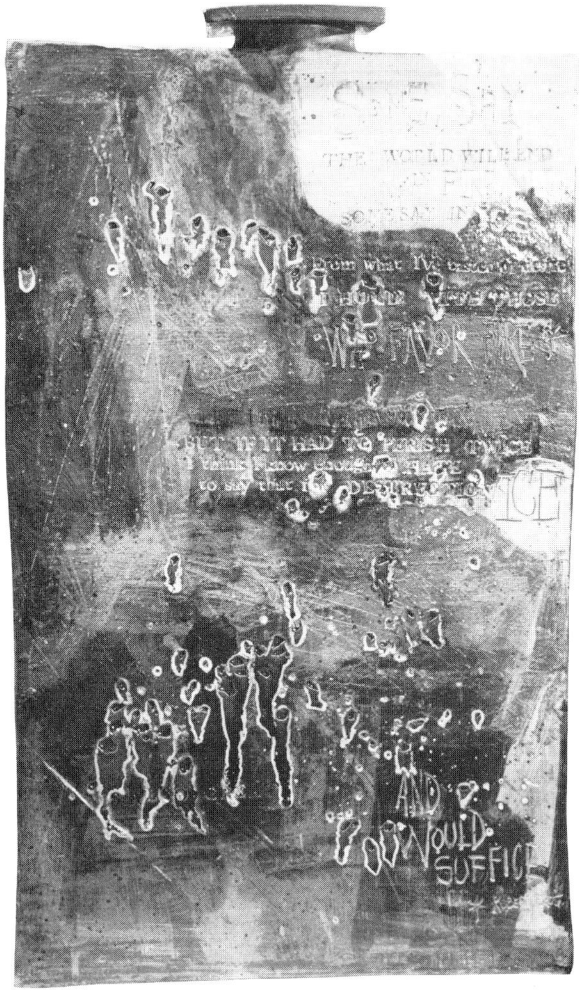

Figure 11-11. William Wyman, "Homage to Robert Frost," stoneware vessel, handbuilt, decorated with slips, engobes, stains and pressed and incised decorations, 1962. Everson Museum of Art Permanent Collection.

Many studio-potters of the late 50's and early 60's found the surfaces of their vessels fields for active graphic decorations that sometimes took their clues from activities in the area of drawing, painting and graphics of that same time period.

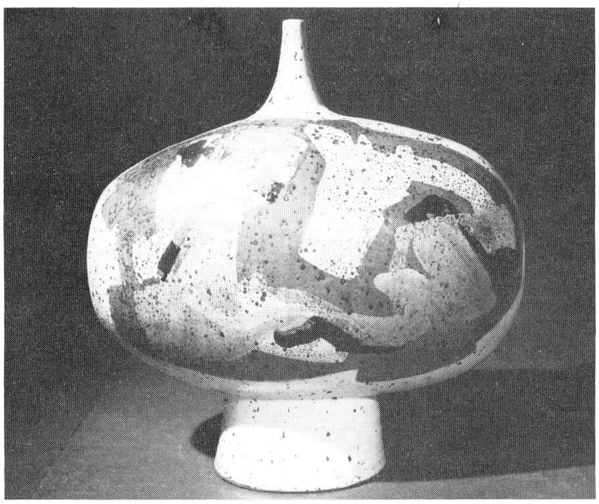

Figure 11-12. Charles McKee, Branch Vase, stoneware, wheel thrown and altered, white glaze, wax resist with orange, blue, brown and black brush decoration, 21″ × 21″, 1960, Everson Museum of Art Permanent Collection.

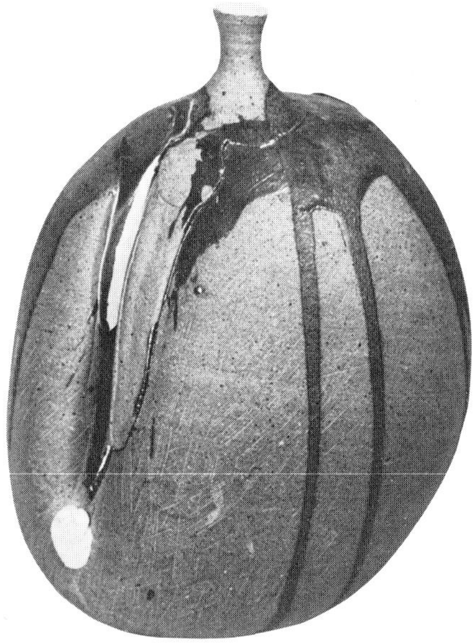

Figure 11-13. James Wozniak, Bottle Form, stoneware, wheel thrown and altered; partially glazed with green matt glaze; 15″ × 8″; 1963. Collection of the artist.

McKee. His approach to creating visual tensions by dramatic interplays of broadly painted slips and glazes is typical of the newly celebrated Abstract Expressionist influence that was making itself felt during the late 1950's and early sixties in American pottery (Fig. 11-12).

After 1957, American pottery was marked with an increasing exuberance, boldness and irreverence. Some potters pushed their materials to its limits by subjecting them to stresses of sharply changing forms and powerful dimensions. The sources of influences were varied and complex. Involvement in the innovative handling of form, color and texture cannot be ascribed to any one single force, but the painting, and to some degree the sculpture of the period reinforced the trend.

Relationship to Contemporary Sculpture

New techniques in pottery paralleled the approaches of some American sculptors who worked with welded metals, and who committed themselves to contemporary idioms by their new methods. Sculpture began to be characterized by additive processes and configurations of generalized gesture and posture in space; what Herbert Read calls "space drawing." An analogy may be drawn with the forcefulness of non-figurative painting. The sculptor was involved with the total process and was in a position to be able to perceive changes in form and to conceptually exploit them. The noticeably greater emphasis on raw forms and surfaces contrasted with a considerable body of earlier work that depended on refinement of surface and form. The forged, welded and hammered constructions of Seymour Lipton, Theodore Roszak and David Smith exemplify a more direct approach to form, material and technique. In some instances, forms underwent drastic simplifications, while at other times, the destruction of basic shapes such as cubes, spheres or cylinders created new and complex relationships of shape, space, color, texture, and line. These challenges of the limitation of media, form and craftsmanship were similar to the attitudes of potters.

Potters were also aware of changes that were occurring in other areas. Several potters felt that it was the sculptural free forms created by designers and architects for interior furnishings which served as a catalyst for asymmetrical pottery shapes. Others have advanced the opinion that it was a reaction against the rigidity and inflexibility of industrial design that motivated them to seek new solutions to designing their pots. But perhaps more important was the realization by potters themselves that the plastic character of the medium demanded further investigation and experimentation. In order to carry this out, it was necessary to violate established principles set down by a long heritage of ceramic design which upheld utilitarian function as one of its primary aims.

Peter Voulkos

Peter Voulkos exemplifies how some potters began to adopt new attitudes toward pottery during the 1950's. Although Voulkos had been recognized as an outstanding potter as early as 1952, when he was still dealing with a classic form concept (Figs. 11-14, 11-15, 11-16), he gained international attention when he started creating pottery of a more controversial nature. This began with an interest in the work of Picasso. The result of wanting to "live with it [examples of Picasso's work] until I really felt I had absorbed all he had to say" became evident in Voulkos' new approach to pottery.[19] Although his initial concern was with new decorative methods, one can sense an unrest and dissatisfaction in his work which eventually led him to consider other possibilities of altering the total pottery form.

In 1954, he painted his classical urns and vases with figure and flower motifs similar to those seen in Picasso's work. His treatments of highly stylized human heads and other figurative motifs gained Voulkos international recognition.[20] This type of work was repeatedly chosen for awards in regional and national shows, as in 1956, when he was awarded a prize in the San Francisco Pottery Association's Exhibition (Fig. 11-17).

Although Voulkos recognized "Picasso's ability to detach himself from the centuries old tradition in the ceramic arts,"[21] the influence was short lived. Voulkos moved into new directions after 1956, but the inspirations provided by Picasso pointed him toward more radical treatments of structure. Since that time a style of "Abstract Expressionist Pottery" has been identified with Voulkos (Fig. 11-18).

Voulkos was not the first American potter to dismiss traditions of symmetry and challenge the limitations of the wheel,[22] but, he was one of the most outspoken in questioning the traditional values of carrying out preconceived designs. Consider his reply when he was asked how he determined the designs of his forms.

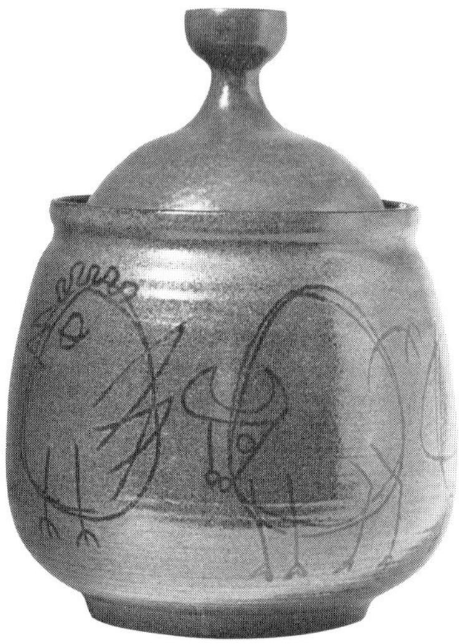

Figure 11-14. Peter Voulkos, Cookie Jar, stoneware clay, wheel thrown, wax resist decoration; Museum Purchase Prize in the 15th Ceramic National Exhibition; 1951; Everson Museum of Art, New York.

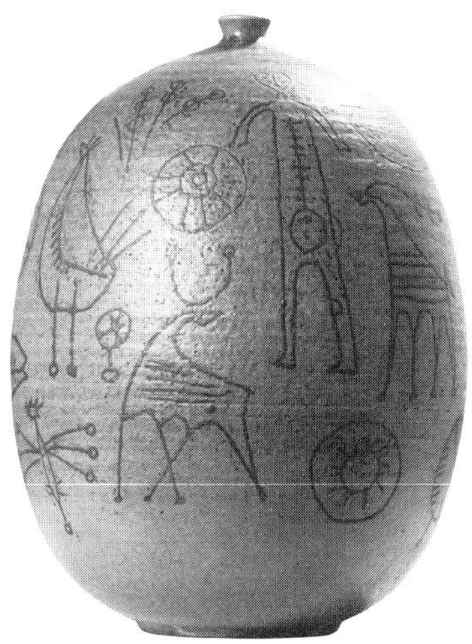

Figure 11-15. Peter Voulkos, Rice Bottle, earthenware, wheel thrown, greenish glaze with yellow glaze; figures in wax resist decoration; ca. 1951. Courtesy the Everson Museum of Art, Syracuse, New York.

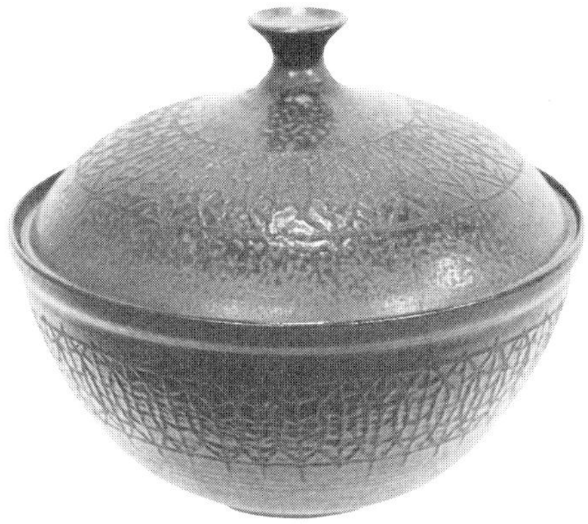

Figure 11-16. Peter Voulkos, Tureen, stoneware, wheel thrown, gray-green glaze over slip trailed decoration; ca. 1953. Everson Museum of Art Permanent Collection.

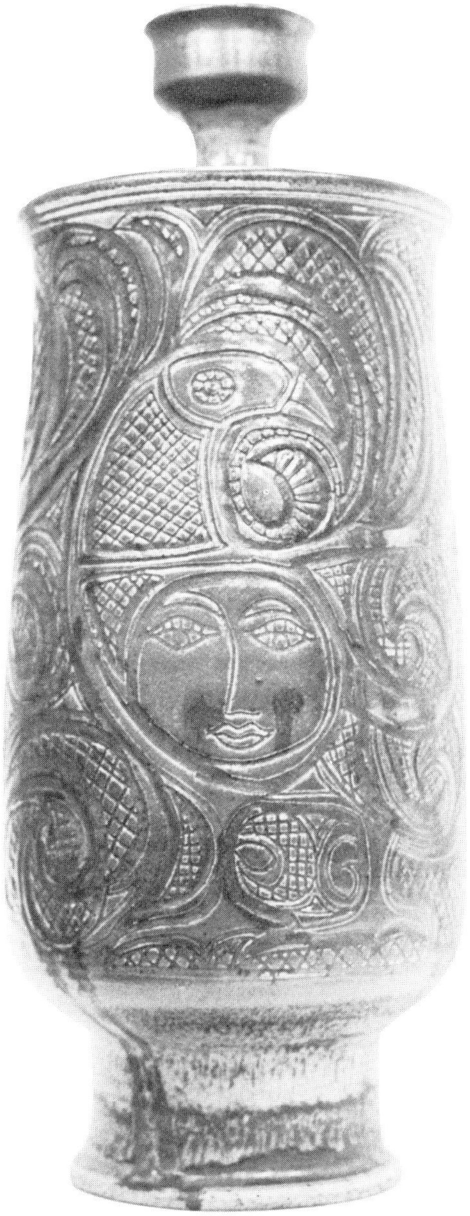

Figure 11-17. Peter Voulkos, Covered Jar, stoneware, wheel thrown, incised decoration, light brown glaze, approx. 15″ high; Everson Museum of Art Permanent Collection; ca. 1954.

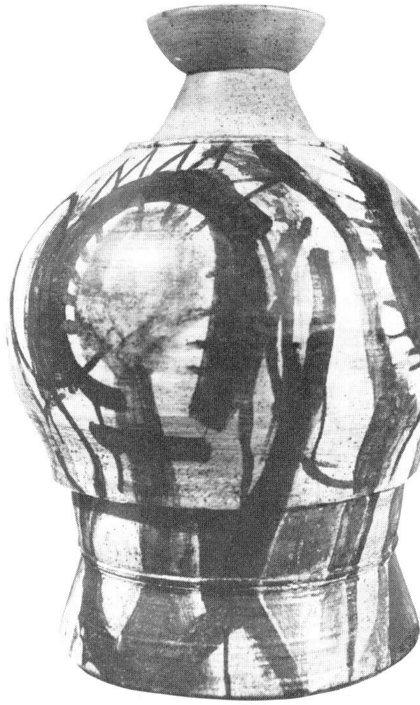

Figure 11-18. Peter Voulkos, Covered Jar, stoneware, wheel thrown, brush decorated, approx. 26″ high. Everson Museum of Art Permanent Collection; 1958.

> Depends on the piece. Of course if I'm making a plate or a bowl I assume its going to be a plate or a bowl. Most of the times when I work I work in the dark, but sometimes I have just a vague idea of something and I want to bring it into being. I think it gets down to the creative act, actually: The reason that I do it is because I don't know about it and I want to find out about it. . . . If I knew what it was going to be in advance—if I had a visualization that I could draw on a piece of paper there'd hardly be any point in my doing it.[23]

With this attitude, Voulkos increased the pace and intensity of experimentation with form, space, color and texture. It carried him far beyond the traditional unity found in works that came from the wheel (Fig. 11-19). In 1957, he made a variety of forms whose sculptural entities were created by combining separate forms into one unit. For example, a totem effect resulted from placing six similar shapes one above the other, varying their direction and angles slightly. Another form made in a similar manner was more complex because designs, unrelated to the over-all form, were cut into the separate sections (Fig. 11-20).

A year later, a more radical departure became evident when compositions evolved which simultaneously utilized throwing and slab construction. Thrown sections were pressed on clay boxes, slabs were inserted between these, and parts of rounded pots protruded from among these combinations. Various kinds of slips were added with a directness and boldness that aided in reinforcing, while at the same time contrasting with, these weighty monumental forms. Voulkos' thirst for change was further reflected by configurations whose imperfect, yet vigorous, quality expressed a search for personally meaningful forms. They also symbolized his willingness to repudiate traditional values of craftsmanship. In a 21 inch vase (Fig. 11-21), he used clay slabs and thrown pots and attached them in such a manner that it is surprising they withstood the stresses and strains sustained in stoneware firing.

In succeeding years, Voulkos moved away from forms which had the slightest suggestion of pottery shapes. His configuration expressed an increased state of restlessness, change and searching. A sense of immediacy pervades all of them (Fig. 11-22). This is especially evidenced by the unfinished, raw state in which he allowed his work to remain. Slabs of clay appeared to be barely attached to the main form. Glazing was almost nonexistent.

His own involvement in painting, and his awareness of what was transpiring in the fields of painting and sculpture, played a vital role in his further development. He felt painting to be superior to any craft because "painting is completely free of limitations."[24] Voulkos recognized the free invention and dynamic automatism of such painters as de Kooning, Guston, Gorky, Tobey and Pollock, and it is reasonable to infer that these qualities have influenced his work.

Around 1959 an increased agitation appeared in Voulkos' work. In his sculptural forms, the construction, the decoration, the shifting of forms, the breaking down and building up of structures were all indicative of a process of vital action. One can still sense how, in the process of assembling various forms, decisions were made under the stress of immediate feelings, of changing relationships. The material bespeaks having been pushed to its physical limits through beating, paddling, scoring, laminating, scratching, tearing or otherwise having been manipulated by unorthodox methods. The result was a radical reduction and even elimination of the thrown

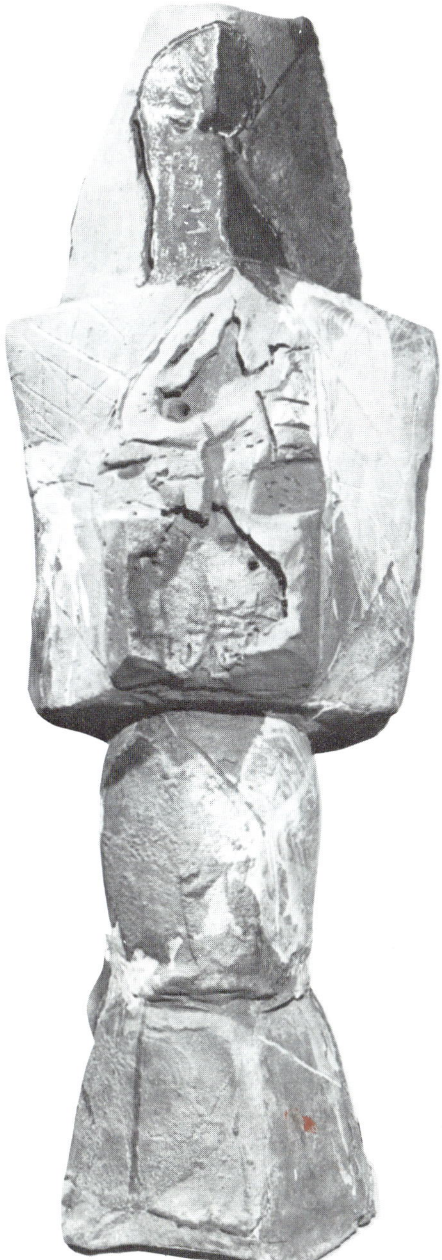

Figure 11-19. Peter Voulkos, Totem Sculpture, stoneware clay, handbuilt and thrown, altered forms, raw slips and glazes. Courtesy of the Everson Museum of Art, Syracuse, New York.

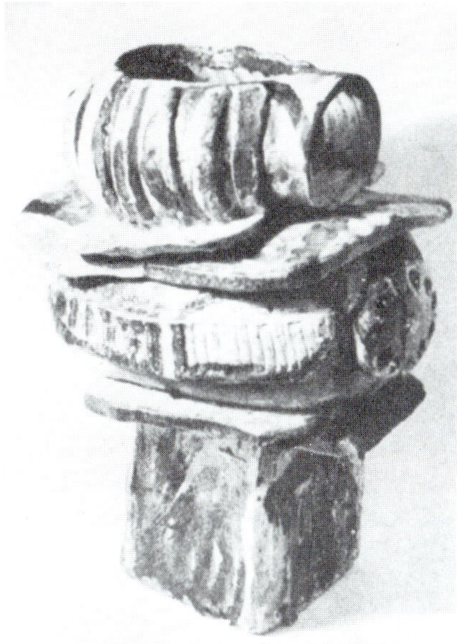

Figure 11-20. Peter Voulkos, Ceramic Sculpture, stoneware clay, wheel thrown forms and slabs, white and brown slips; Private Collection.

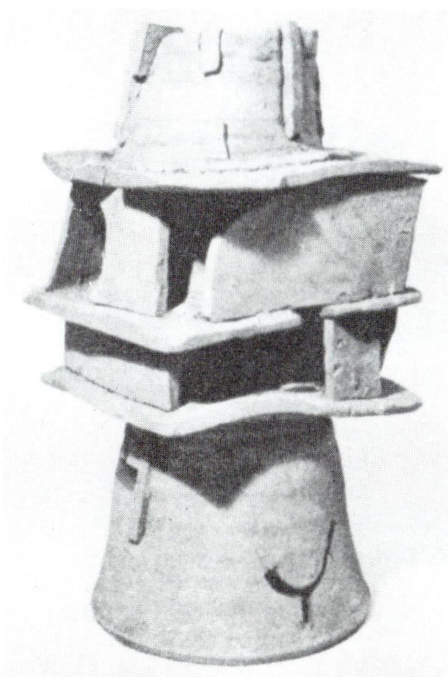

Figure 11-21. Peter Voulkos, Vase, stoneware, wheel thrown and slab constructed; ca. 1957; Private Collection.

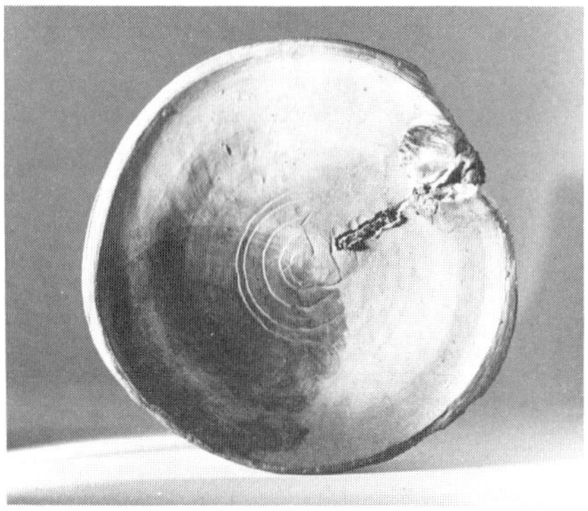

Figure 11-22. Peter Voulkos, Plate #1, stoneware, wheel thrown and altered, brown and orange glaze, Prize winner in the 22nd Ceramic National Exhibition; 1962; Everson Museum of Art Permanent Collection.

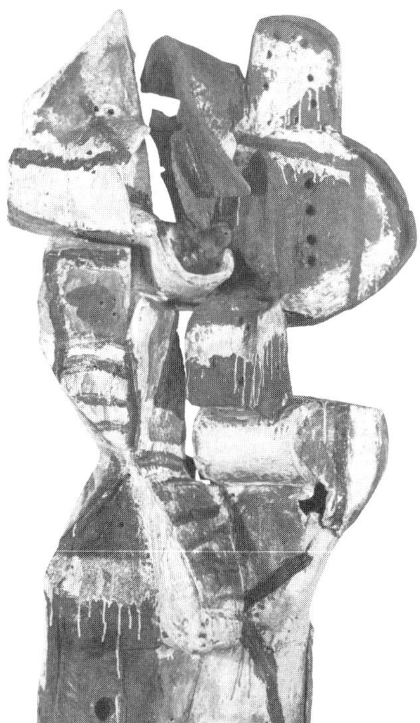

Figure 11-23. Peter Voulkos, Untitled Sculpture, stoneware, handbuilt, white and black slips, unglazed, approximately 6 ft. tall; 1958-59; Quay Gallery, San Francisco, California.

form. Stylistic devices of decorating were generally abandoned so that an irreducible quality of the raw, naked material was reached (Fig. 11-23 and Plate 11).

Voulkos' presence, his teaching, and his work should not be underestimated in evaluating the growth of American studio-pottery during the last few years of the 1950's. Outstanding potters throughout the country worked with him. Some of these are John Mason, Malcom McClain, Paul Soldner, Jerry Rothman, Micheal Cohen, Robert Sperry, Win Ng, Henry Takemoto and Stephen DeStaebler, among many. Their comments relative to Voulkos' influence indicate why he had become the established leader in American ceramics during this period. Robert Sperry recounted:

> The work and attitude of Peter Voulkos while he was working at the Archie Bray Foundation were things which influenced me most. He brought a new vitality and strength to American pottery which was unknown before.[25]

Micheal Cohen placed importance on Voulkos' presence, "because he responded to Abstract Expressionism in clay when no one else did, and I needed that at the time."[26] Jerry Rothman admired Voulkos' approach to working with clay, while Paul Hatgil pointed out that "he lifted the craft from the minor niche it occupied and developed it into a field with full expression."[27] Other leaders in American studio-pottery have also acknowledged Voulkos' importance.[28]

The work of numerous other potters began to reflect Voulkos' controversial direction in ceramics (Plate 12). His work and attitudes received widespread exposure through exhibitions and reviews in magazines. In addition, through workshops and his teaching positions at the Archie Bray Foundation and the University of California at Berkeley and Los Angeles his influence was further extended. Students and potters started to emulate Voulkos' attitudes and form concepts. Their thirst for breaking with past traditions was reinforced by the popularity of Voulkos' venturesome excursions into three-dimensional clay forms. Several potters were able to assimilate and refine Voulkos' influence so that some other personally distinctive work began to emerge (Plate 13).

Jerry Rothman and John Mason had one of their first important exhibitions in 1957 at the Ferrus Gallery in Los Angeles. It was a controversial exhibition because of the radical departure in using pottery shapes for sculptural free-form constructions. The exhibit consisted mainly of clay forms whose references to traditional concepts of pottery were completely negated. The work of Rothman resembled tree or plant-like shapes. Strong, simple cylindrical bases, terminating with active interplays of shapes and textures, suggested the intricacies of seed pods or some other organic form (Fig. 11-24).

The work of John Mason illustrates a similar approach. Although he did not combine thrown pots, his work was characterized by an interest in the sculptural possibilities of pottery. After throwing, the pot was altered by paddling, pushing, gouging and cutting. The resulting forms expressed Mason's search for new concepts by challenging the traditional precepts of pottery. J. Bennet Olson forecast the new, seemingly inevitable, direction of pottery when he evaluated this exhibition.

> There was no flippancy or tongue-in-cheek approach here. These are artists-craftsmen seriously pushing aside convention to make room for ceramics in architectural design, in landscape design—in and beyond the areas usually reserved for sculpture.[29]

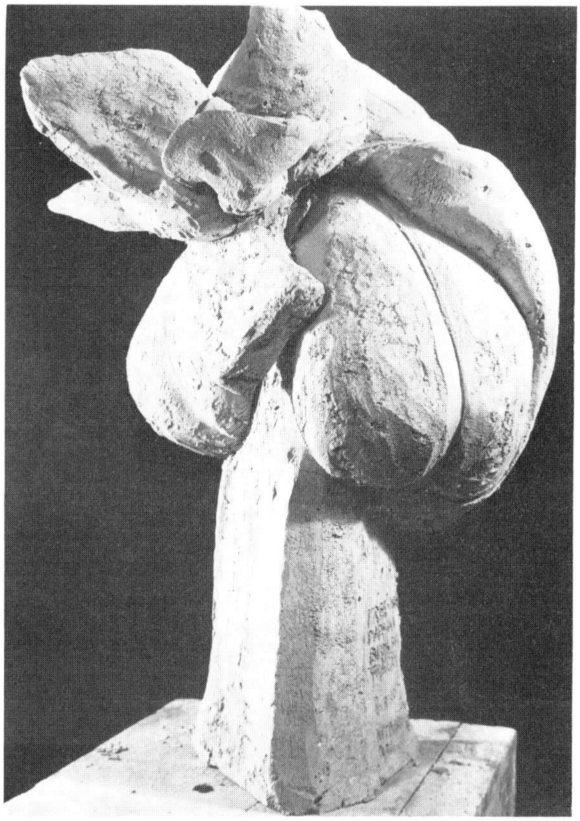

Figure 11-24. Jerry Rothman, "Not in Central Park #3" stoneware, handbuilt, 24" high, 1963, Everson Museum of Art Permanent Collection.

The use of unrefined forms and surfaces found favor among numerous ceramic artists of the early 1960's who subscribed to an abstract expressionist attitude of dealing with a highly charged form of self expression.

Exploration of Form and Scale

The recognition given to this type of work, as well as an increased awareness of what was transpiring in the area of sculpture began to make itself felt in the work of other potters. Each developed a distinctive approach to dealing with altered or assembled forms in clay. Malcom McClain and Henry Takemoto are examples of Voulkos' influence, but who nevertheless created work that still retained their individual marks of distinction. McClain often dealt with forms that still had some slight references to bottles, only because the tops sometimes terminated with spouts. The remainder of the forms were often complex networks of interchanging planes created by beating deep depressions into the clay.

Takemoto's earlier work consisted mainly of large, bulbous handbuilt pots. But around 1958 he began dealing with more fanciful assemblages where separately thrown parts were playfully combined. Attenuated necks, short protrusions, swellings and cumbersome looking bases all encouraged imaginative interpretations.

One of a number of people who studied and worked with Voulkos and who went on to become a highly respected leader in American ceramics is Rudy Autio. Of particular note are his large stoneware vessels which were constructed with slabs. Their joining and fastening was accomplished with instinctiveness and sureness, thereby retaining a freshness that has become an identifying characteristic of Autio's production. The fact that most of his pieces are based in a container-like structure is almost incidental. More important are the contrasts and tensions he creates which are the result of his spirited building technique and painterly applications of slips and glazes in starkly contrasting colors. This highly emotive handling of materials and tools creates a powerful sculptural structure (Fig. 11-25).

A number of potters who had abandoned the wheel completely and who chose not to work with the same sense of bravura as cited in previous examples, amplified a personal approach through more carefully assembled slab constructions. Among them were Theodore Randall whose combination of slab box and thrown base (Fig. 11-26) illustrates how some ceramists arrived at a more contemporary image through assembling various parts. Betty Feves stacked box-like structures on top of each other, allowing some of them to be closed, while other parts remained open, thereby revealing an interior structure that is almost reminiscent of unfinished architectural forms. Allowing parts to remain unglazed and contrasting highly finished areas to rough surfaces further adds to a feeling of well controlled boldness (Fig. 11-27).

Most notable among the numerous people who began seriously working with these constructions is Win Ng. His use of clay slabs in building hollow block forms was typical of this innovative direction in American ceramics during the late fifties and early sixties. Of his work Mr. Ng says:

> I am exploring and integrating that interval in space occupied by the structure and composing within that interval. There is something in the space within a pot that is mysterious and alive. I want to explore that space, this enclosed intensity, draw it to the surface, and so impose relationships between the body and the surface.[30]

At times the suggested space was opened and the interior penetrated to expose a complex

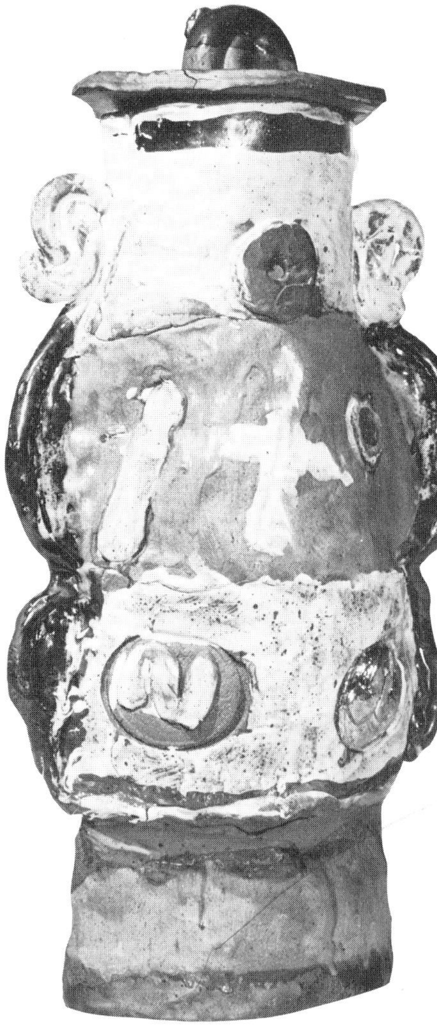

Figure 11-25. Rudy Autio, Covered Jar, stoneware, handbuilt, 28 1/2″ × 14″; Everson Museum of Art Permanent Collection; ca. 1965.

The utilitarian function is negated in favor for more expressionistic considerations.

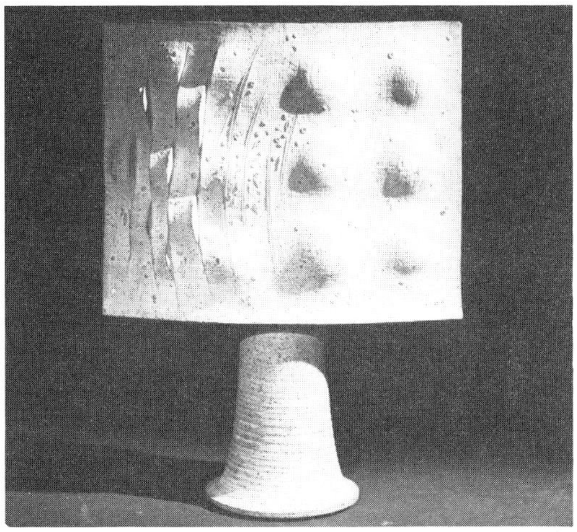

Figure 11-26. Theodore Randall, Footed Slab Vase, wheel thrown and handbuilt, 17″ × 4″ × 10 1/2″; raw clay exterior, glazed interior; 1961; Everson Museum of Art Permanent Collection.

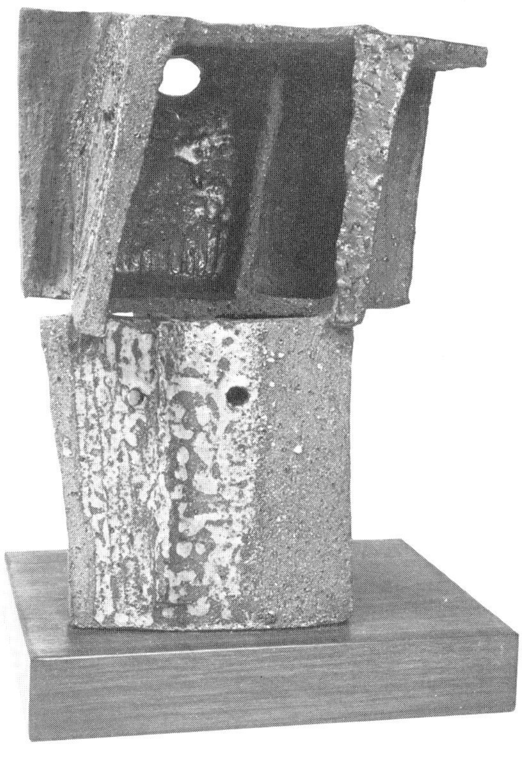

Figure 11-27. Betty Feves, "Persona," stoneware, handbuilt slab construction; ca. 1964; Everson Museum Permanent Collection.

network of other, smaller structures. When the entire piece remained closed, however, he imposed a lively field of painted surfaces. This was done with boldness and freedom. The application of simple, wide areas of tan, dark brown, blue and white slips related these forms to three-dimensional abstract paintings (Fig. 11-28). Mr. Ng's constructions have become consistent prize winners in regional and national ceramics exhibitions.

These attitudes toward form, construction, decoration and function have continued as an integral part of contemporary American ceramics (Fig. 11-29). A three foot tall stoneware box by Douglas Johnson of Wisconsin is just one example of how numerous ceramic artists have continued to pursue this particular direction with slight variations of their own ideas. In Johnson's piece the uninhibited handling of the clay remains well intact by a complete absence of any surface decorations. The structure is stained with iron and cobalt containing washes in order to accent the raw, natural quality of the clay (Fig. 11-30).

David Weinrib was another artist whose recognition as a potter was essentially gained through his slab constructed forms. His initial involvement in clay was with large decorative tiles. Most of these were imbedded in cement and then used to supplement a variety of interior and exterior architectural settings.[31] A natural outgrowth or progression from the tile was the slab construction. Exploration of the use of a flat, upright tile created a diversity of forms. Though his new configurations were not sculpture *per se,* they did suggest a sculptural concept (Fig. 11-31). His hollow forms were architectonic in feeling, since slabs suggest walls which imply structure—that is, sculpture or architectural sculpture. Open space was also investigated in Weinrib's work.

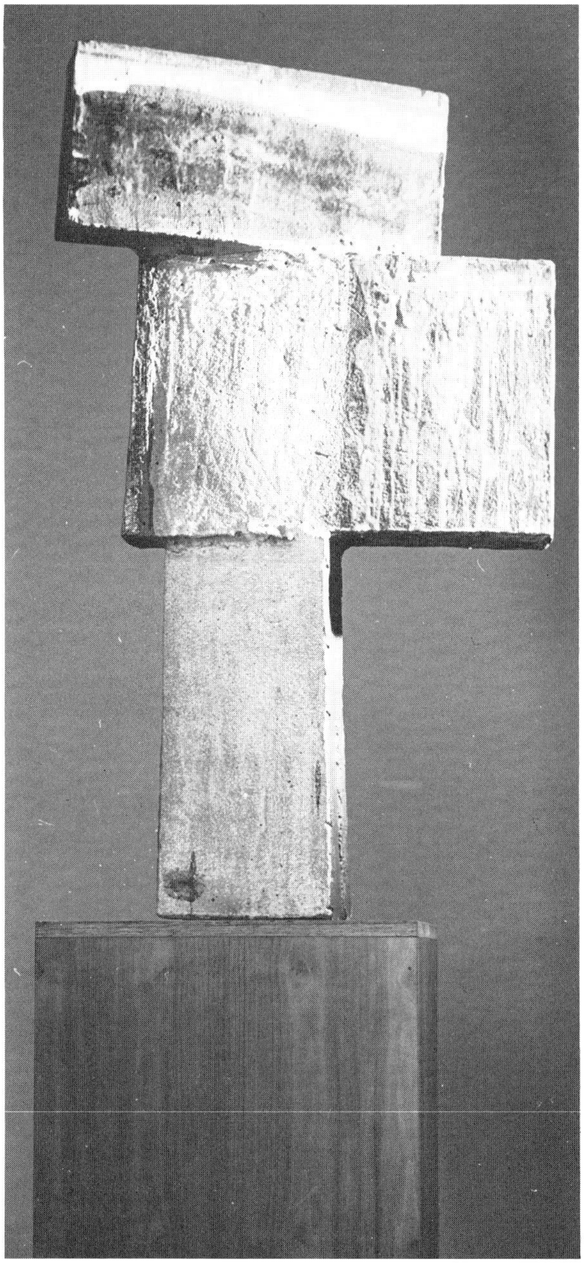

Figure 11-28. Win Ng, "Directions," stoneware block construction, 36″ × 23″, grey, white and brown glazes. By assembling several slab constructed forms, some ceramic artists were able to deal more effectively with large scale sculptures.

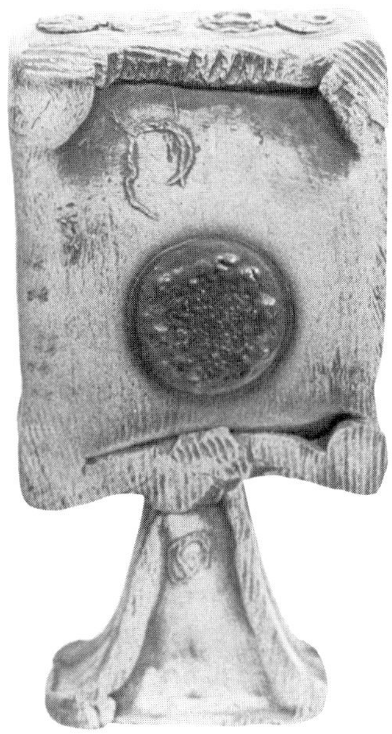

Figure 11-29. Michael Cohen, Branch Vase, stoneware clay, stained body with blue circular decoration, approx. 12″ tall; ca. 1960; Everson Museum of Art Permanent Collection.

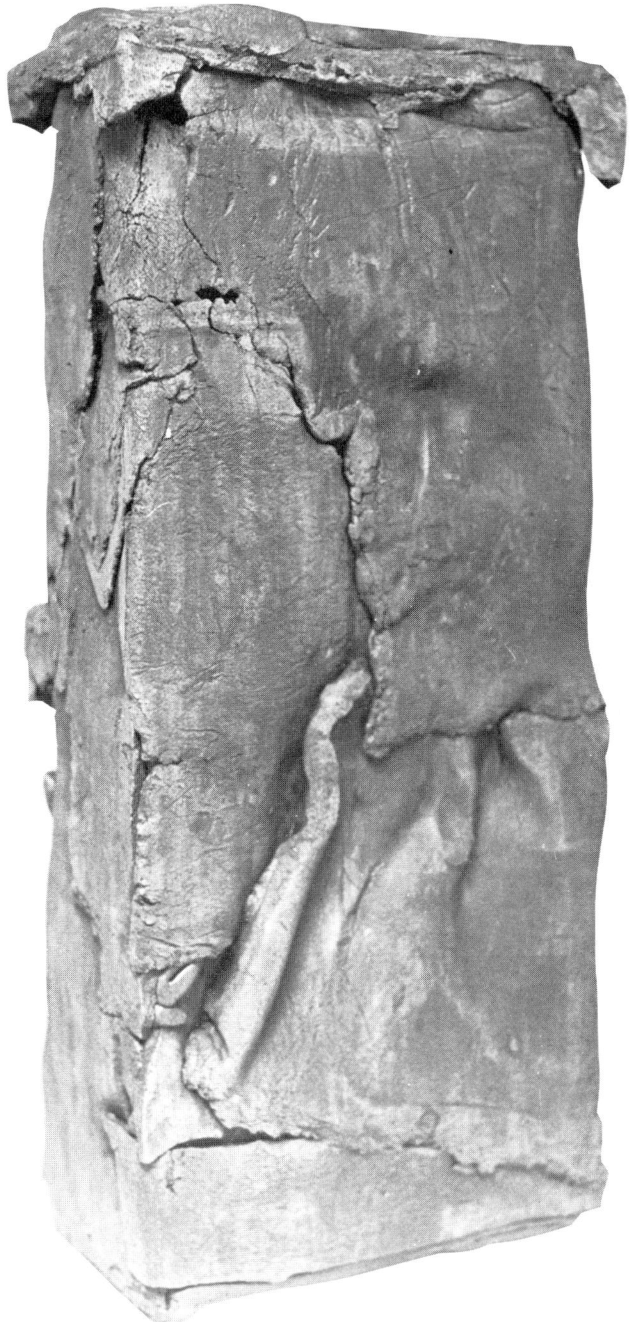

Figure 11-30. Douglas Johnson, Branch Vase, stoneware, handbuilt, 3 ft. tall, stained with washes of iron oxide. Collection of the artist.

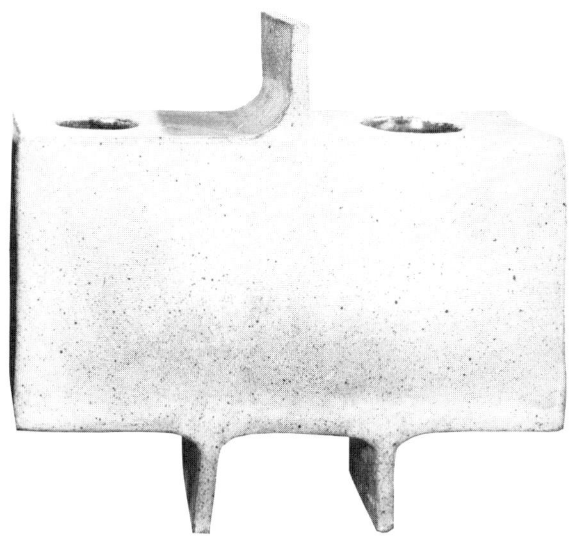

Figure 11-31. David Weinrib, "Slab Built Pots," stoneware; exterior unglazed, interior glazed; 1957, Everson Museum of Art Permanent Collection.

At times he combined obvious pot elements such as spouts with sculptural elements such as boxes. This does not mean that the basic idea of three-dimensional form suffered from what might appear as uncertainty or lack of conviction. It merely points out that his work, like several others', overlapped the objectives of contemporary pottery and sculpture.

The work of Antonio Prieto is further evidence of the influence that sculpture had upon ceramics during the closing years of 1950. Although Prieto claimed that his work was not consciously influenced by past or present activities in art,[32] it might be surmised that his large constructions, over three feet in size, reflected sculpture (Fig. 11-32).

Prieto's production alternated between these types of forms and some exquisitely designed utilitarian pottery (Fig. 11-33). At times he was able to fuse these two elements. Its scale is accented by bold white, black and yellow glazes. The work is typical of sculptural orientation. It is imbued with a positiveness, strength and tense balance of contour, form, color and texture. Like Weinrib, Prieto achieves an expression in clay that is not marked by an extreme technique or material. Instead, his work is characterized by disciplined craftsmanship and formal certainty.

A conscious concern for monumental size was yet another outgrowth of sculptural attitudes toward pottery. Whereas previously most pots were not more than 24 inches high, the late fifties and early sixties saw a dramatic increase in scale. This was accomplished in several ways. Since it is physically difficult to throw anything over 30 inches in height in one piece, some potters resorted to joining several pots together, either directly on the wheel or after they were leather hard. Paul Soldner and Carlton Ball are noted for this, although other

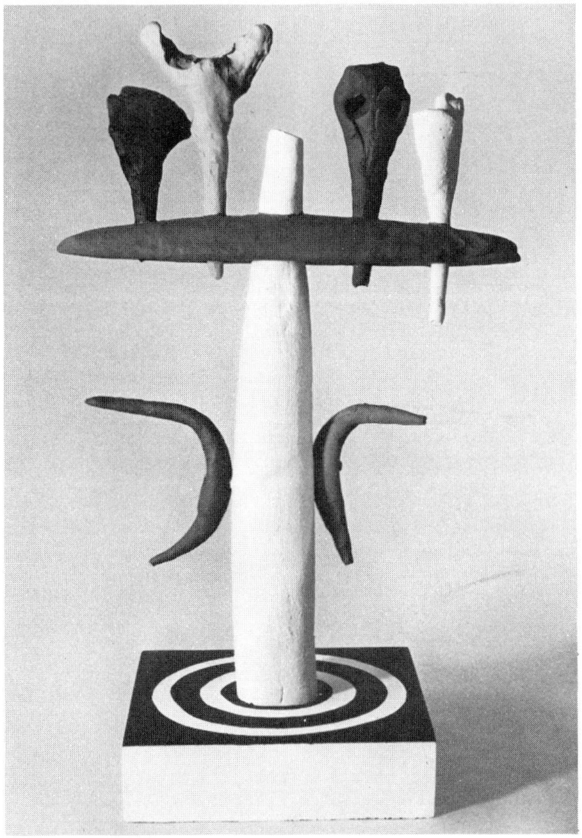

Figure 11-32. Antonio Prieto, Ceramic Sculpture, handbuilt, multicolored slips and glazes, over 3 ft. high. Courtesy of Mills College Art Department, Oakland, California.

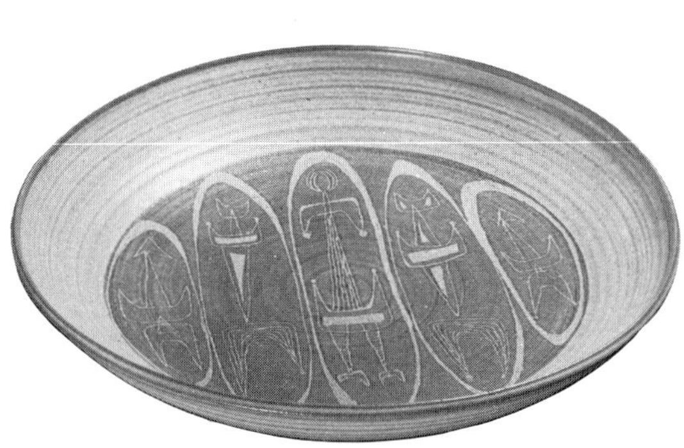

Figure 11-33. Antonio Prieto, Bowl, stoneware, wheel thrown, slip and sgraffito decoration; 18″ diameter.

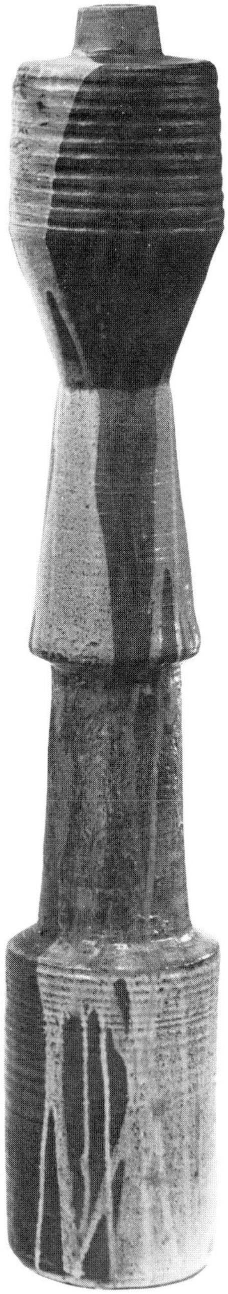

Figure 11-34. Paul Soldner, Floor Pot, stoneware, wheel thrown, brown and white glazes, reduction fired, 68″ tall, 1956. Collection of the artist.

potters have adopted their methods. Through their desire to produce large pieces, Soldner and Ball used a method of throwing which was not widely practiced. They were able to create pieces as high as five and six feet by throwing a large cylinder, adding to it coils of thick clay and pulling it up to the desired height. This was repeated as often as necessary, and the only limitation was the size of the kiln which had to accommodate the pot for firing. Of this particular technique Soldner said:

> I once threw clay up to eight feet with the wall no thicker than one inch at the base. However, this is only a technique and of use only as a means to expressing new ideas (for me) in clay. I find that the long scale puts me in a field of exploration which is void of centuries of examples and without contemporary influences. Therefore, all problems presenting themselves in this foreign form need to be solved by my own devices.[33]

Soldner's large pots, produced in this manner from 1956 through 1959, were glazed by pouring slips and glazes over the entire surface in a loose, asymmetrical pattern. This aided in breaking up the vertical thrust as well as providing a severe contrast to the symmetrical character of the form (Fig. 11-34). At other times he decorated only one of the sections with active calligraphic brush work.

Though only a few potters followed this particular method of throwing, it did become popular to work with a number of forms thrown at the same time and then assembled when they turned leather hard. This enabled potters to increase the proportions and sizes of their work. Potters in other parts of the country were also increasing the scale of their work.

Of particular note was the work of Toshiko Takaezu, whose large pieces were sometimes made from three or four separately thrown pots and by stacking them on top of each other achieved unusual effects of vertical rhythmic movements (see Fig. 9-8). The size and scale of these combined forms conclude at the top with small spouts. These pieces are only remotely related to traditional concepts of pottery through insignificant openings at the top. They are merely terminating elements and actually emphasize their nonutilitarian character.

Preceding examples illustrate that the increase in size was not motivated by a desire to create large pots merely for the sake of bravado. Rather, the integration of numerous forms, frequently supplemented by various types of decorations, appears to be a reflection of much contemporary sculpture and painting, particularly in terms of dealing with more massive proportions. In this new synthesis the potter concerned himself with creating forms that pushed more dramatically into space.

Not everyone absorbed the influences of activities in other areas of the arts after World War II to the same degree. Those who would not dismiss tradition so easily sought, instead, more subtle variations within the confines of the formal, or slightly asymmetrical form. Those who preferred to venture into unknown realms of plastic, three-dimensional expression found an opportunity for free action, for improvisation. They found little support or inspiration by looking to the past—even their immediate past. Hence, a group of ceramic artists emerged in the late 1950's and early 1960's whose efforts with clay created even more radical treatments of form and space, more remarkable painted effects and more fundamental, yet more complex concepts of structure.

This did not imply that they consciously sought the novel, for the different or unique piece of work which might be accepted in a

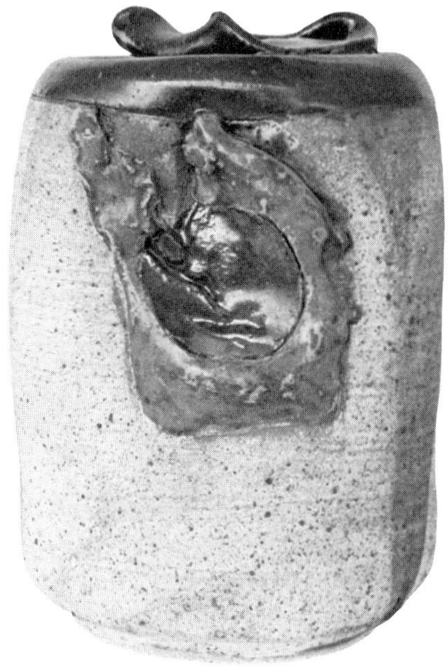

Figure 11-35. Roland Jahn, Vase, stoneware, wheel thrown and altered, partially glazed with applied decoration; 1961. Collection of the author.

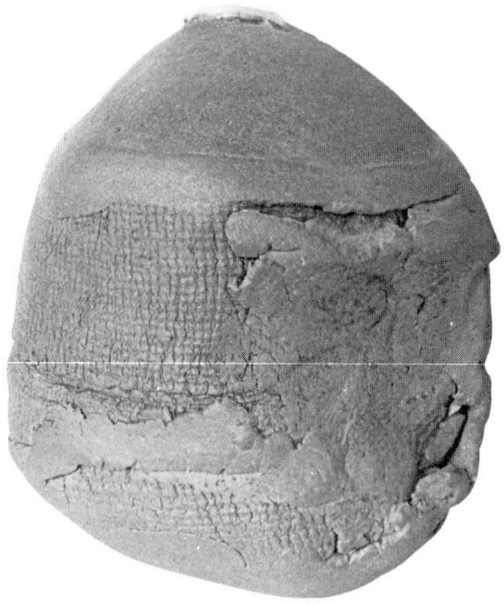

Figure 11-36. Robert Winokur, Pot, stoneware, handbuilt, unglazed, 6″ × 6″, 1960. Collection of the author.

competitive exhibition. Rather, it means that the skilled, perceptive potter who was trained as an artist had the conceptual freedom to experiment with new forms, surfaces and colors; that he could, and perhaps had an obligation to, risk, venture, and make mistakes freely in the hopes of creating for himself a meaningful form of self-expression (Fig. 11-35). A bulk of work already exists which reveals that artistic caution and prudence have been overshadowed by even more profuse varieties of attitudes and forms in ceramic expression than in the initial experimental years of the 1950's (Fig. 11-36).

Notes

1. This decorative approach can be distinguished from that of the Japanese influence by the absence of its calligraphic implications. The most noticeable difference was that decorations evolving from the Oriental influence were somewhat more calculated in contrast to the less cerebral, almost violent forms of those that emanated from influences of contemporary painting.
2. "Biographical Sketches: Ted Bielefeld," *Design Quarterly*, 42:55 (1958).
3. "Biographical Sketches: Dennis Chaseck," p. 55.
4. Biographical Sketches: Angelo Garzio, p. 57.
5. "Biographical Sketches: Hal Rieger," p. 62.
6. "Biographical Sketches: Joan Pearson," *Design Quarterly*, 42:61 (1958).
7. "Crafts Museum Opens," *Crafts Horizons*, 16:41 (December, 1946).
8. "Pablo's Pixilated Picasserole's," *Crafts Horizons*, 18:15-20 (May-June, 1958).
9. Stanley Rosen, Professor of Art, Bennington College, Bennington, Vermont, correspondence to author.
10. William Perry, Associate Professor of Art, Alfred University, Alfred, N.Y., unpublished correspondence.
11. Val Cushing, Associate Professor of Art, Alfred University, Alfred, N.Y., unpublished correspondence.
12. Roger Corsaw, University of Oklahoma, Norman, Okla., unpublished correspondence.
13. Glenn Nelson, Professor of Art, University of Minnesota, Duluth, Minn., unpublished correspondence.
14. Wesley Mills, Professor of Art, Carnegi Technical Institute, Pittsburgh, Pa., unpublished correspondence.
15. Rudy Autio, Missoula, Mo., unpublished correspondence.
16. Ward Yowry, Long Beach, Calif., unpublished correspondence.
17. William Wyman, North Weymouth, Mass., unpublished correspondence.
18. Louis B. Raynor, Professor of Art, Michigan State University, East Lansing, Mich., unpublished correspondence.
19. Conrad Brown, "Peter Voulkos," *Craft Horizons*, 16:12 (September-October, 1956).
20. Ibid., p. 14.
21. Ibid., p. 14.
22. Others were Toshiko Takeazu and Harold Nash.
23. "Report from the First National Conference of American Craftsmen," *Crafts Horizons*, 17:25 (July-August, 1957).
24. Conrad Brown, p. 12.
25. Robert Sperry, Associate Professor of Art, University of Washington, unpublished correspondence.
26. Micheal Cohen, Newton Centre, Mass., unpublished correspondence.
27. Jerry Rothman, Paramount, Calif., and Paul Hatgil, University of Texas, unpublished correspondence.
28. Among those who confirmed this to the author through correspondence or interviews were Theodore Randall, Marc Hansen, Herbert Sanders, Maija Grotell, Richard Peeler, William Wyman, Norman Schulman, Charles McKee, James McKinnel, Jolyn Hofsted, James Wozniak and Erwin Whitaker.
29. J. Bennet Olson, "Exhibitions," *Craft Horizons*, 12:41 (September-October, 1957).
30. Yoshiko Uchida, "Win Ng," *Craft Horizons*, 20:33-34 (January-February, 1960).
31. Oppi Untracht, "David Weinrib . . . A Potter Turns to Tiles," *Ceramics Monthly*, 4:20-21 (February, 1956).
32. "Biographical Sketches: Antonio Prieto," *Design Quarterly*, 42:61 (1958).
33. "Biographical Sketches: Paul Soldner," *Design Quarterly*, 42:62 (1958).

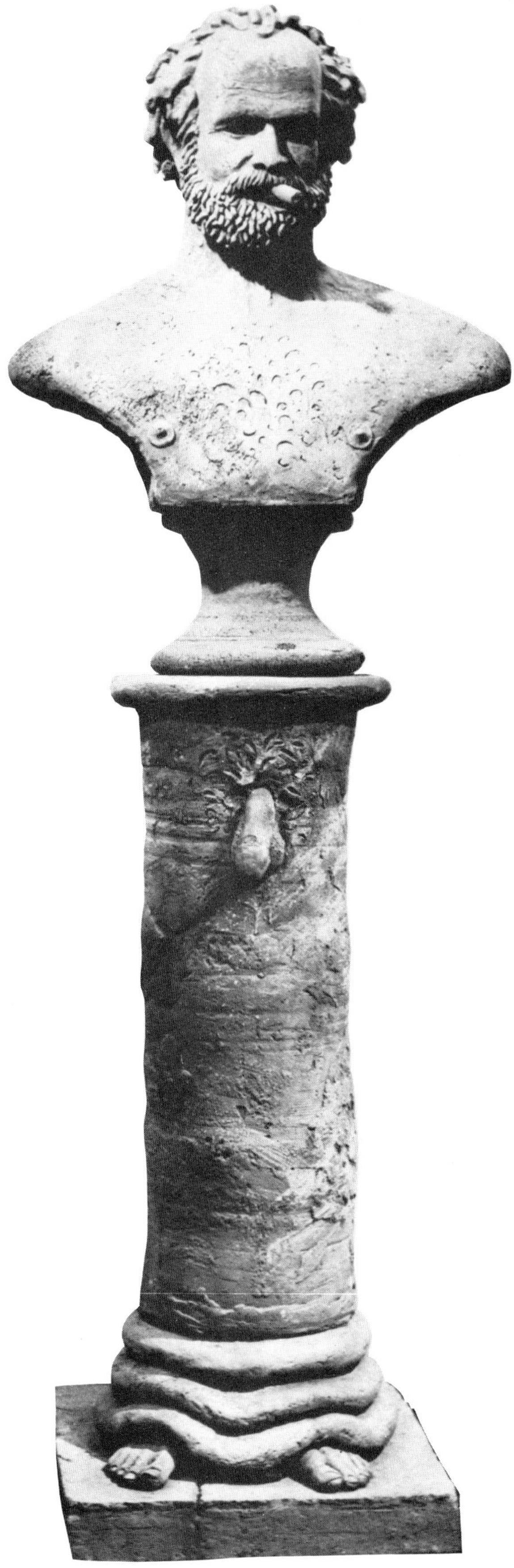

Robert Arneson

Developments During the 1960's 12

Although Peter Voulkos has been largely responsible for providing American potters with a catharsis which aided in promoting attitudes of exuberance and vitality, most mature artists who came under his influence did not sheepishly follow in his path. Some pursued their own identities and through long, patient searching arrived at forms that distinguishes them from each other. Their common denominator was one of a spiritual nature; an attitude toward ceramics, art, work and life. Each of them has made a vital contribution to American ceramics. Collectively they provided Americans with a new, almost revolutionary way of looking at ceramics which, in preceding times, had been couched in the prototypes of Oriental or European aesthetics.

John Mason was among the first group of young potters who studied under and worked with Peter Voulkos and whose spirit of free experimentation resulted in the adoption of Abstract Expressionism in ceramics. By 1958 Mason seemed committed to the idea that a pot need not necessarily assume a vessel form; that the invariable symmetry of the wheel could be a point of departure for creating more vigorous statements of personal expression.

Mason achieved this best by altering the shape of the pot through cutting, denting or otherwise distorting the basically circular design. By adding low-fire, brightly colored glazes he further increased a distorted sense of balance. This exploration of form and surface for its expressive potential signalled the direction that Mason's work would assume in the future. He soon abandoned any clues about the "pot-as-a-vessel" idea in favor of a much more dynamic, massive and weighty expression which manifested itself in a series of monolithic, totem-like configurations.

These towering sculptures, built with a directness and spontaneity which the soft clay encourages, conveyed tensions and animation which are visual clues to the aggressiveness with which Mason's work has become identified. Allowing the clay at times to remain undecorated, with the exception of a few spots of bright glaze, reinforces the power of these growing, twisting organic free-forms (Fig. 12-1).

Mason also became well known for his large wall reliefs which employed a similar approach to construction and surface treatment as seen in his free standing sculptures. Dealing with scales of from six feet high to over ten feet wide, he imparted these topographical explorations with a dynamism and rigor that was the result of actually stepping into the mural while he pounded, pushed, and cut the clay into a complex puzzle-like assemblage. Glazing a few areas with bright, primary colors created dramatic contrasts to the otherwise unglazed stoneware clay.

By the mid-1960's Mason began to deal with a more limited range of shapes. In favor of the organic columns he now developed a series of more simplified geometric forms with the cross or X as the dominating shape. He retained a sense of power in these by working with scales of up to six feet tall and glazing them in vivid reds and yellows (Fig. 12-2).

Mason was one of a number of young ceramic artists who serves as a good example of how some potters during the middle 1960's abandoned their association with traditional pottery and began to fashion for themselves works of ceramics that easily distinguished it

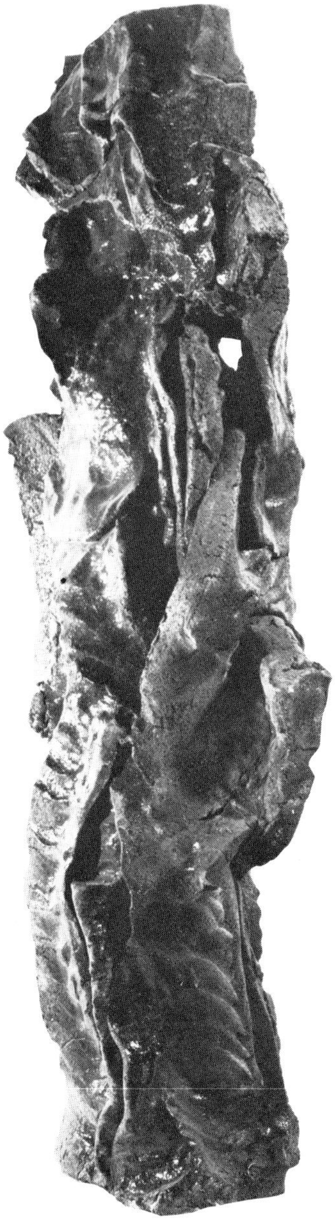

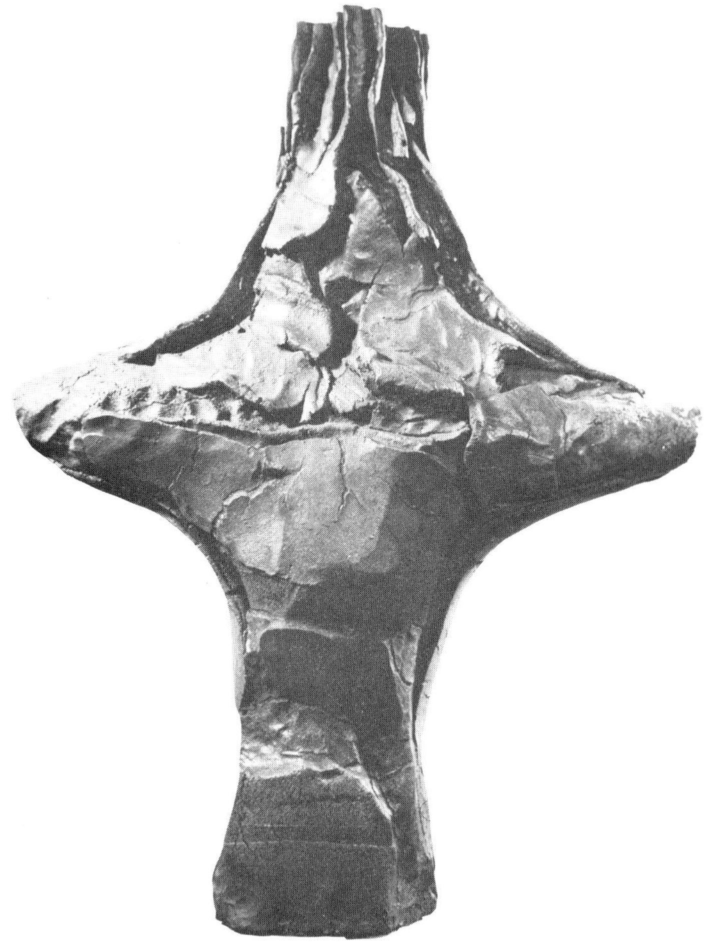

Figure 12-2. John Mason, "Cross Form-Dark Brown," 1963, stoneware clay, handbuilt, 66″ high. Courtesy of the artist and Hansen Fuller Gallery, San Francisco.

Mason's massive clay sculptures served as an indication how some studio-potters of the mid-1960's abandoned their association with traditional pottery in order to fashion for themselves a more personal form of self-expression.

Figure 12-1. John Mason, "Vertical Sculpture," 1960, stoneware clay, handbuilt, 66″ high. Courtesy of the artist and Hansen Fuller Gallery, San Francisco.

Mason's towering sculptures are a good example of how some artists working in clay reflected the dynamic energy often associated with abstract expressionism.

as works of art rather than fictile objects of the hand-crafts. It was a time when the conventions of the ceramic media and its value as an art form came under serious questioning. Through his work, Mason contributed to the growing belief that utilitarian considerations may interfere with the expressive function of art—that works of art made of clay must aim new questions at the nature of existence. This kind of introspection seemed to be accomplished best when an aesthetic experience was presented in its purest form, as in his large, minimalist sculptures.

Identifying closely with the abstract expressionists who dealt with ceramics in a highly energized, almost violent act of "becoming" is the work of Stephen DeStaebler. His large ceramic sculptures represent a liberating force from the constraints of the preciousness that characterized so much American ceramics during the preceding ten to fifteen years. He combined his interest for monumental proportions (sometimes to heights of nine feet) with his fascination for capturing and retaining the natural, rock-like quality of clay. This brought his personal expressions into close proximity of a primeval state of the earth.

Among his most impressive contributions to the development of American ceramics are his more recent involvements with figurative content clarified through the human form. When working on a more abstract level, he resorts to implied land formations. In the latter, DeStaebler skillfully manipulated large slabs of clay by tearing, pounding, denting, cutting, almost mutilating the clay in order to convey a sense of rawness and spontaneity. This was sensitively balanced by treating the surfaces with dry, matt glazes or stains, thereby achieving close resemblances or analogies to the earth. Whether these mammouth formations hung on a wall, stood by themselves or layed on the floor, DeStaebler's work always conveys a feeling of transition. The pieces do not reside in a state of dormancy, but instead, exude a kind of quiet mystery—like a volcano—that seems to harbor pent-up energy which could be released at any moment.

Thus, when he invested his pieces with cuts, crevices, cracks and chasms they served not as mere decorative motifs, but rather as elements which suggest that beneath the surfaces and in between the various openings are harbored some mysterious forces which could reveal themselves at any time. Even in his gigantic thrones, which bisect the form, suggest that there is potential for other concealments to reveal themselves (Fig. 12-3).

When DeStaebler resorted to the human figure for his subject matter, he retained much of the same qualities of his landscapes. Because of the large scale (sometimes up to eight feet tall) and the handling of the clay and its surface, his figures convey a quiet, almost occult sense of the past. The images are not gestural; they seem, instead, to be receding into their large, pedestal-like forms. The absence of heads, in fact, their fragmentary compositions achieved by leaving out parts of the anatomy, all add up to a sense of incompleteness, of decaying or crumbling (Fig. 12-4). This highly personal, poignant approach to self-expression has established DeStaebler as one of the important leaders of contemporary American ceramics.

Funk Art in American Ceramics

One of the more perplexing idioms in contemporary American ceramics of the 1960's is Funk art. It defies clear, easily definable

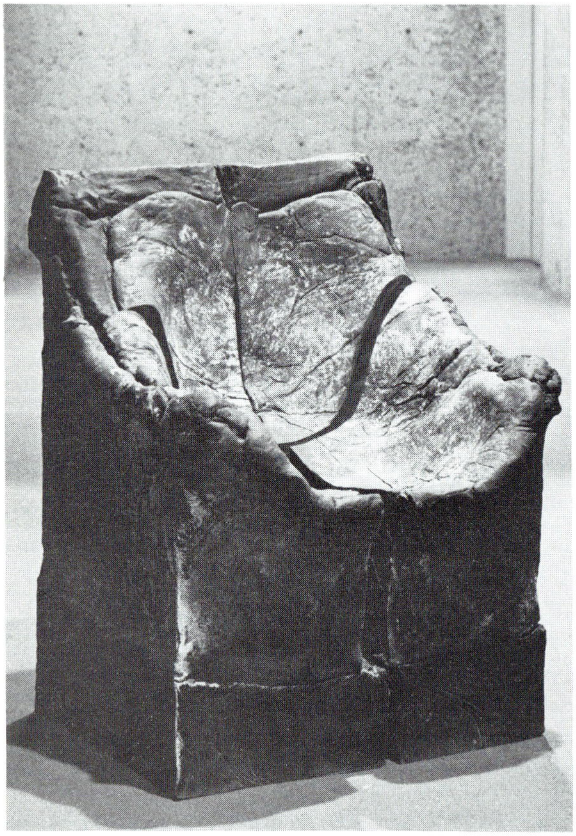

Figure 12-3. Stephen DeStaebler, "Bisected Throne," stoneware clay, handbuilt, 43" h × 34" l × 33" w, 1973. Courtesy of the artist.

DeStaebler's use of monumental proportions and the raw, rock-like quality of clay brings his work into close proximity of primeval states of the earth.

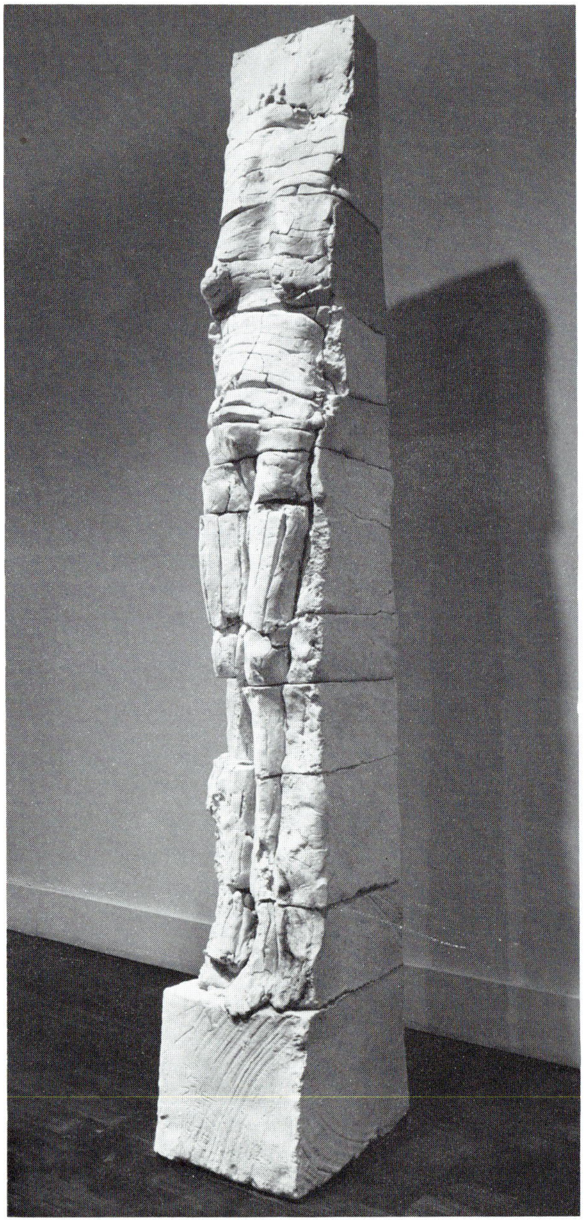

Figure 12-4. Stephen DeStaebler, "Standing Woman with Yellow Calf," stoneware clay, handbuilt, 85" h × 17" l × 16" w, 1976. Courtesy of the artist.

A feeling of quiet mystery prevails in DeStaebler's monumental figurative sculptures.

categorization. Begun essentially in California, it is equally difficult to find a logical relationship to its historical antecedents. Although it is often identified with some aspects of Surrealist painting and sculpture, it should be noted that Funk ceramics possesses some obvious characteristics that set it apart from Surrealism.

In terms of subject matter, Funk ceramics frequently is bizzare, grotesque, inelegant, and in fact, rather ugly. Of special interest to numerous artists working in this mode of expression were ideas that conveyed associations of lewd, sensuous and voluptuary feelings. Erotic images, exploited to their most heightened psychological potency lent themselves particularly well for evoking a wide range of responses that may include complete outrage, disgust, laughter or bewilderment.

Unlike most Surrealist painting and sculpture, which often sought to create new meaning by juxtaposing familiar objects in a different environment, Funk ceramic objects became transformed articles and ideas and thereby focused new meanings on the final forms. Clay lent itself especially well for this, since its pliable quality can be easily used for distortion. The ready availability of a wide range of colors and the ease with which the clay can also be made to imitate almost any other material, added to the rich vocabulary needed by the ceramic artist in order to create rich, sumptuous and engaging surfaces.

As early as 1960 there were signs that a new movement was developing, which was challenging the Abstract Expressionist syndrome. It could be seen in some "pots" by people such as Peter Voulkos, Manuel Neri and James Melchert. Before 1960 their forms, even when dramatically distorted, could still be viewed with some sense of utilitarian purpose. But thereafter, much of their ceramics assumed a more intense uselessness. Hence, the rather clear abandonment not only of traditional notions of well integrated plastic and visual relationships, and acceptance of an overbearing and irreverent impracticality signalled a new era in the development of American ceramics. It became popularly accepted as Funk art ceramics.

Robert Arneson

One of the prime instigators of the Funk art influence in ceramics was Robert Arneson, a former student of Voulkos. In 1961 he created his first series of pop bottles thrown on the wheel and then capped with the usual bottle cap. When he stamped it with the phrase "No Return" Arneson signalled his identity with the newly emerging Funk art ceramics movement. His "Six Pack" of 1964, showing twisted, soft soda bottles, complete in a case made of clay, reinforced his allegiance to this new action in ceramics. His entire production, in fact, assumed a highly complex interchange of object-making, of incorporating words, phrases and deliberately misspelled titles and of combining these into highly personal and symbolic references.

Arneson, and others like him working in clay, never lost sight of infusing the popular item with a strong sense of personal involvement and intimate associations. Whether the subject matter was a six pack of bottles, a toaster with an emerging hand of 1965, a typewriter with lacquered fingernails replaced as the keys or a clay brick of 1966 with the word "Waterbrick" stamped on it, Arneson's modeling of the object project a strong physical and emotional presence. None of his work could ever be identified with the cool, detached Pop art syndrome as seen in the work of painters or sculptors of other mediums. Working in clay allowed Arneson to explore more fully the parody of everyday objects and their witty associations. Whereas someone like Claes Oldenburg would transform a hamburger or fan into a monument whose main concern became one of pure aesthetics, Arneson's commitment to dealing with real-life situations resulted in his work always projecting some aspect of human presence. His plate series of 1971 are not just passive selections of everyday objects. They are poignant reminders of human activities, an idea that sets his creative productions at quite opposite ends in contrast to Pop artists, especially those working in New York.

Arneson's prolific production often included a number of inspirations which emerged simultaneously. While he was involved in the more referential "encounters" of everyday experiences, he also investigated the more enigmatic, surreal concepts which dealt with the idea of juxtaposing objects in unfamiliar, strange and bizzare fashion.

Of particular note were a series of cups started in 1971 which resulted in the "Mountain Cup" that depicts a sumptuously glazed rock with a handle attached to it, sitting on a richly glazed saucer. The cup series are among the most Magritte-like creations, in that they come close to the idea of using familiar references which, when they are combined in unorthodox fashion, will evoke something else—usually something unfamiliar. Even their clear, crisp finishing in terms of form, decoration and glaze is similar to the careful renderings of Magritte's paintings.

Arneson's profuse production is, at times, dizzying, ranging in subject matter from a series of plates that illustrate throwing techniques ("How to Make the Big Dish Plate" of 1967) to the renditions of his home and surrounding landscape (Plate 14). But perhaps no one particular body of work established him more as one of the pre-eminent leaders of American ceramics than have his series of busts. All of them are self portraits and address themselves to a pun about how he relates to ceramics and to every-day situations or how he sees himself as an important historical figure (Figs. 12-5, 12-6, 12-7). See Fig. 12-0.

Arneson's early interest in wanting to become a professional cartoonist seems to linger in the self portraits, however slightly. Though the configurations of his own heads are seldom animated and refined as one would usually find in a good cartoon, Arneson nevertheless resorts to strong distortions and, at times, even some form of suspended gesture. In his "Crazed" portrait of 1972 he portrayed himself in a scream whose power is accented by thick, syrupy glaze that literally drips from his teeth and beard (Fig. 12-8). In his "Hollow Gesture" which depicts him with his tongue sticking out, one sees yet another example of how Arneson skillfully orchestrated and reinforced an irrational view of himself. The piece is glazed with vivid, low-fire colors and illustrates how Arneson, as well as others who came under his later influence, abandoned straightforward representation of nature in favor for a new, poetic strangeness (Fig. 12-9).

Among his most imposing contributions which reaffirmed Arneson's leadership in contemporary ceramics was his "Fragments of Civilizations" of 1972. Although several writers have attempted to align the piece with

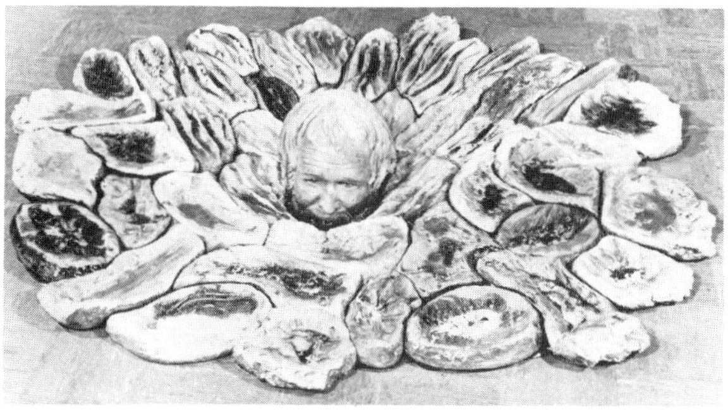

Figure 12-5. Robert Arneson, "Stream A Head," clay, glazed in multicolor glazes, handbuilt, 13" × 70" × 65", 1974. Courtesy the Museum of Contemporary Art, Chicago, Illinois.

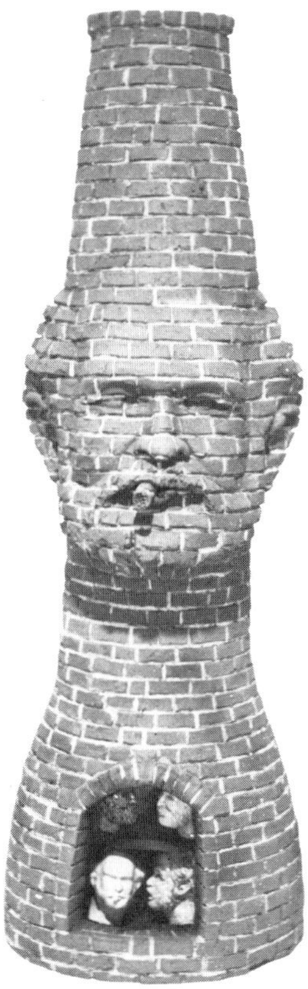

Figure 12-6. Robert Arneson, "Kiln-Man," Terra Cotta, handbuilt, 36" tall, 1971. Courtesy of the artist.

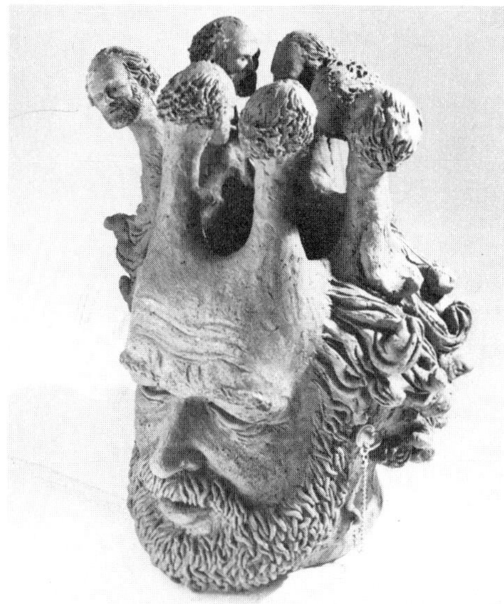

Figure 12-7. Robert Arneson, "Huddle," Terra Cotta, handbuilt, 1973, from the 1974 Robert Arneson Retrospective Exhibition. Courtesy of the Museum of Contemporary Art, Chicago, Illinois.

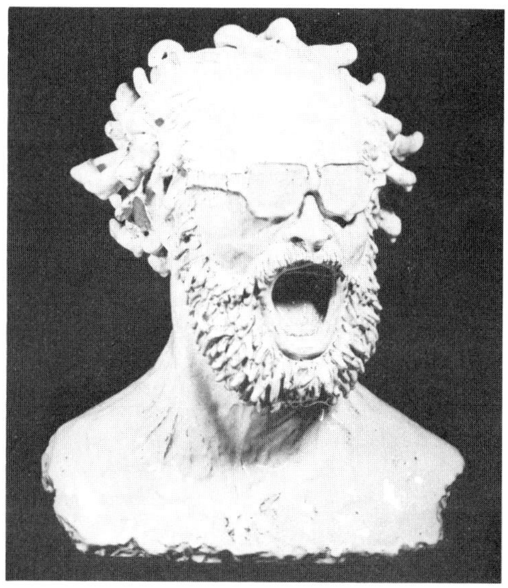

Figure 12-8. Robert Arneson, "Crazed," glazed ceramic, handbuilt, 22" × 19", 1972. Courtesy of the artist and Hansen Fuller Gallery, San Francisco.

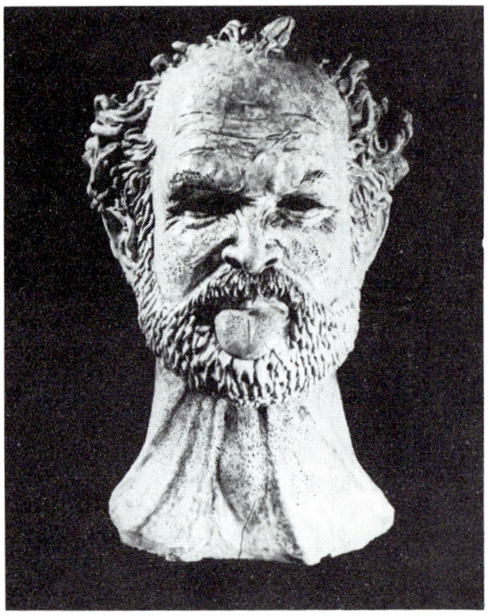

Figure 12-9. Robert Arneson, "Hollow Gesture," glazed ceramic, handbuilt, 1971. Courtesy of the artist and Hansen Fuller Gallery, San Francisco, California.

Arneson frequently abandoned naturalistic representation in favor for a more distorted and humerous view of himself.

Figure 12-10. Robert Arneson, "Fragments of Civilization," Terra Cotta, handbuilt and cast, approx. 15′ × 20′, 1972. Courtesy of the artist, Hansen Fuller Gallery and the John Michael Kohler Art Center, Sheboygan, Wisconsin.

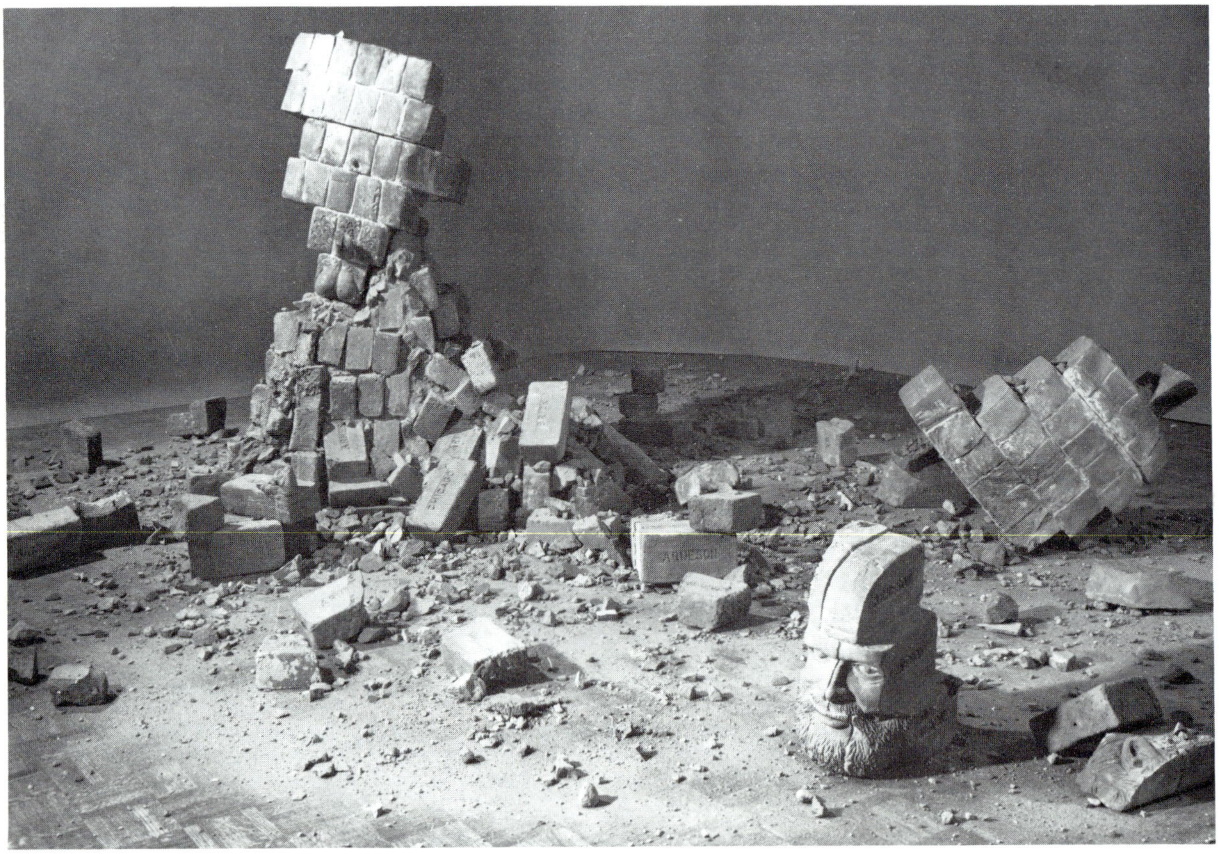

an overt concern that Arneson may have had with past civilizations, or the demise of contemporary society, Arneson himself pointed out that it was merely the outgrowth of an ongoing dialog which he has carried on with himself. In reference to this he explained that "I try not to take myself too seriously, and when I think I might be, its time to knock over a big piece"[1](Fig. 12-10).

Although Arneson's artistic output during any given period may appear to be somewhat confusing, due mainly to the wide range of subject matter with which he deals at one time, one of the unifying factors is his distinctive sense of humor. Sometimes self-effacing, other times sardonic, it is always somewhat aggressive and creates confusion and discomfort. Those who were confronted with Arneson's work, as well as the sculptures by others who came under his influence, may have realized that Funk art ceramics was robbing pottery of its traditional function and identity. In large part this was achieved through the elements of surprise, shock, contradiction and disorientation.

The seemingly haphazard manner with which some Funk art ceramics were executed in no way reflects what may appear to be a lack of sound craftsmanship. Manuel Neri's "loops" of 1961, Arneson's vexatious telephone "Call Me Lover" of 1965, James Melchert's "Leg Pot" and "Anti-Slant Wall Sculpture" of 1966 all employ a direct, spontaneous handling of clay. This seemed to heighten the expressive impulsiveness often associated with the casualness of one part of the Funk art allegiance (Plate 15).

But at the same time, a number of ceramic artists also appeared to be taking clues from other artists who were working within the Funk philosophy, though not in ceramic materials. Sculptors such as Robert Hudson, Mowry Baden, Harold Paris, Jerrold Ballaine and Don Potts, for example, were working in plastics, wood, metals, fabrics and rubber. Careful construction and finishing resulted in images that were hard-edged, shiny and super clean. In similar manner, some artists using clay took great care to construct and finish their pieces with an exactitude that conveyed a feeling of almost having been machine made. This allowed for maximum clarity in expressing the abstract and the literal qualities.

For example, Kenneth Price started a series of egg-like shapes in 1962 from which protrude embryonic and other subdued genitalia. These were carefully built and covered with repeated layers of paint and reflect an impeccable craftsmanship and draftsmanship recruited for promoting a greater sense of formality within the panorama of Funk art ceramics.

Many of the nation's art journals such as *Art Forum, Art in America, Art News, Craft Horizons* and *Ceramics Monthly,* as well as various catalogs from art museums and galleries who held exhibitions or ceramics, transmitted the ideologies and form concepts of Funk art ceramics. Although the most enthusiastic proponents of this newly formed art were located in California, other parts of the country also had its popular practitioners. Curt Hoard, for example, of Minnesota created a series of flintlock guns whose barrels metamorphosed into soft, limp phalic symbols (Plate 16).

Kenneth Vavrek, while still located in La Crosse, Wisconsin made a series of bullet forms in 1969. They were carefully constructed with various building techniques and skillfully glazed in bright, multicolored combinations to suggest erotic and politically oriented relationships. The idea of multiplicity of meanings in these artists' creations was also popular with a number of Funk art ceramists. At first glance their well crafted forms and seemingly innocent content may well have elicited a passive response. But closer scrutiny reveals more perplexing relationships couched in a kind of post-Freudian imagery such as the bullet and the phallus (Fig. 12-11).

Paul Dresang of Wisconsin tranformed every-day objects such as kitchen utencils, drills, fans and mix-masters into sensuous, almost lewd configurations. These were dramatized not only through their skillful redefinition of the orginal subject matter, but by also imbuing them with a sense of color and surface that was directly aimed at the viewer's sybaritic nerves (Fig. 12-12). In similar manner, Judy Onofrio of Rochester, Minnesota, handled clay with directness and sensitivity in creating a series of hearts whose folds and crevices give clues to other anatomical references. Supplemented with airbrushed underglazes and acrylic paints of soft, fleshy colors she effectively conveys feelings of ephemeral erotica (Fig. 12-13). When erotic symbols are incorporated a more disquieting sensuality is in contention with a kind of superficial abstraction.

More subtle, but nonetheless convincing in transmitting feelings of a more ethereal eroticism can be seen in the sculptures of Henry Gernhardt (Fig. 12-14) from Syracuse, New York and Ruth Duckworth of Chicago, Illinois (Fig. 12-15). In both cases, though the overall configurations identify with pseudo-landscape ideas, the unexpected orifices, bulges, and breast forms are symbolic in content and evocative in feeling.

These and other examples cited are testament to the popularity and importance of Funk art ceramics as it emanated from California and spread to various other parts of the country during the late 1960's and early 1970's. It

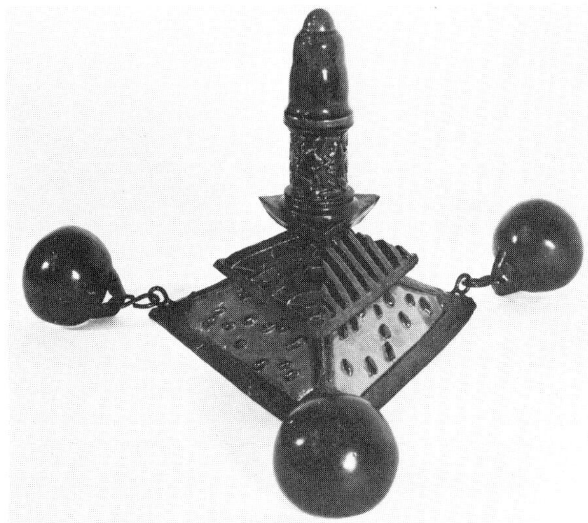

Figure 12-11. Kenneth Vavrek, "Air Cooled Tangarine," stoneware, handbuilt and thrown parts, multicolored glazes and metalic lusters, ca. 1971. Courtesy of the artist.

Numerous artist-potters of the late 1960's and early 70's combined elements of Funk and Pop art in creating provocative statements related to the social climate of the times.

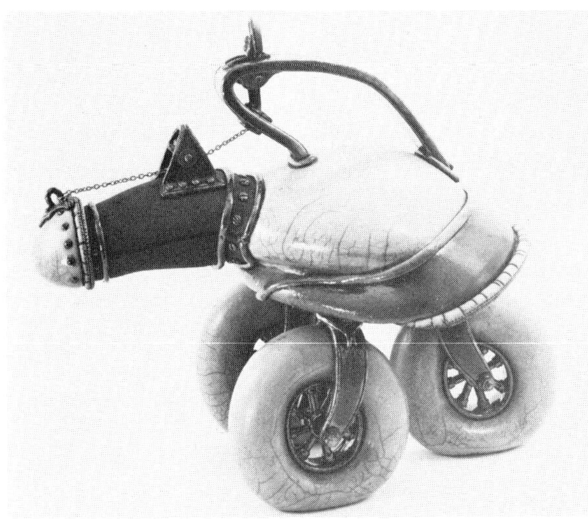

Figure 12-12. Paul Dresang, ceramic sculpture, wheel thrown and altered with handbuilt parts and chain; approx. 18″ long × 18″ high; 1975; Raku fired. Courtesy of the artist.

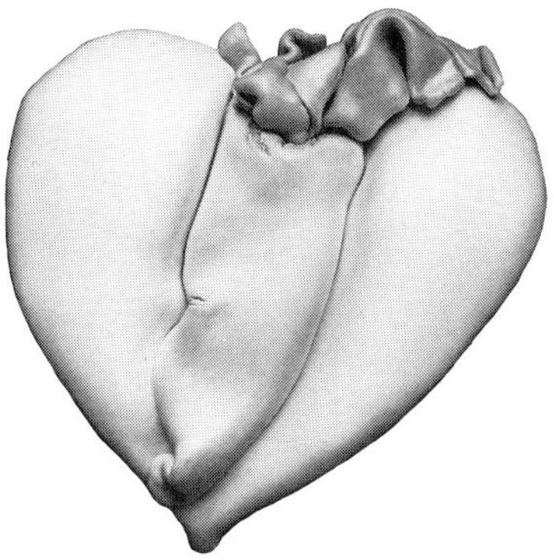

Figure 12-13. Judy Onofrio, "Soft Form," white earthenware, handbuilt, glazes and acrylic paints, 24″ diameter, 1977. Collection of the artist.

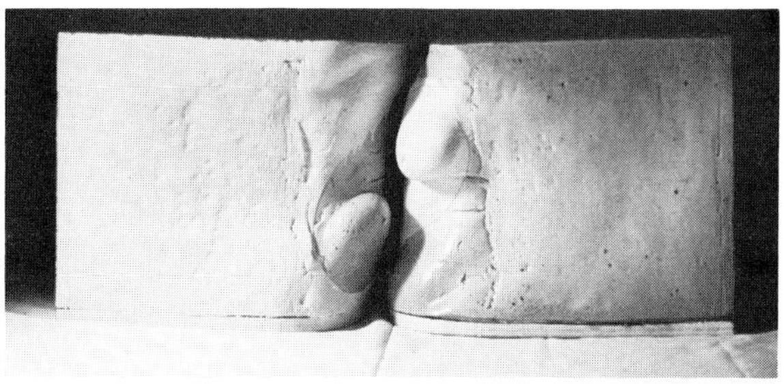

Figure 12-14. Henry Gernhardt, "Grand Canyon," stoneware, handbuilt, 20″ h × 50″ l, ca. 1972. Courtesy of the artist.

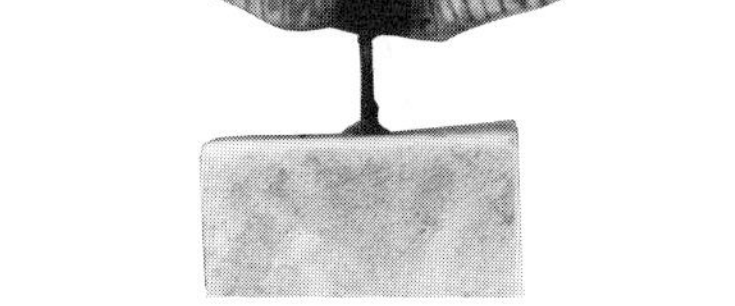

Figure 12-15. Ruth Duckworth, Sculpture, porcelain, 10″ w., handbuilt, ca. 1972. Courtesy of the artist.

exerted strong influences not only among the younger, more venturesome artists, but also made itself felt in the constantly evolving ideas of some older, more established ceramic artists.

Influences of Fantasy and Surrealism

Out of the spirit of Funk art ceramics there developed yet another very distinctive approach to dealing with private visions in clay. During the early 1960's a number of ceramic artists addressed themselves to the problem of incorporating subject matter in their statements which was quite different from the Funk artist. This newly emerging work depended heavily upon using references from the external, "real" or rational world. But by fragmenting and then reincorporating them into a composite, these artists achieved an iconography of fantasy, whim and surrealism that often approximated the irrational, strange and enigmatic. Their main task seemed to be to transform objects associated with the external world into a sense of metaphysical remoteness. The viewer was thereby provided with a new sense of excitement, or an accessibility to a new, though highly personal and mysterious experience.

James Melchert of California was among the earliest artists who used identifiable objects and symbols and by transposing them into new settings, caused one to seriously reconsider the validity of representationalism. In a series of games that he devised in 1967 he resorted to the use of fragmented parts of human anatomy and also of nonfunctional items such as spheres and functional objects such as clothes-hangers and juxtaposed them in such a manner as to confront the viewer with an unpredictable order of ideas (Fig. 12-16). If it was a game, it was not to be partaken in; it was not to be played with or in. One's daily association with the shapes he used became mystified through their segmented, seemingly unrelated nature to conventional perception. Thus one was obliged to become involved in his "games" in a mysterious, imaginary way.

Pattie Warashina of the University of Washington and David Middlebrook of the University of Kentucky are further examples of how some ceramic sculptors chose to faithfully reproduce objects with their external appearance left well intact. But the final impact often assumed cryptic forms by juxtaposing them in such a way that one would not ordinarily encounter them in the conventional world. Middlebrook's swimming pool sinking into an apple (Fig. 12-17) reflects the popular idea of how a number of artists shared the notion that the reverse rational order of things can create statements of surprise, contradiction and disorientation. It was a literal (though not necessarily conscious) way of creating confusion and discomfort which had not been dealt with previously in the same manner.

More doctrinaire and articulate was some sculpture by Warashina whose "Car Kiln" (Plate 17) rendered in red bricks projects a sense of mystery, but whose inscrutable meaning is more easily understood by the title. Thus, although the bricks of the car and the contour of the automobile are faithful reproductions, the contrast of the stylized flames coming out of the vehicle and the overall orchestration of these separate elements create a cumulative mental impact that is contrary to physical law and conventional reality. The general effect is one of defying common sense, an idea that was becoming more popular with

Figure 12-16. James Melchert, "Game on Black Field," cast earthenware and painted plywood, 72″ × 72″, 1972. Courtesy of the artist.

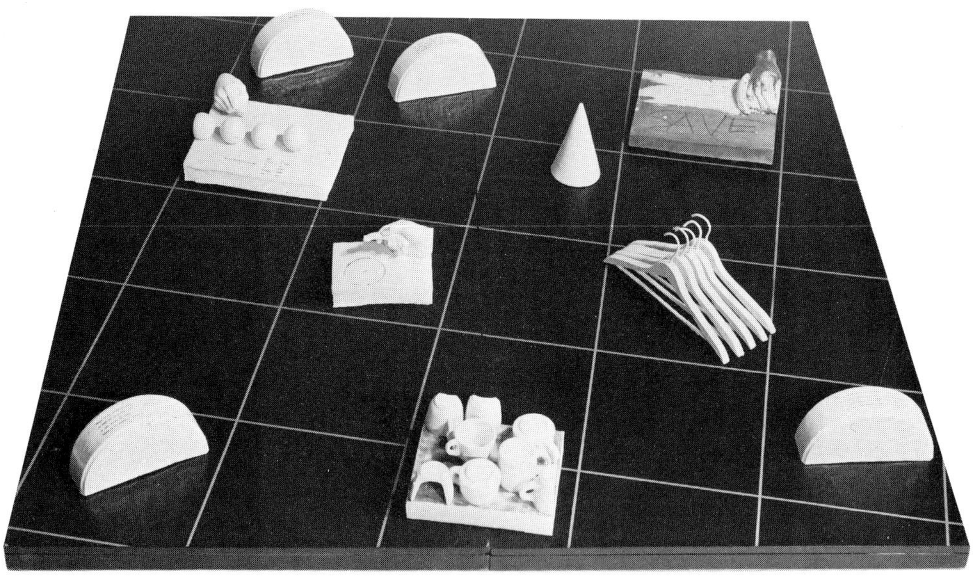

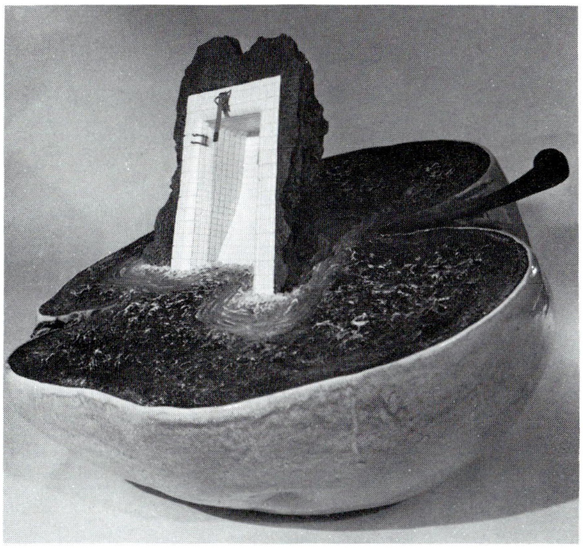

Figure 12-17. David Middlebrook, "Soft Core," stoneware, low-fire glazes, wooden stem and wooden diving board; 44" × 36", ca. 1973. Courtesy of the artist.

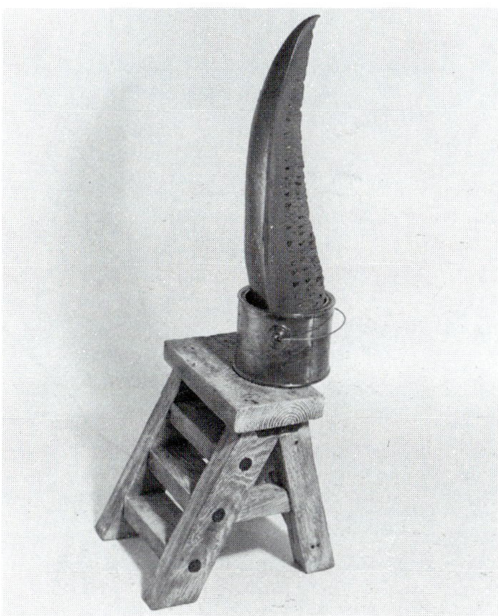

Figure 12-18. David Middlebrook, "Southern Comfort," stoneware clay, low-fired glazes, lusters and textured glazes; handbuilt, 42" × 17" × 17", 1976. Courtesy of the artist and the Quay Ceramics Gallery, San Francisco, California.

numerous other ceramic artists in various parts of the country during the late 1960's and early 70's.

James Stephenson of Pennsylvania State University made some large cone-like structures and set them outside amidst pedestrian and vehicular traffic (Fig. 12-20). Henry Gernhardt of Syracuse constructed vessels with emerging heads (Fig. 12-21), while Verne Funk of Peoria, Illinois painstakingly built simple boxes, plates and cylinders which were supplemented with sumptuous, sometimes erotic lips and open mouths (Figs. 12-22, 12-23, 12-24). Most of the artists working in this vein gave meticulous attention to faithfully reproduce the physical appearances of the literal elements which they incorporated in their total compositions. Although a heightened sense of clarity is well illustrated through their astute craftsmanship, combining these separate parts in an unorthodox manner aided in giving their work an enigmatic presence.

Richard Shaw of Hollywood, California is one of a number of young ceramic artists who enthusiastically embraced the newly adopted area of fantasy which relied heavily on incorporating figurative content as its underlying force. Starting in 1965 his couches and stuffed chairs, decorated with cows in landscape settings or ships sinking into the ocean, reflect a curious combination of nostalgia and Funk. Shaw's continual refinement of ideas and ceramic techniques eventually led to more distinctive innovations, especially in the area of complex assemblages made from variously cast pieces of earthenware or porcelain.

As if to subscribe to one aspect of the surrealists' idea of constructing images from accidentally found and "discovered" materials, Shaw made casts of items that are generally not associated with "high art." Sticks, stones, branches, pieces of cardboard and various

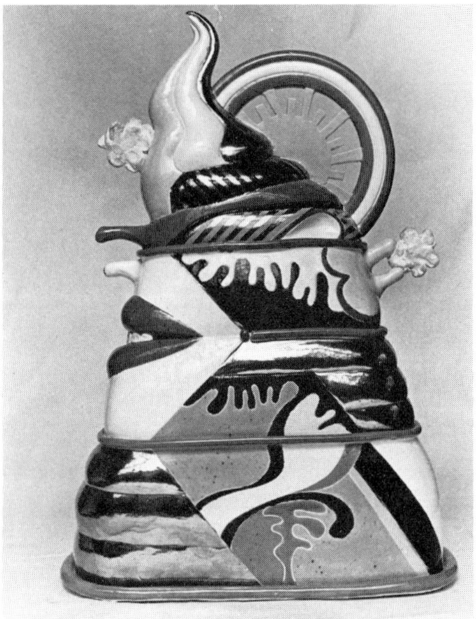

Figure 12-19. Patti Warashina, "Ketchup Kiss," earthenware, handbuilt, low-fire glazes and lusters, 36″ h, ca. 1972. Courtesy of the artist.

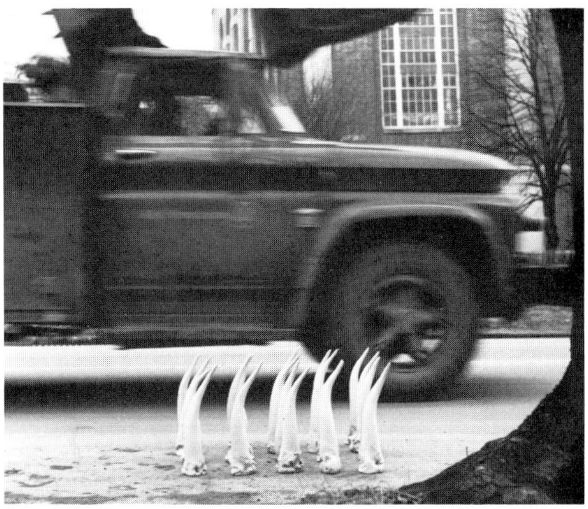

Figure 12-20. Jim Stephenson, "Clay Horn Series," stoneware, handbuilt, decorated with white slip, unglazed, each approx. 18″ high, 1971. Courtesy of the artist.

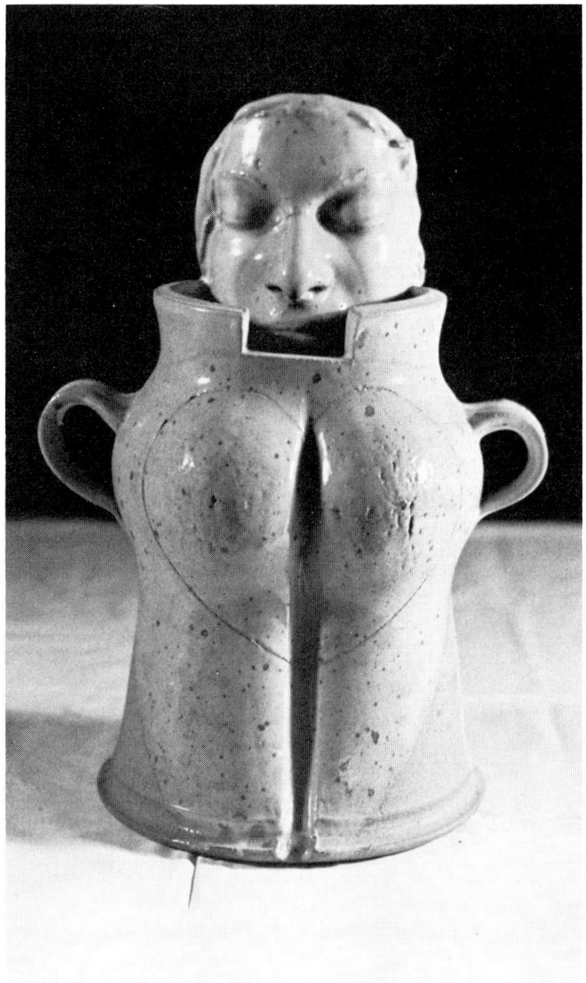

Figure 12-21. Henry Gernhardt, "Wishing Well," stoneware, wheel thrown and handbuilt, white opaque glaze, 18″ high, ca. 1972. Courtesy of the artist.

Numerous artists resorted to using parts of the human anatomy and traditional pottery vessels, and by combining them in unusual ways were able to transmit feelings of mystery.

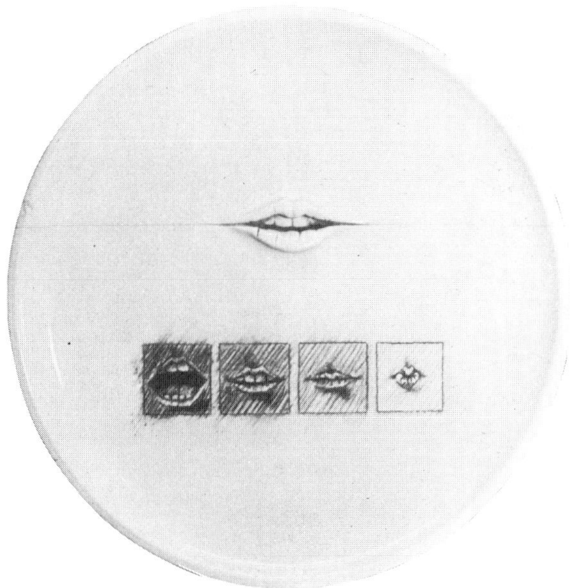

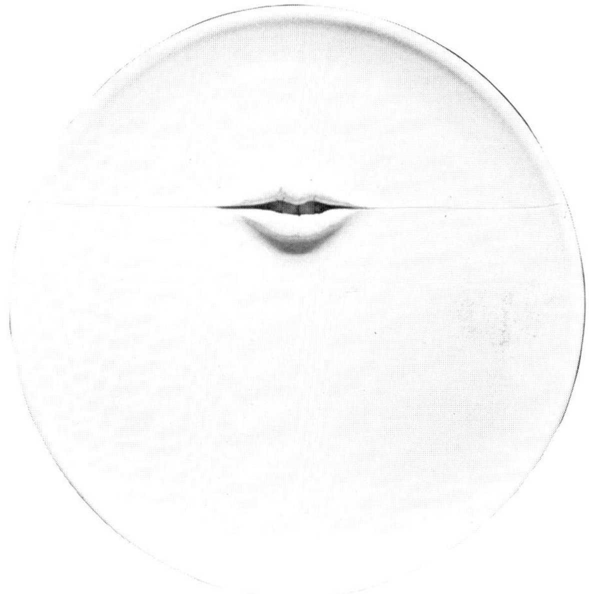

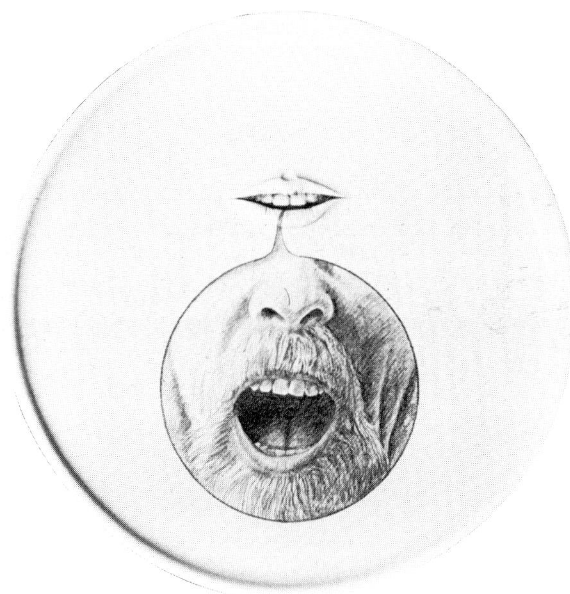

Figure 12-22. Verne Funk, Plate, earthenware, wheel thrown and modelled, underglaze pencil drawing, transparent glaze; 12″ diameter, ca. 1971. Courtesy of the artist.

Figure 12-23. Verne Funk, Plate, earthenware, wheel thrown and modelled, transparent glaze; 12″ diameter, ca. 1971. Courtesy of the artist.

Figure 12-24. Verne Funk, "Funk Plate," white earthenware, wheel thrown and modelled, underglaze pencil drawing, transparent cover glaze, 17 1/2″ diameter, ca. 1972. Courtesy of the artist.

Funk's ceramic pieces achieve an enigmatic presence by combining familiar elements in an unfamiliar setting.

other paraphernalia became an important part of his visual repertoire. In order to best illustrate their real identities, these objects were painstakingly treated with a wide array of popularized decorative techniques such as underglazes, ceramic stains, china paints, overglaze decals, metallic lusters and a wide range of glazes.

A natural extension of these techniques and ideas directed Shaw toward even more innovative explorations of the decal and silkscreening process which allowed him to reproduce any visual material in multicolor form with uncanny exactness. These were translated into complicated designs on cast porcelain plates. What sets them distinctively apart from the ideas of synthetic cubism of Picasso or Braque and the *tromp l'oeil* of William Harnett's or Aaron Bohrod's still life paintings is that they are cast in porcelain. The real-life character of the paper-thin porcelain makes them even more startling than if they had been dealt with as illusion on paper or canvas.

Not only is it the strangeness of the subject matter of Shaw's creations that give it distinctiveness; it is also a sense of precariousness, a nervous balance, that prevails which often gives his work a special provocative power (Plate 18). The idea of casting numerous parts and then assembling them into complex, tension-laden incongruous conglomerate forms increased in popularity during the 1970's, and young artists throughout various parts of the country began to pursue this new line of investigation with enthusiastic virtuosity (Figs. 12-25, 12-26, 12-27).

It is generally agreed that creative thinking is an imaginative act and that its processes lie quite near the realm of fantasy (Fig. 12-28). In the broadest sense of the term, fantasy underlies all art. But some artists deal with the idea of fantasy more directly as their form of expression than do others. In the case of American ceramics, a number of artists, starting as early as 1960, have sidestepped the more incongruous and mystifying aspects of surrealism (especially its symbolic implications) and have dealt with the problem of fantasy in a more direct and more complete means of creating their own world of make-believe.

The work of David Gilhooly from California is an example of how some ceramists went to great lengths to create for themselves an entire kingdom which centered around a particular fantasy. In his case a large, continuing body of work and great time and energy was directed at building a world of animals whose imaginary function is not, however, so far removed from the lives of ordinary, everyday people.

Gilhooly's initial forays into ceramic sculpture around 1965 led to a series of footstools and other renditions of exotic animals such as crocodiles, monkeys, cats, pigs, and poodles. These were supplemented by his interest in reproducing various kinds of food, with the all-American donut among the most conspicuous and popular items.

By 1970, Gilhooly had discovered his love for the frog and toad as the main theme for creating a mythical civilization. He embarked on a venture to create a Frog-World which was essentially based on developing frog-like creatures whose relationships closely identify with man's own history. Familiar human political figures, religious personages, artists and even gangsters ("Frog Capone," "Frog Washington." "Madonna and Frogs and the Nineteen Saints") all aided in the confusion of attempting to determine just what is human and what is frog. An unsettling kind of ambiguity exists in Gilhooly's work which adds to

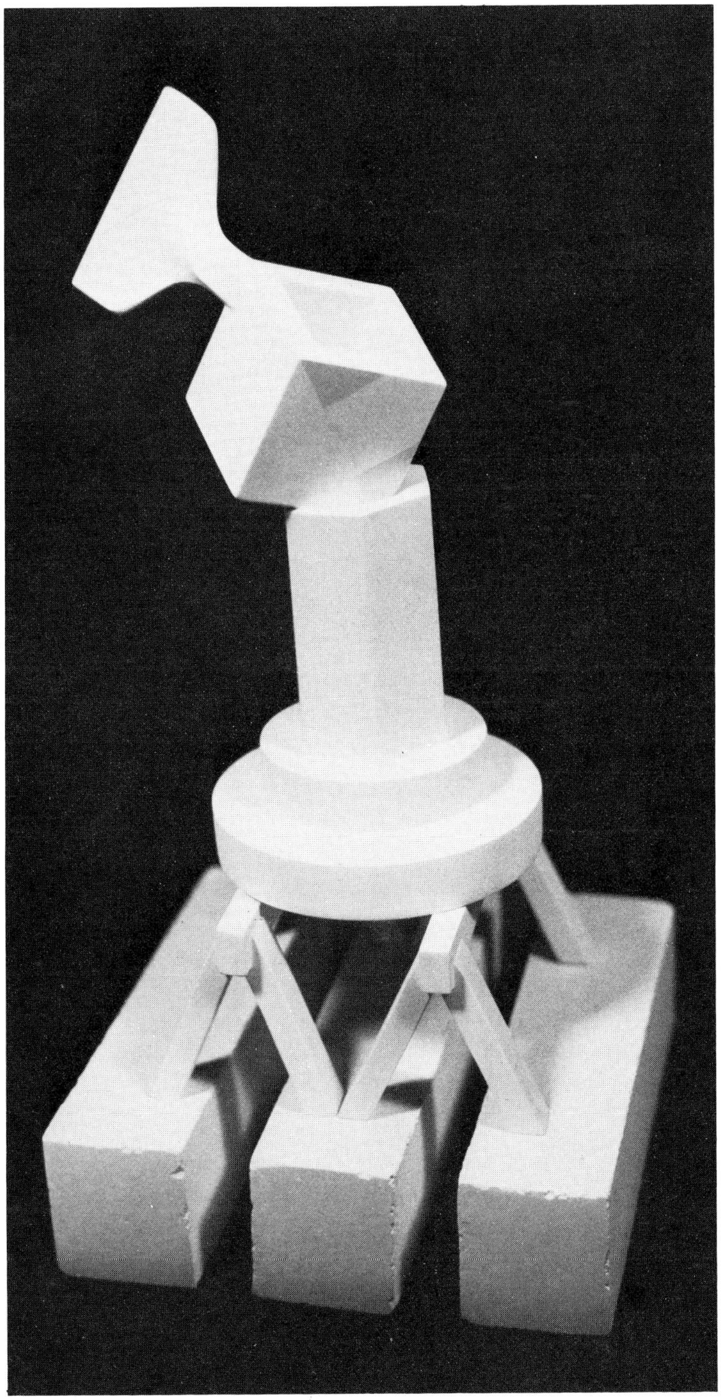

Figure 12-25. Bruce Ostwald, Untitled, white earthenware, cast and handbuilt, underglazes and transparent overglaze; 17″ h × 9″ w; 1977. Courtesy of the artist.

the notion of the Funk/Fantasy/neo-Dada/Surreal idea of wholesale rejection of traditional aesthetics (Fig. 12-31).

Another young artist who has been generally identified with the Funk art movement, but who is more appropriately connected with the world of fantasy, fun and humorous defiance is Clayton Bailey. Although he started with his absurd non-functional teapots in Wisconsin around 1962, his more interesting contributions to the evolving art of American ceramics seemed to reach more maturity and recognition after he settled in California.

It was there that Bailey refined his "Kritters," those witty, zany and often outrageous creatures which were half human, half animal. Sometimes immersed in water, his creatures would emerge from ingeniously constructed, electronically operated containers, confronting the viewer with peculiar sounds and noises. Bailey's free-wheeling mind created a rich array of mortals, including a large collection of rubber latex fetishes. But the more notable efforts came about when he assumed a new role of masquerading under the guise of Dr. George Gladstone.

Behind this new identity as a scientist Bailey proceeded to create a legend of the Precredulous Era, a time that he places before the Stone Age. This imaginary epoch served as the main catalyst for Bailey's voluminous creations of skeletal relics made from clay (Plate 19). They were crafted with exactness in order to resemble conventional paleontological remains. To the casual observer they may, in fact, appear to have been the result of a highly scientific excavation. Bailey has caused considerable notoriety by placing his Kaolithic fossils on California beaches and building sites and having them "discovered" by unsuspecting, serious-minded people who were not familiar with his tongue-in-cheek extravaganza.

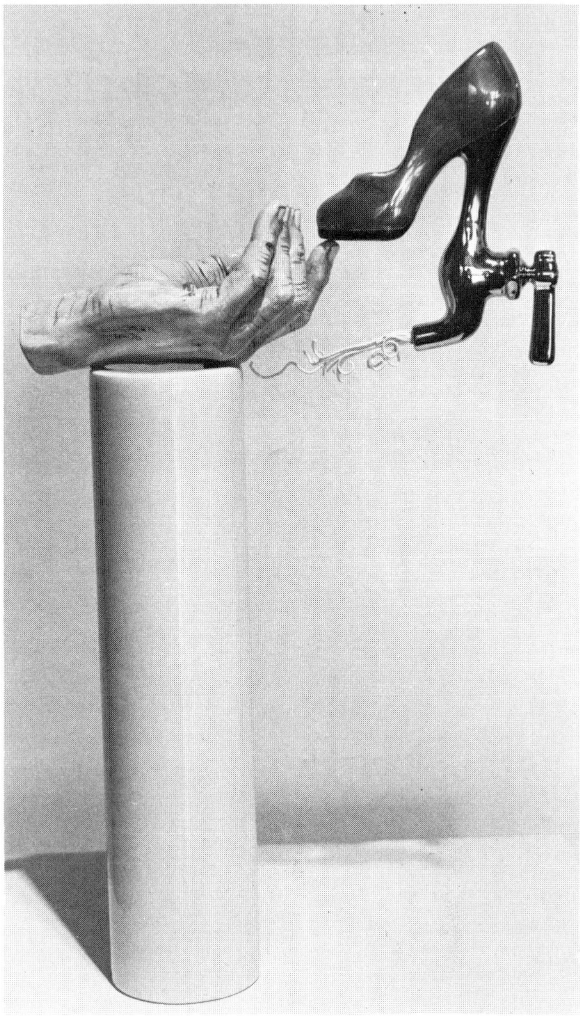

Figure 12-26. Lukmen Glasgow, "Tap-Shoe," clay, cast and handbuilt, multiple low fire glazes and lusters, 23″ h, 1977. Courtesy of the artist and Jacqueline Anhalt Gallery, Los Angeles, California.

A sense of mystery prevailed among the work of numerous, young ceramic artists who created compositions in a strange manner by combining conventional subject matter in new, bizzare fashion.

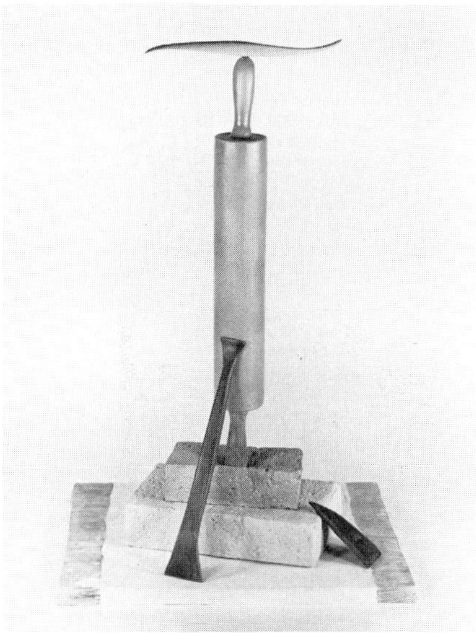

Figure 12-27. David Furman, "The Scale of Justice," ceramic, cast and handbuilt, variety of underglazes and cover glazes; 12″ × 15″ × 24″; 1976. Courtesy of the artist and Jacqueline Anhalt Gallery, Los Angeles, California.

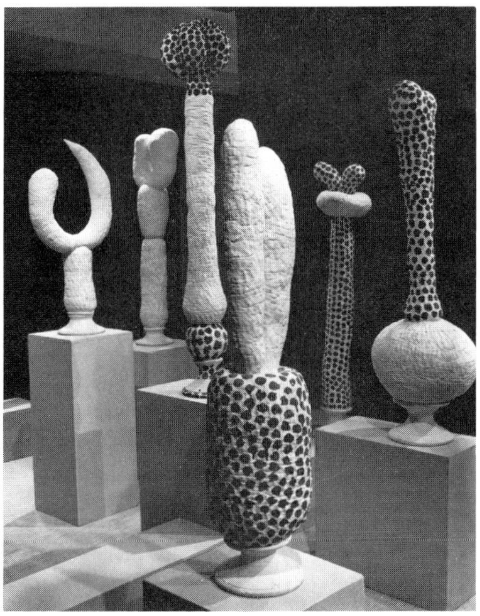

Figure 12-28. Dave DonTigny, "Clay Hybrids," stoneware, handbuilt and thrown, underglazes and variety of cover glazes, ranging from 3 to 5 ft. high. Courtesy of the artist.

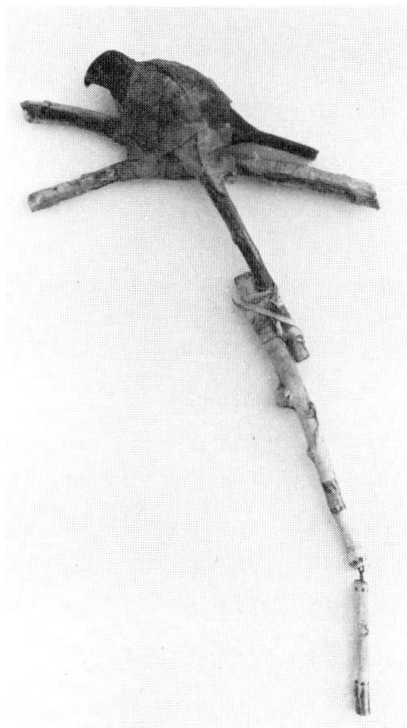

Figure 12-29. Jim Adamson, "Bird Wall Piece," earthenware clay and mixed media; handbuilt, 22″ high; 1977. The Quay Ceramics Gallery, San Francisco.

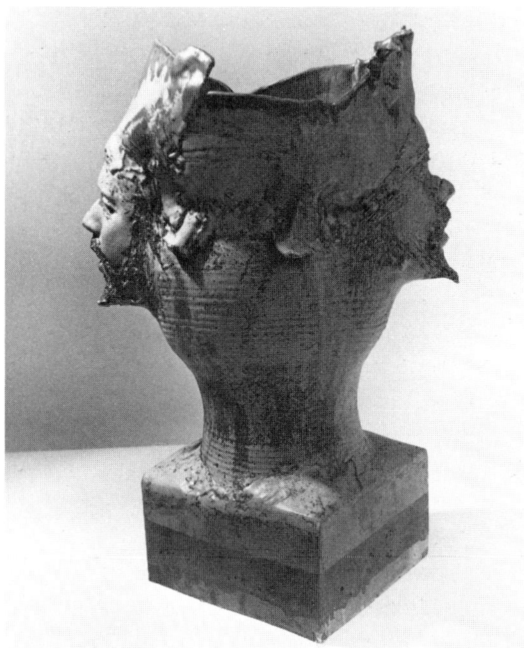

Figure 12-30. Bruce Grimes, "Floor Vase," stoneware, wheel thrown and handbuilt, 30″ tall, ca. 1972. Courtesy of the artist.

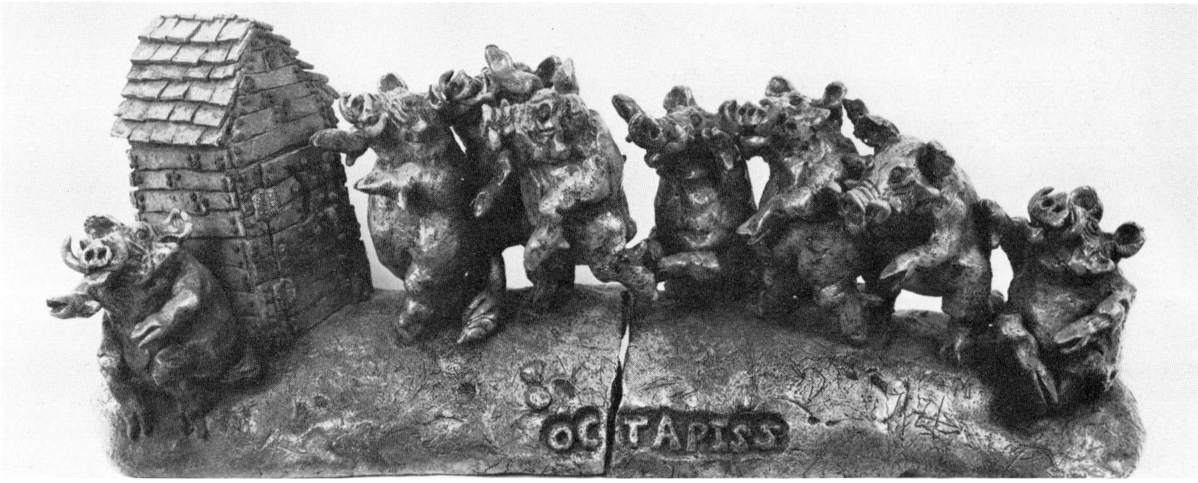

Figure 12-31. David Gilhooly, "Octapiss," earthenware, multicolored glazes, handbuilt; 1975. Courtesy, the ARCO Center for Visual Art, Los Angeles, California.

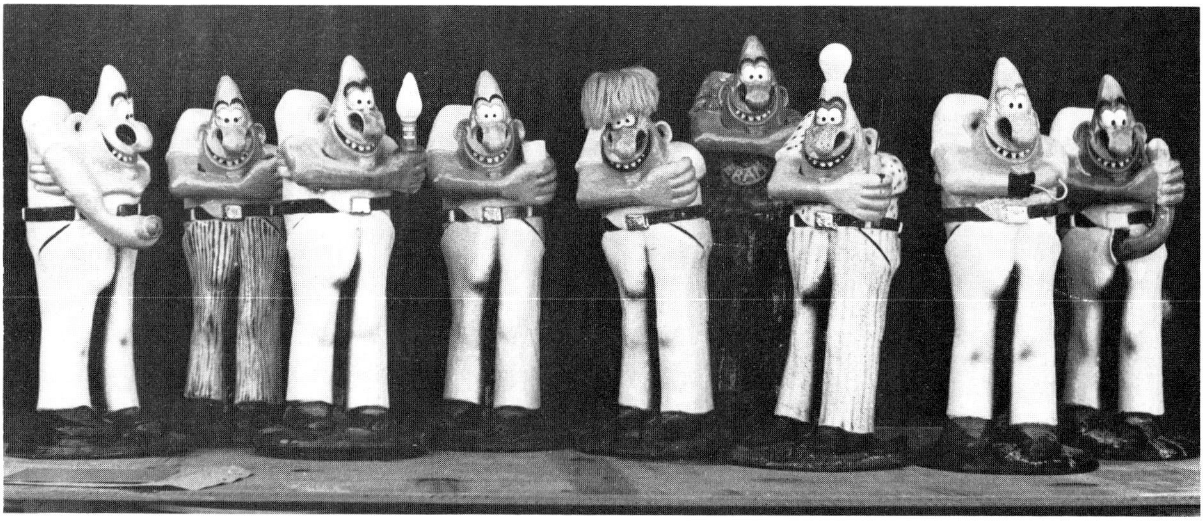

Figure 12-32a. Clayton Bailey, "Demented Pinhead Figures," cast parts and handbuilt, combined with mixed media, underglazes, variety of low fired glazes and lusters; average height 18″; 1971. Courtesy of the artist and Wonders of the World Museum, Port Costa, California.

Bailey's sculptures have received wide acclaim for its outrageous humor and ingenious defiance of "good taste."

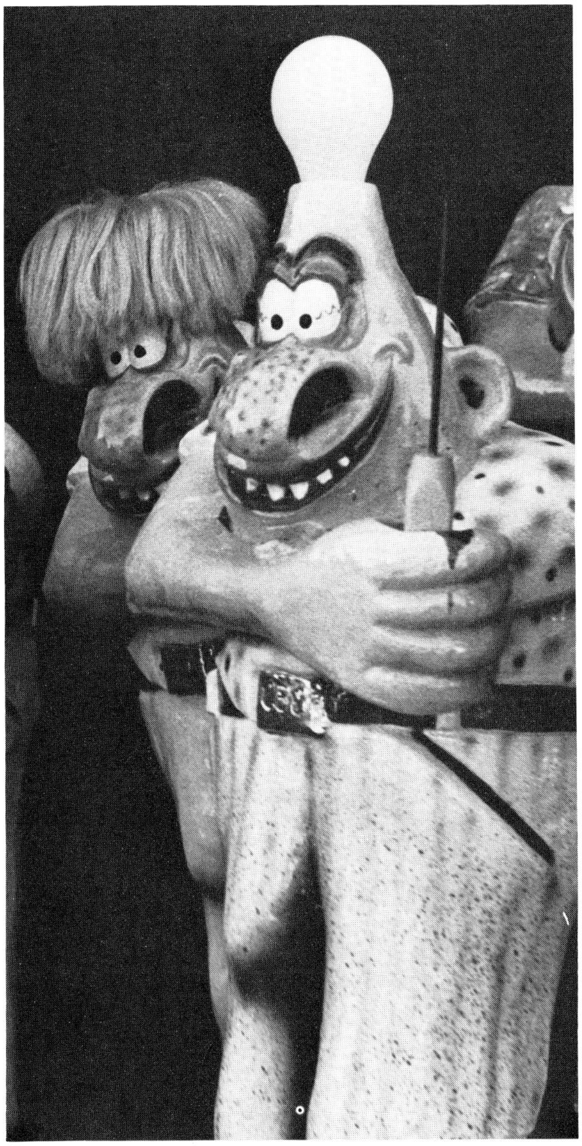

Figure 12-32b. Clayton Bailey, "Demented Pinhead Figures," 3 feet tall.

In order to better legitimize his buffoonery Bailey has designed and constructed a number of gadgets to aid him in substantiating his "discoveries." One such item, the Fossil Tester, sounds a siren when it comes in contact with a Kaolithic specimen. This is but another effort to help bring to the attention of the public his amazing discoveries. In contrast to other artists who have been involved in similar efforts of creating mythical cultures, Bailey takes his venture to a more complete conclusion by actually housing his "finds" in his Wonders of the World Museum in Port Costa, California. It is here that the viewer is confronted with Bailey's total vision of awesome specimens (Fig. 12-32a and Fig. 12-32b). If Bailey's humorous confusion of art and life were not detected in this setting, one could easily be convinced to believe in the existence of the Precredulous Era.

The popularity of fantasy as compared to Funk or Pop art in ceramics became widespread in America during the 1960's and 70's. The idea of using ordinary subject matter or common objects and then transforming them into zany, irreverent and absurd statements has long been the preoccupation of Jack Earl of Vermont. While he was still at the Toledo Museum School of Art during the sixties, he became involved in creating his penguin kingdom. Sustaining the interest in irony and wit which is generally associated with Funk and Pop, Earl also took great delight in the use of visual puns. He imbued his penguins with some humanoid considerations both in form and titles. His "Flower Basket Penguin" cast in porcelain was supplemented with a lengthy explanatory title in which he says:

> One time I was picking flowers and I looked up and there was a penguin picking flowers too and it had its basket full, so then we stopped picking flowers

and I never picked any again, but the penguin does all the time.[2]

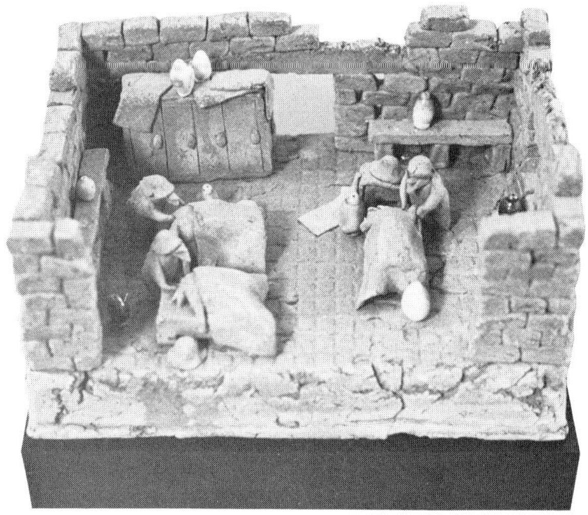

Figure 12-33. Doug Baldwin, "Undergraduate Rub Down Room," from the series of "The Great Duck Ceramic School," earthenware clay, handbuilt, partially slip decorated; 1976. Courtesy, Gallery Rebecca Cooper, Washington, D.C.

Doug Baldwin of the Maryland Institute of Art also developed an intense interest in creating a fantasy world consisting of ducks. In all of them a delightful sense of humor prevails, especially when he made a monumental setting of his "Great Duck Ceramic School" which features thirty-five rooms in which various activities are carried out by the ducks in creating ceramic pottery (Fig. 12-33).

In similar manner, Art Morrison of Cedar Rapids, Iowa and a product of the University of California at Davis, expanded his fantasy concept of art, history and life by transforming and reinterpreting some aspects of the present and the past. Finding analogies between the Sumerian and Assyrians of the Fertile Crescent of Mesopotamia, Morrison created a cultural group that could easily have inhabited the midwest, or more particularly, Iowa.

Using historical prototypes, he has developed an imaginary history of ancient Iowa and his "Farmounians." These creatures, who have their own class system, complete with gods such as Bacornius and Trickinosos, are not depicted in human form (Fig. 12-34). Instead they are rendered as pigs walking upright on "corntainers" or on ancient-looking ceramic reliefs known as Pigtaglyphs. To complete his interest in searching for "Farmounica," its legends and myths, Morrison serves one with additional "infarmation"

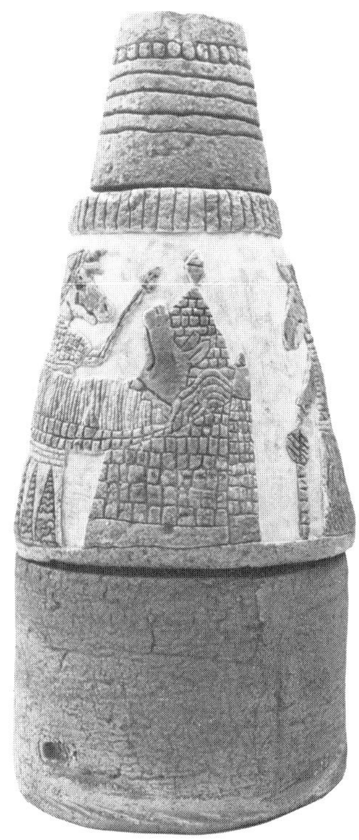

Figure 12-34. Art Morrison, "Trickinosos Levitating to the Planet Uranus," white earthenware, handbuilt, stains, low fire glazes and lusters, 18″ × 8″ × 9″; 1977. Courtesy of the artist.

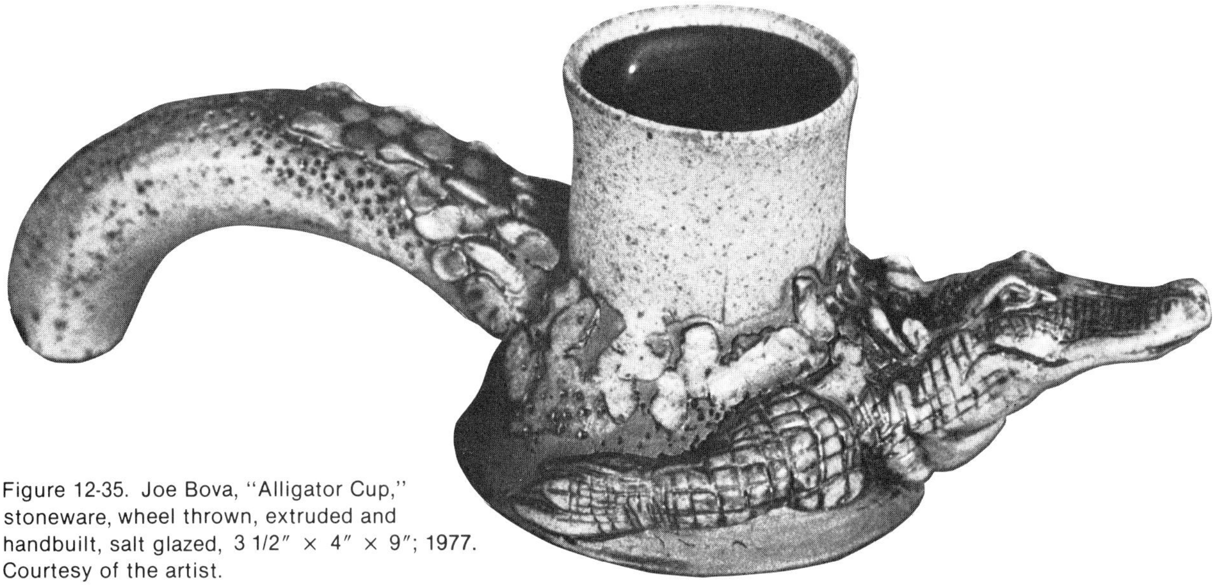

Figure 12-35. Joe Bova, "Alligator Cup," stoneware, wheel thrown, extruded and handbuilt, salt glazed, 3 1/2" × 4" × 9"; 1977. Courtesy of the artist.

such as color photographs of Marmounian architecture, writings, puns and a newly invented word vocabulary to aid in a better understanding of this highly amusing, personal dialog.

Joe Bova of Baton Rouge is yet another example of how numerous, young artists throughout the United States took refuge in the fantasy world of ceramic sculpture. Relying on the unique culture, landscape, flora and fauna of southern Louisiana, he creates objects of dual purposes. In his "Alligator Cup" (Fig. 12-35) any utilitarian consideration is obviously overshadowed by the zoomorphism of the stylized alligator. Humor abounds consistently as in his fish with eagle's wings or humanoid ducks. To this effect he explains that . . .

> . . . I am constantly thinking about humor, but when I make a piece, rather than begin with humor as the idea, I prefer to have a subject as an idea and impose my humor upon that subject extemporaneously.[3]

Most ceramists whose work was infused with the cross-influences of Pop, Funk, Surrealist and Fantasy art developed for themselves some individual identities. The newly celebrated popularity of subject matter, uses of colors and surfaces and serious reconsiderations of craftsmanship were in strong contrast with the more abstract expressionist aesthetic and became one of its more effective contenders. Other considerations relating to more complicated surface treatments created even more diversity.

Influences of Pop Art on Ceramics

Among the well entrenched influences on contemporary ceramics such as Abstract Expressionism, Surrealism, Fantasy and Funk, the activities of Pop art became yet another decisive force in shaping the diversity of contemporary American ceramics. In contrast to the influences illustrated in previous discussions where the selection of subject matter and the execution of the final statement often involved a kind of high pitched emotionalism, the Pop (ceramic) artist was relatively passive in the subject matter that was chosen. The preference for ideas and how to deal with them visually did not seem to involve the same type of philosophical speculating as one saw, for example, in work associated with the Abstract Expressionist or Funk art syndrome. Instead, the Pop artist working in clay appeared to be taking a kind of delight in choosing a common object and celebrating its prominence as a part of our everyday life and culture. Nor did there seem to be any attempts made to focus upon the object as one that may have had particular aesthetic merit of and by itself.

The artist working in clay who was being influenced by the Pop art movement, like his counterpart executing ideas on canvas or paper, did not view society in critical terms. He was content to merely take from society in a rather accepting manner those forms which symbolized most directly the current urban environment. Although several ceramic artists relied on the use of imagery taken from everyday life and from the mass media, some objects created a more dramatic presence by virtue of exaggerating its size, color or surface.

For example, an oversized reproduction of an M&M candy bar, a hot dog, a cigarette or a soft drink bottle are items that previously would not have been included within the sphere of most ceramic artists' repertoire. But now they were being viewed in a more familiar way. A critical factor in this seems to also have rested with the viewer. Because of the acquaintance attached to the everyday object, many artists were prompted to place them in a new art context, thereby focusing the viewer's attention upon the conditions of contemporary life.

At times, artists whose reputations had become well established through other mediums and other forms of self-expression, ventured into the area of ceramics. It was Roy Lichtenstein, primarily assocatied with Pop art painting who produced some ceramic forms which have been widely accepted as "fine art." This approval is perhaps due to the fact that the ceramics came from a person whose stature as a recognized painter brought with it a greater sense of importance.

In 1965 Lichtenstein began his collaboration with Hui Ka Kwong, a nationally recognized ceramic artist from New York, in casting the first female heads and his "Ceramic Sculpture" of black and white earthenware dishes. The latter were often stacked and assembled into complex, free-standing sculptures. The problem of orchestrating a unit which conveyed the feeling of leftover, dirty dishes required alterations of the original pieces by either adding or subtracting various parts.

More important, however, was Lichtenstein's approach to decorating the cups, saucers and female heads. Relying on his familiar dots which had been popularized through his paintings, and which were a familiar symbol of the printing industry, Lichtenstein had to redefine how to use them on a three-dimensional object. He chose to use the dots, stripes of black glaze and the white background of the forms to create complex inter-relationships between the shapes and their surface decorations. The result was often a further complication of the already existing baroqueness of the heads and stacked dishes (Plate 20).

But aside from the aesthetic considerations of these pieces is the idea that Lichtenstein's brief venture into ceramics dramatized some problems which were also being dealt with by

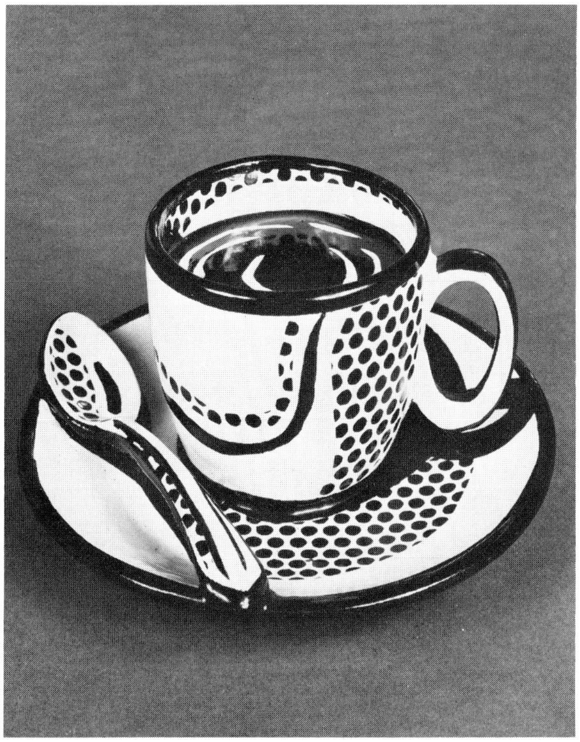

Figure 12-36. Roy Lichtenstein, "Ceramic Sculpture 5" white earthenware, cast and handbuilt, white glaze and black and orange overglaze, 3 1/4" tall, ca. 1965; from the collection of Leta and Mel Ramos, Oakland, California. Courtesy, The Art Galleries, California State University, Long Beach, California.

other potters. Using dimestore items, such as a cup or saucer and then decorating it with a highly inventive, painterly convention created a sense of contradiction. This, in turn, helped to convey an uneasy sense of ambiguity. The idea of using common crockery and elevating it to a position of "high art" by transforming it through *avant garde* decorative approaches had not been dealt with in the same manner by other American artists working in clay.

In contrast to other potters who had been working with the cup shape in many personal ways, Lichtenstein was not concerned with making cups, or even to deal with the idea about cups. His was more an excursion into the realm of paradox; of creating a work of art which

> . . . alluded to the banal, to trivia, to the anonymous industrial object, yet remained finally what has been described as the 'first sculpture about painting.'[4]

Most young ceramists affected by the Pop art influences chose not to use clay for transforming familiar objects into new symbols of meaning, but rather as a means for reproducing as exactly as possible the object as it actually existed. Karen Massaro's painstakingly executed boxes of candy made in porcelain, her slip cast bars of various soaps and pencils or her hand built towels and washcloths were all presented to the viewer without make-believe. Peter Vandenberg's and Victor Spinski's garbage cans (Plate 22) and David Middlebrooks's large carrots suspended on over life-sized clothes hangers are further testament to how some ceramic artists during the early 1970's engaged in the idea of selecting objects that were not only interesting to look at, but which also reflected the belief that the final selection and execution of the form should be prompted by a familiarity of our present-day society (Plates 21 and 23).

A number of artists working in clay who did not concern themselves exclusively with reproducing objects exactly as they may have been chosen from our seemingly inexhaustible supply of commercialism did, however, incorporate various elements in their work that clearly identified it as coming from our Pop culture (Fig. 12-39). It was not unusual to see symbols such as the stars, chevrons, stripes, various letters of the alphabet or even complete slogans or words such as "Love" or "Coke" appear on various works (Fig. 12-40).

Although Michael Frimkes was deeply preoccupied with re-creating the classical pottery shapes of ancient Greece and China, his final solution in terms of the overall effect of his decorations brings him well within the Pop art tradition. By resorting to cartoon images in portraying contemporary events he not only identified himself with an important part of American Pop culture, but he also used it as a means for repudiating the popularity of Funk art. Referring to this he explained that

> . . . they were doing all the things I'd wanted to do—coke bottles, urinals—so I decided to rebel against that Mickey Mouse stuff and get into historical shapes.[5]

Victor Spinski of Delaware created new machines that do not perform, but which take their cue from our overabundance of contraptions. Dick Hay of Indiana resorted to adopting various kinds of foods and created monuments to the all-American Dagwood sandwich (Plate 24), whereas Rodger Lang's observation that "fruit pie is, after all, a very American food"[6] resulted in a series of variations on the pie (Fig. 12-41). James Melchert of California investigated the lower case "a" as his basic

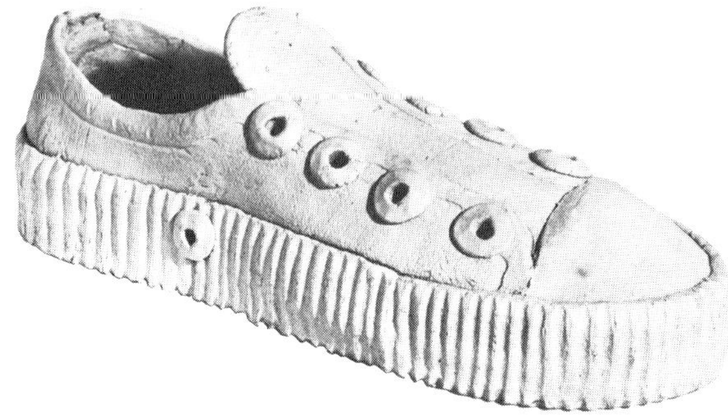

Figure 12-37. Joseph A. Pugliese, "Harry" earthenware clay, handbuilt, enamels, 12 1/2″ long; 1968. Courtesy of the artist.

Pugliese was among a number of ceramic artists who copied objects that are generally associated with our consumer society.

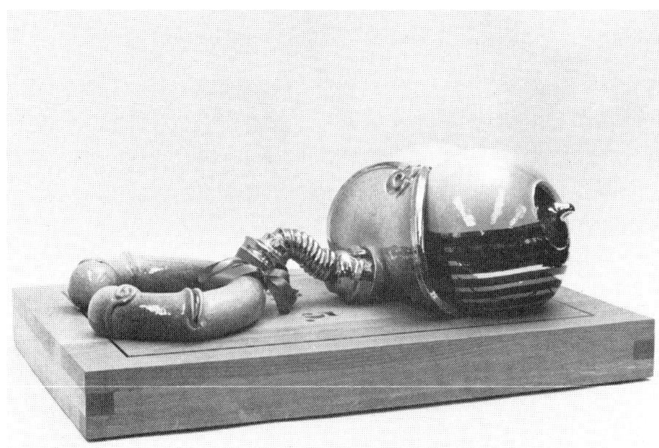

Figure 12-38. Dick Hay, "Male Pacifier," stoneware, handbuilt, 40″ × 28″, low fire glazes and lusters; 1975. Courtesy of the artist.

The subject matter and use of bright colors reflects the cross influences of Pop and Funk art in Dick Hay's sculpture.

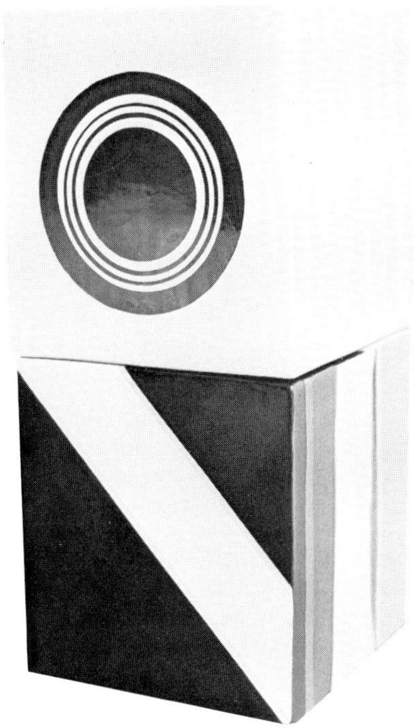

Figure 12-39. Maurine Weaver, "Cube Construction," white earthenware, press molded and handbuilt, low fire glazes and metallic lusters; 12″ h × 6″ w, 1977. Courtesy of the artist.

Figure 12-40. Mel Ruben, "7-Up Wall," earthenware, handbuilt, acrylic paint, 18″ × 14″; 1976. Courtesy of the Gallery Rebecca Cooper, Washington, D.C.

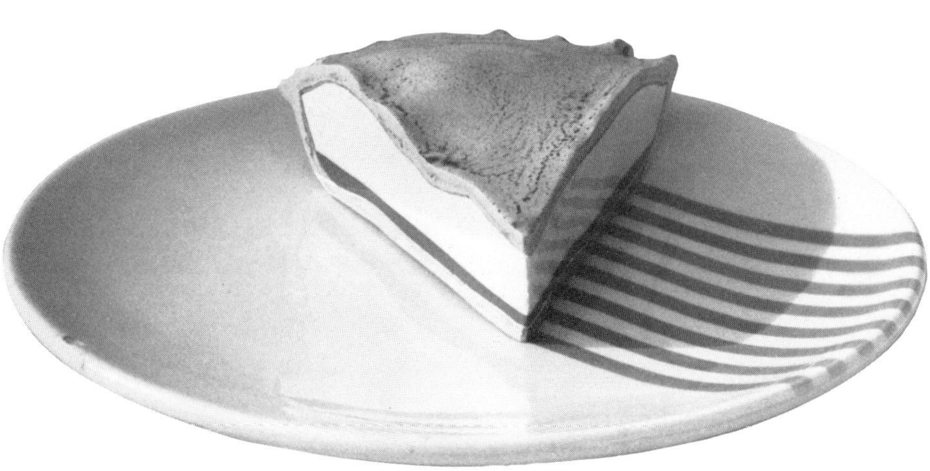

Figure 12-41. Rodger Lang, "Bluestripe Pie #2," earthenware, opaque underglazes, translucent underglazes and earthenware cover glazes, handbuilt and cast; 10″ diameter × 3 1/2″ h. Courtesy, the artist.

motif which then became small homages to one of the most frequently used letters in the alphabet.

Of equal concern to numerous ceramic artists and an obvious influence from Pop art was the use of bright, often primary colors seen not only in paintings, but also in our urban environment through billboards, neon signs, cars, clothing, home furnishings and other accessories. The ready availability of a wide range of brightly colored glazes, underglazes and liquid metals such as gold, platinum and copper made it convenient for the ceramic artist to adopt the color spectrum of our sugar-coated commercial advertising. Even if the three-dimensional form with which the ceramic artist was working did not identify with any particular Pop art configuration, the use of bright, flashy colors fulfilled his wish to be contemporary, to be part of his time.

Hui Ka Kwong's free-standing clay sculptures of 1968 are an appropriate example of how numerous artists utilized the newly adopted commercial glazes for gracing their work with jazzy colors (Plate 25). Through the use of this newly heralded visual vocabulary artists were able to impart their work with a similar expressive potency as did his predecessor of the Abstract Expressionist vein; the bright colors and metallic surfaces frequently resulted in violent visual distortion, conflicting linear directions and clashing dissonances (Fig. 12-42). The cumulative result was often one of creating visual and visceral shock. This was not unlike the brazen commercial advertising found in various communications media whose sole intent it was to assault the senses in order to gain attention and implant in the viewer a lasting mental image.

By taking an object popularly associated with contemporary culture some artists

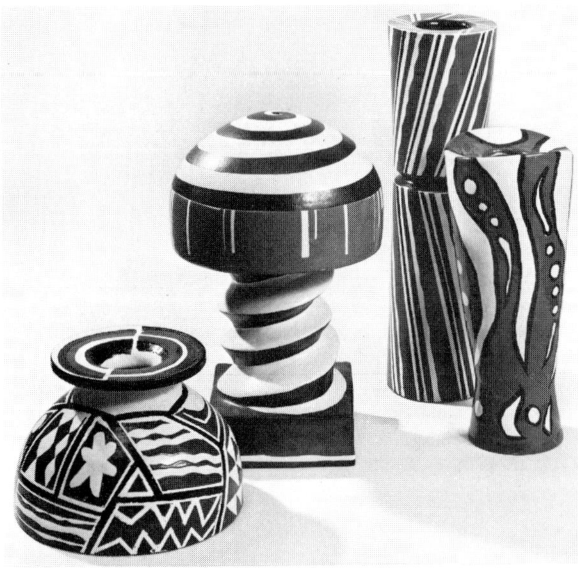

Figure 12-42. Hui Ka Kwong, "Ceramic White Ware," wheel thrown, multicolored low fire glazes, sizes varied from 10″ to 18″; ca. 1972. Collection of the artist.

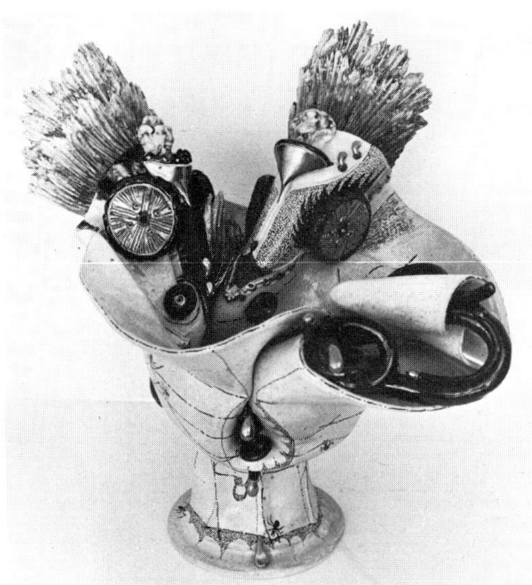

Figure 12-43. Arthur Nelson, "Collision of the Fire Dragsters," stoneware, thrown and handbuilt, 22″ × 21″; low fire glazes, metallic lusters and china paints; ca. 1973. Courtesy of the artist, California College of Arts and Crafts, Oakland, California.

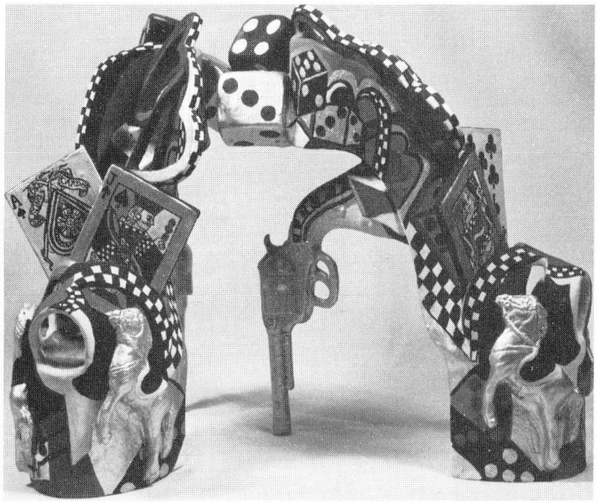

Figure 12-44. Toby Buonagurio, "Gun Shoes," ceramic, cast and handbuilt, painted with acrylics, 12 1/2" high, 1974. Courtesy, Gallery Rebecca Cooper, Washington, D.C.

Some artists incorporated numerous objects into complex compositions in dealing with statements about contemporary American Pop culture.

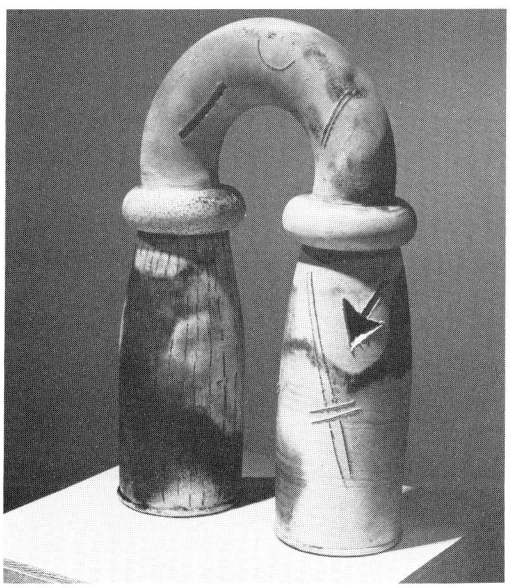

Figure 12-45. Bill Farrell, "Smoked Popeye," stoneware, wheel thrown and assembled, 24" × 12" × 6"; 1977. Collection of the artist.

changed them sufficiently in order to blur the exact clarity of their derivation (Figs. 12-43 and 12-44) (Plate 26). Bill Farrell of Chicago adopted the familiar popeye symbol and combined it with hard-edged, bright colors that reinforced their Pop art identity. As early as 1968 he also introduced neon lights which framed these sculptures, thereby heightening their affiliation with the comic strip society (Plate 27).

But by 1977, though he dealt with other ideas during the intervening years, he treated the popeye form with a more severly reduced, unglazed surface. Like many others working in clay, Farrell turned to the magic of smoking his pieces which imparted them with similar elements of the "controlled accident" that had been associated with the reduction firing, pit firing, garbage firing and the Raku and salt glazing processes. His most recent work thus represents a synthesis of a Pop art form with the more romantic, intuitive response to surface and color (Fig. 12-45).

Influences of Drawing and Graphics

Potters have always delighted in romanticizing the surfaces of clay vessels, and the history of ceramics is resplendent with examples of fine decorations that grew out of specific cultural dictates. But in America, with the popularization of "personal expression" well entrenched by the 1960's, ceramic artists embarked on a course of more intense interest in embellishing the clay surfaces of their work.

Particularly noteworthy were the efforts of a number of younger artists who were able to assimilate newly developed techniques and redefine older, well established ways of decorating. The extensive use of underglazes, overglazes, airbrush painting and underglaze pencils have been referred to. Of new interest was the use of photo silkscreening and other related techniques which allowed the artist to deal more graphically with reproducible images lifted from other, already existing sources (Plate 28).

Among the numerous artists who had access to sophisticated photographic equipment and knowledge and skill of its demanding technique was Robert Engle of Ohio. In 1968 he fashioned traditional pots and experimented with transferring photographic images onto the entire surface so that the vessel itself was treated almost as a photographic paper. The fact that it was round added to a subtle sense of distortion which helped to create an interesting contrast between the connotative imagery and the traditional pot. Most of the subject matter used by Engle relied on personages identified with the Pop art cult. Jean Harlow, Brigitte Bardot, Bertrand Russel and Ernest Hemingway, among others, were recurring personalities in Engle's, as well as other ceramic artists' works who subscribed to this innovative idea.

Since 1968 and continuing today, Erik Gronborg of Las Vegas has integrated silkscreened motifs from photographic or printed materials with drawn and relief patterns to create nostalgic renditions of the past as well as contemporary "events." He skillfully fused Funk elements such as his softly formed vessels and nude female figures with recognizable historical images such as the Statue of Liberty. These literal images are often contrasted with abstract shapes of stained clay to brightly colored areas of glaze. This complex combination of various elements infuses his objects with an unmistakable contemporary Funk-Pop art origin. (Plate 29).

Although John Stephenson of Michigan has achieved distinction for creating good pottery over a long period of time, his forms which incorporate collage elements from newspaper galley proofs have proven to be particularly popular (Fig. 12-47). Carefully organized into good graphic compositions, they represent a sound synthesis of two-dimensional decoration with three-dimensional form.

Howard Kottler of Seattle, Washington has achieved national and international acclaim through his inventive use of "decalcomania" which involves a process of transferring pictures of designs from specially prepared paper to ceramics. Often relying on patriotic motifs and slogans, Kottler used porcelain plates, mass produced by industry, as a convenient means for dealing with his quasi-surreal, highly poetic expressions (Fig. 12-49). Many of his ideas are associated with American political and social events. In a plate of 1968, for example, he used decals of Lincoln's bust and by reconstructing it with various other images such as the Capitol dome and guns, he created an imposing, yet subtle commentary.

The popularity and wide diversity of graphically illustrating on clay surfaces during the late 1960's and early 70's is further exemplified through the work of Susan and Stephen Kemeneffy of Pennsylvania. Their large Raku sculptures and platters have always served as convenient vehicles for freely drawn and spirited painted figurative images (Fig. 12-50a and 12-50b). Curt Hoard of Minnesota actually recruited the talents of his young child and her friends to adorn his dome shapes with relatively naive drawings in underglaze colors (Fig. 12-51). Robert Ransom of Los Angeles relied on sophisticated combinations of photo silkscreening, underglaze painting and the reflective quality of platinum to produce engaging graphic illusions on manufactured bathroom tiles (Fig. 12-52).

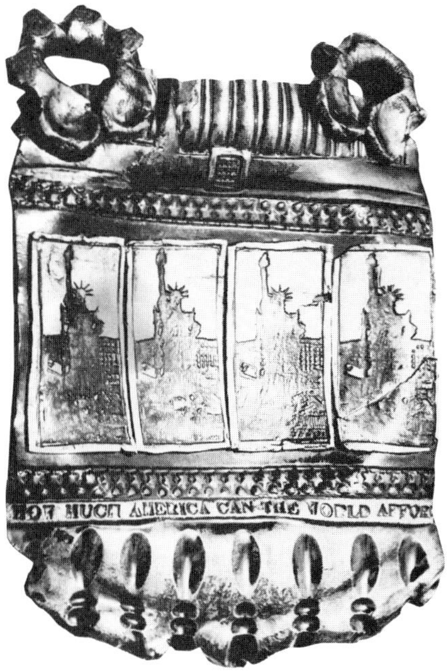

Figure 12-46. Erik Gronborg, "Plate," handbuilt stoneware, low fire glazes and stains, 15″ × 18″; 1971. Courtesy of the artist.

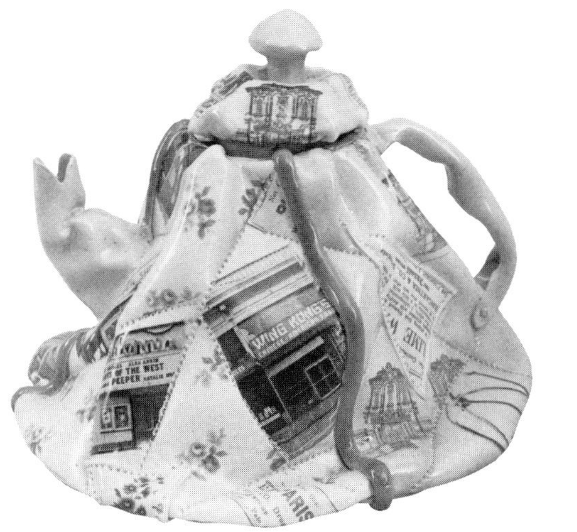

Figure 12-48. Nancy Selvin, Untitled tea-pot, quilted handbuilt, decals and photo silkscreened decorations; 1975. Courtesy, the Quay Gallery, San Francisco, California.

The use of various graphic techniques such as photo-silkscreening, transfer decals and reverse printing from galley proofs became a popular method of decorating by numerous studio-potters during the 70's.

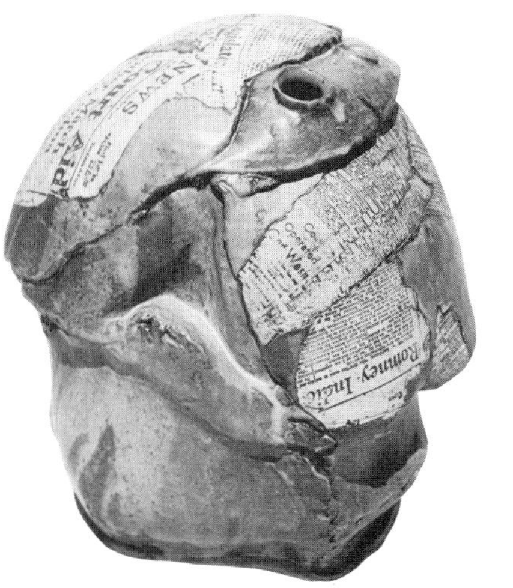

Figure 12-47. John Stephenson, "Floor Vase," stoneware, handbuilt, slab constructed with newspaper impressions, approx. 18″ high; 1968. Courtesy of the artist.

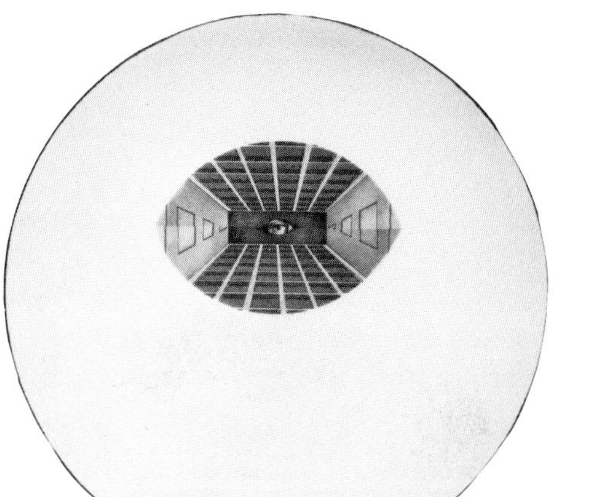

Figure 12-49. Howard Kottler, "Pupil Reflex Plate," porcelain, cast plate with ceramic decals and silver luster; 10″ diameter, 1968. Courtesy of the artist.

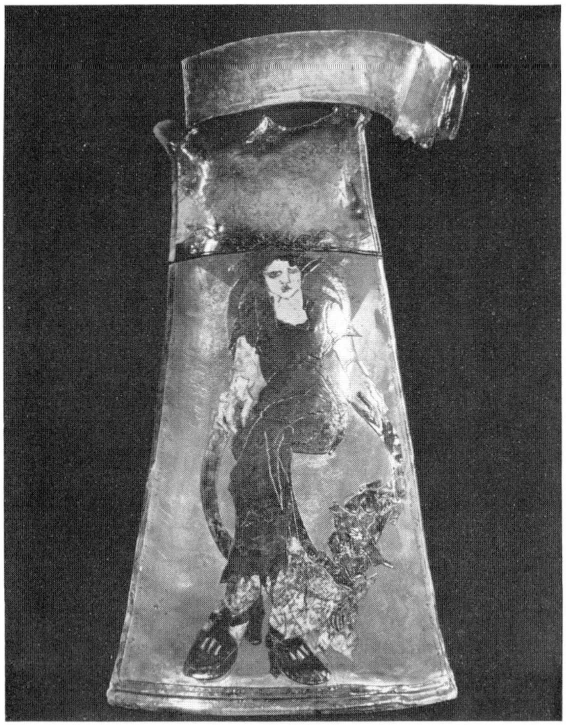

Figure 12-50a. Susan and Stephen Kemeneffy, "Raku Covered Jar," handbuilt, incised and multi-colored glaze decoration; 48" tall; 1977. Courtesy of the artists.

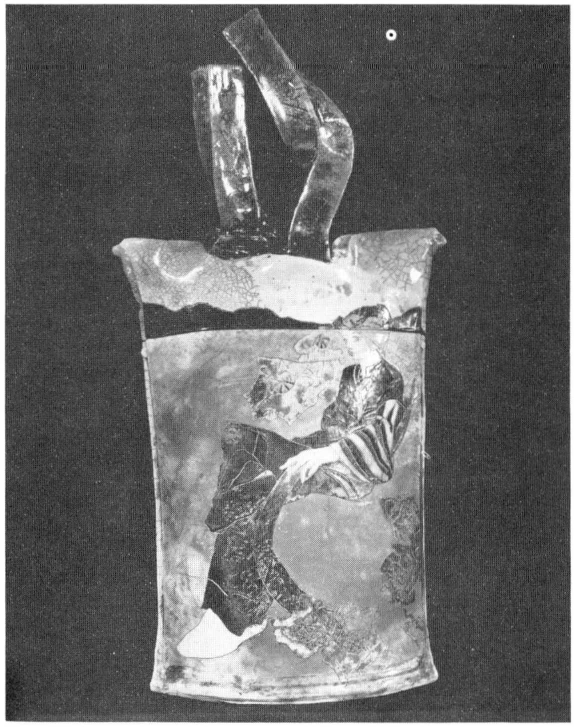

Figure 12-50b. Susan and Stephen Kemeneffy, "Raku Covered Jar," *Western Lady;* approximately 4 feet tall (48 inches).

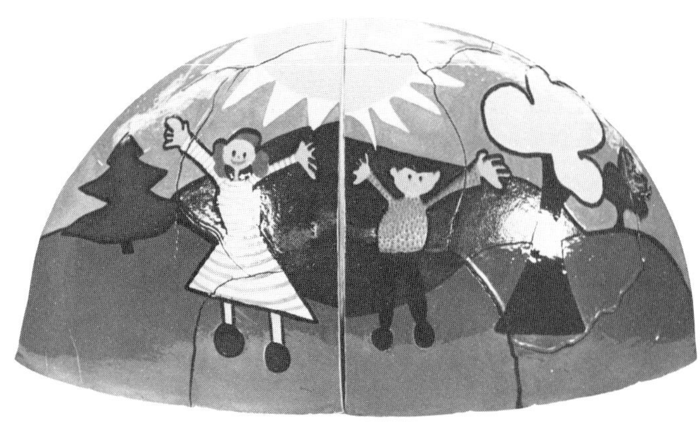

Figure 12-51. Curt Hoard, "Children's Landscape," stoneware, handbuilt, multicolored underglazes, transparent cover glaze; approx. 36" × 18"; 1975. Courtesy of the artist.

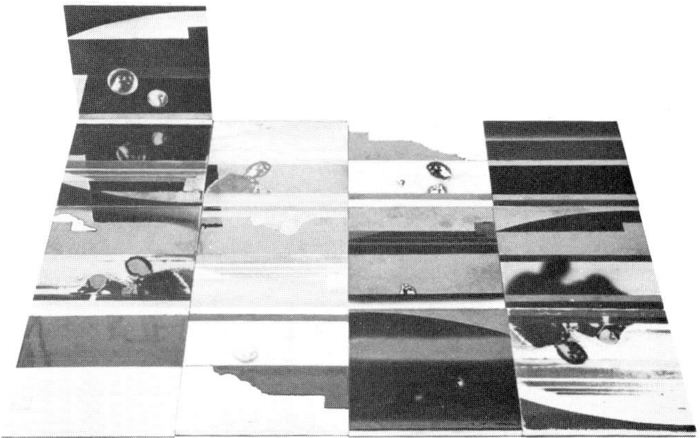

Figure 12-52. Robert Ransom, "Peepers," earthenware tiles, photo silkscreened images, low fire glazes and metallic lusters; approx. 24″ × 24″; 1973. Collection of the author.

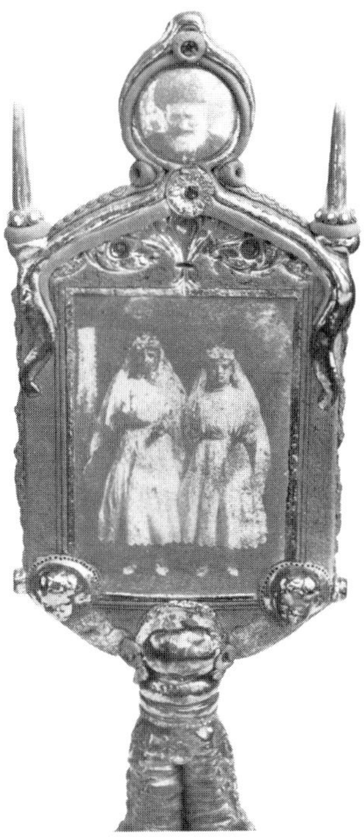

Figure 12-53. Marc Sijan, Ceramic Sculpture, stoneware clay, handbuilt, photo silkscreened images, low fire glazes and lusters. Courtesy of the artist.

The efforts illustrated by these examples are yet another part of a larger, newer generation of ceramic artists that emerged during the 1970's. They aided in giving contemporary ceramics a distinctive American quality (Fig. 12-53). Of special interest was the immediate impact of the final result. Any (graphic) material or technique that could be directed toward that end-product seemed acceptable (Fig. 12-54).

Although their images were sometimes reflective of a particular phase of our Pop culture (Fig. 12-55), the problem of dealing with literal imagery on clay is a concern with which some ceramic artists have always occupied themselves. In large part this was due to the fact that most ceramists in America were being trained in art programs of colleges, universities and professional art schools where there was less inclination toward the romanticism of the traditional potter. More stress was placed on synthesizing the concepts and percepts of other disciplines within the arts, such as drawing, design, painting, sculpture, jewelry and weaving. In ceramics this meant a stronger preoccupation with the unique, one-of-a-kind item for which various surface embellishments of a graphic nature seemed to lend itself very well (Fig. 12-56 and Plate 30).

A close adjunct to the renewed interest of dealing with photographic reproductions and drawing on ceramic forms, and also with the new popularity of photo-realist painting, were the concerns of a number of younger ceramic artists who explored the possibilities of documenting in minute detail the surface effects of visual experiences. Although associated with the Pop art movement, some people working in clay chose subject matter which did not, however, necessarily reflect preoccupations with our consumer society. Instead,

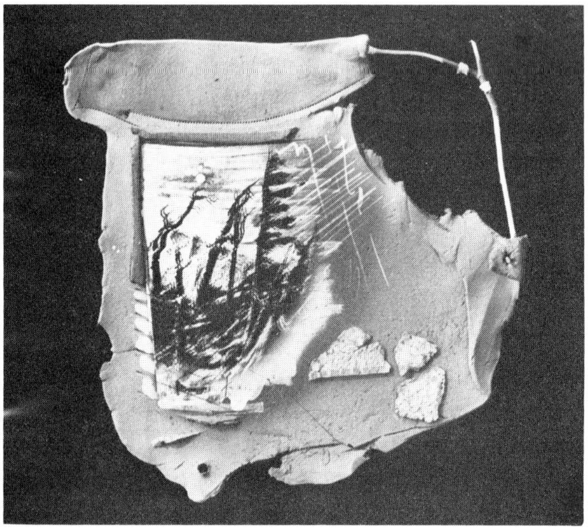

Figure 12-54. Daniel Engelke, "High Country Impressions," earthenware, handbuilt, photo emulsion, wood and leather; 12″ × 13″ h, 1977. Courtesy of the artist.

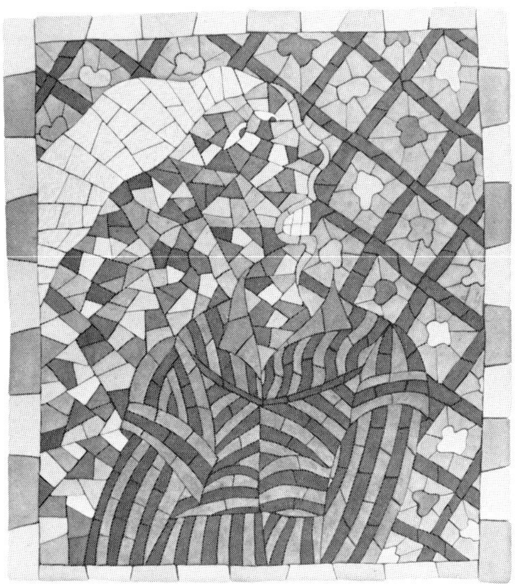

Figure 12-55. Tom Rippon, "Wall Mosaic," porcelain, handbuilt, 38″ × 29″; 1977. The Quay Ceramics Gallery, San Francisco, California.

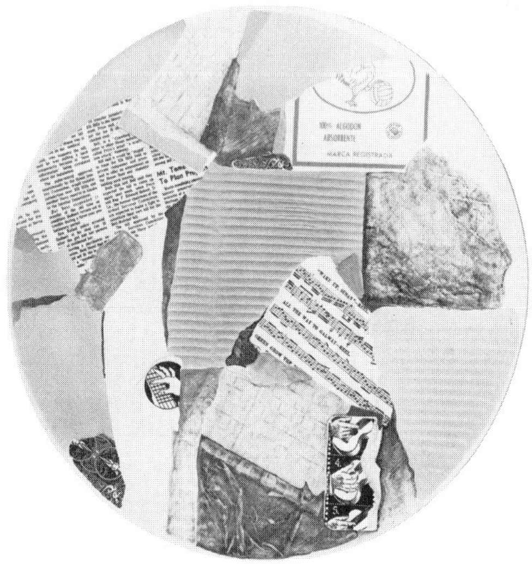

Figure 12-56. Richard Shaw, "Music Plate," porcelain, cast and handbuilt, china paints and decals; 17″ diameter, 1976. Courtesy, the Quay Gallery, San Francisco, California.

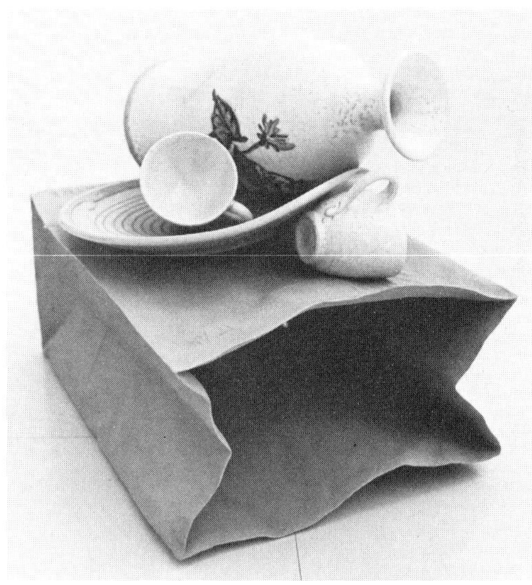

Figure 12-57. Vernon Patrick, "Bags," stoneware, cast and handbuilt, thrown parts; underglazes and decals; 1975. Courtesy, the Quay Ceramics Gallery, San Francisco, California.

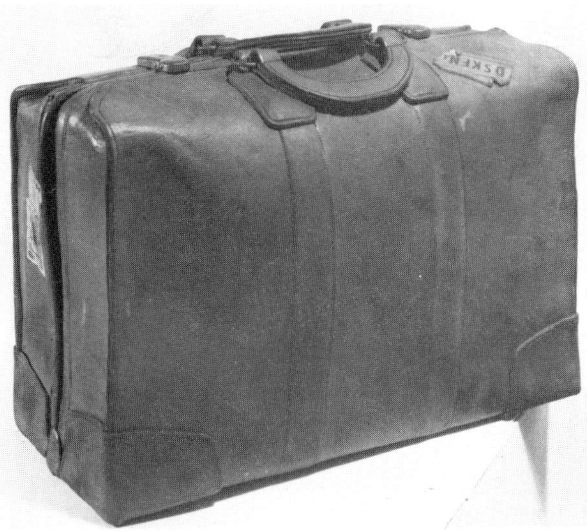

Figure 12-58. Marilyn Levine, "Dsken Suitcase," stoneware, handbuilt, oxide stains, 13" × 19" × 7 1/2"; 1972. Courtesy, the O.K. Harris Gallery, New York, New York.

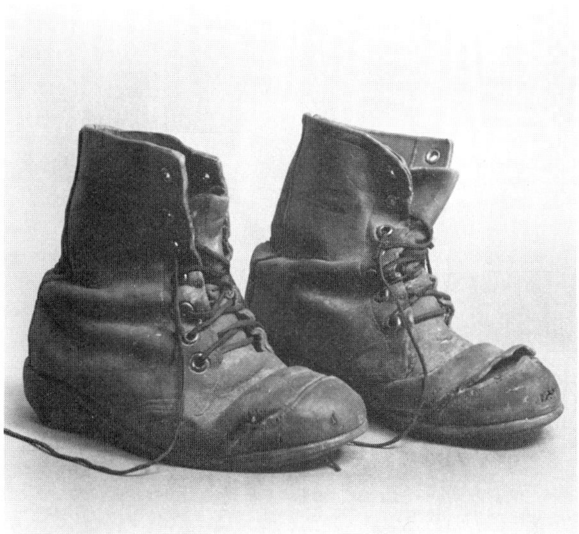

Figure 12-59. Marilyn Levine, "Steel Toed Boots #2," stoneware, handbuilt, oxide stained, 8" × 11" × 4 1/2"; ca. 1973. Courtesy, the O.K. Harris Gallery, New York, New York.

they dealt with objects that tended to grow out of intensely personalized experiences.

High levels of manual dexterity and keen observation were required to copy paper bags (Fig. 12-57) by Verne Patrick or leather suitcases, belts, jackets and purses by Marilyn Levine into clay counterfeits (Fig. 12-58). Levine's work has frequently, and erroneously, been associated with the Pop art attitude. Although she executed her work with such verisimilitude that one must actually touch the work in order to tell that it was made of clay, the emotive qualities it conveys sets it distinctively apart from any Pop references (Fig. 12-59).

Her work cannot be viewed without sensing the presence of human drama; the worn, tired, torn, limp, faded and dusty objects all give hints that some sort of long, involved human activity has occurred.

Like many other artists, particularly painters of the super-realist mode, Levine also challenges conventional attitudes toward reality. As if testing orthodox ways of perception she states that

> . . . you see a soft material and you feel a hard material. Something you know should be soft feels hard. I'm interested in the dichotomy that creates.[7] (Plate 31)

Elements of Conceptual, Systemic and Serial Art

Concurrent with all the other styles and attitudes during the late sixties and early seventies was the emergence of even more radical departures from traditional concepts of ceramics. Their main sources of influence came from the activities of artists working in the Systemic, Serial or Conceptual art philosophies (Fig. 12-60). While most ceramists of the past had dealt with traditional problems of composition, i.e., the harmonious integration of major and minor elements and principles of "design," the newer influences on ceramics resulted in less concern for the ordering of internal relationships. In de-emphasizing compositional characteristics as they had been dealt with previously, some ceramic artists began working with a modular approach to repeating one or two shapes in order to form a system of patterns which then created larger overall units.

Although the problem of composition could not be eliminated completely, the idea of conveying the mode of construction (repetition of the same module) and the inherent qualities of the material (clay) focused greater clarity on the final form as seen in Jim Stephenson's "Sagging Tile Wall" (Fig. 12-61).

John Mason is sometimes identified with bringing the greatest influence of this formalist attitude to contemporary ceramics through his large, sequential configurations made of manufactured fire bricks (Figs. 12-62, 12-63, 12-64). But other artists throughout various parts of the country had also dealt with similar emphasis.

Dismissing traditional orientations of compositional relationships in favor for experiencing a single unit made of repeated modules was the work of Stephen Kaltenbach. In 1965 he created a series of geometric clay forms which were similar in concept to the constructions of Donald Judd's boxes. Kaltenbach's elongated, slightly curved forms produced a sensuous richness of surface and color and also complex shadows when they were assembled into simply massed organizations.

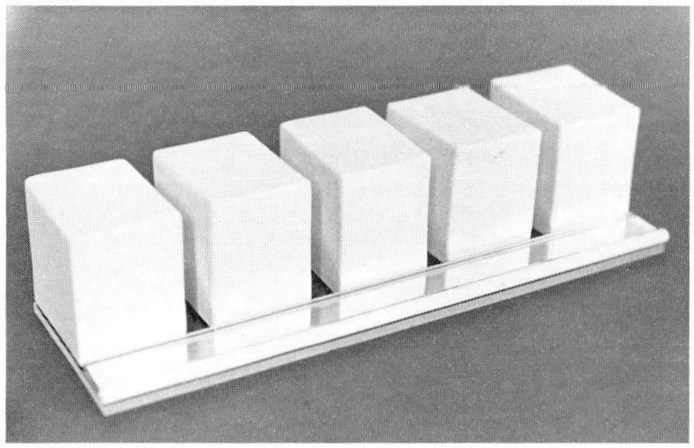

Figure 12-60. Maurine Weaver, "Multiple Cube Construction," earthenware, plexiglass and mirror; low-fire glaze; handbuilt and press molded; 17 1/2″ long × 3″ high × 4″ deep. Collection of the artist.

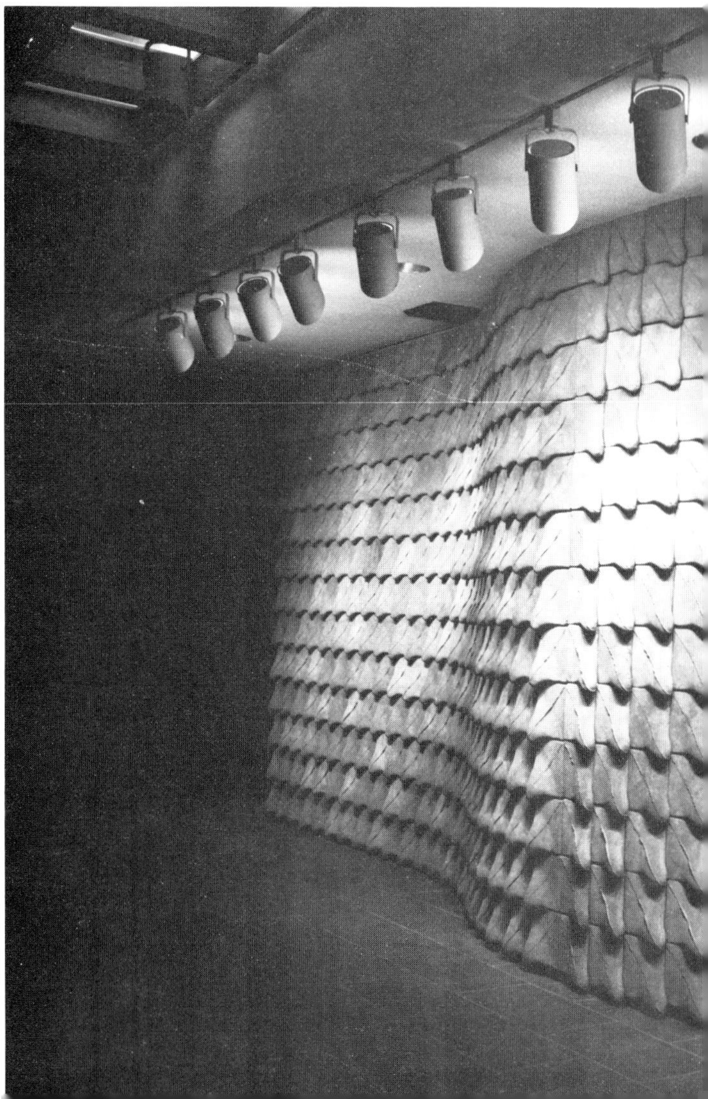

Figure 12-61. Jim Stephenson, "Sagging Tile Wall," brick clay, press molded and handbuilt; 9′ × 32′; 1977. Courtesy of the artist.

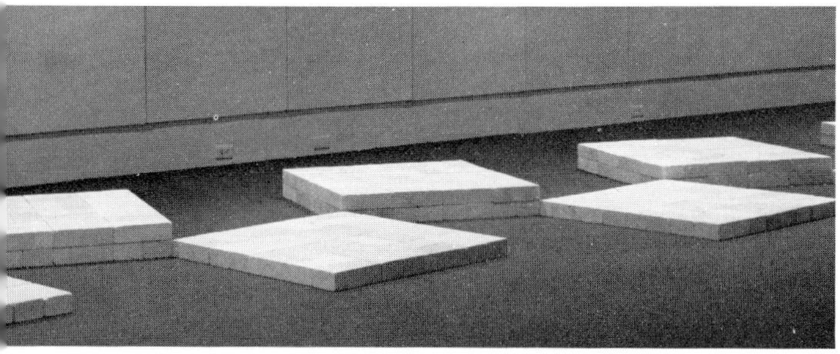

Figure 12-62. John Mason, "LAICA" Firebrick sculpture, 5 in. × 36 ft. × 7 ft.; hand constructed; 1977. Courtesy, the Hansen-Fuller Gallery, San Francisco, California.

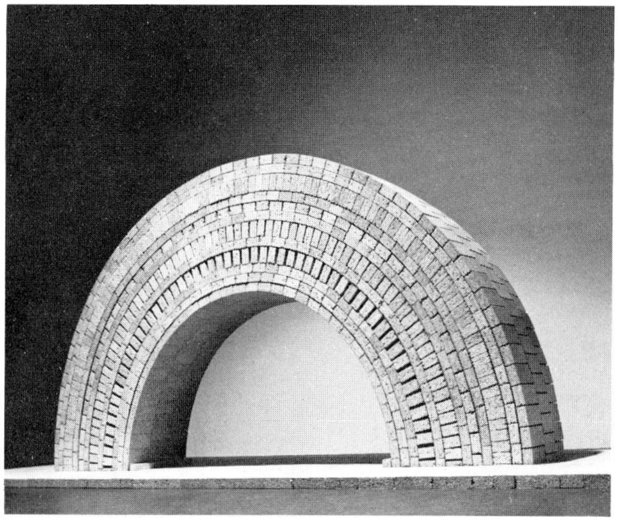

Figure 12-63. John Mason, "Arch," Firebrick sculpture, (model/particle board) 16″ × 20 1/2″ × 22 1/2″; handbuilt, 1976. Courtesy, Hansen-Fuller Gallery, San Francisco, California.

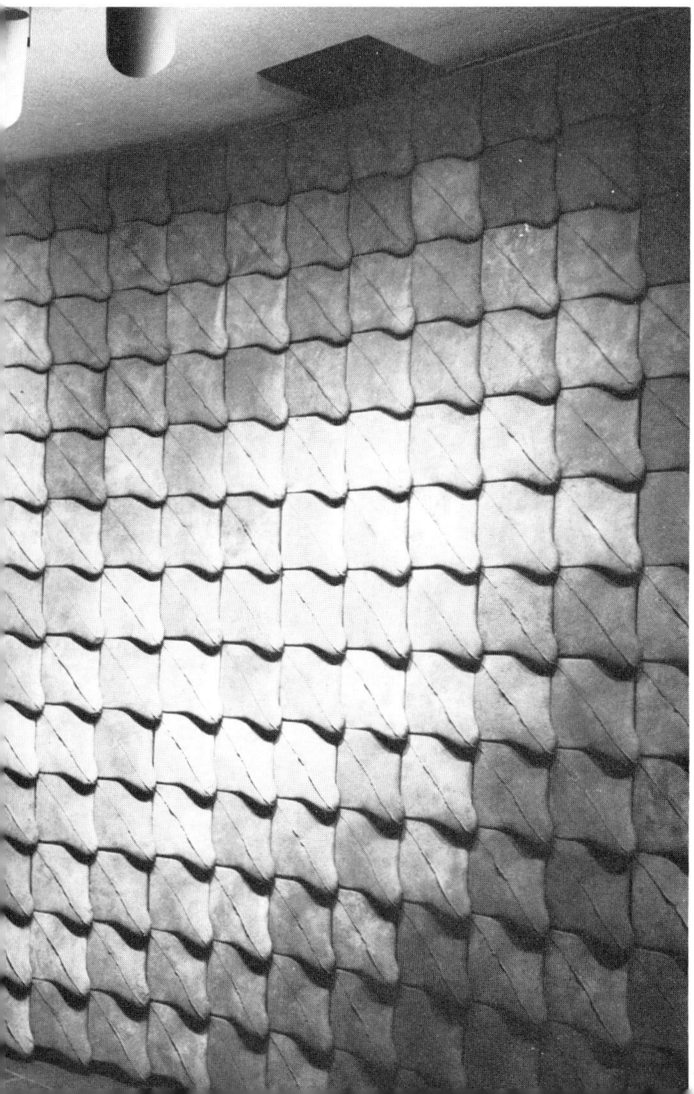

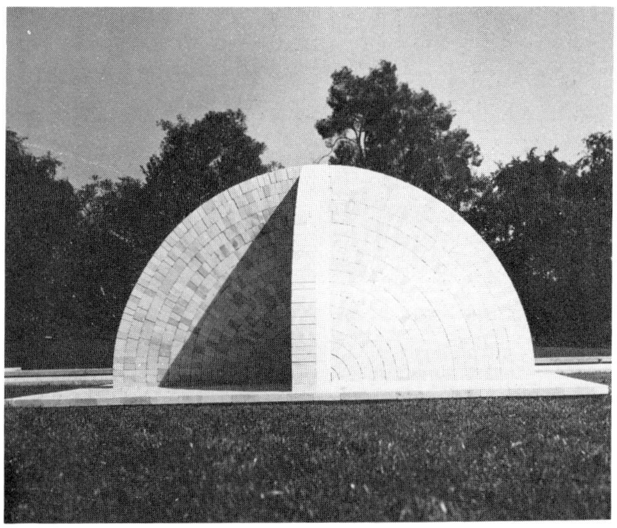

Figure 12-64. John Mason, "Firebrick Sculpture-Pasadena," Firebricks, handbuilt, 84″ high × 198″ diameter; 1974. Collection of the Norton Simon Museum of Art at Pasadena, California.

Gene Koss of New Orleans relied on large tubes of extruded clay pipes (Fig. 12-65) to convey sensations of actual rather than implied space and form. These stacked elements of clay pipes further espouse a formalist attitude of eliminating many of the subjective or expressive qualities which had been of such importance to most ceramic artists of the past.

John Bowitz's unglazed, raw bisque bricks not only illustrate his lack of concern for illusion, but also reinforced his interest for clarity of structure by presenting his modulated configuration in relatively clean, simple, precise terms. The handmade bricks convey an uncontrived, factual attitude toward form and the material's intrinsic character (Fig. 12-66). George Hageman of Ohio dealt with similar attitudes toward creating more reductive forms in which one moves from the particular (single module) to a more general construct. In his instance the cross motif was variously interpreted with the use of bags of clay, fire bricks, masking tape and pieces of wood (Fig. 12-67). Their simple format and large construction of over eight feet engages the viewer in an elementary visual experience. Compared to most ceramic sculpture of the past which was usually viewed from a particular vantage point, these pieces could be comprehended from many different (visual) positions (Fig. 12-68).

Much less geometric, but nonetheless dependent on the idea of repetition of particular units is illustrated in the quasi-environmental work of Doug Hanson. Using large, hand built boulders, gravel and stainless steel cubes in various combinations, he synthesized various influences of Systemic, Minimalist, Conceptual and Environmental art. His "Indented Rocks" of 1974 is a typical example of how

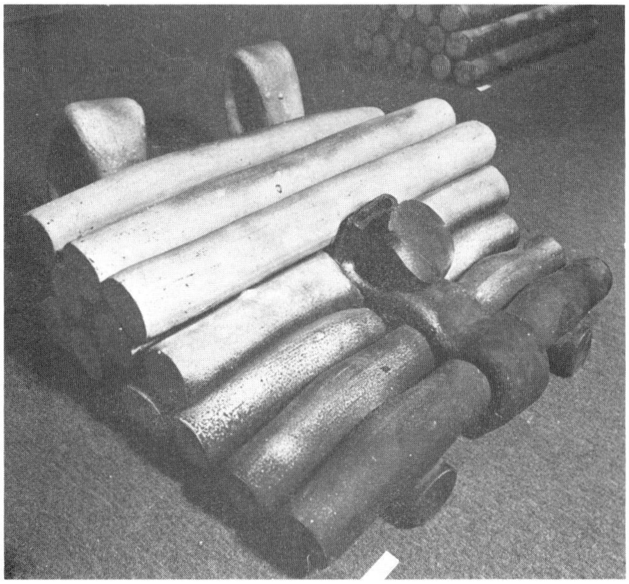

Figure 12-65. Gene K. Koss, "Stone Boat Stack," stoneware clay, extruded and handbuilt, sandblasted surface; 3′ × 4′; 1976.

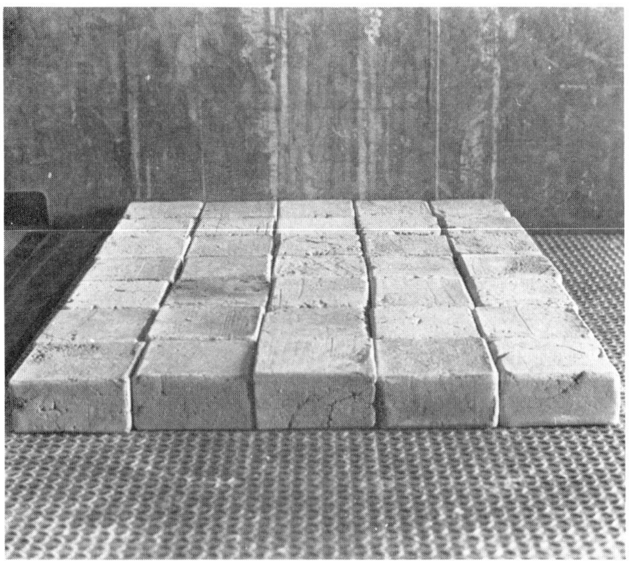

Figure 12-66. John Bowitz, Untitled Assemblage, solid bisque fired clay, handbuilt, unglazed 4″ × 36″ × 30″; 1972. Collection of the artist.

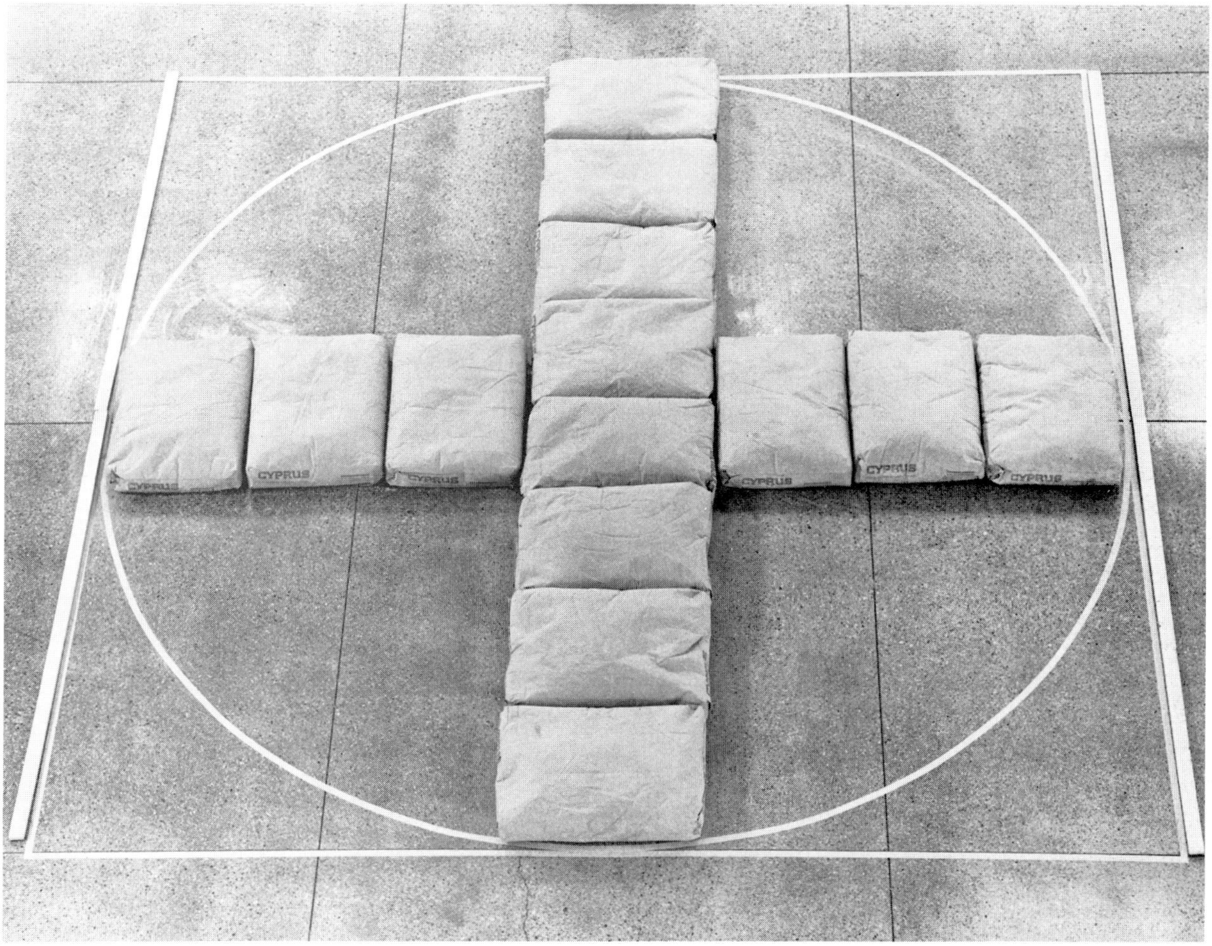

Figure 12-67. George Hageman, "Cross," Bagged clay, masking tape and wooden strips; hand assembled, 10′ × 10′; 1977. Courtesy of the artist.

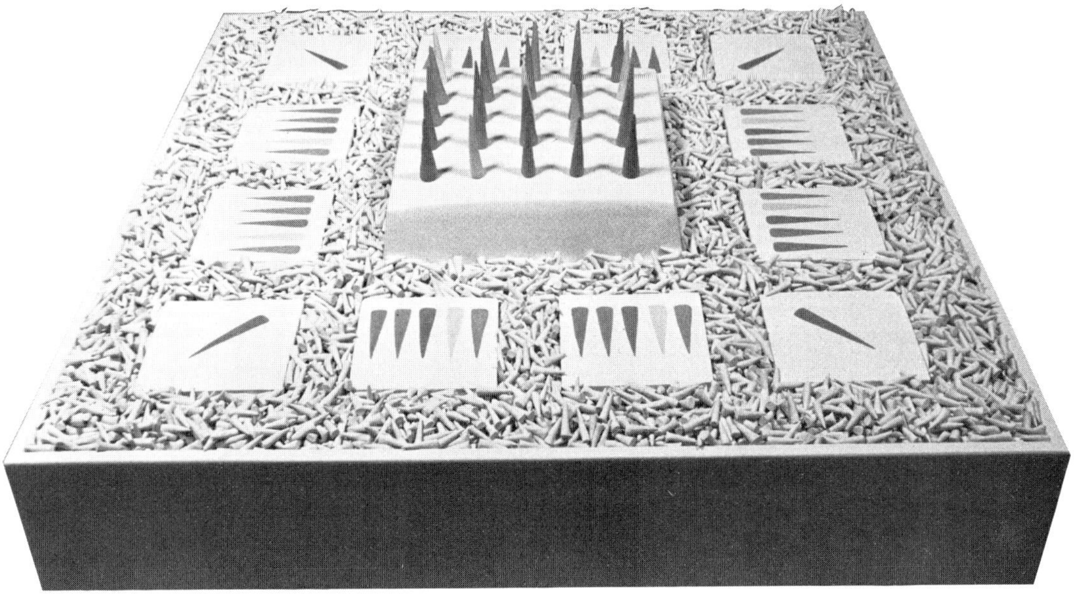

Figure 12-68. John Thames, "Position for Veneration," earthenware clay, handbuilt, wood base; entire unit 42″ × 42″ × 6″; 1976. Collection of the artist.

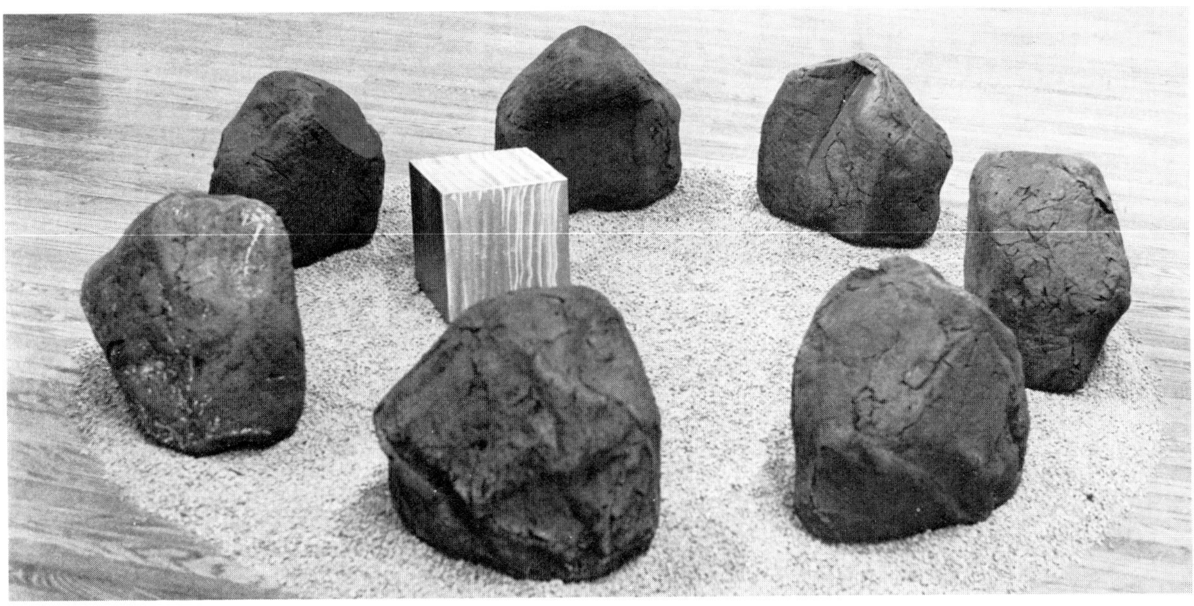

Figure 12-69. Doug Hanson, "Indented Rocks," stoneware, handbuilt, combined with gravel and steel cube; entire unit approx. 8′ diameter; 1974. Courtesy of the artist.

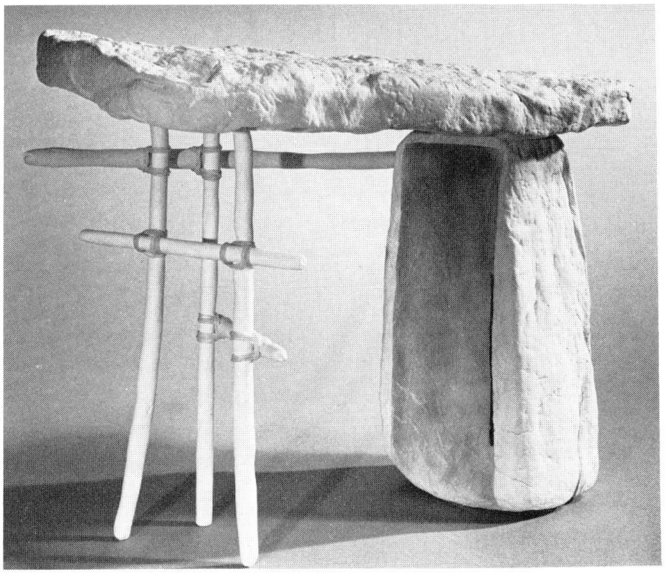

Figure 12-70. Curt Heuer, "Paradolmen #3," earthenware, handbuilt, combined with waxed linen and iron wire; 8 1/2" h × 11" w × 5" d; 1977. Collection of the artist.

Precarious balances add to a sense of mystery in Heuer's construction which rely on combining several elements into a cohesive unit.

some ceramic artists adapted these various influences in fashioning for themselves statements that were directed toward the problem of how repeated objects can relate to an existing environment (Fig. 12-69).

The separate elements in any of these examples are seldom unique or precious, which was not the case of most work in previous discussions. Instead, artistic identity was achieved essentially by the manner in which the artist organized the various units and the space in which they existed. Consequently, the traditional pedestal or glass case was also being replaced quite frequently by the floor or exterior landscape of the gallery or museum. Those who elected to deal with these new problems therefore had to seek other alternatives for physical and visual support of their ideas. The ceramic artist of the late 1960's and early 70's who focused upon these particular ideas was also less thought of as a "craftsman," "artist-potter," or "artist-craftsman." He was, instead, well within the vanguard of the (other) visual arts because he was also deeply involved in and committed to dissolving the traditional boundaries of pottery and free-standing ceramic sculpture (Figs. 12-70, 12-71, 12-72).

Perhaps the most radical shifts of emphasis can be seen in the work by a small group of young artists who subjected their work to visible changes induced by nature. Closely aligned to the concept of a "happening," these people relied even more directly on the transitory aspects of life. Not even finishing the clay in the traditional manner by firing it in a kiln, a piece was allowed to remain sitting in a gallery, outdoors or in water. Various elements such as rain, wind, light, heat or snow was then allowed to act upon it and literally change its composition and eventual form (Fig. 12-73).

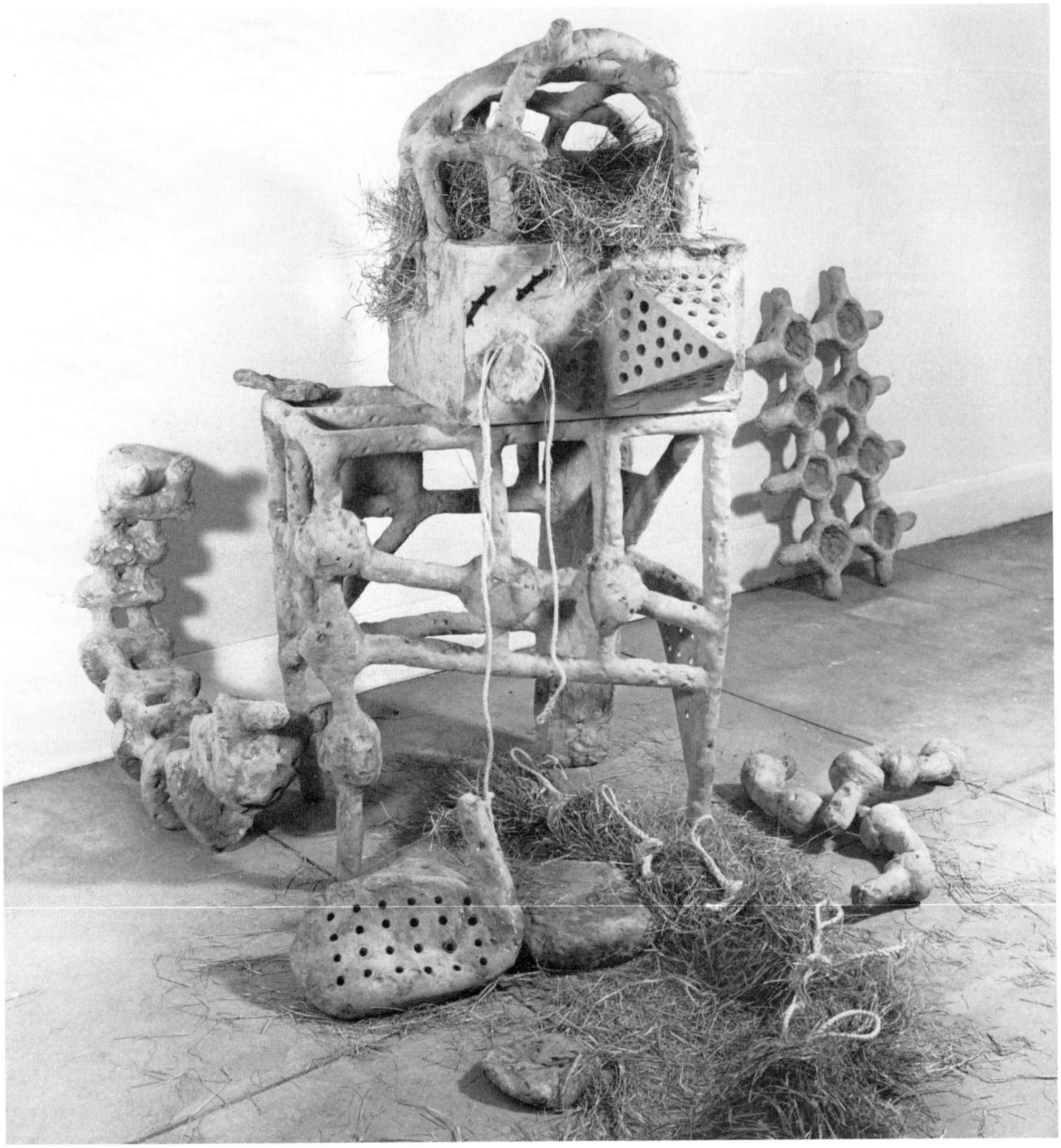

Figure 12-71. Ken D. Little, "First Situation with Hay," ceramic, combined with rope and hay; handbuilt; 52" high; 1973-74. Courtesy of the artist.

Ceramic artist such as Little created environments and "happenings" that have aided in breaking down the traditional barriers of the artist-craftsman.

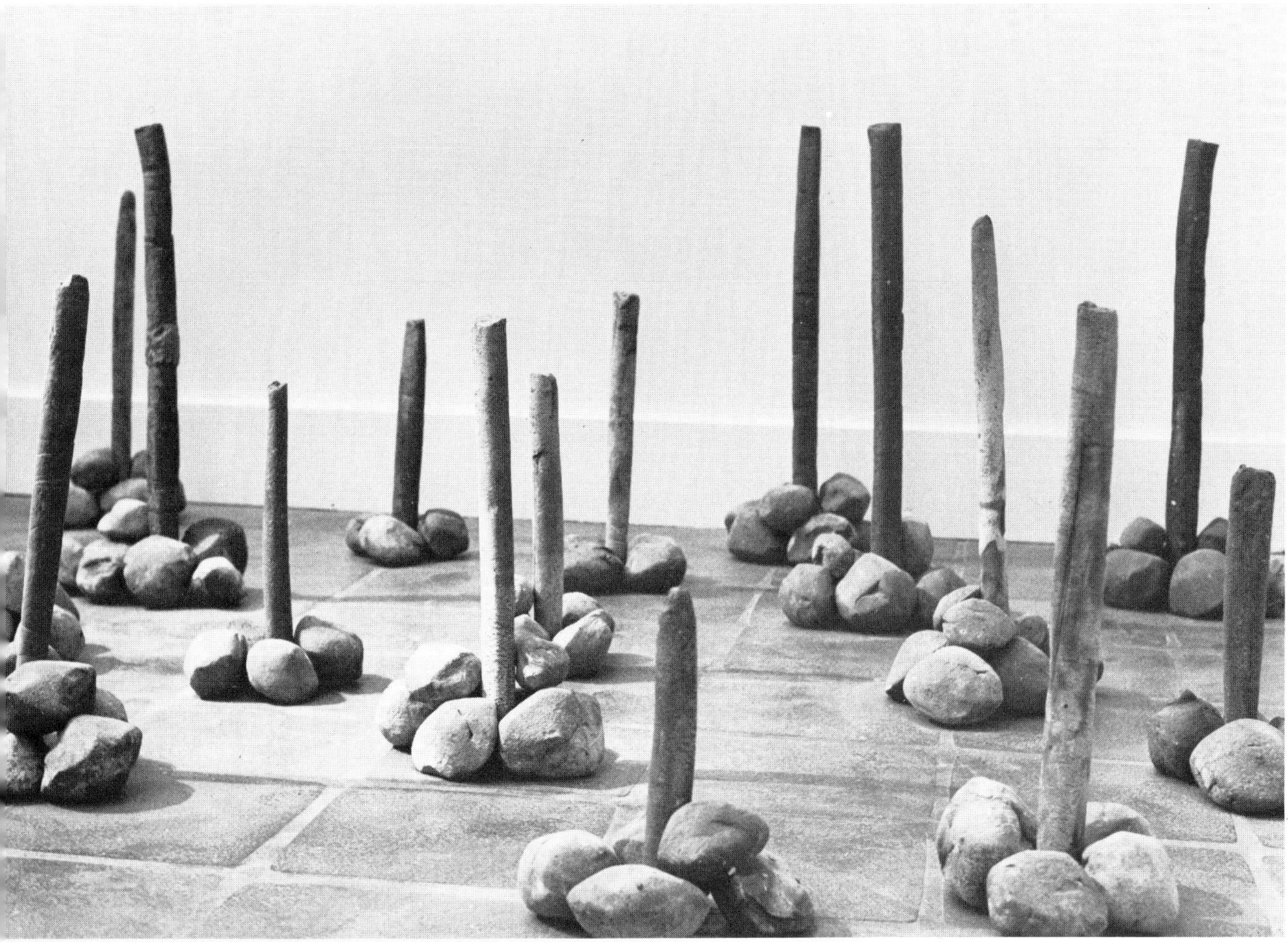

Figure 12-72. Susan Babson, "Sticks and Stones," stoneware, handbuilt; 12′ × 6′ × 28′; 1977. Courtesy, Santa Anna College Art Gallery, Santa Anna, California.

The environmental sculptures by artists such as Babson often utilized the floors of galleries for their displays, thereby challenging the traditional attitudes of sculptures on pedestals.

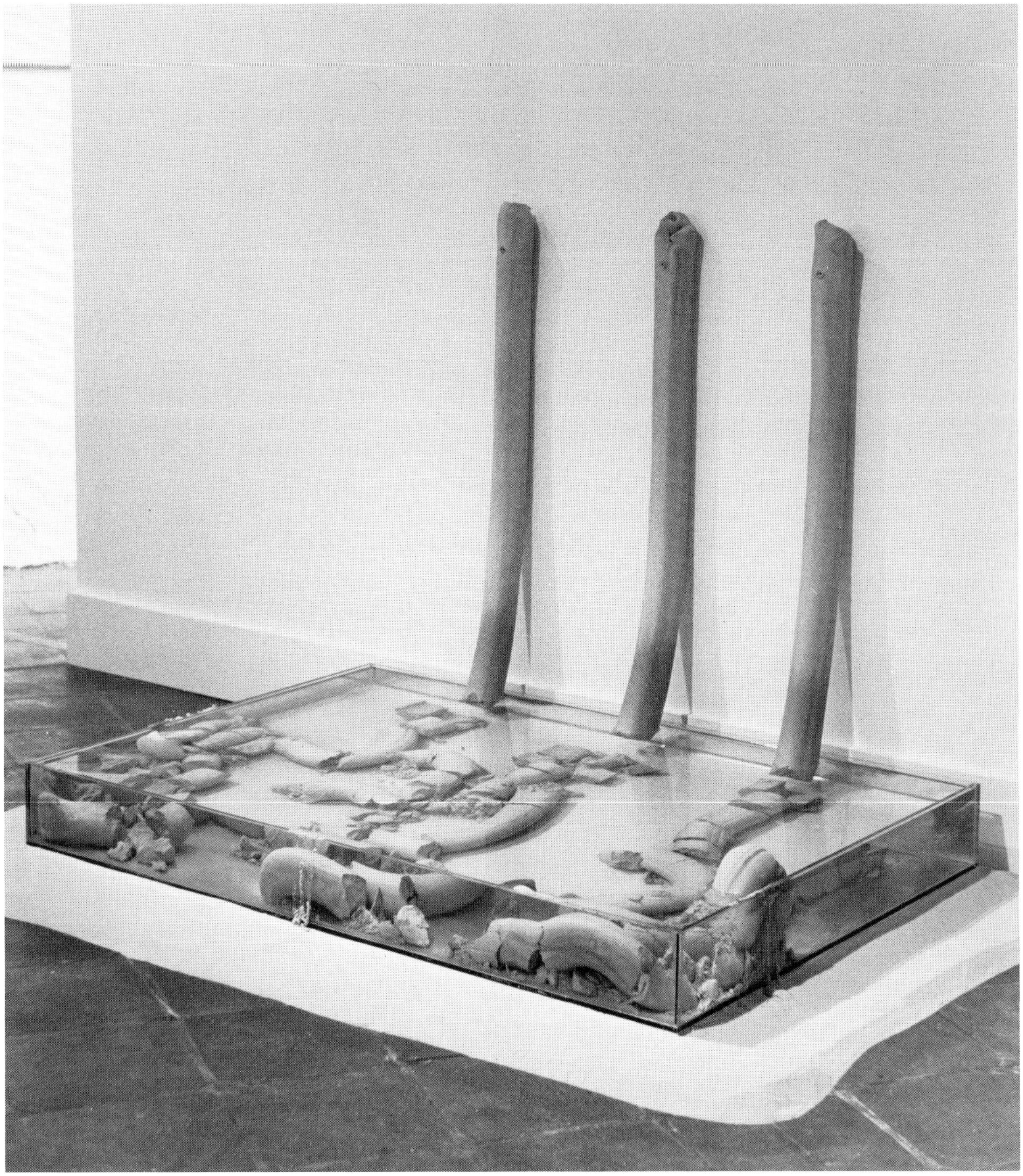

Viewed as a rebellion against any traditional notions of the ceramic heritage, this attitude finally brings the ceramic artist to the point where the work disintegrates and returns the material to its natural state. Only the "performance" of the piece, and at times the mental and emotional participation by the viewer remained as the most integral part of the entire aesthetic experience.

Notes

1. "Interview with the Artist," Exhibition Catalog, *Civilizations*, John Michael Kohler Arts Center, Sheboygan, Wisconsin, Sept. 1977.
2. "Clayworks: 20 Americans," Exhibition Catalog, Museum of Contemporary Crafts, New York, N.Y. (June 1971).
3. Joe Bova, Professor of Art, Department of Art, Louisiana State University, Baton Rouge, Louisiana, unpublished correspondence.
4. "Roy Lichtenstein: Ceramic Sculpture," *Ceramics Monthly*, 25:5 (May 1977), p. 40.
5. Mary F. McChesney, "Michael Frimkes and the Cultured Pot," *Crafts Horizons*, XXXIII:6 (December 1977), p. 62.
6. "Clayworks: 20 Americans," *Op. Cit.*, p. 27.
7. Susan Peterson, "The Ceramics of Marilyn Levine," *Crafts Horizons*, XXXVI:1 (February, 1977), p. 63.

Figure 12-73. George Geyer, Untitled Ceramics, clay, sand, glass and water; handbuilt; width—5 ft. 6 inches × 3 ft. 8 inches in length × 48 inches high; Exhibited at "Definition Clay, L.A." Courtesy, Santa Anna College Art Gallery, Santa Anna, California, 1977.

Among the most radical directions of contemporary American ceramics is the work by artist who subject their creations to visible changes induced by natural or man made phenomenons, which finally results in the disintegration of the "object."

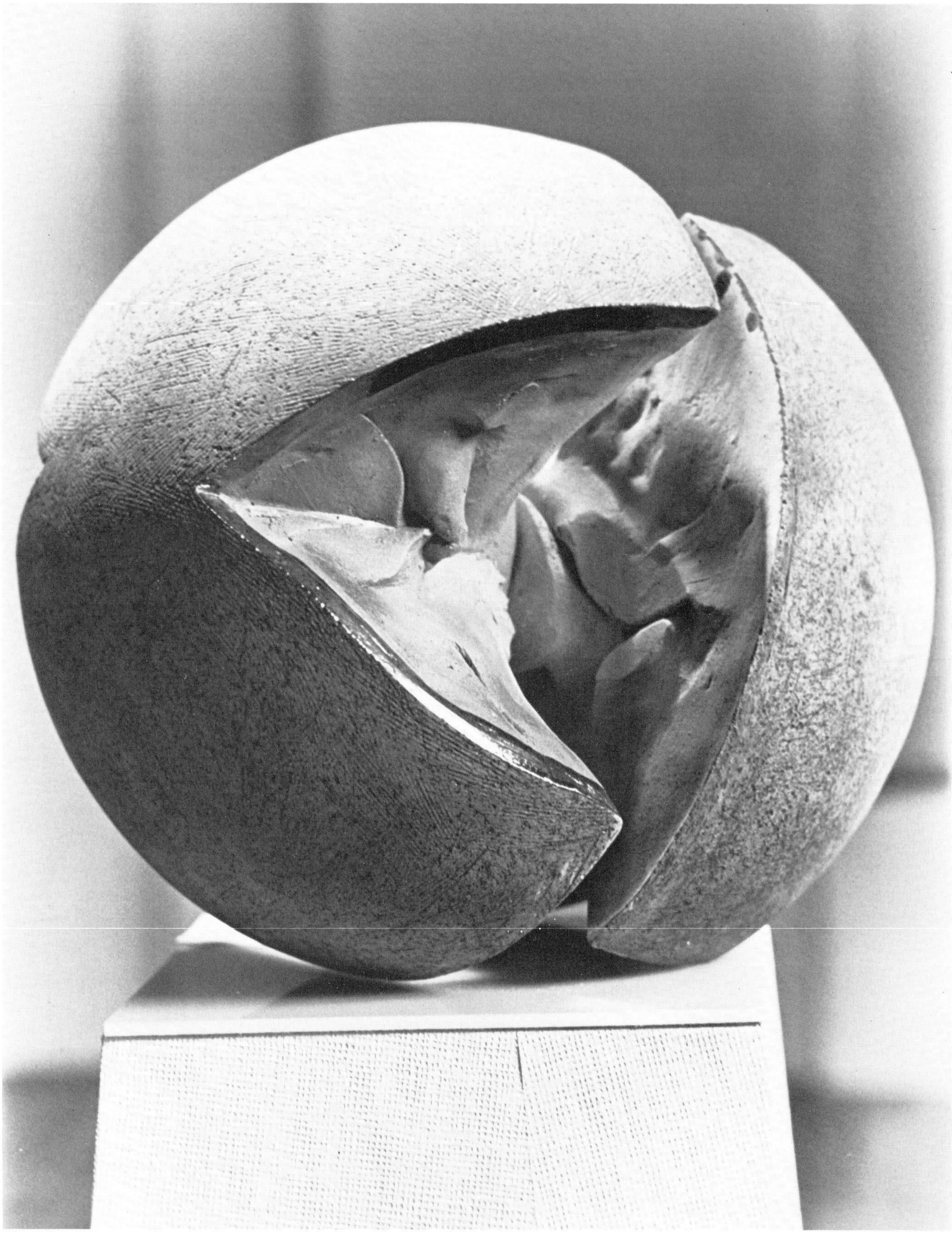

Paul S. Donhauser

Individual Continuity in the 1970's 13

There have always been a number of potters and ceramic sculptors whose work lies quite outside the general tendencies which have been discussed in previous chapters. Their work usually does not gravitate toward any particular movement, style or philosophy. Though their final solutions are quite diverse, their foundations are often grounded in or identified with the principle of a vessel. But they are not the least perceived as pottery *per se.*

More often than not, their structures give hints that within them are contained some mysterious energy which contributes to a kind of ceremonial quality. For example, Paula Winokur's porcelain "Celadon Landscape" extends into an idea of a container. Skillfully camouflaged, only close scrutiny will reveal lids that invite further exploration and discovery (Fig. 13-1).

Richard DeVore has consistently made vessels that are an embodiment of an extremely personal concept. Like shells found at sea, they reveal subtle visual and tactile surprises upon close examination. Their multiple staining, glazing and firings gives them a time-worn character. The insides of these seemingly simple bowls contains small convolutions whose quiet, mysterious nuances add to interesting relationships of interior/exterior space (Figs. 13-2, 13-3).

David Cox from Utah, draws upon a combination of hard-edged, Minimalist construction and a soft, interior tunnel that moves the viewer in and out of the form with gentle persuasion. Its larger than life size scale invites physical as well as visual interaction (Fig. 13-4).

For years Ralph Bacerra has worked with pottery and ceramic sculptures. Whether they are clay vessels or free forms that resemble some sort of creatures, they always deal with subtle imbalances caused by skillful contrasts of organic shapes against hard edged, precisely glazed stripes, dots or other tightly controlled patterns (Fig. 13-5).

Ron Nagle has been a long established potter whose reputation as a highly individual artist stems mainly fron his series of cups which he began around 1962. By 1967 they evolved to such a level of intimate iconography that he devised for them their own, private environments by placing them in beautifully constructed plexiglass and wood boxes. Eventually the cups became free-standing sculptures whose function did not in the least rely on being used for any particular utility. They depended more and more on an idea about a cup and eventually had only a very small orifice that was obviously not designed to hold or dispense liquid. The forms became more architectonic and their slight tilts seemed to challenge laws of gravity. Panels of soft and bright colors sometimes clashed on the cylindrical shapes which further added to the proposition that utilitarian function need not be a prerequisite for dealing with the idea of beauty (Plates 32 and 33).

While Paul Soldner's presence in the development of ceramics has been acknowledged for several decades, his leadership has come about mainly through a keen interest in the area of Raku. Although Raku was not new to American potters, (Bernard Leach discussed it at length in his book, *A Potter's Book* of 1940) Soldner has been largely responsible for helping to develop a distinctively American sense of it.

Using vessel forms thrown on the wheel and then usually altered, or resorting to hand-built

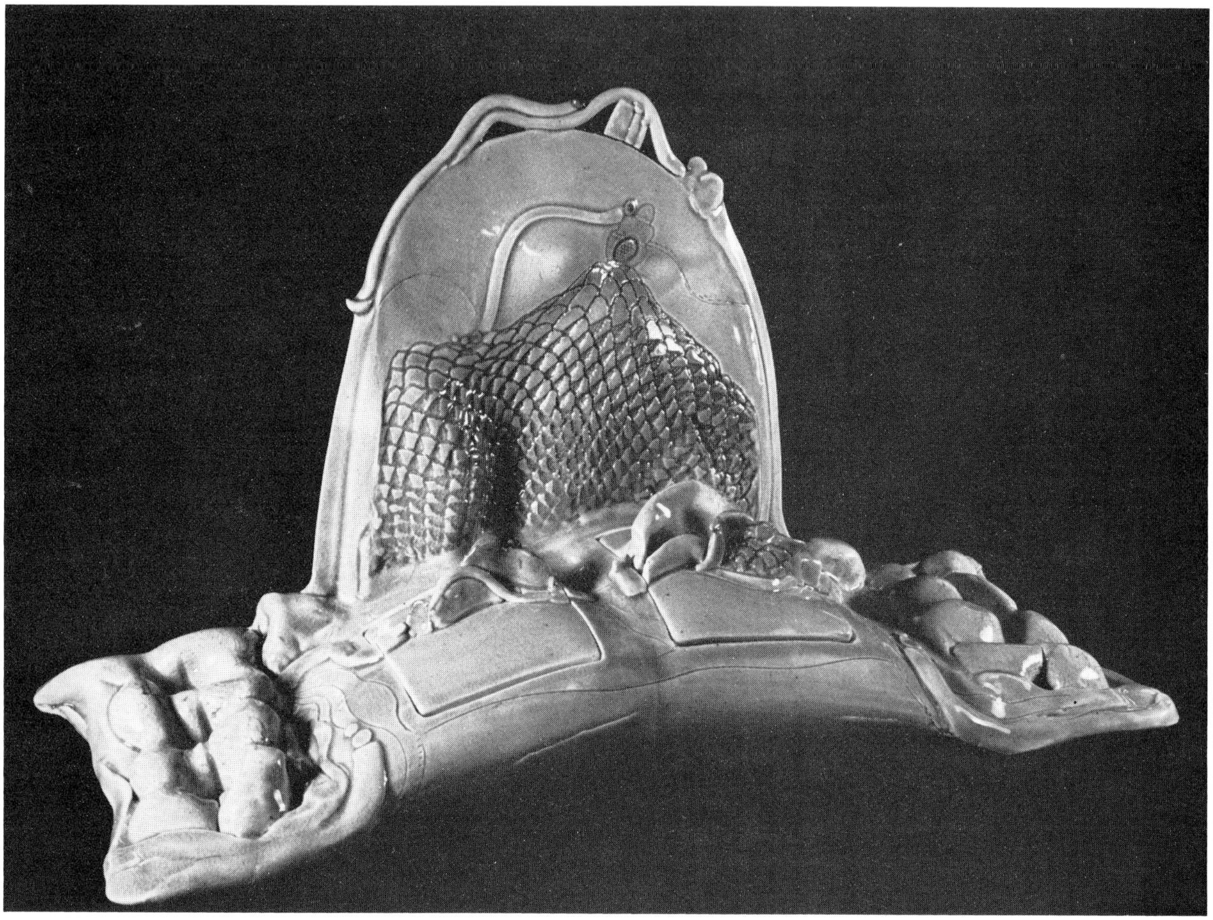

Figure 13-1. Paula Winokur, "Celadon Landscape," porcelain, extruded and handbuilt; celadon glaze; 1977. Courtesy of the artist.

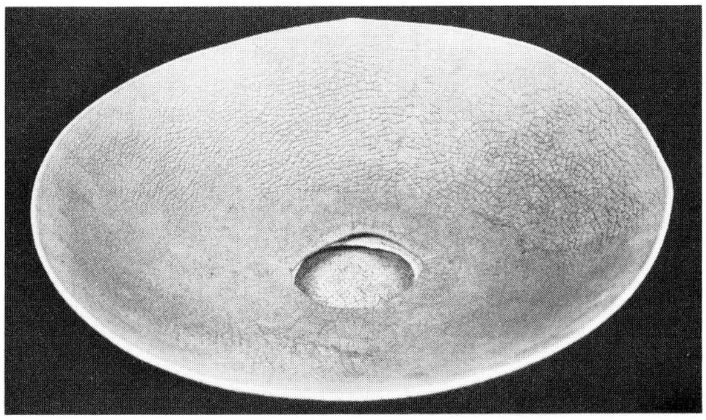

Figure 13-2. Richard E. DeVore, stoneware, 14" diameter, 1977. Courtesy of the artist.

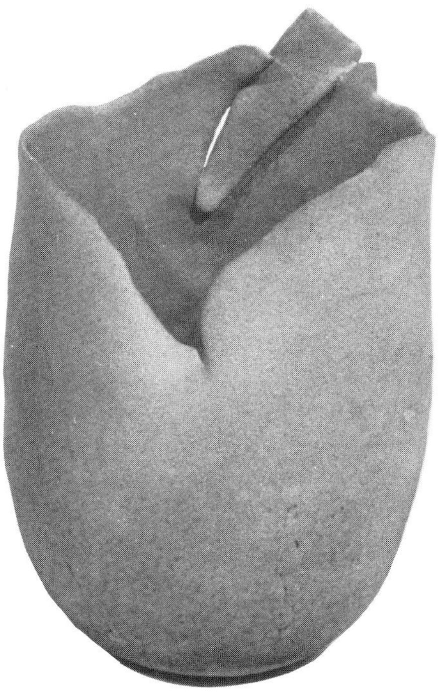

Figure 13-3. Richard E. DeVore, stoneware, 12" × 8"; 1973. Courtesy of the artist.

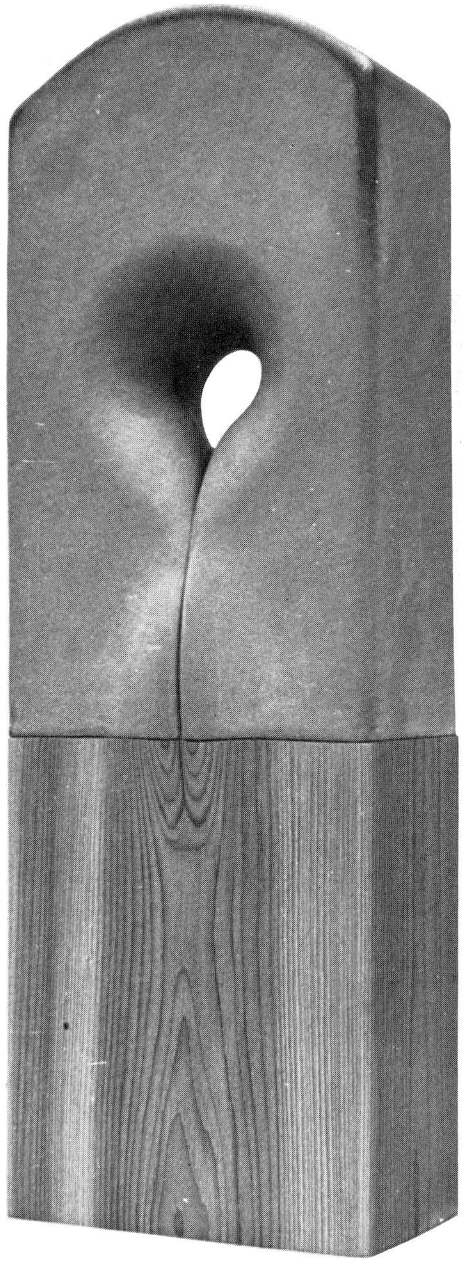

Figure 13-4. David Cox, Untitled Sculpture, stoneware, and cedar wood; unglazed; handbuilt; 9" × 5" × 24"; 1976. Courtesy of the artist and the Weber State College Permanent Collection.

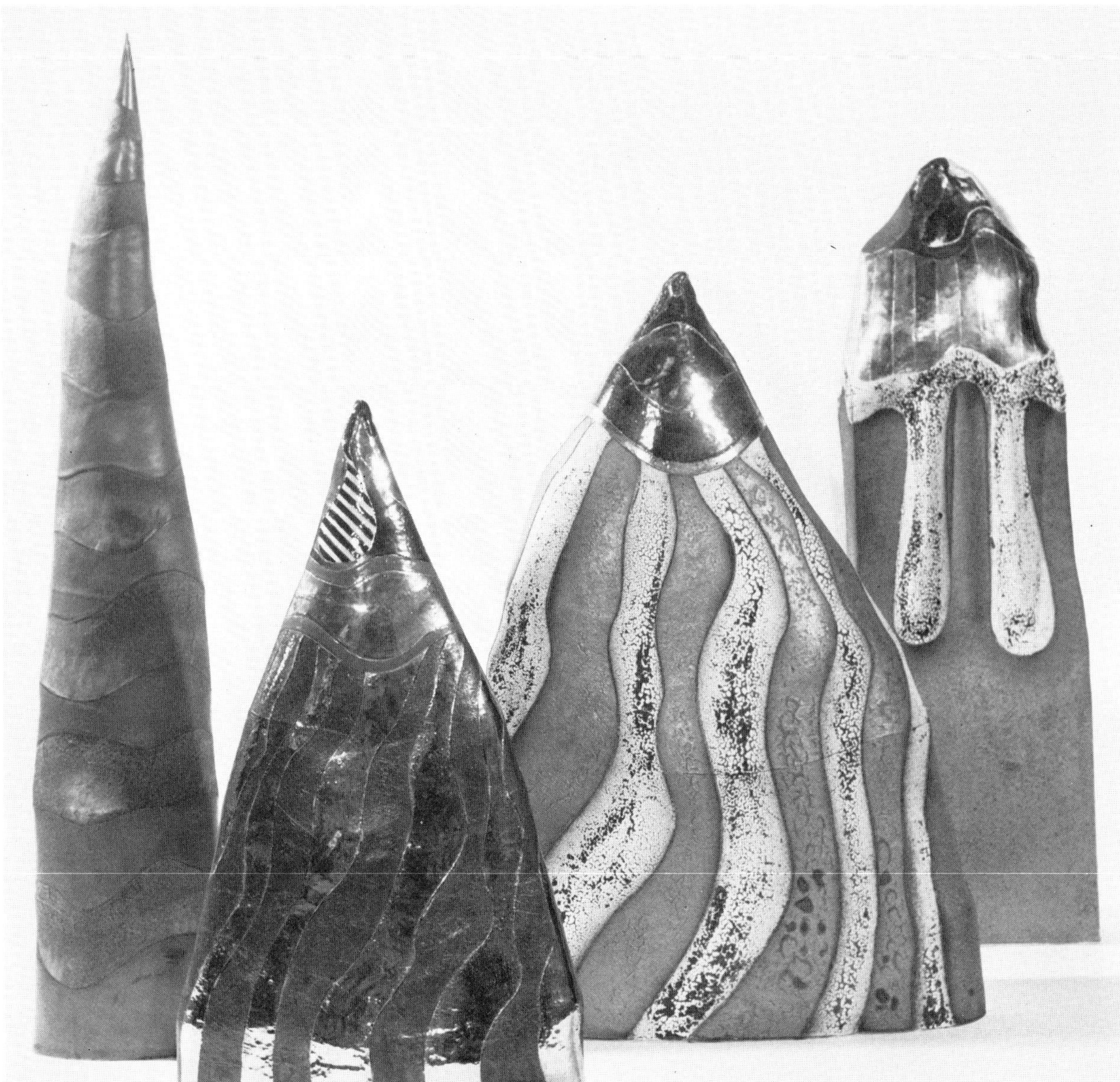

Figure 13-5. Ralph Bacerra, "Red Stripe," "Silver Stripe," "Ruby," and "Chief" from left to right; stoneware, handbuilt, multicolored low fire glazes and lusters; 1970; from the exhibition of "Everson Museum Ceramics '70 Plus Woven Forms." Courtesy, the Everson Museum of Art, Syracuse, New York.

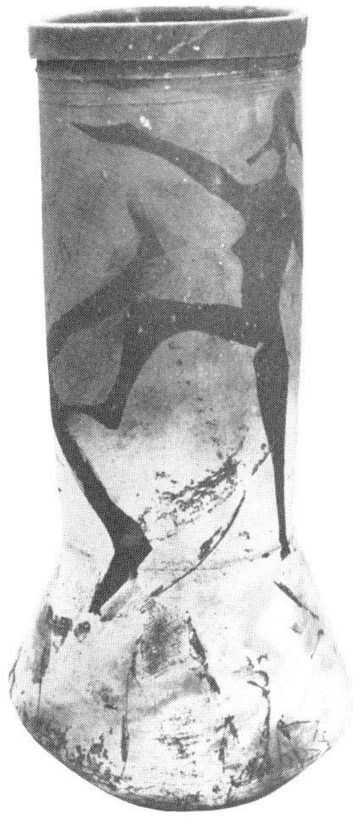

Figure 13-6. Paul Soldner, Raku Vase, Raku clay body, wheel thrown and altered, 20″ × 7″, salt bisqued, figures stenciled with clear glaze, black-orange and green, post fire smoked; 1977. Courtesy of the artist.

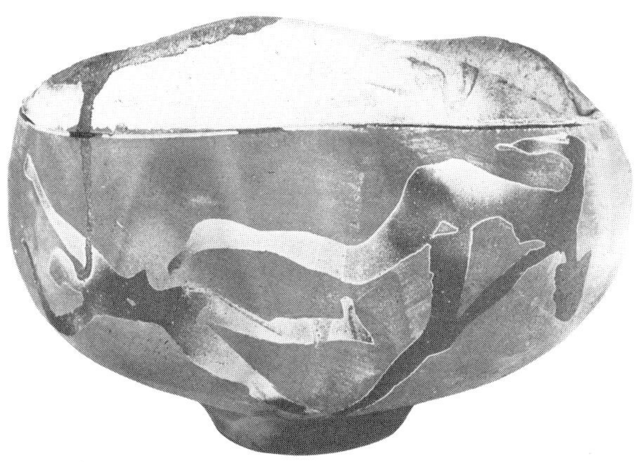

Figure 13-7. Paul Soldner, Raku Vessel, Raku clay body, wheel thrown and altered, unglazed, iron and copper oxide stencil design; post fire smoked; 18 1/2″ × 12″ h; 1976. Courtesy of the artist.

platters, he often embellished them with motifs derived from the human figure. By endless experimenting with various slips, engobes, glazes and smoking techniques, Soldner has created a wide range of complex designs and lyrical surfaces (Figs. 13-6 and 13-7).

Through his teaching position at Scripps College, his studio-school in Colorado, his numerous workshops, lectures and demonstrations throughout the United States, Raku has become an integral part of the ceramic artists' repertoire. By the mid and late 1960's Raku in America had become synonomous with Paul Soldner. It appeared particularly suitable for the American temperament which seems to demand immediate and often repeated results (Fig. 13-8).

These few examples illustrate how a number of potters developed an uncompromising sense of independence from being identified with any particular trend or fashion. Although they may operate within a broad framework of pottery, their continual refinement of highly personal approaches toward form, surface and color gives their work a highly individual distinction. They have not been swept into the tides of momentary fashion. Instead, they are the best propagandizers of the idiom "to do your own thing."

To the potter who was deeply committed to a traditional form concept, to a way of life that involved making unpretentious pottery for everyday use, the new wave of experimentation and selfconscious creation of "for-exhibition-only" pieces may have proved to be a dilemma. But in retrospect this did not prove to be true. Despite the emphasis on self-expression, of "doing your own thing," of challenging established tenets about good taste, of constantly searching for the new, the novel, and the innovative, large numbers of potters remained true to their commitment of creating well designed and expertly made—yet individually created—pottery (Fig. 13-9).

The contributions by numerous leaders in American ceramics during the first half of this century became the foundation for following generations of potters who dedicated themselves to the ideal of creating sound, utilitarian work. Although hundreds, perhaps thousands, literally engaged in making pots, a number of them have remained conspicuous through some personal mark of distinction (Fig. 13-10). They are emblematic of the wide diversity of attitudes and interests that exist to this day across the United States (Fig. 13-11, Plate 34).

Although these potters often worked on a small, mass-production basis, each piece was individually conceived and made with great care, setting it distinctly apart from the impersonal items of industry. Among the many respected studio-potters fashioning a living through his work is John Glick from Farmington, Michigan. Although the mainstay of his production has dealt with pottery for use, such as tea sets, plates, covered jars and dishes, he also ventured into the "one-of-a-kind" products that allowed for some playful experimenting (Fig. 13-12).

Karen Karnes of New York has always maintained a commitment to producing strong, simple forms for decorative and utilitarian function. Her robustly thrown covered containers are free of superfluous decorations, relying on salt glazing for reinforcing the strength and sureness of her forms (Fig. 13-13).

Kenneth Ferguson of Kansas City has maintained a strong interest in creating pottery which considers function as the main criteria for artistic excellence. He became best known during the early 1960's for his large covered

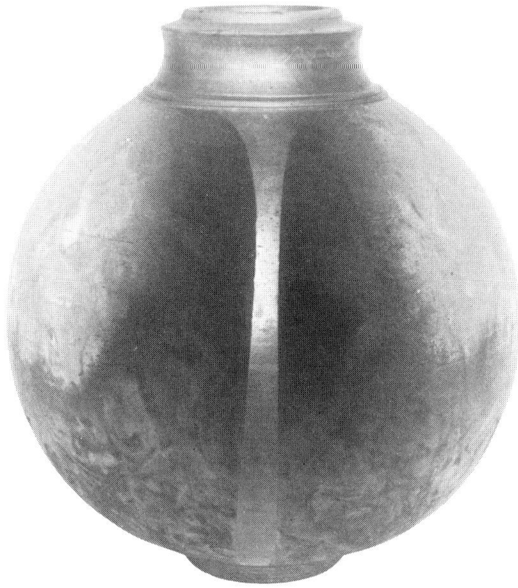

Figure 13-8. Harvey Sadow, "Entrance to the Land of Souls," from the Earth/Sea Vessels, wheel thrown, partially glazed with matt glazes, Raku fired, 16" × 12"; 1977. Courtesy of the artist.

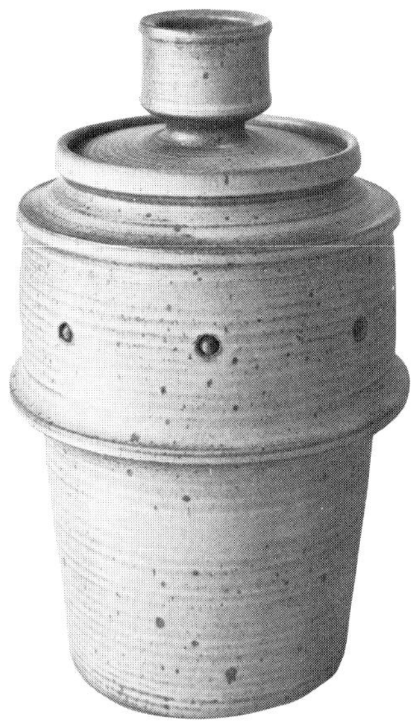

Figure 13-9. Roger Corsaw, Lidded Jar with inserts; stoneware, wheel thrown, 15 1/2" high; 1974. Collection of the artist.

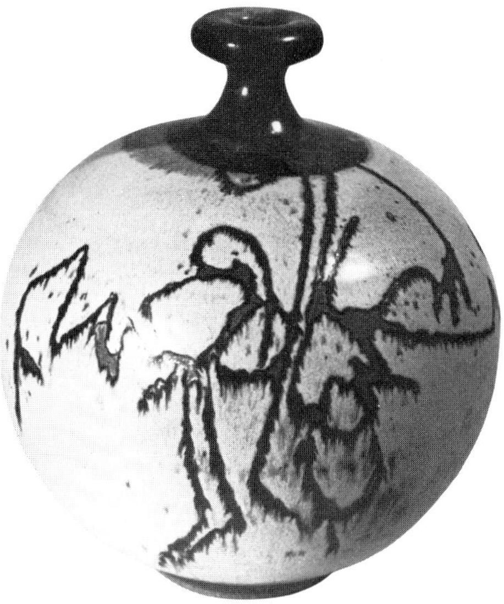

Figure 13-10. Robert Sperry, Bottle Form, stoneware, wheel thrown, slip decoration under matt stoneware glaze; 1964.

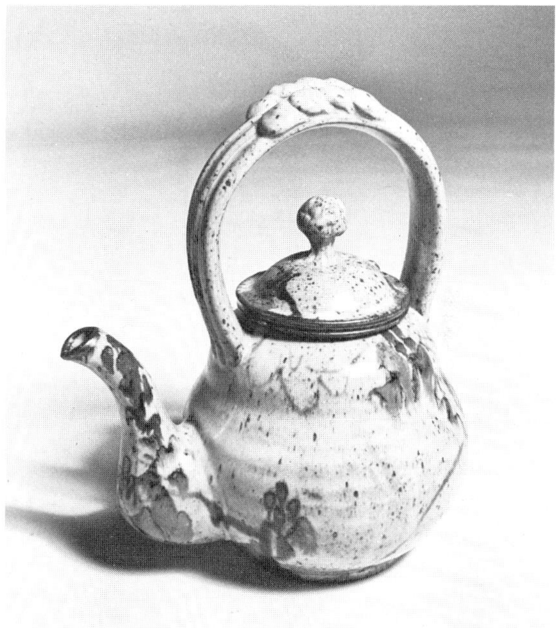

Figure 13-12. John Glick, Teapot, stoneware, reduction fired, pressmolded spout, wire-cut handle; 11" high; 1975. Courtesy of the artist.

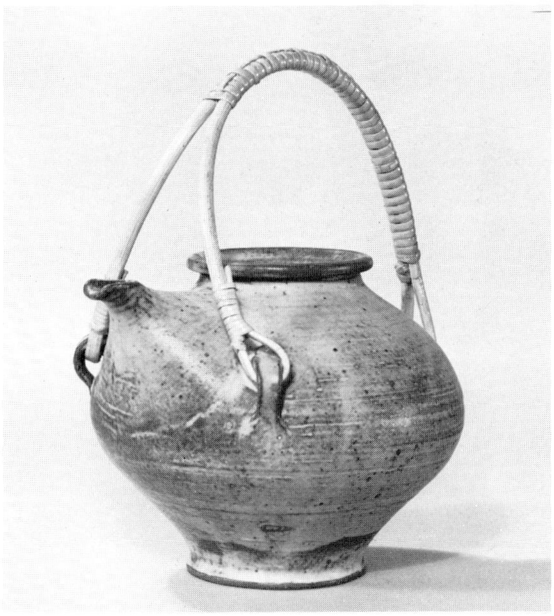

Figure 13-11. Donald Frith, Teapot, stoneware, wheel thrown, light brown glaze, bamboo handle; ca. 1965. Courtesy of the artist.

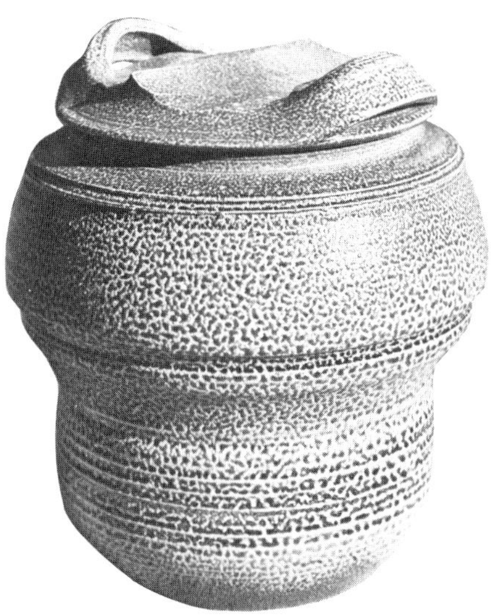

Figure 13-13. Karen Karnes, Covered Jar, stoneware, wheel thrown, salt glazed; 20" high; ca. 1974. Courtesy of the artist.

jars (Fig. 13-14), tea pots, pitchers, platters and bowls which were characterized by a directness of throwing and finishing by allowing the finger ridges to remain as an integral part of the pot's structure. His forms were simply glazed, relying on rich surfaces to enhance the stoneware quality of the clay. In recent years Ferguson has widened his interest by also dealing with the platter in a more decorative manner in which the human figure serves as the main motif.

Robert Winokur of Pennsylvania has maintained his interest in resolving the problems of skillfully integrating utility with visual harmony. His recent containers, fired in salt kilns, are clear statements of sound ceramic structure and inventive visual organization (Fig. 13-15).

David Shaner of Montana, long a respected potter of functional ceramics, continues to provide unpretentious work whose main purpose is to fill the utilitarian needs of the home. Working mostly in stoneware reduction firing, his pots are sometimes thought of as derivative of contemporary Japanese traditions (Fig. 13-16). But he conveys a personal imprint by imbuing much of his work, particularly the large plates and platters, with motifs that are indicative of the vast landscape of his Montana residence (Fig. 13-17). Various glazes which are overlapped by pouring create rich interplays of positive-negative space relationships. This results in his work being devoid of the mannerisms which so often dominate the self-conscious efforts of many other potters (Figs. 13-18 and 13-19).

Vivika and Otto Heino from California, who for several decades have been regarded as leaders of American studio-pottery, continue to create pottery essentially made for practical purposes. Their work is distinctive for its intimate understanding of the media and a

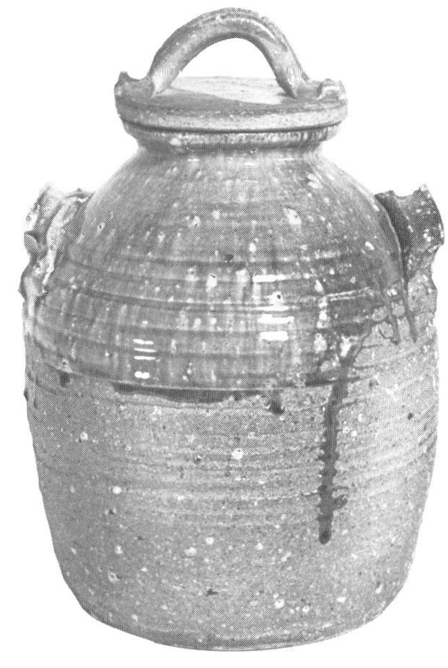

Figure 13-14. Kenneth Ferguson, Covered Jar, stoneware, wheel thrown, partially glazed, fired in wood burning kiln; approx. 15″ high; 1967. Courtesy of the artist.

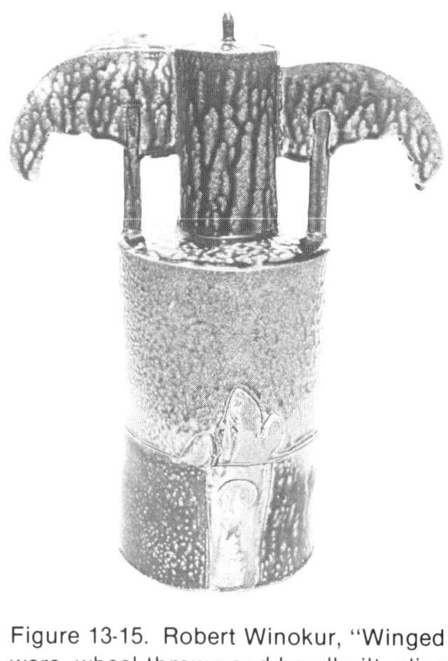

Figure 13-15. Robert Winokur, "Winged Vessel," stoneware, wheel thrown and handbuilt, slips and engobes covered with blue wood ash glaze, salt glaze fired; 18″ high; 1977. Courtesy of the artist.

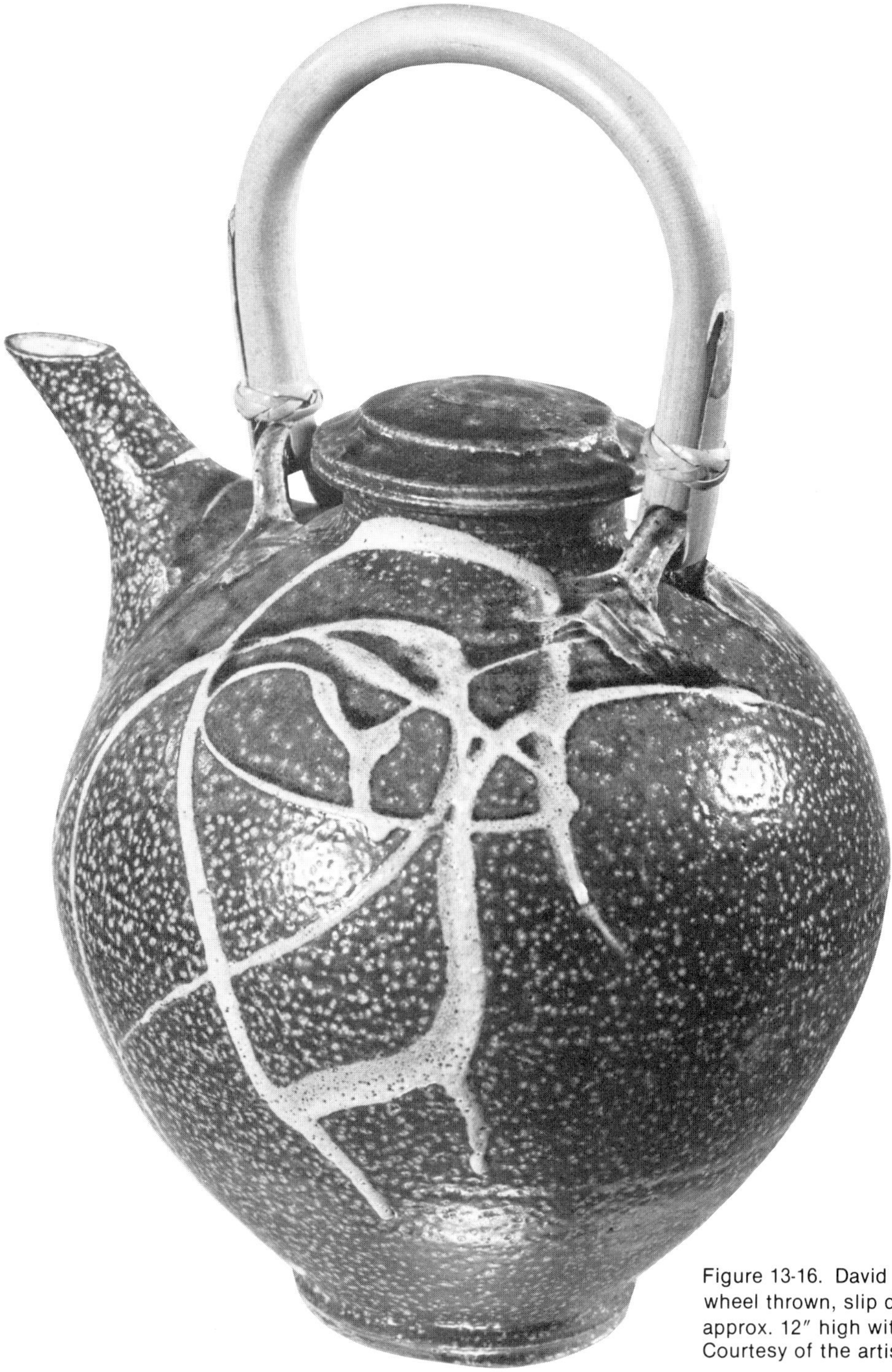

Figure 13-16. David Shaner, Teapot, stoneware, wheel thrown, slip decoration, salt fired; approx. 12″ high with handle; ca. 1974. Courtesy of the artist.

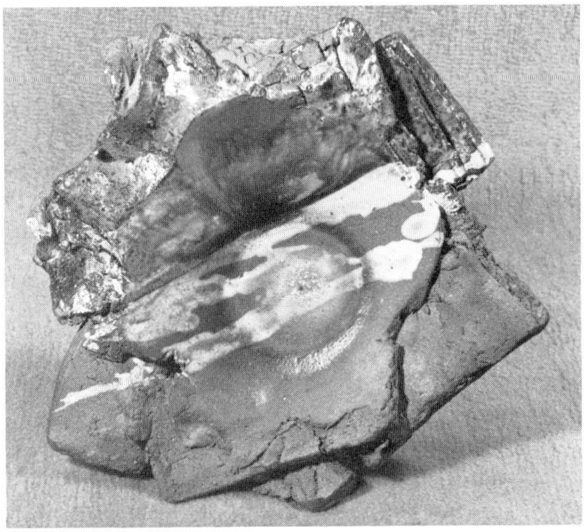

Figure 13-17. David Shaner, Slab Dish, stoneware, hand-built partially glazed; 20″ diameter; ca. 1975. Courtesy of the artist.

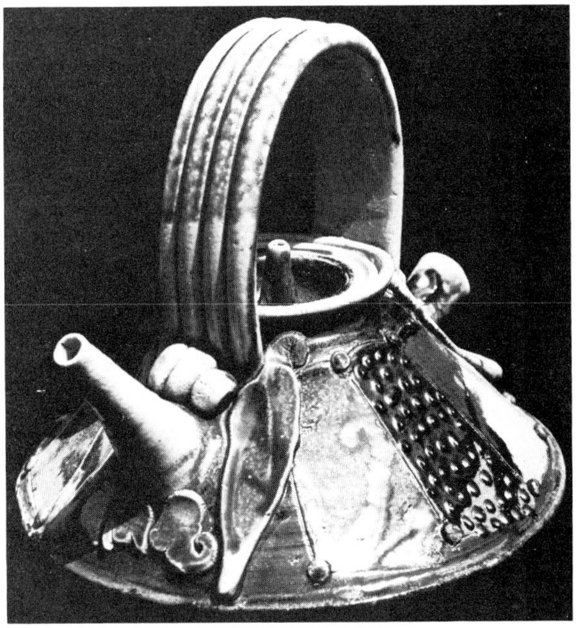

Figure 13-18. William Warehall, Teapot, porcelain, wheel thrown; applied decorations, slips and glazes; 10″ × 10″; 1977. Courtesy of the artist.

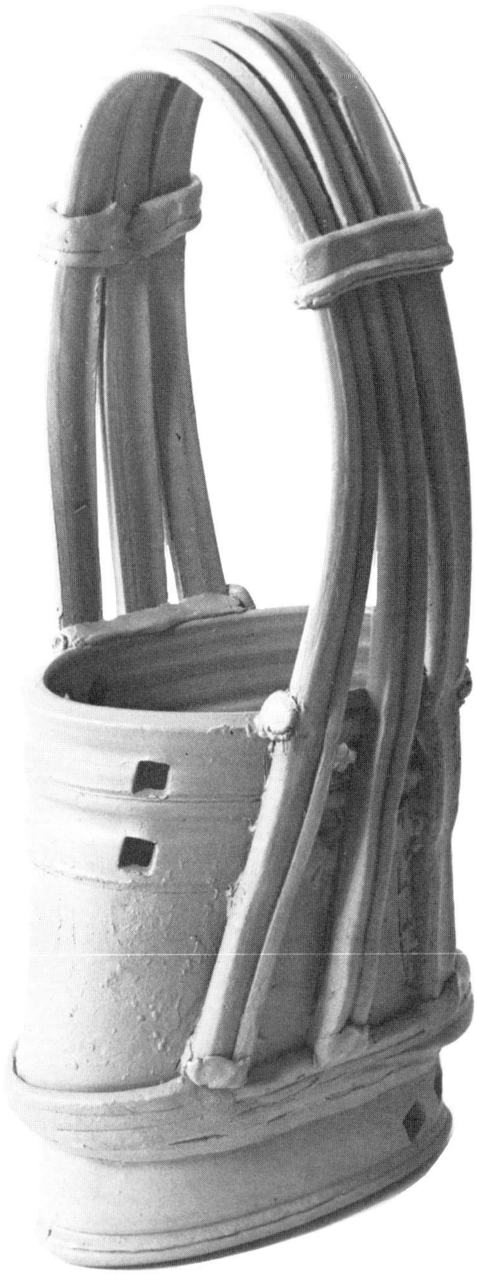

Figure 13-19. Betty Woodman, "Basket," earthenware, wheel thrown, altered, pulled handles; Terra Siggalata; 21″ tall; 1977. Courtesy of the artist.

sensitive response to the needs of providing pottery produced with conviction and integrity. Their vases and covered jars, for example, exude a kind of forthrightness and dignity that is reflective of their continued efforts to capture the essential beauty of clay as it is formed on the wheel and then decorated in such a way that it enhances the structure of the pot (Fig. 13-20).

Warren MacKenzie of Minnesota who has often been identified as one of the best disciples of Bernard Leach's philosophy and style, has maintained an unswerving commitment to creating pottery for every-day use (Figs. 13-21, 13-22). In a time when many potters are agonizing over whether or not a clay object is regarded as "craft" or "art," MacKenzie has provided a resounding ring of optimism and enlightenment. He pointed out that

> I am a potter; maker of containers and useful objects. The repetition of form and ideas over months and even years allows them to sink into the subconscious and to surface again, transmuted by changes in myself and my environment. . . . Expression and communication as a combination of conscious and unconscious controls seems to me to be the most important goal of the hand potter or any other creative person.[1]

The high regard for MacKenzie and his work is best substantiated by his numerous awards, exhibitions and especially by the consistent invitations to present workshops, lectures and demonstrations throughout the United States over the past twenty years. His presence has provided a reassuring sense of variety and continuity in the growth and development of the American artist-potter (Figs. 13-23 and 13-24).

Rudolph Staffel from Pennsylvania where he also teaches at the Tyler School of Art, has been involved in ceramics for well over thirty years. His reputation as a major figure in American ceramics has been gained mainly through his interest and research in the area of translucent porcelain. Through empirical research and intuitive probing, Staffel has concentrated on capturing the structural and lyrical properties of light which gives his pottery an ephemeral luminosity. This interest in light and its integral structural and decorative relationship to a translucent porcelain pot has resulted in a prolific production of work which dramatizes a relatively new form-concept based on interior-exterior space. It has established Staffel as one of a number of eminent artist-potters in America (Fig. 13-25).

Perhaps no one has been singlehandedly more responsible for the resurgent interest in the art of salt glazing than Donald Reitz of Wisconsin. Shortly after arriving at the University of Wisconsin, Reitz realized the limitations that traditional stoneware glazes held for his personal and artistic development. Seeking a more direct method of decorating and firing which would afford maximum opportunities for improvising, Reitz pursued salt glazing with intense ingenuity. After much experimenting he developed a wide and rich vocabulary of colors, textures and other surface embellishments that gives his pottery strength and distinction (Fig. 13-26 and Plate 35). Numerous exhibitions, awards, lectures and workshops throughout the nation and other continents have established him as one of the important leaders that have reinforced American studio-pottery with a sense of professional integrity (Fig. 13-27).

Robert Turner of Alfred, New York has been an acknowledged leader of studio-pottery for well over twenty years, both as a potter of expertly crafted functional items and as a highly respected teacher at Alfred University.

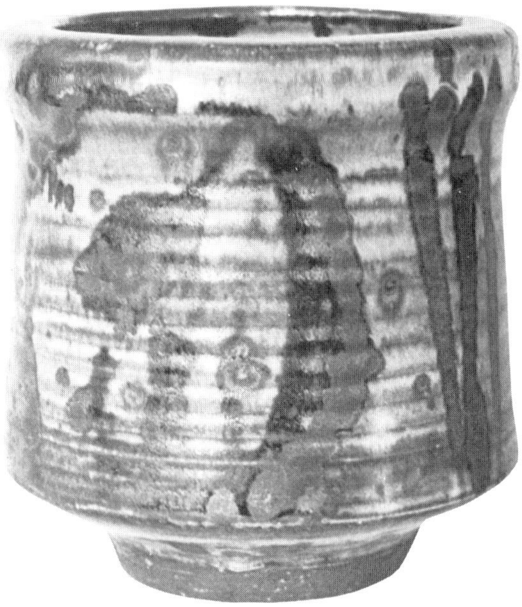

Figure 13-20. Vivika Heino, Vase, stoneware, wheel thrown, iron slip decorated, opaque reduction-fired glaze; 6″ h × 4 1/2″ w; 1963. Collection of the author.

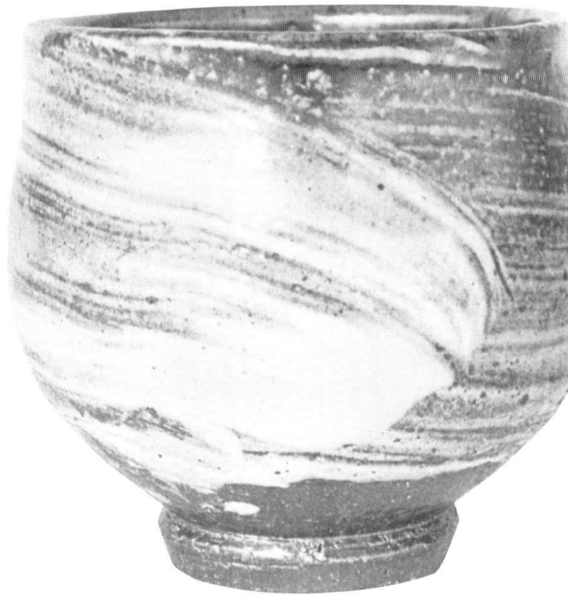

Figure 13-22. Warren MacKenzie, Pot, stoneware, wheel thrown, white slip decoration, salt glaze fired; 3″ × 3″; 1964. Collection of the author.

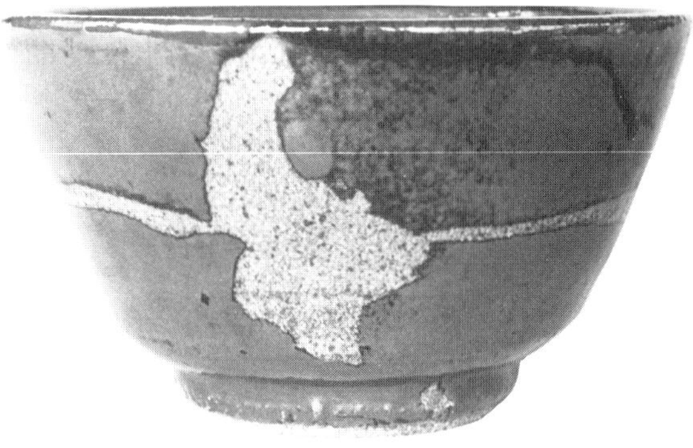

Figure 13-21. Warren MacKenzie, Bowl, stoneware, wheel thrown, wax resist decoration over grey glaze and covered with iron saturated reduction-fired glaze; 8″ × 3 1/2″; 1977. Collection of Maureen Weaver.

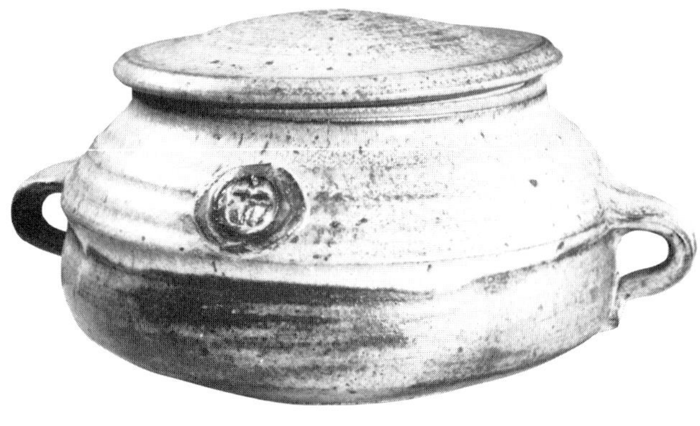

Figure 13-23. Angelo Garzio, Casserole with pulled handles; stoneware, volcanic ash glaze, reduction fired; 13″ × 11″ × 6 1/2″; ca. 1973. Courtesy of the artist.

Angelo Garzio is a good example of the American studio-potter who have maintained a strong commitment to produce well made functional pottery amidst the flurry of the more avant garde activities of contemporary ceramics.

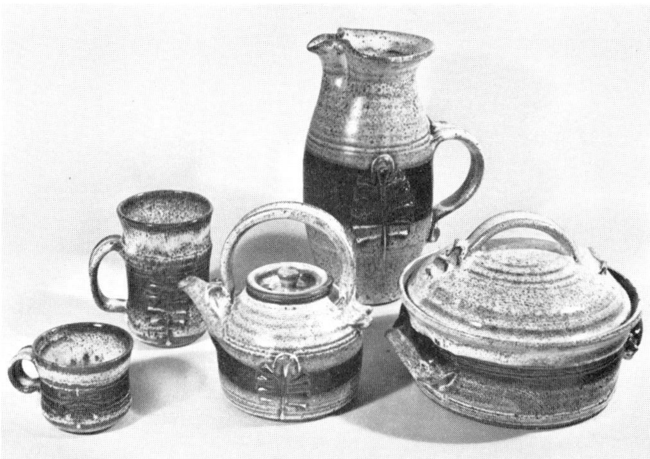

Figure 13-24. Richard Peeler, Production Pieces, stoneware, wheel thrown, stamped decorations, fluid slips covered with opaque glazes; 1973. Courtesy of the artist.
The work of Richard Peeler, and other production potters like him, represent one of the best continuing links in history of American studio-pottery.

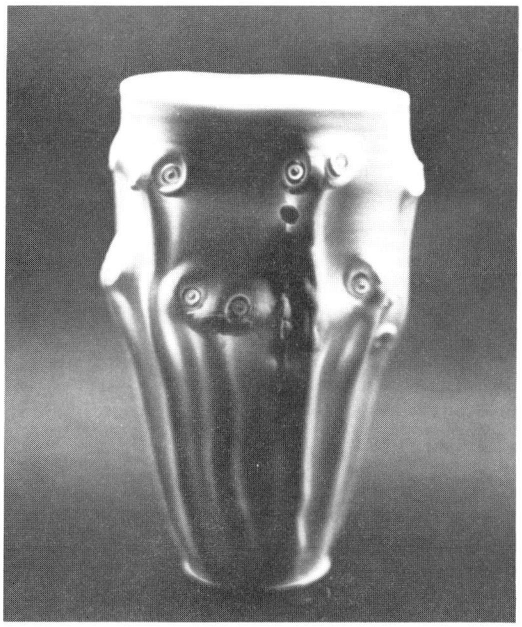

Figure 13-25. Rudolf Staffel, Vase, translucent porcelain, wheel thrown and altered; transparent glaze; 12″ tall × 5 1/2″ wide; ca. 1973. Courtesy of the artist.

Turner's work conveys a sense of extreme simplicity of design and austere surface. He pointed out that

> . . . the natural processes with clays and glazes at stoneware temperatures are appropriate when one is interested in the expression of enduring values seen in natural objects.[2]

Although his pots are intended for practical use, their successful merging of form and surface creates feelings of purity and utter simplicity and need no particular utilitarian assignment in order to be viewed as an expression of artistic sensibility (Figs. 13-28, 13-29).

A number of other potters did not consider utility as a primary principle of beauty. Instead, they pursued an approach to decorating and glazing which places their work essentially in the realm of decorative ceramics. For example, Beatrice Woods of California maintains her interest in conventionally thrown forms, but imbues them with exotic, lustered surfaces. Harrison McIntosh provides a sense of continuity even to this day in his utilitarian and decorative pottery which are noted for their over-all patterns achieved through sgraffito, incising or brush work (Fig. 13-30). Carlton Ball continues to develop a wide range of decorative approaches on large vessels, especially by using wax resist processes which he helped to popularize during the early 1950's when he was at the University of Wisconsin and at Illinois Southern University. Lastly, Laura Andreson and Herbert Sanders, long and well established leaders in American studio-pottery, have continued their fascination for refining elegant crystalline glazes on sensitively thrown shapes (Figs. 13-31, 13-32). These and many other potters continue as an important link in the development of American pottery whose foundations are essentially

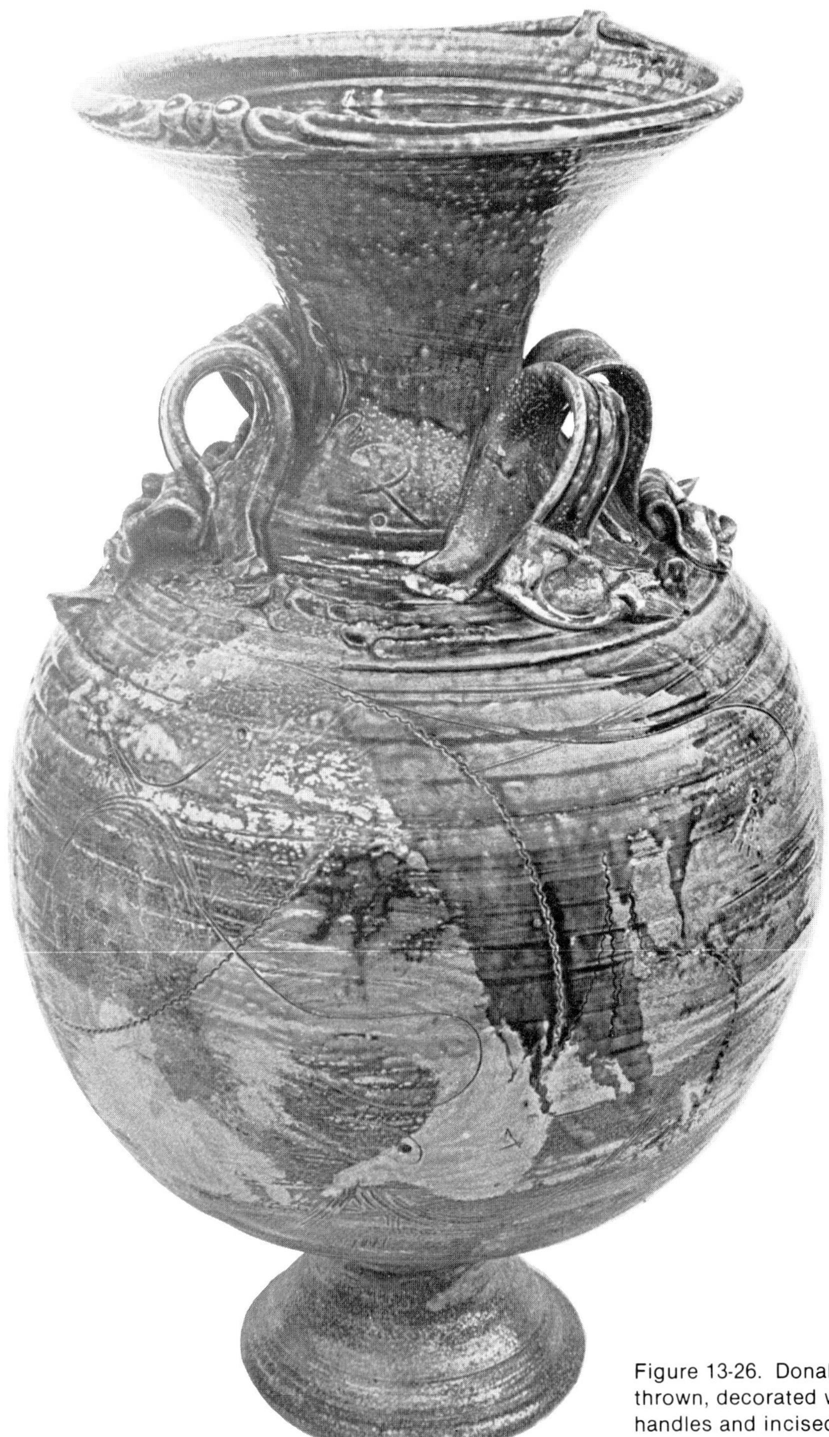

Figure 13-26. Donald Reitz, Vase, stoneware, wheel thrown, decorated with various slips and oxides, pulled handles and incised design, salt glazed; 43″ h × 24″ w; 1974. Courtesy of the artist.

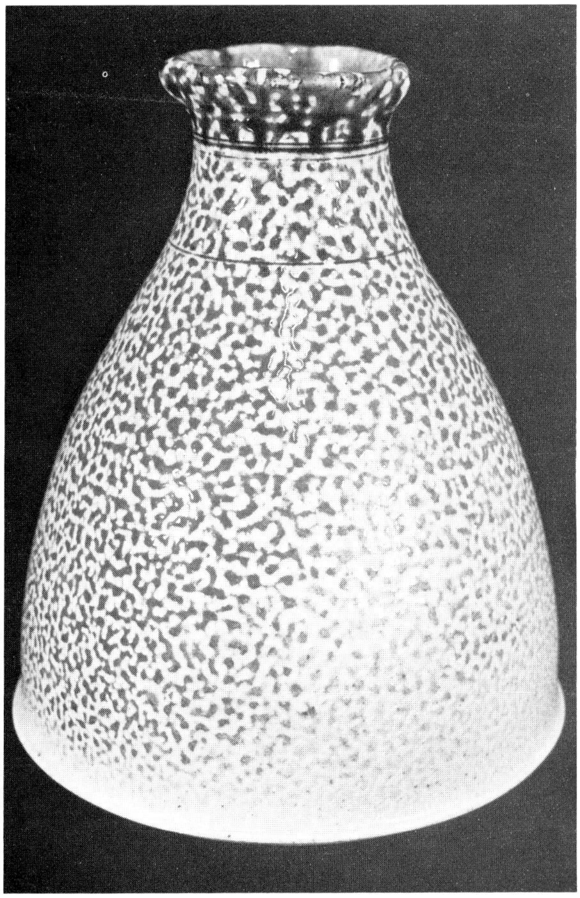

Figure 13-27. Tom Turner, Vase, porcelain, wheel thrown, copper red reduction salt glaze; 10″ × 8″, 1976. Courtesy of the artist.

Continuing experimentation with different clay bodies, slips, glazes and firing techniques has given new meaning to the traditional use of salt glazing.

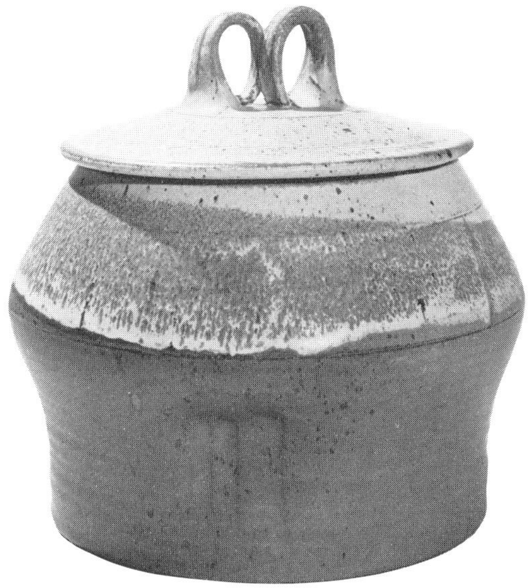

Figure 13-28. Robert Turner, "Storage Jar," stoneware, wheel thrown, pulled handles, stamped decoration, matt glazes; 1966. Prize winner in the 24th Ceramic National Exhibition. Courtesy of the Everson Museum of Art, Syracuse, New York.

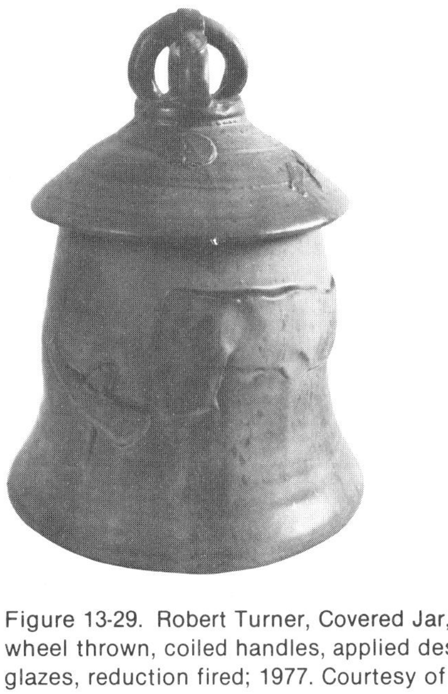

Figure 13-29. Robert Turner, Covered Jar, stoneware, wheel thrown, coiled handles, applied designs, matt glazes, reduction fired; 1977. Courtesy of the artist.

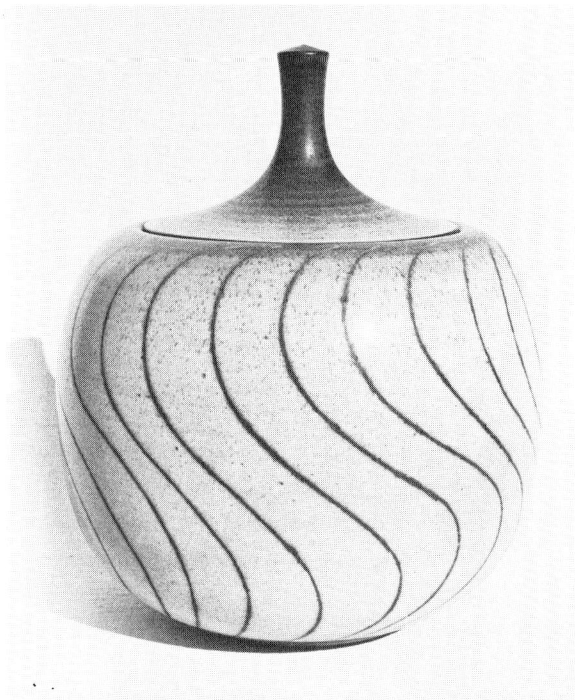

Figure 13-30. Harrison McIntosh, Covered Jar, stoneware clay (cone 5), wheel thrown; beige matt glaze, grey and black wax resist decoration; 9 1/2″ × 8 1/8″. Courtesy of the artist.

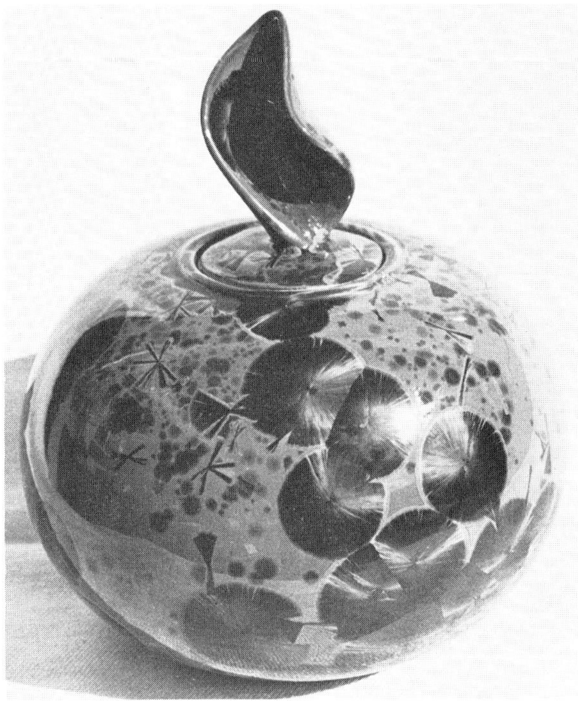

Figure 13-31. Herbert Sanders, Covered Jar, porcelain, wheel thrown, hand constructed handle on lid; crystalline glaze; approx. 10″ w × 12″ h; ca. 1972. Courtesy of the artist.

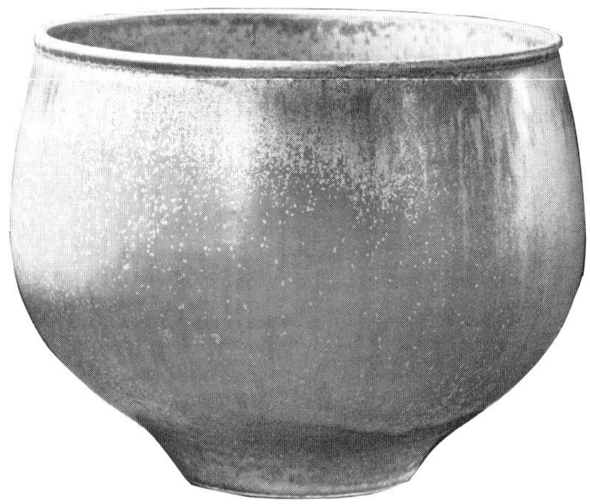

Figure 13-32. Laura F. Andreson, Vase, porcelain, wheel thrown, brown iron crystal glaze; 5 1/2″ × 6 1/2″; 1961. Collection of the artist.

based on European and Oriental prototypes (Fig. 13-33).

A Retrospective View

Through an examination of potters, their work, and other social, economic and educational circumstances related to pottery, insights have been gained into the changing role of the American studio-potter. From colonial times to approximately 1970, several shifts in emphasis are noted as regard purposes, designs and techniques in pottery.

During colonial times, the potter fulfilled immediate utilitarian needs. He seldom made overt claims to being an artist. However, mechanization in the 19th century replaced the need for individuals to produce pottery by hand. Thus, a division of labor within the total ceramic process became more evident. Painters and sculptors designed and decorated pottery, while chemists and technicians dealt with glazes, clay bodies and firing. Copies and imitations of the past and of other countries were the mainstay of most commercial potteries. At the same time, several companies began to produce art-ware. The notion of making "one-of-a-kind" pottery became increasingly popular. The people associated with the production of this type of ware were loosely referred to as artist-potters.

An important outgrowth of commercial pottery was that some people reacted against its limitations, i.e., mass production of imitations and copies. Several ceramists established themselves as artists, independent of industry. The popularity of china painting was a reflection of the growing dissatisfaction with the impersonal character of commercial pottery.

Although the people associated with china painting perpetuated form concepts similar to those of the ceramics industry, a number of important ideas were implemented which became instrumental in further developments in studio-pottery. First, the independent potter had to be skilled in all aspects of the pottery process. Secondly, a good background in art, especially in drawing, was deemed necessary to deal with the problem of decorating. Lastly, a concern for dealing with each pot as an individual work of art once more promoted the idea of the hand-crafts. A number of people emerged from the china painting movement as leaders of this early form of the studio-potter.

The lack of reliable information, as well as the inadequacy of available training, necessitated the creation of schools that could fulfill the need for training in all aspects of pottery. Alfred University was a pioneer in preparing potters in technical and artistic aspects of ceramics. Its numerous graduates established themselves in various parts of the country and perpetuated the ideas that prevailed at Alfred. The ideas nurtured at Alfred orientated around traditional concepts regarding design and craftsmanship. By 1935, several other schools implemented programs similar to that at Alfred.

At the same time, a growing awareness of the importance of the crafts was being dealt with through various types of organizations. The most popular of these was the Society of the Arts and Crafts. Although this group accomplished little to improve the artistic quality of pottery, it did bring about a better public awareness of the hand-crafts. The Society also served as a prototype for numerous other organizations which, since the turn of the century, have become well established throughout the country. The activities of the various groups have significantly aided in promoting

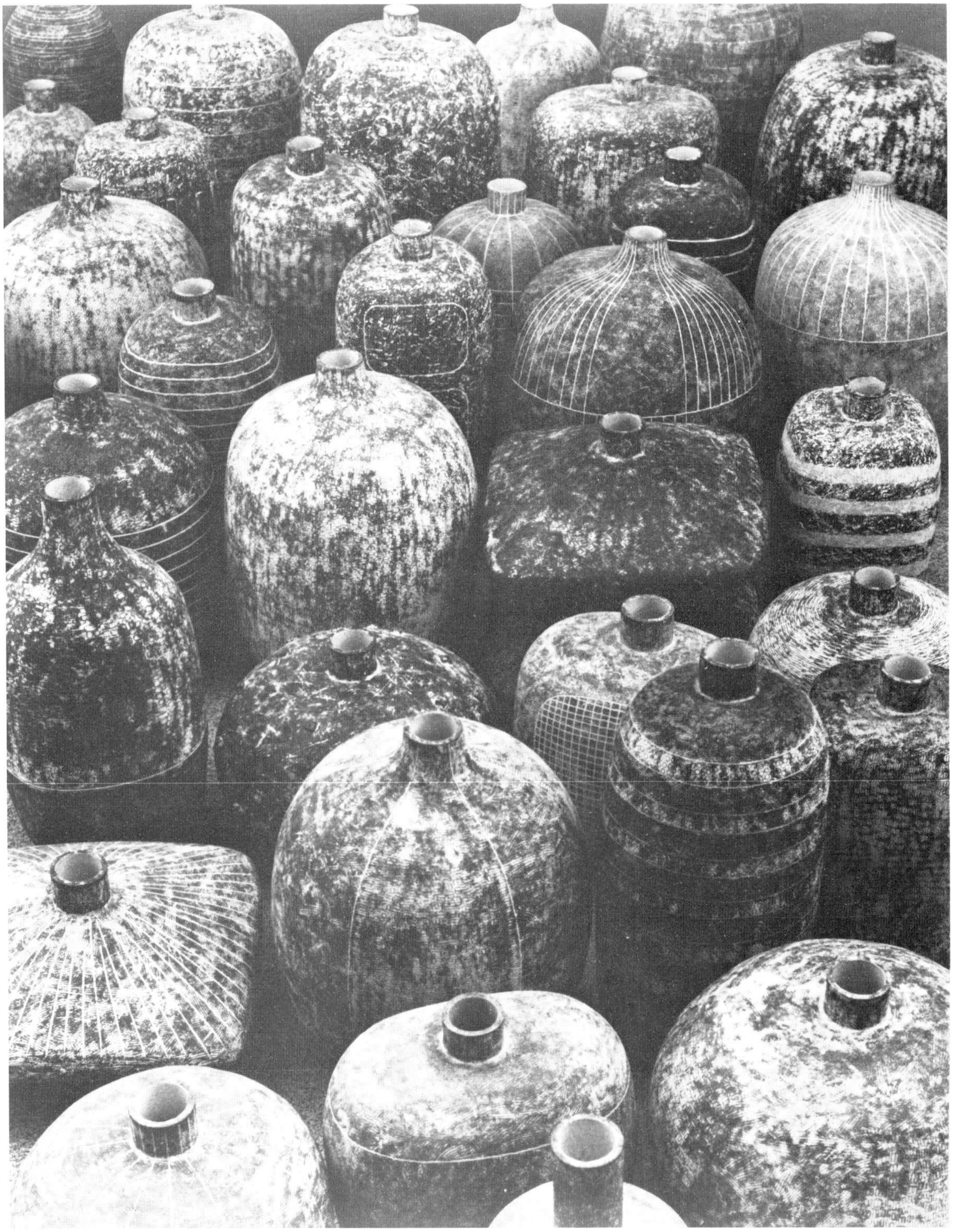

the art of the potter during the first three decades of the twentieth century.

After 1930, a number of European-trained artists came to America where they became well established studio-potters. Their presence influenced students and potters and created a diversification of styles, techniques and attitudes. In addition, the insurgent interest in industrial design, associated with the International Style, encouraged a further proliferation of existing forms of self-expression in pottery.

Relatively little activity occurred from 1938 to 1945, but after World War II an increase in developments was noted. Growing numbers of potters, trained in Europe and the Orient, made themselves felt on the contemporary scene. American potters were quick to assimilate their influences. Other influences emanated from contemporary Japanese pottery, Scandinavian design and other sources of the industrial design syndrome of the 1940's. Studio-pottery thus became characterized by a diversity of forms, building techniques and approaches to decorating.

After 1945, several parallel movements developed which added to the complex growth of American studio-pottery. Increased enrollments in colleges and universities and its accompanying expansion of art programs was one example. The idea that a potter should be trained thoroughly in artistic and technical considerations became well established in ceramics courses offered in departments of fine art. Increased information through more research and consequent publishing added to the existing body of knowledge. The willingness of more museums to exhibit contemporary pottery aided in giving stature to potters as artists. Hence, the scope of self-expression was broadened in ceramics.

Activities in other areas of the arts, such as contemporary painting and sculpture, made themselves felt in the form concepts of several potters who were trained between 1950 and 1960 (Fig. 13-34). Pots were characterized by an increasing exuberance of building and decorating techniques. Although some did not abandon tradition in terms of design, they did become involved in decorative innovations. This led to further investigations of the three-dimensional character of the pot. In so doing, traditional notions of form, craftsmanship, firing techniques, and decoration were questioned and challenged. The result was that a type of work emerged during the late 1950's which did not rely on precedence (Fig. 13-35).

The work of some potters, produced toward the end of 1950, signaled a complete departure from the conventional pot form. At times, any utilitarian consideration was negated. That a form was thrown on the wheel became of less importance than the transformation that could occur by beating, gouging, scratching, tearing, or otherwise altering the form. Hence, a form concept developed which was distinctively American. Pots were imbued with a dynamism, spontaneity, and freedom of expression that associated it closely with Abstract Expressionist painting and sculpture. Indeed, the new forms in pottery were clear manifestations of the concepts and percepts brought to the field by artists who were exposed to a much different background than their predecessors.

Figure 13-33. Claude Conover, Series of vases, stoneware, handbuilt, slab constructed, stained with colored clays and fired to cone 8; sgraffito designs. Heights vary from 12″ to 36″; ca. 1972-74. Courtesy of the artist.

Many studio-potters elect to work with a particular shape which is investigated for long periods of time. The results are subtle variations of form, decoration and surface as seen in the work of Claude Conover.

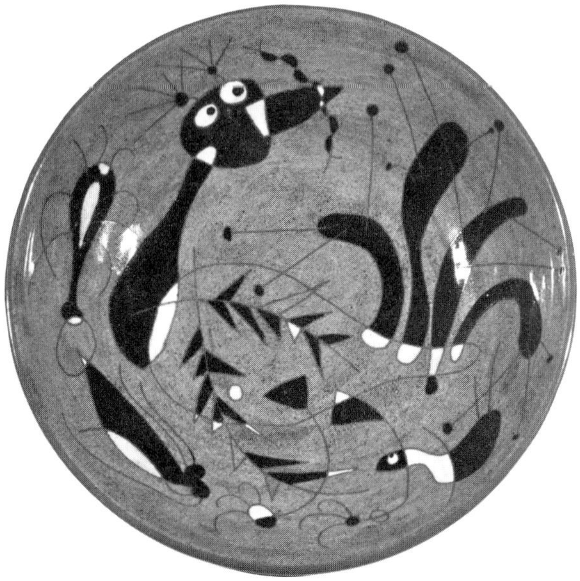

Figure 13-34. Karl Martz, Low Bowl, red earthenware clay, wheel thrown, black and white slip decoration, transparent cover glaze, 1952. Private Collection of Mr. and Mrs. Rudolf Gottfried, Bloomington, Indiana.
Numerous studio-potters during the early 1950's were influenced in their decorative approaches by activities in contemporary painting.

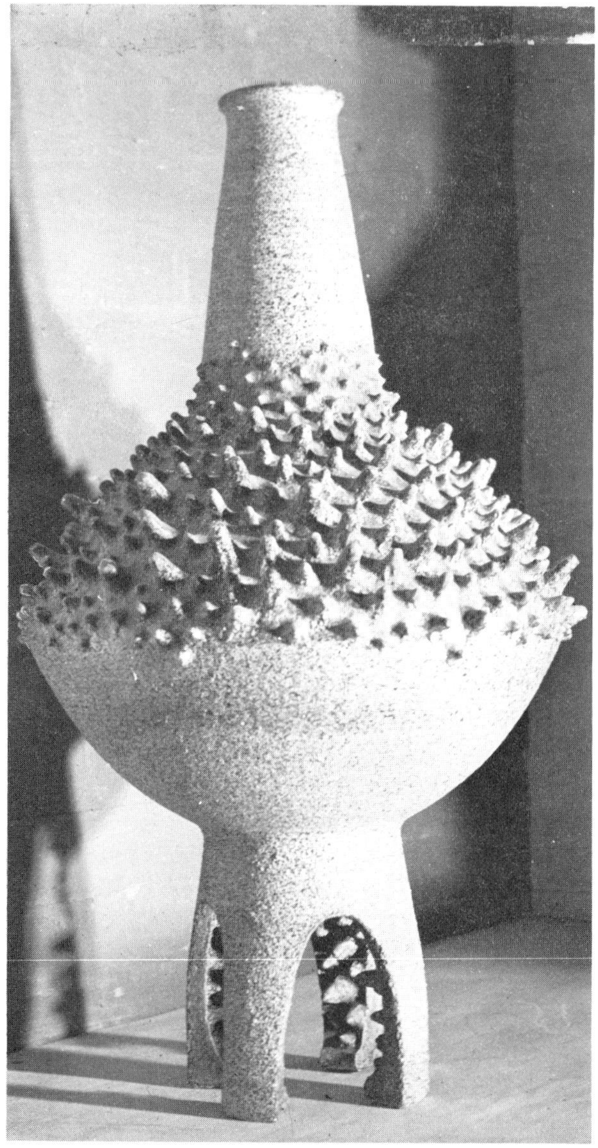

Figure 13-35. Lyle Perkins, Vase, stoneware, wheel thrown and altered, applied clay decoration, partially glazed; 30″ high; 1957; Butler Museum of American Art Permanent Collection, Youngstown, Ohio. Courtesy of the artist.
A spirit of experimentation with forms, decorations and glazes characterized much pottery during the 1950's.

The pottery produced by these artists constituted one part of the creative efforts of numerous American potters. A variety of other approaches still existed. But the new, venturesome excursions into the realm of complex concepts of structure placed the work of American studio-potters in contention with pottery produced throughout the world. By 1960, the potter had become established as a part of the mainstream of modern art, and had become an artist-potter.

If the 1950's were indicative of a time when the crafts in general were undergoing an identity crisis, then the 60's was a time when ceramics, in particular, was going through a phase of new technical, visual and philosophical exploration. With the aid of established ceramics programs in most major art departments of colleges and universities, with increased availability of techincal, artistic and historical information through books, magazines and exhibits; with more opportunities for receiving acknowledgement from competitive exhibitions, invitational theme shows and the creation of numerous shops and galleries, the artist-potter indulged in assimilating a wide range of new materials, tools and techniques and pursued more vigorously to exhibit and sell the fruits of his labor.

Among the more notable shifts of emphasis in the sixties was an increased use of techniques which, although known to many potters, were previously not a serious part of their vocabulary in searching for new or unique expressions. For example, commercially prepared underglazes, china paints, low fire glazes and metallic lusters lent themselves conveniently for hand or airbrushing. The latter tool had been essentially reserved for use in commercial art, but potters began to see its potential also for complex graphic decorations. Underglaze pencils allowed the ceramist to draw on the clay with the same sensitivity and skill as his compatriot in the area of graphics or painting. In similar manner, the ready access of ceramic decals, photo silkscreening and photographic emulsions that could be combined with clay became an additional source for enriching the ceramic artists' repertoire for visual communication.

An insurgent popularity of slip casting and press molding, using as models everything from newspaper galley proofs to found objects and part of the human anatomy widened the ceramic artist's resources in fashioning for himself a more distinctive vocabulary. Even the ready availability of commercially made clays and casting slips (or at least their "foolproof" formulas) alleviated the time consuming tasks of endless experimenting and trial-by-error frustrations with which his predecessor of ten or fifteen years had to concern himself.

Better built wheels, more efficient and safer kilns, more powerful clay mixers, more workable information about kiln building and more detailed discussions about problems related to glaze-making and firing techniques gave the ceramist of the 1960's a newly found freedom not previously known to the American artist-potter.

Armed with this vast array of information and skill, the ceramist was thus able to more easily embark on the adventure of searching for growth and recognition as an artist.

The decade from approximately 1960 to 1970 represented an era of, what now seems like, an overindulgence in attempting everything that was available in order to infuse the attack upon an (clay) object with as much tension and explosiveness as possible. Some people even relinquished the traditional approaches to glazing in favor for using commercial paints. Automobile laquers, enamels and any combination of paints frequently appeared as plausible solutions to the alternatives of glazing. The fact that the paints may not have remained permanently on the clay surfaces seemed of little concern to those who entertained the idea that a work of art need, perhaps, be no more lasting than a human life.

The 1960's and early seventies can therefore be characterized as a period during which American ceramics underwent one of its most convulsive changes; not gradual evolution, but impetuous reaction against many traditionally held values that espoused "good taste" and serene beauty. Thus, alongside the faithful producers of well made and sensitively designed ceramics for everyday use, there emerged a new ceramic tradition. It was an expression based not so much on eclecticizing and repeating the accepted standards of the past, as it was a signaling of a new era based on ebullition, ferment and high pitched psychological intensity (Figs. 13-36, 13-37).

It is understandable, therefore, that many artists working in clay, armed with an endless array of techniques, tools and equipment took advantage of this new spirit of independent action to fashion for themselves highly personal contingencies (Plate 36). There were no specific styles, no clearly defined attitudes that dominated (Fig. 13-38). There were not even particular heros or gurus whose presence either through their teaching, exhibitions, or their own work served as an exclusively dominant force. Whatever one's specific predisposition was, it could be identified with by any one of a number of highly respected ceramic artists in almost any part of the country (Fig. 13-39).

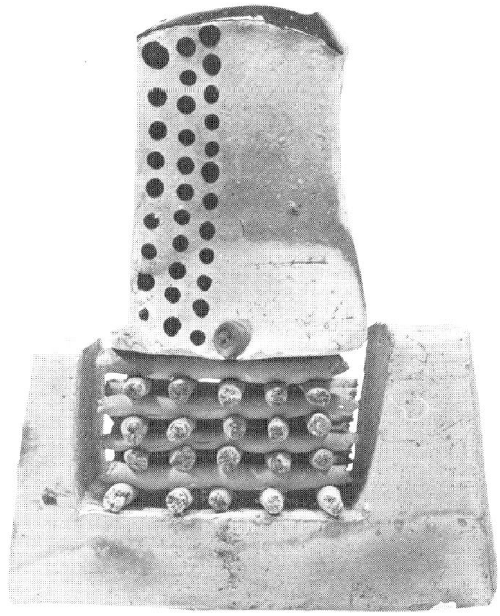

Figure 13-36. Ron Gallas, Construction, brick clay, handbuilt and extruded, partially decorated with low fire glazes; approx. 18″ × 12″; 1977. Courtesy of the artist.

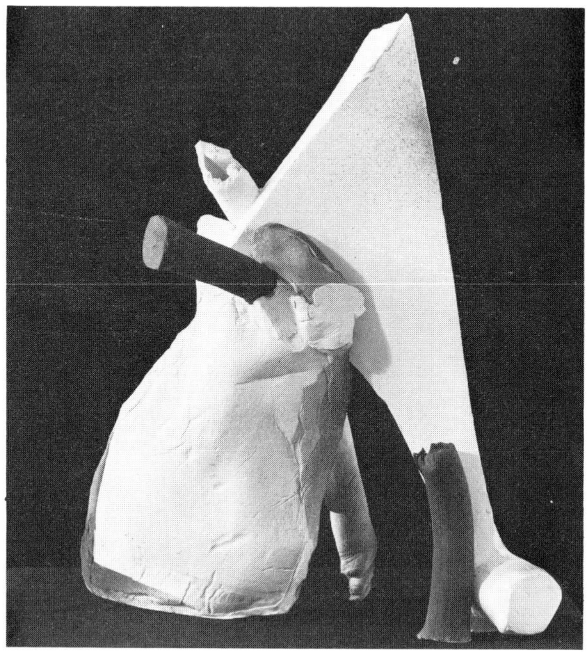

Figure 13-37. Donna Nicholas, "Wedge II," white earthenware clay, handbuilt; low fire matt glazes; 24″ h × 18″ w × 15″ d; 1977. Collection of the artist.

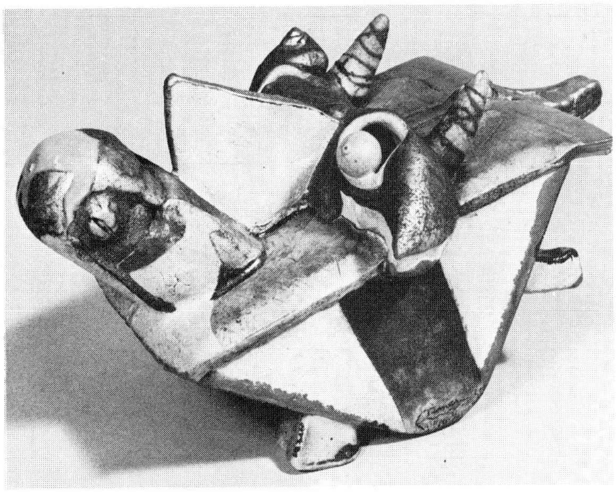

Figure 13-38. James L. Tanner, "Mobitur" P.F.O. Series, stoneware, handbuilt, slip decorated and melted copper wire, luster glazes; 16 1/2″ × 11″ × 9 1/2″; 1977. Courtesy of the artist.

Tanner's work is typical of the spirit of experimentalism that prevailed during much of the early and mid 1970's when many studio-potters were searching for a highly personal form of self-expression.

Figure 13-39. Viola Frey, "Sphinx Self Portrait," Whiteware clay, handbuilt, underglazes, 4 ft. × 6 ft.; 1976. Courtesy of the artist.

Fantasy, combined with a sense of humor which was usually self directed, played an important part in the work of numerous ceramic artists throughout the United States during the early 1970's.

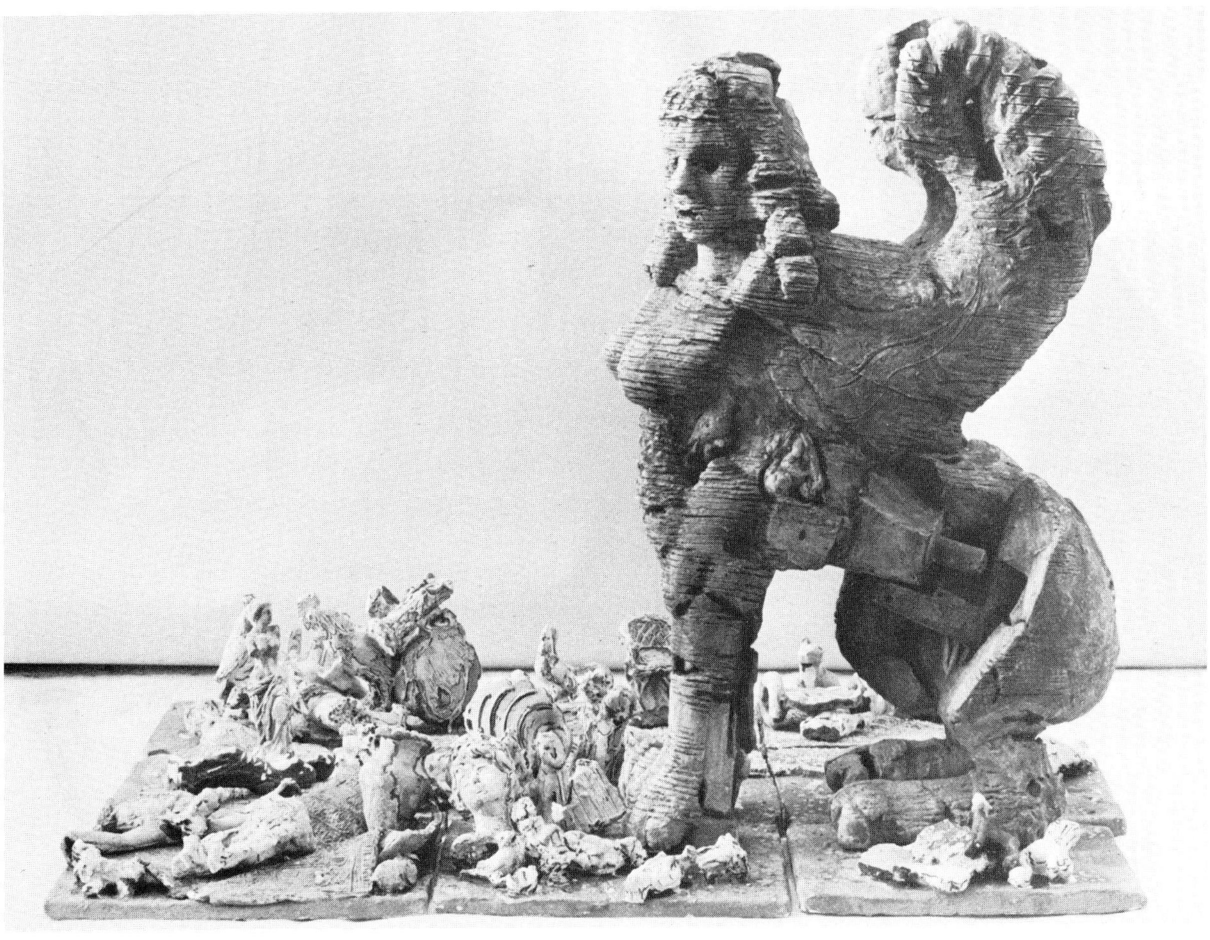

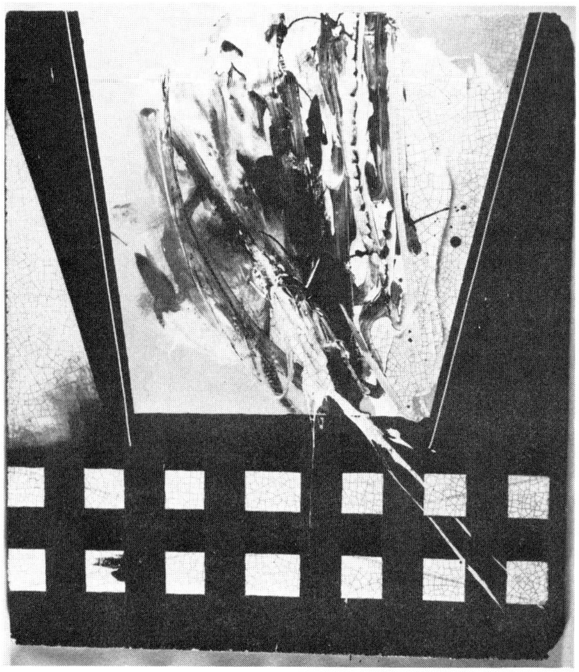

Figure 13-40. David Tell, "Wall Construction," Raku clay, slab constructed, Raku fired, multicolored underglazes; 18″ × 22″; 1974. Courtesy of the artist.

By combining the skills and perceptions of other areas within the visual arts the studio-potter of the 1970's continued to challenge traditional notions of the ceramic arts.

Figure 13-41. Bruria, "Breath" porcelain, cast and hand-built, opaque glaze; approx. life size; 1977. Courtesy of the artist and Jacqueline Anhalt Gallery, Los Angeles, California.

These provocative forms give some indication of the wide diversity of styles and attitudes that characterized the 1970's.

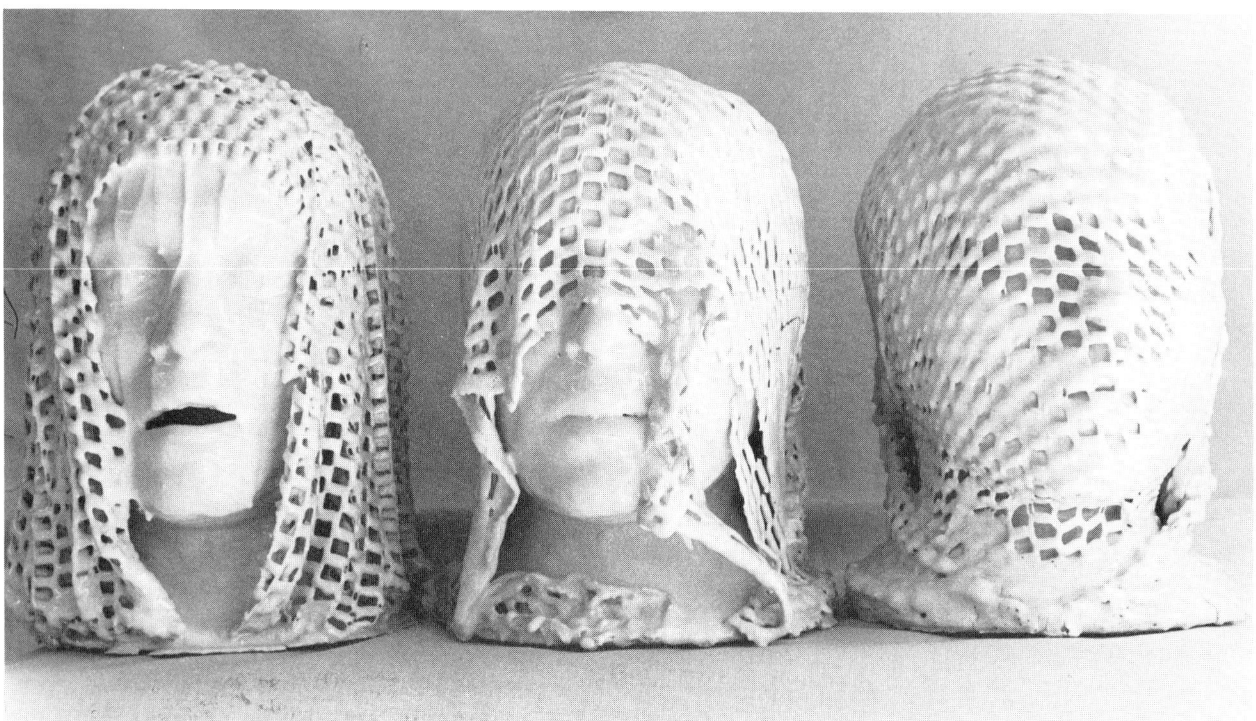

Although one generally looked either to the West or East Coasts for identifying special trends and its leaders, one could seek out reputable practitioners of any particular idiom within the confines of other states or regions. The mythical power structure that was of such great influence on the younger people during the late 1950's and early 1960's began to dissipate under the influx of young graduates from colleges and universities who spread their gospel of "doing your own thing" as they assumed influential teaching positions in various parts of the country (Fig. 13-40).

Even when an attempt was made to use invitational exhibitions as a means for gaining some sort of overview of what was transpiring on the contemporary scene, the best observations that could be extrapolated were of a presumptuous nature. For example, the exhibition "Clayworks: 20 Americans," held at the Museum of Contemporary Crafts in New York City, was typical in reflecting the realization that contemporary attitudes in American ceramics crossed all stylistic and expressive boundaries. With the exception of utilitarian function, no conspicuous attitude, state of mind, sentiment or mood prevailed. If any common denominator moved through the complex labyrinth of the 1970's it was the idea that a multiplicity of meaning in regard to personal expression not only be tolerated, but in fact, encouraged.

Thus, the exhibit at the Museum of Contemporary Crafts was a typical example of the numerous and complex sets of attitudes of the times. Paul J. Smith referred to this when he commented:

> . . . the kind of work shown in this exhibition is possible and meaningful only in the context of our affluent, "fee-form" American society. To intellectualize further by attempting to state what all this means would be presumptuous on our part. The main issue is that these creations have a strong presence—that is the real and valid statement.[3]

A continual form of nervous restlessness prevailed during the early seventies and continues today. Great emphasis was placed on more experimentation. Often the art of the ceramist was left unrealized in the enthusiasm for further exploration. They pushed materials and ideas to their limits in search for new and vital forms; forms not necessarily restricted by preconceptions, but forms with which they could identify themselves. The ceramic scene thus became infused with a bewildering variety which did not seek to duplicate the known formulas of established ideas, but rather to create new and provocative forms (Plates 37 and 38).

The multifaceted aspects of contemporary art, like that of life in general, seems to have also expanded the perceptions of the ceramic artist. While numerous ceramists pursue the more traditional modes of making clay vessels based on precepts of the past, others are constantly challenging the frontiers of newly emerging styles and attitudes. It is the latter group that continues to be the strongest contending force in breaking down the traditional role of the "artist-potter," "studio-potter," or "artist-craftsman" as he was variously identified in the past (Fig. 13-41).

Notes

1. John Reeve, "Warren MacKenzie and the Straight Pot," *Crafts Horizons*, XXVI:3 (June 1976), p. 19.
2. Biographical Sketches, *Design Quarterly*, Walker Art Center, Minneapolis, Minnesota, Numbers 42 and 43, 1958, p. 63.
3. Paul J. Smith, Introduction to the Exhibit Catalog, "Clayworks: 20 Americans," Museum of Contemporary Crafts, of the American Crafts Council, New York, New York, June, 1971.

Bibliography

Books

Barber, Edwin A. *The Pottery and Porcelain of the United States.* New York: G.P. Putnam's Sons, 1909.

Binns, Charles F. *The Potter's Craft.* New York: D. Van Nostrand Co., Inc., 1910.

Cox, Warren. *Pottery and Porcelain.* New York: Crown Publishers, 1945.

Crafts in the Southern Highlands. Southern Highlands Handicrafts Guild, Asheville, North Carolina, 1958.

Crawford, Jean. *Jugtown Pottery.* John F. Blair, Publishers, Winston, Salem, North Carolina, 1958.

Eaton, Allen. *Handicrafts of New England.* New York: Harper and Brothers, Publishers, 1949.

Frackelton, Susan M. *Tried by Fire.* New York: D. Appleton Co., 1886.

Hamlin-Duncan, Julia, and D'Amico, Victor. *How to Make Pottery and Ceramic Sculpture.* The Museum of Modern Art, New York: Simon and Schuster, 1947.

Koch, Robert. *Louis C. Tiffany, Rebel in Glass.* New York: Crown Publishers, 1964.

Leach, Bernard. *A Potter's Book.* Hollywood-by-the-Sea, Florida: Transatlantic Arts, Inc. 1960.

Norwood, Nelson. *50 Years of Ceramic Education.* Alfred, New York: New York State College of Ceramics, 1950.

Ramsay, John. *American Potters and Pottery.* Clinton, Mass.: Colonial Press, Inc. 1939.

Rhead, Frederick M. *Studio Pottery.* St. Louis: People's University Press, 1910.

The Rookwood Book. Cincinnati, O.: The Rookwood Pottery Co., 1904.

Spargo, John, *Early American Pottery and China.* New York: Garden City Publishing Co., 1926.

Stiles, Helen. *Pottery in the United States.* New York: E.P. Dutton and Co., 1940.

Watkins, Laura W. *Early New England Potters and Their Wares.* Cambridge: Howard University Press, 1950.

Williamson, Scott. *The American Craftsman.* New York: Crown Publishers, 1940.

Periodicals

"American Pottery." *Scribner's Magazine,* 32:640 (November, 1902).

"The American Woman's League. Its Plan and Purpose." *Everybody's Magazine,* 4:1-5 (December-January, 1908-1909).

"An Open Letter to Bernard Leach from Marguerite Wildenhain." *Crafts Horizons,* 13:43-44 (May-June, 1953).

Atherton, Carlton. "Arthur Baggs, Distinguished American Ceramist." *Design,* 19:10-11 (March, 1947).

Barber, Edwin A. "The Pioneer of China Painting in America." *New England Magazine,* 13:33-48 (Sept. 1895).

Binns, Charles F. "The Arts and Crafts Movement in America." *The Craftsman,* 14:276 (June, 1908).

———. "Clay in the Potter's Hand." *The Craftsman,* 4:162-66 (May, 1904).

———. "Craft of the Potter." *The Craftsman,* 9:856 (March, 1906).

———. "Education in Clay." *The Craftsman,* 55:162 (June, 1903).

———. "The Progress of Ceramic Art." *Transaction of the American Ceramic Society,* 5:24 (1902).

"Biographical Sketches: Angelo Garzio." *Design Quarterly,* ed., Meg Torbert, 42:55 (1958).

Boyton, K.L. "Trio at Gustavsberg." *Ceramics Monthly,* 2:14-16 (August, 1954).

Brown, Conrad. "Peter Voulkos." *Crafts Horizons,* 18:15-20 (May-June, 1958).

———. "Toshiko Takeazu." *Crafts Horizons,* 19:26 (March-April, 1959).

Brownson, James. "Midwest Craftsmen's Seminar." *Ceramics Monthly,* 1:10 and 28 (February, 1953).

Carey, Sheldon J. "Improvisations on the Wheel." *Ceramics Monthly,* 12-14 (April, 1953).

Cox, Paul E. "Why Use More Than One Clay in a Body Mixture." *Journal of the American Ceramic Society,* 29:48 (March, 1946).

"Crafts Museum Opens." *Crafts Horizons,* 16:41 (December, 1956).

The Craftsman. 20:1 (April, 1911).

Emerson, Gertrude. "Marblehead Pottery." *The Craftsman,* 21:671-73 (March, 1916).

Gray, Walter, E. "Latter-Day Developments in American Pottery." *Brush and Pencil,* 9:241 (January, 1902).

———. "Latter-Day Developments in American Pottery—II." *Brush and Pencil,* 9:290-291 (February, 1902).

———. "Latter-Day Developments in American Pottery—III." *Brush and Pencil,* 9:359 (March, 1902).

———. "Latter-Day Developments in American Pottery." *Brush and Pencil,* 10:36 (April, 1902).

"Gropius and His Bauhaus." *Newsweek Magazine,* 12:21 (December 12, 1938).

Guild, L. "They Brought Style to the Machine." *House and Garden,* 65:54-55 (January, 1934).

Gummerus, O.H. "Wellsprings of Scandinavian Design." *Crafts Horizons,* 16:30 (July-August, 1956).

Hald, Arthur. "Stig Lindberg, Artist in Clay." *Crafts Horizons*, 14:11-15 (October, 1954).

Higgins, J.W. "Design for Mass-Production." *American Magazine of Art*, 26:40-41 (September, 1933).

Leader, Mary. "The Frackelton Story." *Exclusively Yours*, 13:6 (February, 1961).

Lerch, John. "Yankee Pottery Goes Abroad." *Country Life*, 73:108-112 (December, 1937).

Locke, Josephine. "Some Impressions of L'Art Nouveau." *The Craftsman*, 1:200-04 (August, 1902).

"Marguerite Wildenhain." *Crafts Horizons*, 16:31 (November, 1956).

"Marguerite Wildenhain." *Design Quarterly*, ed., Meg Torbert, 42:63-64 (1958).

McChesney, Mary F. "Michael Frimkes and the Cultured Pot." *Craft Horizons*, XXXIII:6 (December, 1977).

McLennan, T. "The Art Industries of America-IV, China Decorating." *Brush and Pencil*, 13:134 (June, 1905).

Mendenhall, Lawrence. "Cincinnati's Contribution to American Ceramic Art." *Brush and Pencil*, 17:47-61 (February, 1906).

Milliken, William M. "Ohio Ceramics." *Design*, 38:17-18 (November, 1936).

Northland, Mary. "Paul Revere Pottery." *House Beautiful*, 36:82-83 (August, 1914).

"Notable Arts and Crafts Exhibition." *Brush and Pencil*, 20:81 (February, 1907).

Olson, Bennet J. "Exhibitions." *Crafts Horizons*, 12:41 (September, 1957).

"Pablo's Pixilated Picasserole's." *Crafts Horizons*, 18:15-20 (May-June, 1958).

Papas, George. "Ceramics Teaching in American Colleges." *College Art Journal*, 16:332-35 (1957).

Perry, Aaron. "Decorative Pottery of Cincinnati." *Harper's Monthly*, 23:834-35 (May, 1881).

Peterson, Susan. "The Ceramics of Merilyn Levine." *Craft Horizons*, XXXVI:1 (February, 1977).

"Planning and Operating a Studio Pottery." *The Potter*, 1:25-28 (December, 1916).

Plumb, H. "The Pewabic Pottery." *Magazine of Art*, 2:64 (January, 1911).

"The Potters of America: Examples of the Best Craftsmen's Work for Interior Decorating." *The Craftsman*, 27:302 (December, 1914).

"Principles of Handicrafts." *Handicrafts*, 2:2 (April, 1902).

Rawson, Jonathan Jr. "Teco and Robineau Pottery." *House Beautiful*, 33;151 (April, 1913).

Reeve, John. "Warren MacKenzie and the Straight Pot." *Craft Horizons*, XXVI:3 (June, 1976).

"Report from the First National Conference of American Craftsmen." *Crafts Horizons*, 17:25 (July-August, 1957).

Rhead, Frederick. "America as a Ceramic Art Center." *Fine Arts Journal*, 22:193 (April-May, 1910).

Rhodes, Daniel. "Contemporary Pottery and High Fire." *Ceramics Monthly*, 1:11 (January, 1953).

Robineau, Adelaide. "American Pottery." *The Art World*, 3:155 (November, 1917).

———. "Hand Made Lunch Sets." *Keramic Studio*, 26:63 (July-August, 1922).

"Roy Lichtenstein: Ceramic Sculpture." *Ceramics Monthly*, 25:5 (May, 1977).

"The Rookwood Pottery." *The Craftsman*, 3:248 (January, 1903).

Ross, Denman W. "The Arts and Crafts: A Diagnosis." *The Craftsman*, 7:335 (October, 1904).

Rugg, Harold. "The Creative Artist in Industrial America." *Scholastics*, 30:17-18 (April, 1937).

Sargent, Irene. "Some Potters and Their Products." *The Craftsman*, 4:255-57 (July, 1903).

———. "The Wavey Line." *The Craftsman*, 2:135 (April, 1902).

Scharff, Robert. "A Studio Session with Edwin and Mary Scheier." *Craft Horizons*, XII (May-June, 1952).

Scherer, Mary. "The Developments in American Pottery." *Journal of the American Ceramic Society*, 7:645 (August, 1924).

Solon, L.V. "Sweden's Solution of ths Art Industry Problem." *Architectual Record*, 65:375-76 (April, 1927).

"Story of Paul Revere Pottery." *The Craftsman*, 25:205-07 (November, 1913).

Uchida, Yoshiko. "Win Ng." *Crafts Horizons*, 20:33-34 (January-February, 1960).

Untracht, Oppi. "David Weinrib . . . A Potter Turns to Tiles." *Ceramics Monthly*, 4:20-21 (February, 1956).

"Vally Wieselthier." *Design*, 39:46-47 (November, 1937).

"The Van Briggle Pottery." *Brush and Pencil*, 9:2 (October, 1901).

Whitcomb, Charlotte. "A Unique Turkish Coffee Set." *Brush and Pencil*, 8:135 (May, 1901).

Wright, Livingston. "Girl's Club Establishes Pottery and Ultimately Makes It a Financial Success." *The Art World*, 2:578-79 (September, 1917).

Reference Works

French, Myrtle. "Pottery and Porcelain." *Encyclopaedia Brittanica*, 1947, vol. 18. Chicago: Encyclopaedia Brittanica Co., 1947.

Bulletins

Avery, Louise C. *A Memorial Exhibition of the Work of Charles F. Binns.* Bulletin of the Metropolitan Museum of Art, no. 30, p. 108, May, 1935.

"Backus, Lulu S." Bulletin of the American Ceramic Society, no. XXI, May, 1942.

Bach, Richard F. *Art in Industry.* Bulletin of the American Ceramic Society, no. 3, pp. 284-88, August, 1924.

Baggs, Arthur E. *A Dream Come True.* Bulletin of the American Ceramic Society, no. 6, pp. 286-87, August, 1928.

Busbee, Juliana. *Jugtown Pottery: A New Way for Old Jugs.* Bulletin of the American Ceramic Society, XVI, no. 10, October, 1937.

Cox, Paul. *American Ceramics for Interior Decoration.* Bulletin of the American Ceramic Society, no. 5, pp. 420-22, September, 1925.

Knight, Paul F. *Commercial Feldspars in the United States.* Bulletin of the American Ceramic Society, no. 13, pp. 532-33, January, 1930.

Mary Louise McLaughlin. Bulletin of the American Ceramic Society, no. 17, p. 225, May, 1938.

McCabe, L.R. *National Ceramics Association Founded in 1891.* Bulletin of the American Ceramic Society, no. 82, p. 373, September, 1938.

McLaughlin, M.L. *Her Own Story.* Bulletin of the American Ceramic Society, no. 17, pp. 218-19, May, 1938.

McMahon, J.F. *Charles F. Binns.* Bulletin of the American Ceramic Society, no. 27, p. 176, April, 1938.

Rhead, Frederick. *American Ceramic Society Exhibition.* Bulletin of the American Ceramic Society, no. 1, pp. 15-16, May, 1922.

———. *Research in Ceramic Decorative Processes.* Bulletin of the American Ceramic Society, no. 5, pp. 330-31, May, 1921.

Smoot, Jack. *Development of an Art Program at NYA Resident Project.* Bulletin of the American Ceramic Society, XXI, May, 1942.

Newspapers

"University City." *The St. Louis Republican Newspaper,* (St. Louis, Missouri), col. 3, p. 15 (June 14, 1911).

Unpublished Material

Perkins, Dorothy W. "Education in Ceramic Art in the United States." Unpublished doctoral dissertation, The Ohio State University, 1956.

Perkins, Lyle. "An Investigation of Experimentalism as Applied to Creativity and Ceramic Media." Unpublished doctoral dissertation, The Ohio State University, 1956.

Exhibition Catalogs

Adams, Franklin. "Two Decades of Newcomb Pottery; Pieces from 1897 to 1917." *Exhibition Catalog,* Newcomb College, New Orleans, La., February, 1963.

Bach, Richard F. "Foreword." *Catalog of Contemporary Ceramics of the Western Hemisphere,* Corcoran Gallery of Art, Washington, D.C., March 4, 1942.

"Clay Today." *Exhibition Catalog,* New Gallery, School of Fine Art, State University of Iowa, December, 1963.

Cowan, Guy R. *Catalog of the Fourth National Robineau Memorial Ceramics Exhibition.* Syracuse Museum of Fine Art, Syracuse, New York, 1935.

Exhibition Catalog of the 5th National Ceramics Exhibition. Syracuse Museum of Fine Art, Syracuse, N.Y., 1936-1937.

Exhibition Catalog of the 7th National Ceramics Exhibition. Syracuse Museum of Fine Art, Syracuse, N.Y., 1938-1939.

Exhibition Catalog of the 12th National Ceramics Exhibition. Syracuse Museum of Fine Art, Syracuse, N.Y., 1948.

Exhibition Catalog of the 14th National Ceramics Exhibition. Everson Museum of Art, Syracuse New York, October, 1949.

"Exhibition of Contemporary Ceramics." intro. Charles F. Binns, *Exhibition Catalog,* W. & J. Sloane, Co., New York, (undated). (Maija Grotell dated the exhibition as being in 1925.)

"Forms from the Earth: 1000 Years of Pottery in America." *Exhibition Catalog,* The Museum of Contemporary Crafts, New York, 1961.

"Interview With the Artist." Exhibition Catalog, *Civilizations,* John Michael Kohler Arts Center, Sheboygan, Wisconsin, September, 1977.

Olmsted, Anna W. "Foreword." *Exhibition Catalog,* 2nd Annual Robineau Memorial Exhibition, Syracuse Museum of Fine Art, Syracuse, N.Y., 1933.

———. *Exhibition Catalog.* 5th National Ceramics Exhibition, Syracuse Museum of Fine Art, Syracuse, N.Y., 1936-1937.

Rhodes, Daniel. "The Twentieth Century." Exhibition Catalog, "Forms from the Earth: 1000 Years of Pottery in America." The Museum of Contemporary Crafts, New York, pp. 8-11, 1961.

Smith, Paul J. "Clayworks: 20 Americans." Introduction to the *Exhibition Catalog*, Museum of Contemporary Crafts of the American Crafts Council, New York., 1971.

Government Publications

Federal Security Agency. *Statistics of Higher Education; Biennial Survey of Education in ths United States, 1947-48.* Office of Education, Washington, D.C., Government Printing Office, 1948.

Appendixes

Appendix A

Samplings of Articles Which Articulated Responses for and Against Design Concepts of Art Nouveau

S. Bing, "L'Art Nouveau," *The Architectural Record,* XII (August, 1902), pp. 279-285.

Hector Guimard, "An Architect's Opinion of L'Art Nouveau," *The Architectual Record,* XII (June, 1902), pp. 127-133.

W. Hamilton, *The Aesthetic Movement in England,* London: Reeves and Turner Co., 1882.

A.D.F. Hamlin, "L'Art Nouveau: Its Origin and Development," *The Craftsman,* III (December, 1902), pp. 129-143.

"L'Art Nouveau—What It Is and What Is Thought of It—a Symposium," *Magazine of Art* (New York), (March-June, 1904), pp. 38-40.

Gabriel Mourney, "Interview on Art Nouveau with Alexander Charpentier,' *Architectual Record,* XII (June, 1902), pp. 121-125.

"Plant Forms in Ornament," *Design,* XXXV (September, 1902), p. 24.

Jean Schopfer, "L'Art Nouveau, An Argument and Defense," *The Craftsman,* IV (October, 1903), pp. 229-238.

"Secession Art in Europe: Its Growth, Meaning and Failure," *The Craftsman,* XIII (1908), pp. 36-49.

"Tiffany and Company at the St. Louis Exposition," *The Craftsman,* VII (October, 1904), pp. 169-183.

Oscar Lovell Triggs, "Chapters in the History of the Arts and Crafts Movement," *Bohemia Guild of the Industrial League,* 1902.

Gleason White, "Some Glasgow Designers and Their Work," *The Studio,* XII (1898), p. 48.

Appendix B

List of Members of the American Society of the Arts and Crafts Formed Between 1890 and 1907.

Colorado: Arts-Crafts Society, Denver

Connecticut: Arts and Crafts Club, Hartford; Arts-Crafts Society, Wallingford

Illinois: Chicago Society of Arts and Crafts; Bradley Arts and Crafts Club, Peoria; Society of Arts and Crafts, Rockford

Indiana: Arts and Crafts League, Evansville

Maine: Portland Society of Arts and Crafts

Maryland: Handicraft Club of Baltimore

Massachusetts: Whittier Home Association of Arts and Crafts, Amesbury; Society of Arts and Crafts, Boston; Society of Deerfield Industries; Arts and Crafts Society, Haverhill; Hingham Society of Arts and Crafts; Melrose Society of Arts and Crafts; Norwell Society of Arts and Crafts; Wayland Society of Arts and Crafts

Michigan: Society of Arts and Crafts, Detroit

Missouri: Arts and Crafts Society, Kansas City; Society of Applied Arts, St. Louis.

Montana: Society of Arts and Crafts, Deer Lodge; Helena Society of Arts and Crafts

New Hampshire: Handicraft Workers of Peterboro

New Jersey: Arts and Crafts Society of New Jersey, East Orange

New York: National Society of Craftsmen, New York City

North Carolina: Arts and Handicrafts Guild, Greensboro

Ohio: William Morris Society, Columbus

Oregon: Portland Arts and Crafts Society

Pennsylvania: Arts and Crafts Guild, Philadelphia

Rhode Island: Handicraft Club, Providence

South Carolina: Handicraft Guild, Charleston

Source: Eaton, Allen H., *Handicrafts of New England,* New York; Harper & Brothers Publishers, 1949, p. 289.

Appendix C

A List of Published Research by Charles F. Binns

"The Use of Equivalent Weights in Ceramic Compositions," *Transactions of the American Ceramic Society*, I (1899), pp. 7-14.

"The Grinding of Flint and Spar," *Transactions of the American Ceramic Society*, IV (1902), pp. 281-82.

"Improvements in Apparatus for Clay Analysis," with E.S. Babcock, Ibid., p. 355.

"Sulphur and Sulphates," *The Clay Worker*, XLVIII (January, 1907), pp. 76-77.

"The Functions of Boron in the Glaze Formula," *Transactions of the American Ceramic Society*, X (1908), pp. 158-74.

"The Behavior of Granular Limestone in Burned Clay," Ibid., XIV (1912), pp. 218-26.

"A Note on Rational Analysis and Glaze Fit," Ibid., XV (1913), pp. 177-83.

"Efflorescence and How To Stop It," *Brick and Clay Record*, XLII (November 18, 1913), p. 1017-18.

"A Comparison of Some Kaolins in Respect to Grain Size," *Transactions of the American Ceramic Society*, XVIII (1915), pp. 131-38.

"Vermillion Color from Uranium," *Journal of the American Ceramic Society*, III (November, 1920), pp. 913-14.

"Low-fired Procelain," Ibid., V (January, 1922), pp. 913-14.

"A Chromium Red Glaze," *Journal of the American Ceramic Society*, X (February, 1927), pp. 73-74.

"Experiment in Egyptian Blue Glaze," *Journal of the American Ceramic Society*, XV (May, 1932), pp. 271-72.

"Matte Glazes at High Temperatures," *Transactions of the American Ceramic Society*, VII, Part 1 (1905), p. 115.

"The Development of the Matte Glaze," *Transaction of the American Ceramic Society*, V 50 (1903), no page number.

Appendix D

A List of Some Studio-potters Graduated from Alfred University, 1910-1940

R. Guy Cowan

Dr. William G. Whitford

Myrtle French

Harold Nash

A.A. Ayers

O.T. Frazer

Roger D. Corsaw

Hal Riegger

J. Sheldon Carey

Jane Hartsook

Louis B. Raynor

Dr. Glenn Lukens

Dorothy Perkins

D.F. Teague

This list constitutes some graduated of Alfred University who have been recognized as outstanding potters and teachers of ceramics. During a period of time from 1910 to 1940 the actual number of graduates from Alfred's Ceramic Art and Design Division totaled 226. This did not include graduates from its Ceramic Engineering and Technology Division.

Appendix E

A List of Potters in America, 1930-40

Arthur E. Baggs, Columbus Ohio
Charles F. Binns, Alfred University
H. Bailey, Newcomb Pottery
Paul Bogotay, Ohio State University
Ede F. Curtis, Wayne, Pennsylvania
A.R. Deyer, Cleveland, Ohio
Edris Eckhardt, Cleveland, Ohio
George Fetzer, Columbus, Ohio
Marion Fosdick, Alfred University
Maija Grotell, New York City
Charles Harder, Alfred University
Edgar Littlefield, Ohio State University
Glen Lukens, University of Southern California
Dorothea O'Hara, Darien, Connecticut
Winifried Phillips, Wauwatosa, Wisconsin
Victor Schreckengost, Cleveland, Ohio
Leon Volkmar, Bedford Village, New York
Roger Corsaw, University of Oklahoma
R. Guy Cowan, Syracuse, New York
Louise McLaughlin, Cincinnati, Ohio
Karl Martz, Nashville, Indiana
Charles Mosgo, Cleveland, Ohio
Henry Varnum Poor, New York
Carl Walters, Woodstock, New York
J. Sheldon Carey, Providence, Rhode Island
William Manker, Claremont, California
John Foster, Detroit, Michigan
Maria Martinez, Sante Fe, New Mexico
Harold Nash, Cincinnati, Ohio
Gertrude and Otto Natzler, Los Angeles, California
Beatrice Wood, North Hollywood, California
Carlton Atherton, Ohio State University

Appendix F

Representative Sampling of Galleries and Museums Which Have Accommodated the Circuit Shows from the Syracuse National Ceramics Exhibitions

Newark Museum, Newark, N.J.
Cincinnati Art Museum, Cincinnati, Oh.
Newcomb Memorial College Art Gallery, New Orleans, La.
Brooks Memorial Art Gallery, Memphis, Tenn.
University of Minnesota, Minneapolis, Minn.
University of Pittsburgh, Pittsburgh, Pa.
Columbus Gallery of Art, Columbus, Oh.
Currier Gallery of Art, Manchester, N.H.
Worcester Art Museum, Worcester, Mass.
Cleveland Museum of Art, Cleveland, Oh.
San Diego Museum of Art, San Diego, Calif.
San Francisco Museum of Art, San Francisco, Calif.
Oberlin College
Munson-Proctor Institute
Memorial Art Gallery, Rochester, N.Y.
Albright Art Gallery, Buffalo, N.Y.
Cranbrook Academy of Art, Bloomfield Hills, Mich.
Baltimore Museum of Art
Metropolitan Museum of Art, New York
Butler Institute of Art, Youngstown, Oh.
City Art Museum of St. Louis
Corocoran Gallery of Art
Detroit Institute of Arts
Isaac Delgado Museum of Art, New Orleans, La.
John Herron Art Institute, Indianapolis, Ind.
Kansas City Art Institute
Milwaukee Art Center
Museum of Fine Arts, Houston, Texas
Philadelphia Museum of Art
St. Paul Gallery of Art, St. Paul, Minn.
Whitney Museum of American Art, N.Y.
Indiana University Art Gallery

Appendix G

Sampling of Galleries and Museums Which Sponsored Exhibitions of Ceramics.

The Chicago Art Institute, Chicago, Illinois, "Pottery of Marguerite Wildenhain

Brooklyn Museum, Brooklyn, New York, Group Exhibitions and the Work of Bernard Leach.

Albright Art Gallery, Buffalo, New York, "Designer Craftsmen of New York"

Corcoran Gallery of Art, Washington, D.C., "Annual Area Exhibition of Art" (included section in pottery)

Milwaukee Art Institute, Milwaukee, Wisconsin, "Annual Designer Craftsmen Exhibition"

Spe Art Museum, Louisville, Kentucky, "Designer-Craftsmen, U.S.A."

Isaac Delgado Museum, New Orleans, Louisiana, "Mexican Pottery"

Butler Art Institute, Youngstown, Ohio, "Autumn Annual Ceramics Exhibition"

Philbrook Art Center, Tulsa, Oklahoma, "German Ceramics"

Henry Art Gallery, Seattle, Washington, "Pottery of Carlton F. Ball"

Crocker Art Gallery, Sacramento, California, "Annual Arts and Crafts Show"

Detroit Institute of Art, Detroit, Michigan, "Scandinavian Pottery"

Denver Art Museum, Denver, Colorado, "Denver Ceramic Exhibition."

Portland Museum of Art, Portland Oregon, "Pottery of Bernard Leach"

Tucson Art Center, Tucson, Arizona, "Area Craftsmen"

Mulvane Art Center, Topeka, Kansas, "Pottery of Bernard Leach"

Joslyn Art Museum, Omaha, Nebraska, "Midwest Designer Craftsmen Show"

Witte Memorial Museum, San Antonio, Texas, "Regional Exhibition of Crafts"

Long Beach Art Center, Long Beach, California

De Young Museum, San Francisco, California, "California Ceramics"

Appendix H

A List of Crafts Organizations in the New England Area

A list of organizations in the New England area that sought to duplicate the efforts of the League of New Hampshire Arts and Crafts.

The Maine Crafts Guild, University of Maine

The Portland Society of Arts, Seat Memorial Gallery

Vermont Arts and Crafts Service, State Department of

Education, Vermont

Vermont Handicrafts Guilds

Worcester Guild of Artists and Craftsmen, Worcester, Mass.

The Handicraft Club of Providence, Providence, Rhode Island.

Glossary of Ceramic Terms

Absorption
The capacity of a (ceramic) material to soak up water.

Albany Slip
A clay which is mined in the vicinity of Albany, New York. It is often used as a decorating slip under glazes, but can also be used by itself as a slip-glaze. Without any additional ceramic chemicals, the slip will usually fire to a dark brown or black color at cones 7 to 10.

Alkalies
Usually a base compound consisting of sodium, potassium and other alkaline earths which serve as fluxes for low fire glazes.

Ash
The ashes of various vegetable matter such as trees, leaves, straw, hay (and other foreign matter) used as the primary ingredient in some high fire glazes. Popularized by the Far East, it has become a convenient source for a variety of glazes since it contains from 40 to 70 percent silica, 5 to 20 percent alumina and in smaller, varying amounts of lime, potash and magnesia.

Aventurine
A term given to glazes that are composed of soda, lead or boric oxide which, if large amounts of iron oxide are present, and cooled very slowly, will form a crystalline surface.

Banding
A method of applying glazes or slips with a brush or slip trailer to a pot while it is rotating on a wheel.

Ball clay
A sedimentary clay which is extremely fine-grained and plastic. Used as a plasticizer in clay bodies, especially porcelain. Although it contains some impurities, it usually fires out to a white color.

Ball mill
A jar, usually made of porcelain, which is filled with quartz pebbles and rotated on a machine in order to mix and grind glazes to a fine consistency.

Basalt ware or basaltes
A black, unglazed stoneware body, usually unglazed. Developed by the Wedgewood potteries in England around 1772.

Bas-relief
A raised or indented pattern which remains close to the surface planes.

Batch
A term generally used in glaze calculation to describe a glaze made up of varying chemicals that have been weighed out to specific weights in order to melt at predetermined temperatures.

Bisque firing
Usually the first firing of clay objects designed to drive off chemical water and carbonaceous material. Although the clay is strong enough to be handled after bisque firing, it is usually not impervious to liquids. Most bisque firings are done between cones 010 and 05.

Bisque or bisquit ware
Unglazed ceramic objects.

Bone china
A clay body that resembles porcelain, but which is only fired to around cone 6. Mainly used by industry for casting dinner ware and decorative items. It contains large amounts of bone ash and is often referred to as soft-paste porcelain.

Bone dry
A term to describe clay which has not been fired and has no moisture content other than that which it may absorb from natural humidity.

Burnishing
A method of smoothing the surface of leather hard clay with a wooden or metalic instrument.

Carving
A method of decorating clay, usually in its leather hard state by cutting into its surface with some sort of implement.

Casting or slip casting
A process of forming a clay object by pouring liquid slip into a mold (usually made of plaster) and allowing it to build up a thick enough layer of clay so that it can be removed in one piece.

Celadon
A French term for jade-like green colors which are derived from iron bearing glazes in reduction firings.

China
A general term referring to white-ware bodies which are fired lower than true porcelain.

China paints
Low fire glazes that contain various coloring stains and sufficient fluxes in order to melt at temperatures lower than most low-fire glazes. They are usually applied over glazes which have already been fired and allow for a wide variety of colors.

China clay (see also kaolin)
A white firing, highly refractory clay which is used extensively in compounding procelain and whiteware bodies and also as a source of alumina in glazes.

Clay
A general term to describe decomposed granite. Although clay is often thought of as being free of foreign substances, it often contains numerous impurities which renders it in a variety of colors such as white, grey, buff, brown, green and black. Depending upon the original site of decomposition, clay may be variously classified as primary or sedimentary clay, and upon further processing are sometimes referred to as ball clays, kaolins, earthenware, stoneware, fire clay or slip clays.

Coiling or coil building
A term to describe a building process of pottery or sculpture whereby the walls are constructed with rope-like coils of clay.

Crackle glaze
A glaze that shows a fine network of cracks which are the result of tensions created by differences of shrinkage between the clay and glaze during the cooling period of firing.

Crawling
A term to describe the separation of glaze from the clay body, thereby revealing the underlying surface.

Crazing
Excessive crackle in the glaze.

Cone or pyrometric cone
A small triangular pyramid made of ceramic materials that are compounded to melt at predetermined temperatures. When the cone bends, it is usually an indication that a desired melting temperature of a glaze has been achieved. The cone can also serve as an indicator of how fast the temperature is rising during a firing. (See also Pyrometer.)

Crystal or crystalline glazes
Glazes that are characterized by large clusters of flower-like crystal designs. The crystals are achieved by introducing iron or rutile in glazes that contain high amounts of silica and low amounts of alumina, and upon very slow cooling, form unpredictable designs of varying sizes of crystals.

Delft ware
An earthenware clay developed in Holland during the seventeenth century in the hopes of imitating Chinese porcelains. The objects were usually covered with a white, opaque tin oxide glaze which gives it a slightly bluish tint.

Della Robbia ware
Earthenware or Terra Cotta sculptures usually made in low relief for architectual adornement and covered with a tin-enamel glaze which has an off-white appearance. It was most popular in Florence, Italy where it was produced by the family of Lucca della Robbia during the fifteenth century.

Devitrification
Loss of glossiness of a glaze which is due to the recrystallization during the cooling period of the firing.

Dipping
A technique of glazing ceramic objects by immersing them in a large quantity of liquid glaze.

Earthenware
Low fire clays that usually mature at or below 2,000 degrees Fahrenheit. Although much weaker than stoneware, it will hold water if glazed with an appropriate earthenware glaze.

Eggshell porcelain
A porcelain body which is made of extremely thin walls, and of a particular combination of various ceramic materials that renders it translucent. Because of its non-plastic nature, eggshell porcelain is usually made from slip molds.

Egyptian paste
A low-fire, self-glazing clay which was developed in ancient Egypt. Used most frequently in making ceramic jewelry or as inlays for ceramic vessels or sculpture.

Empirical formula
A glaze formula which breaks down the various glaze chemicals into their molecular equivalents.

Engobe
Generally regarded as a slip which is used for decorating green or bisque ware. It differs from a natural slip such as Albany slip in that it is made up of clay, flint, feldspar, flux and various oxides or stains in order to render it in various colors. It is usually covered with a transparent or opaque glaze.

Faience
A French term for tin-enamel glazed earthenware which was extensively used in Spain and then popularized in Faenza, Italy during the Renaissance.

Feldspar
A common mineral found among most igneous rocks from which some clay and glaze materials are derived.

Filler
A material of little or no plastic quality which is used to promote even drying and low shrinkage in clay bodies. Often used in ceramic sculpture in the form of grog, sand, pearlite or sawdust.

Fire clay
A clay that is relatively coarse and is used mainly in the industrial manufacturing of bricks, tiles and muffles. Since it contains more fluxing power than most pure clays it is also used in small parts within a total clay formula by some studio-potters.

Flashing
The flame in an open fire kiln touching ceramic wares and changing the color of their surfaces in an unpredictable manner.

Flux
A substance which promotes the melting of silica in a clay body or glaze.

Foot
The base of pottery vessels.

Frit
A mixture of various glaze materials which is first melted in a crucible and upon cooling, is ground into powder form. The process eliminates toxic effects and the solubility of such compounds as raw lead, borax and soda ash. Used as a major flux for low and medium fire glazes.

Glaze
A combination of various ceramic materials suspended in water and applied to a ceramic piece by pouring, brushing or spraying. The various ingredients are predetermined to melt at specific temperatures, and upon cooling, will form a glass of various refractory qualities.

Glaze firing
A firing cycle designed to reach the melting temperature of glazes which coincides with the maturing of the clay body upon which the glaze has been applied.

Grés
A French term to describe stoneware.

Green ware
Ceramic sculpture or pottery which has not been fired.

Grog (see also fillers)
Usually a fire clay which has been fired and then crushed and screened into various particle size. It is used to retard shrinkage and insure even drying when working with large pieces and thick walls. It is also used to create surface textures either by including it in the clay body or by pressing it into the clay while it is still plastic or leather hard.

Hard paste
A hard, white, translucent porcelain body which is fired to cone 12 or higher.

High relief
A deeply carved design on pottery, sculpture or tiles.

Igneous
A phenomenon created under conditions which involves intense natural or manmade heat.

Impressing
A method of decorating clay by stamping or pressing objects or tools into the soft surface.

Incising
A decorative method of engraving into unfired clay.

Ironstone china
A term generally used for identifying mid temperature, soft paste porcelains which were manufactured in the United States during the eighteenth and nineteenth century.

Iron oxide
Usually found in the form of black or red iron oxide and used chiefly as a colorant for clay bodies and glazes. Although primarily thought of as a colorant for brown and tan glazes, it can also produce vivid blues (when combined with rutile) and subtle greens under reduction firing conditions. (See also reduction firing.)

Jiggering
An industrial method of producing plates by placing a clay slab on a rotating wheel and then superimposing on it a template which trims off the excess clay, thereby creating the underside of the form.

Jollying
The reverse process of jiggering, thereby creating the interior of the plate.

Kaolin
A term used interchangeably with china clay, it is the main constituent of most glazes and porcelain bodies. First discovered in China, it is an anglicized term which means "high hill" and refers to Kao-Lin, a mountain of that country where the clay was first discovered.

Kiln
A furnace made of ceramic materials which is designed to withstand high temperatures for the firing of various ceramic materials.

Kiln furniture
Refractory ceramic materials such as shelves, posts and other equipment placed in the kiln to accommodate clay items for firing.

Kneading
A method of working soft clay in order to remove excess air and to promote uniformed plasticity.

Lead
One of the most common and reliable low-fire fluxes usually found in the form of white lead, lead carbonate, red lead or galena.

Leather hard
A condition of clay when most of the physical water has evaporated, thereby rendering it stiff enough to support itself, but soft enough to allow additions to be made with clay of the same consistency.

Luster
A metalic surface quality that is due to some form of metal having been deposited and melted on the surface of clay or glaze. It is most popularly associated with the oxides and nitrates of silver, gold and copper which are mixed with oils of lavender, applied over a fired glaze and then fired to extremely low (1,200 degrees Fahrenheit) temperatures. Upon cooling the effects often resemble the true metals that they try to imitate.

Majolica
A large range of earthenware pottery and sculpture which relies on a white, tin-enamel glaze for an off-white color. It is frequently decorated with a wide variety of oxides, stains and sulphates over the unfired glaze. Although derived from Spain, via the island of Majorca, it received its main renown in Faenza, Italy during the Renaissance. (See also faience.)

Mat (or matt) glaze
A glaze whose surface does not allow for much transmission of light due to various particles in the glaze which have not gone into a complete melt, usually due to the inclusions of barium carbonate, rutile or alumina.

Maturity
A point in the firing cycle where the clay body has reached a state of nonporosity and optimum density. Also the designated temperature at which a glaze has gone into complete fusion.

Mishima
A Japanese decorating method by which an incised design is filled with a contrasting clay or slip.

Mold (see also casting)
A form, usually made from plaster of Paris, as a negative design, which when it is filled with slip or clay, will produce a reverse (or positive) image.

Molecular formula
A glaze formula which expresses the relative proportions of constituent parts of a glaze or clay body.

Muffle kiln
A type of kiln which has an interior lining that protects the ware from being touched by the flame.

Neutral firing
A method of firing a kiln whereby the atmosphere remains free of excess carbon. In a gas-fired kiln this can be achieved by carefully controlling air and gas ratios. In electric kilns it occurs automatically since the source of heat is from the radiation of the kanthal or nichrome elements.

Once fire or single fire
A method of firing which takes the ware through the bisque cycle up to the maturing temperature of the clay body and glaze.

Open firing
A term describing a type of firing in which the flame is allowed to meander through the kiln freely as compared to a muffle type kiln in which the ware is protected from the flame.

Opacifier
A ceramic substance that remains relatively stable in a glaze, and whose suspension in the glaze disallows any significant light to penetrate, thereby rendering the surface opaque. Although tin oxide has been the most popular source for opacifiers, its high cost has created numerous substitutes such as Opax, Zircopax, Superpax and Ultrox.

Overglaze (see also china paints)
Low temperature glazes which are applied on the surfaces of glazes that have already been fired once.

Overglaze colors
Same as overglaze and china paints, designed to melt around cones 016 to 013.

Oxide
Generally referred to as a metalic chemical used for coloring clays, glazes, slips and engobes.

Parian ware
A soft paste, unglazed porcelain developed in England during the nineteenth century in imitation of the Greek Elgin Marbles. It became popular in America after the War of Independence.

Pâte-sur-pâte
A French term which means "paste on paste;" a decorating technique involving the building up of a low relief with repeated layers of slip or engobe.

Peach bloom
A glaze derived from ancient China which has a peach-like coloration. It is in the family of Chinese copper-red glazes that are usually only achieved under carefully controlled reduction atmospheres.

Plaster of Paris
Calcined hydrated calcium sulfate, or gypsum, used in ceramics for making molds, models and even as a flux for glazes.

Plasticity
A description of clay that allows it to be easily manipulated and still retain its shape when used on the potter's wheel, in hand building or press molding.

Porcelain
Usually a strong, vitreous white clay that is fired to cone 12 or higher. Depending on the varying proportions of kaolin, ball clay, feldspar and flint, it can be opaque or translucent.

Pottery
A general term assigned to any type of vessel made from clay.

Pug mill
A machine designed to mix and extrude clay in a plastic state.

Pyrometer
An instrument used for translating heat energy into numerical measurements.

Pyrometric cones (see cones)

Quartz
Same as flint or silica.

Raku
A Japanese term translated to mean "enjoyment of leisure." It is a method of firing ceramics which, when it is still red hot, is placed in a container of combustible materials such as leaves or straw. Upon combustion of the material, incomplete combustion is created by shutting off the oxygen thereby creating excess carbon which affects the clay and glazes in various ways.

Reduction firing
A firing technique which creates insufficient combustion. This, in turn, provides free carbon in the kiln which combines with the oxygen of the clay and glazes and aids in creating a wide variety of various colors and surfaces.

Refractory
A quality that describes ceramics which is able to withstand high temperatures.

Rib
A tool that is fashioned from hard wood or some type metal which the potter uses in fashioning certain types of shapes while the pot is rotating on the wheel.

Rutile
An impure form of titanium dioxide used mainly as a coloring oxide in glazes and slips in order to obtain yellows, beiges and tans. Also used in crystalline glazes and as a special effect to obtain running and streaking qualities in some fluid glazes.

Saggars
Containers made of fire clay in which pots are placed in order to protect them from excess carbon in the kiln.

Sang de beuf
A French term meaning "oxblood" which describes the vivid red Chinese glaze obtained through the use of copper oxide in a glaze when it is subjected to a carefully controlled reduction firing.

Salt glaze
A glazing technique whereby raw salt is introduced into the kiln (usually at 2,300 degrees Fahrenheit or higher) and upon vaporizing, will combine with the silica of the clay and form a glaze.

Sgraffito
An Italian term meaning "scratched out" which describes a decorating technique of scratching through a slip, engobe or glaze before a piece is fired.

Shrinkage
The contraction of clay or glaze due to the evaporation of water or chemical change induced by heat.

Silica
Same as flint or quartz, usually in powdered form.

Slip
Any type of clay that is suspended in water. Used for decorating green or bisque ware and also for joining clay of leather hard consistency together when a piece is constructed of several parts.

Slip glaze
A glaze made chiefly from slip, such as Albany or Michigan Black Bird slip.

Slurry
A creamy mixture of slip and water, usually made from the same body used for making ceramic wares.

Spraying
A method of applying slips or glazes with a spray gun operated with compressed air.

Soaking
Maintaining of a temperature in a kiln for a specific period of time to insure slow cooling and settling of the glaze.

Stain
A ceramic coloring agent which is made by combining coloring oxides with aluminum, flint and flux and then calcining or fritting it and then grinding and washing it in order to render it in a uniformed, fine particle sized form. It is chiefly used as a glaze colorant for overglazes, china paints, engobes, low fire glazes and body colorants.

Soluble
The ability for a ceramic material to be dissolved in water.

Sprigging
A clay relief decoration usually made in a mold which is applied to the leather hard pot.

Stoneware
A high-fire clay which has little or no absorbency when fired to cone 8 or above. In strength it is similar to porcelain, but due to large amounts of impurities it is coarser, more plastic and varies in color from greys to browns.

Temmoku
A term derived from the Japanese, meaning "Mountain of the Eye of Heaven." It is a highly iron saturated glaze which usually results in dark brown to glossy black colors in a reduction firing.

Terra cotta
A red earthenware clay containing grog or sand. It is commonly used for ceramic sculpture or architectural reliefs.

Terra sigillata
An Italian term meaning "stamped earth." It is a slip made of finely decanted particles and was used extensively by the Romans and Greeks for decorating their pots.

Throw or throwing
A forming method of pottery on the potter's wheel.

Tin enamel
A decorative process which is similar to over glazes, in that they are applied over a glaze which has already been fired. It is usually made up of frits, glass and colorants.

Translucent
The ability for light to penetrate a glaze or clay body such as porcelain.

Trimming
A method of removing clay from a leather hard pot, usually while it is rotating on a potter's wheel.

Tromp L'oeil
"Fool-the-Eye" technique of super realism also used in some decorating process in ceramics.

Turning
Same as trimming.

Underglaze
A decoration generally applied to green ware or bisque ware before it is covered with a glaze.

Vitreous
A condition of fired clay which has rendered it hard and nonabsorbant through firing.

Volatilization
A condition in the kiln which causes various glaze elements to turn from a solid to a liquid and then into a gaseous form, as seen in salt glazing.

Wax resist
A wax emulsion or melted wax which is used for decorating pottery so that during the firing the wax will burn off and reveal the surface under it.

Wedging
Similar to kneading of plastic clay in order to remove excess air and render it in a uniformed, working condition. May also involve cutting clay repeatedly on a taut wire to insure greater consistency.

White lead
A major low-fire flux for glazes.

White ware
Ceramics which is essentially white or creamy in color.

Photographic Credits

Whenever appropriate, a particular photographer's name is *preceded* by the figure number.*

Alfred University, Department of Ceramics, 6-0, 6-1.

Laura Andreson, Los Angeles, Calif., 13-32.

ARCO Center for Visual Arts, Los Angeles, Calif., 12-31, Frank J. Thomas, photographer.

Robert Arneson, Davis, Calif., 12-6.

Carlton Ball, University of Puget Sound, Tacoma, Wash., 9-6.

Joe Bova, Dept. of Art, Louisiana State University, Baton Rouge, La., 12-35.

John Bowitz, Morningside College, Sioux City, Iowa, 12-66.

California State University, Long Beach, Calif., 12-36, Irwin Tepper, photographer; Pl. 20.

Charles Counts, Rising Fawn, Ga., 5-4, Edward C. Du Puy, photographer; 5.0, Bill Haddox, photographer.

Chicago Historical Society, Chicago, Ill., 3-6, Pl. 3.

Cincinnati Art Museum, 2-1, 2-2.

Cleveland Museum of Art, Cleveland, Ohio, 7-0, 9-0, 11-6.

Communications Service, Northern Illinois University, DeKalb, Ill., 12-68, 12-70, Barry Stark, photographer.

Claude Conover, Cleveland, Ohio, 13-32.

Roger Corsaw, 6-4, 7-0, 13-9, William H. Allen, photographer.

David Cox, Ogden, Utah, 13-4.

Cranbrook Academy of Art Museum, 8-0, 8-1, 8-2.

Stephen De Staebler, Berkeley, Calif., 12-3, 12-4, Susan Felter, photographer.

Richard DeVore, Department of Ceramics, Cranbrook Academy of Art, 13-2, 13-3.

Ruth Duckworth, University of Chicago, 12-15.

Daniel Engelke, Evansville, Ind., 12-54.

Everson Museum of Art, Syracuse, New York, 2-0, 2-8, 2-9, 7-1, 8-5, 8-7, 8-8, 8-9, Edward Bowman, photographer; 5-1, 6-3, 6-5, 7-2, 7-3, 7-4, 9-9, Oswald Werner, photographer; 9-10, 11-1, 11-2, 11-4, 11-11, 11-12, 11-14, 11-15, 11-16, 11-17, 11-18, 11-19, 11-22, 11-24, 11-25, 11-26, 11-27, 11-28, 11-29, 11-31, 13-5, 13-28, Pl. 5, Pl. 6, Pl. 7, Pl. 8.

Bill Farrell, School of Art of the Chicago Art Institute, Chicago, Ill., 12-45, Ron Gazdon, photographer.

Ken Ferguson, Kansas City, Miss., 13-14.

Viola Frey, California College of Arts and Crafts, Oakland, Calif., 13-39.

Donald Frith, Department of Art, University of Illinois, Champaign, Ill., 13-11.

Verne Funk, School of Fine Arts, Bradley University, 12-22, 12-23, 12-24.

Ron Gallas, Pennsylvania State University, Department of Fine Arts, 13-26.

Gallery Rebecca Cooper, Washington, D.C., 12-33, 12-37, 12-44.

Angelo Garzio, Manhatten, Kans., 13-23.

Henry Gernhardt, Syracuse, N.Y., 11-7, Robert Clark, photographer; 12-14, 12-21.

John Glick, Farmington, Mich., 13-12.

Bruce Grimes, University of Wisconsin, Green Bay, Wis., 12-30.

Erik Gronborg, Solana Beach, Calif., 12-46, Pl. 29.

George Hageman, Dayton, Ohio, 12-57, Sean Wilkinson, photographer.

Hansen-Fuller Gallery, San Francisco, Calif., 12-0, 12-1, 12-2, 12-8, 12-9, 12-62, 12-63, Barbara Mensch, photographer.

Doug Hanson, Mount Vernon, Iowa, 12-69.

Dick Hay, Brazil, Ind., 7-0, 12-38, Pl. 24.

Henry Francis du Pont, Winterthur Museum, Wilmington, Del., 1-2.

Curt Hoard, University of Minnesota, Minneapolis, Minn., 12-51, Pl. 16.

Margie Hughto, Syracuse, N.Y., Pl. 36.

Illinois State University, Department of Art, 9-8.

John Iwata and Paul Donhauser, University of Wisconsin, Oshkosh, University Publications Dept., 3-7, 9-2, 9-4, 9-7, 11-35, 11-36, 12-60, 13-0, 13-20, 13-21, 13-22, 13-36, Pl. 10, Pl. 13, Pl. 15, Pl. 21, Pl. 27, Pl. 28, Pl. 37, Pl. 38.

Jacqueline Anhalt Gallery, Los Angeles, Calif., 12-26, 12-27, 13-41.

John Michael Kohler Art Center, Sheboygan, Wis., 12-10.

Douglas Johnson, River Falls, Wis., 11-30.

Karen Karnes, Stony Point, N.Y., 13-13.

Susan and Stephen Kemeneffy, Edinboro, Pa., 12-47.

Gene Koss, Tulane University, New Orleans, La., 12-65.

Howard Kottler, University of Washington, Seattle, Wash., 12-49.

Hui Ka Kwong, Brooklyn, New York, 12-42, Pl. 25.

Rodger Lang, Lakewood, Col. 12-41.

James Leedy, Pl. 12.

Lightner Museum, St. Petersburg, Fla., Pl. 2.

Ken Little, University of Montana, Missoula, Mo., 12-71.

*Chapter opening figures are designated by 0 numbering system; for example, 6-0, etc.

Karl Martz, Bloomington, Indiana, 13-34, Pl. 4.

Harrison McIntosh, Claremont, Calif., 9-5, San Calder, photographer; 9-11, 9-12, 13-30, Robert C. Frampton, photographer.

James Melchert, Alexandria, Virginia, 12-16, Pl. 26, Ron Chamberlain, photographer.

David Middlebrook, Department of Art, San Jose State College, San Jose, Calif., 12-17.

Mills College, Department of Art, 11-32, 11-33, Young's Photography.

Milwaukee County Historical Society, 2-6.

Milwaukee Public Museum, 1-3, 1-4, 1-5, 1-6, 2-3, 2-4, 2-5, 2-6, 2-7, 3-2, 3-3, 3-5.

Art Morrison, Coe College, Cedar Rapids, Iowa, 12-24.

Museum of Contemporary Art, Chicago, Ill., 12-5, 12-7.

Museum of Modern Art, New York, 11-10.

Harold Nash, Cincinnati, Ohio, 8-6.

Arthur Nelson, California College of Arts and Crafts, Oakland, Calif., 12-43.

Newcomb College, Tulane University, New Orleans, La., 3-2.

Donna Nicholas, Edinboro, Pa., 13-37, Mary Jo Toles, photographer.

Norton Simon Museum of Art, Pasadena, Calif., 12-64, Frank Thomas, photographer.

Oakland Museum, Oakland, Calif., Pl. 6.

O.K. Harris Gallery, New York, N.Y., 12-58, Eric Pollitzer, photographer; 12-59, Vincent Miraglia, photographer, Pl. 32.

Judy Onofrio, Rochester, Minn., 12-13.

Oshkosh Public Museum, Oshkosh, Wis., 1-1, 1-2, 3-0, 4-0, 4-1.

Bruce Ostwald, Department of Art, University of Minnesota, Minneapolis, Minn., 12-24.

Susan Parks, Haydenville, Mass., 10-0.

Richard Peeler, Reelsville, Ind., 11-5, 13-24.

Pennsylvania Photography Service, Pennsylvania State University, 12-28.

Dorothy and Lyle Perkins, University of Massachusetts, 8-10, 13-35.

Joseph Pugliese, California State University, Hayward, Calif., 12-37.

Quay Ceramics Gallery, San Francisco, Calif., 11-23, 12-17, 12-29, 12-48, 12-55, 112-56, 12-57, Pl. 18, Pl. 32, Pl. 33.

Robert Ransom, Los Angeles, Calif. 12-52.

Donald Reitz, Madison, Wis., 13-26, Pl. 35.

Harvey Sadow, Department of Art, University of Wisconsin, Oshkosh, Wis., 13-8.

Herbert Sanders, San Jose State College, San Jose, Calif., 13-31.

Santa Anna College Art Gallery, Santa Anna College, Santa Anna, Calif., 12-69, 12-73, M. Herberg, photographer.

David Shaner, Bigfork, Mo., 13-16, 13-17.

Marc Sijan, Milwaukee, Wis., 12-53.

Paul Soldner, Aspen, Colo., 11-34, 13-6, 13-7.

Robert Sperry, Department of Art, University of Washington, Seattle, Wash., 13-10.

James Stephenson, Department of Visual Arts, Pennsylvania State University, 12-20, 12-61.

John and Susan Stephenson, Ann Arbor, Michigan, 12-47, Pl. 30.

Rudolf Stoffel, Philadelphia, Pa., 13-25.

Gibson Strawn, Northern Illinois University, Pl. 34.

Sam Sweezy, Belmont, Mass., 5-2.

James Tanner, Mankato State University, Mankato, Minn., 13-38.

David Tell, Department of Art, Illinois State University, 13-40, Ken Westphal, photographer.

The American Art Clay Company, Indianapolis, Ind., 9-1.

The Fine Arts Museum of San Francisco, Pl. 11, Pl. 14, Pl. 23, Pl. 27.

Theo Portnoy Gallery, New York, N.Y., Pl. 22.

Robert Turner, Alfred University, Department of Ceramics, 13-29.

Tom Turner, 13-27.

Kenneth Vavrek, Philadelphia, Pa., 12-11.

Helen Vergette, Carbondale, Ill., 9-13.

Walker Art Center, Minneapolis, Minn., 11-20, 11-21.

Patti Warashina, Department of Art, University of Washington, Seattle, Wash., 12-19, Pl. 17.

William Warehall, 13-18.

Irwin Whitacker, East Lansing, Mich., 11-8.

Marguerite Wildenhain, 8-3.

Paula and Robert Winokur, Horsham, Pa., 13-1, 13-15.

Wonders of the World Museum, Port Costa, Calif., 12-32, Pl. 31.

Betty Woodman, Boulder, Colo., 13-19.

James Wozniak, University of Massachusetts, Amherst, Mass., 11-13.

Index